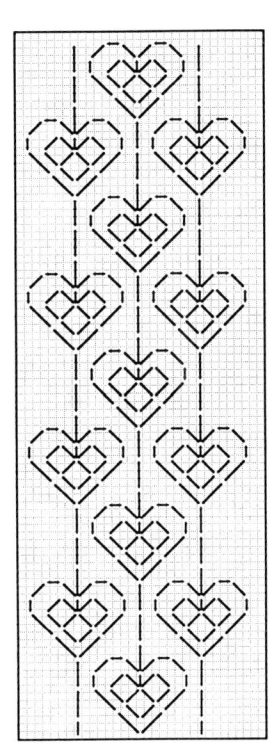

THE HEART OF BLACKWORK

ANN STRITE-KURZ

A STUDY OF
UNCONVENTIONAL
BLACKWORK PATTERNS
FOR
CONTEMPORARY USE

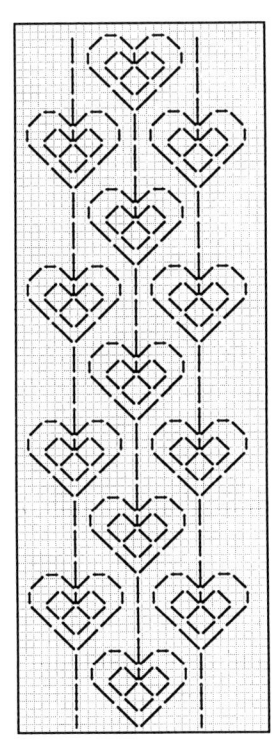
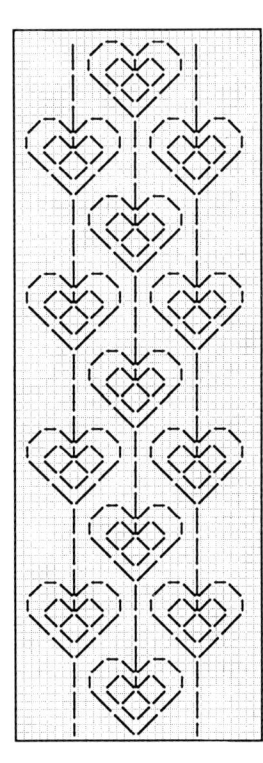

First Printing June 1992

This self-published book was prepared with an IBM personal computer, using WordPerfect 5.0 page composition software with graphic elements generated by PC Paintbrush IV Plus software.

Ann Strite-Kurz
3802 Wrenwood Court
Midland, Michigan 48640-2372

ABOUT THE AUTHOR

Ann Strite-Kurz has been an active teacher of canvas embroidery for the past decade. She received certification in canvas embroidery from the Valentine Museum in Richmond, Virginia in 1982. She also received a Master Craftsman award in canvas from the Connecticut River Valley Chapter of the Embroiderers' Guild of America (EGA).

Ann has traveled extensively throughout the United States and Canada, presenting workshops and lectures to various needlework groups. She has also taught at seminars sponsored by EGA, the American Needlepoint Guild, Callaway Gardens, and the National Academy of Needlearts. In addition, she has taught group correspondence courses for EGA for ten years.

Ann graduated from the Madeira School and has a B.A. degree in American Studies from Sweet Briar College. Her introduction to embroidery was a result of her involvement as a docent in the Keeler Tavern Preservation Society in Ridgefield, Connecticut, and Ann has had extensive training in crewel, counted thread, and silk and metal embroidery as well as canvas embroidery.

Ann currently resides in Michigan with her husband Bill. Their hobbies include photography, tennis, hiking, biking, scuba diving and cross country skiing. They also share three children.

TABLE OF CONTENTS

ACKNOWLEDGMENTS

Many students and peers have encouraged me to publish books on my somewhat innovative pattern treatments on canvas. I chose blackwork as the topic of my first effort not only because it is my favorite medium but because its challenges have been a constant source of interest and pleasure the past ten years.

Several individuals helped to make this book a reality. First a special thank you to Ilse Altherr, my teacher and mentor, who first introduced me to blackwork and encouraged me to take it a step further. I could not have presented my refinements on reversible blackwork technique without her permission to include her pathfinders system in my text. Her continual sharing and assistance in the preparation of a self-published book was most appreciated too.

A special thank you to another friend and advisor, Jane Zimmerman. Jane's high standards of excellence in stitching have been an ongoing inspiration. Her continual sharing of her in-depth knowledge of state-of-the-art computer graphics was a constant source of strength as I struggled to master the personal computer as well.

I particularly want to thank my two proofreaders, Connie Ashman and Natalie Brown, who spent many hours reviewing the material for the book. Their meticulous scrutiny and constructive advice were so valuable in making the book more concise and understandable.

And finally I want to thank my husband Bill for his monumental patience during the preparation of the book. His computer expertise and his publishing experience were so helpful along the way, and his photography skills produced all of the color plates. The book effort was truly a family affair, and I am indeed fortunate to have a partner who is so supportive of my interest in embroidery.

FOREWORD

Blackwork embroidery has always been my favorite form of needlework. As simple linear outlines, usually done in a single dark color on a light fabric, blackwork patterns are the purest form of pattern in needlework. They are unique in that they rely totally on line and contrast for their effect whereas other mediums have additional variables like color, texture, or perforations to further enhance the patterns. In blackwork large scale patterns are bold and dramatic while small scale patterns are delicate and lacelike. Variations in both the density and scale of the patterns allow them to combine in an interesting way to form an overall design, but blackwork is also useful and versatile when combined with other needlework techniques.

As a needle artist, my particular infatuation with pattern in general has moved me to concentrate on developing original patterns of all sorts. My special affection for blackwork patterns caused me to experiment with both the style and the technique used to stitch them. By sharing fifty of my innovative blackwork pattern arrangements in this book, I hope to inspire readers to develop similar creative approaches to blackwork.

It is easy to create original patterns in blackwork since one can transpose the essence of almost any pattern network to a grid or graph and then stitch it in thread. Planning a logical sequence to execute the pattern is a somewhat more complex task, however, so another main focus in this book is to establish guidelines for creating orderly sequences using the reversible method of doing blackwork, which uses the double running stitch. There are many advantages to using this structured method over other more random approaches, and some of the refinements that I have developed make the patterns totally consistent, particularly on canvas.

Traditional blackwork was usually worked in a black silk thread on a fine bleached linen ground. Adapting published "linen" patterns to canvas initially proposed some dilemmas since the printed patterns were often too large in scale and not dense enough to be satisfactory on the coarser ground. By providing some solutions to overcome this problem, I hope to inspire others to use blackwork in new and innovative ways on canvas.

The final goal of the book is to introduce readers to some unconventional styles of blackwork. Conventional stitches usually straddled either two threads or two intersections, but both shorter and longer stitches can be considered on canvas. Instead of simple outlines I often use composite treatments that either superimpose one pattern on top of another or combine a blackwork pattern with another compatible treatment. Embroiderers today can study many historical forms and trends of needlework, but real growth comes in developing new approaches. By sharing some of my innovative ideas on the style as well as the technique of blackwork, I hope to inspire readers to use it in more avant garde ways.

Welcome to my world of blackwork, and enjoy what lies ahead.

IMPORTANT NOTE TO READERS

Any "unconventional" embroidery technique has to be considered an intermediate level of needlework merely because it is assumed that one must know what the "conventional" technique is before one can start to experiment with it in a nontraditional way.

However, it has been my experience that the important thing in understanding any counted needlework is proficiency in reading a chart. I have often had students in classes who think they may be "in over their heads" – as a matter of fact one clever lady showed up wearing a dive mask and a snorkeling breathing tube to indicate just that! After a brief introduction to the subject and a carefully planned "warm-up" pattern for the entire class, these "less than qualified" students have always developed confidence and kept up with the experienced students **as long as** they can follow a chart.

The introductory text that follows is geared to the stitcher who is acquainted with blackwork. However, if any reader studies the glossary of general needlework terms (pages 200-202) and the glossary of terms for the pathfinders system of reversible blackwork (page 37) before reading the text, the analysis of blackwork can be easily understood. In addition, the method comparison charts on pages 5-6 are particularly helpful in understanding the positive and negative features of all three methods of executing blackwork.

After reading the glossary of terms for the pathfinders system on page 37, it would be a good idea to take a doodle cloth and execute both Pattern 1 and Pattern 2 (pages 42-47). The directions for these first two patterns are written for the novice stitcher, and they include detailed discussions of every aspect of a numbered sequence. As you walk through the steps involved, the terminology will clarify itself further, and you will be fully prepared for the comprehensive text and for the later patterns. Most of us learn better by "doing" rather than by reading, and this basic foundation will make the rest of the book more meaningful.

The second glossary of general terms includes words and phrases that are likely to be familiar. However, some terms are listed that even an experienced stitcher may not associate with needlework. Many of my concepts have no precedents in general needlework circles so I often use metaphors or other significant terms from other fields to clarify my points. In other words, a new vocabulary is needed to explain a new idea in the same way that Ilse Altherr developed her pathfinders terminology for reversible blackwork. Therefore if my usage of a word is not clear, please use this second glossary to find a precise definition of my particular application. Because of my mathematical background, I have always used an analytical approach to understanding needlework, and I hope these observations and conclusions are in turn helpful to you.

One final suggestion to less experienced stitchers is to build your skills by executing a sample of each pattern on a doodle cloth, progressing in sequential order. As the patterns are added, I sometimes make references to earlier patterns and charts that are relevant so familiarity with these patterns will broaden your understanding of the points made.

LIST OF COLOR PLATES
(Found Following Page 38)

CHAPTER 1 - INTRODUCTION TO BLACKWORK EMBROIDERY

Blackwork today is generally understood to be a counted embroidery technique that uses linear outlines of symmetrical geometric repeats. This type of patterning existed in ancient times, but the origin and popularity of this style is usually attributed to Spain. Use of these intricate geometric patterns was apparently inspired by the Moors, who conquered Spain in the 8th century. The designs were primarily flower motifs surrounded by scroll or spiral accents, but small animal motifs and geometric shapes were also used that echoed Moorish arabesque styles. Such black linear outlines tend to resemble wrought iron patterns in their delicacy and intricacy. The lacy quality of the patterns also made them a popular substitute for the more tedious handmade lace in edgings for both garments and table linens.

The zenith period for this form of geometric "Spanish work" occurred in England in the first half of the 16th century when Catherine of Aragon, who was the daughter of Queen Isabella and King Ferdinand of Spain, married King Henry VIII. It is assumed that her trousseau included many items that were embroidered in black on white as this style became popular among the ladies of the court as well as with the king, who also wore elaborately embellished clothes.

Henry VIII hired the young Austrian painter Hans Holbein to record the life of the court so one can see the elegant attire of the period in his portraits. Collars and cuffs, however, were often border patterns that appeared to be executed in a structured double running or reversible method since the patterns could be viewed from both sides in these areas. Because Holbein recorded these patterns so realistically in his paintings, reversible blackwork patterns began to be called Holbein embroidery in the 20th century, but the term was not used during this period.

The notion of a form of reversible embroidery was documented one hundred years earlier, however, in one of Chaucer's *Canterbury Tales.* It describes a smock with a

> "...pattern on the collar front and back,
> Inside and out, it was of silk and black..."

Later periods of English blackwork brought further changes in the styles of blackwork, and interest in the reversible outlines waned. Elizabethan blackwork became a form of allover decoration rather than just edgings, and it was used to embellish household furnishings as well as clothing. Designs became elaborate scrolling stems with stylized flowers, leaves and insects that were often filled with small geometric diaper patterns that were stitched in back stitch outlines. Metallic highlights were often added with a silver-gilt thread. Numerous other stitches were also used in these black embroideries so the reversible style was no longer favored.

Today blackwork is enjoying another rebirth in America, and we are no longer limited to using black thread on a fine linen. Any dark shade or color is effective, and the technique can be used on any evenweave fabric or canvas. Since its success depends only on contrast, a light thread can be equally stunning on a medium-dark to dark background.

1

Thanks to the efforts of Ilse Altherr, contemporary embroiderers now have a system of "pathfinders" available that enables them to apply the reversible method to all patterns that form continuous paths of connecting repeats. This pathfinders system is thoroughly explained in Ilse's self published book called *Reversible Blackwork*. However, since all of the patterns presented in this book are charted in reversible sequences, I obtained Ilse's permission to use her terms and to explain the terminology in the glossary at the end of this essay (page 37).

Applying her language, it is easy to study a printed overall pattern, isolate the repeats, and then formulate a logical stitch sequence of rows that will join one segment at a time in a tidy even manner. These maze routes are readily understood when they are broken down into components like the main path, a side trip, and the return trip. These terms are particularly useful when one has to stitch along the side edges of an irregular filling where the regular flow of the sequence is interrupted – these fragments all merely become side trips and are attached accordingly to the nearest uninterrupted row.

REVERSIBLE VS. NON-REVERSIBLE METHODS

Some patterns cannot be done in the reversible technique, but a similar orderly approach of simple running stitch sequence can be used that creates a consistent but different pattern on the reverse side. These patterns are called "one-way" patterns since only the first step of double running stitch is used. The technique is similar to darning or weaving, but instead of parallel rows of stitches in every channel, the rows are more spread out, and outlines are often combined in several directions to form the shapes. Running stitch patterns have a dotted or broken line, and as in darning, the traveling threads are visible in the open areas between stitches.

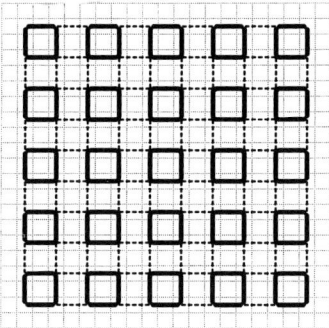

RUNNING STITCH PATTERN
Straight Rows
Box Pattern on Both Sides

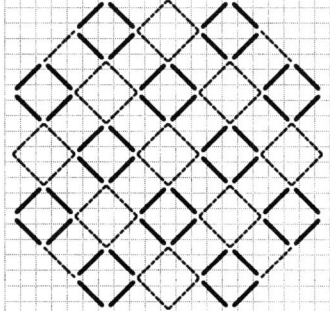

RUNNING STITCH PATTERN
Diagonal Rows
Diamond Pattern on Both Sides

Some patterns have bold isolated motifs that can be worked as separate units in the reversible manner. However, each thread should be ended within a single motif to avoid long unsightly traveling paths between units. In small areas, however, a thin layer of light pellon can be cut to fit the shape before the pattern is applied. If the blackwork pattern is stitched through two layers, these unavoidable traveling paths will not show, and the suggestion of "shadow work" created by the pellon is attractive and creates a nice focal point within a design. One can also use the iron-on pellon to secure the layer firmly before stitching, but I prefer to avoid any modern chemicals that may harm the embroidery at some future date. A few basting stitches can be used to hold the regular pellon until it is stable, and it will not fray around the trimmed edges.

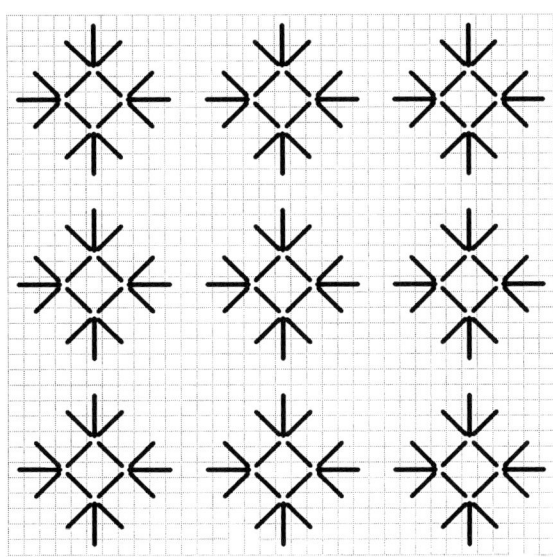

PATTERN WITH ISOLATED MOTIFS

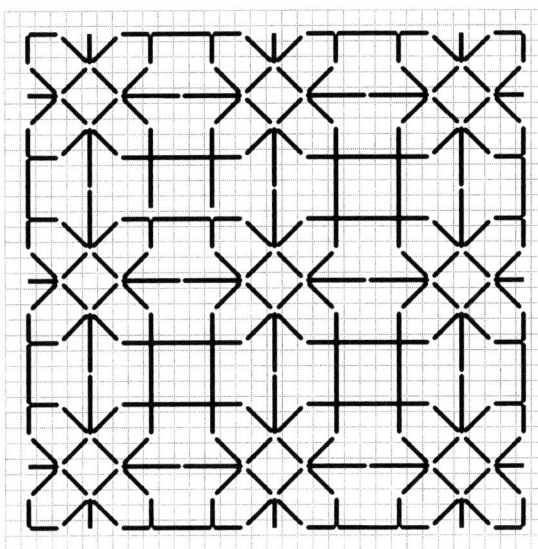

PATTERN WITH CONTINUOUS PATHS

With a dense fabric like aida or hardanger cloth, the random or backstitch method of doing blackwork is fine since shadows from traveling threads are less likely to show through. However, with more porous materials like linen and canvas, unsightly shadows will be obvious in open areas so an orderly method is desirable. As a proponent of the systematic reversible technique, I also find other advantages that make it a superior choice. First, one is less likely to omit a section or to forget a stitch because the sequence will be broken, and one will notice the mistake before the row is completed. The only segment that can be overlooked is a "side trip" since these are completed as you go, but often these segments touch or join the "main path" at several junctures so they can be added later – either on a "return trip" or from an adjacent row once the omission is noticed. If you do not understand the terms used in the previous sentence, please study the glossary provided on page 37.

In addition, this orderly approach makes ripping or backtracking easier since one always knows the path from whence one came. Last but not least, the additional concentration required of the reversible technique adds an extra dimension of challenge and interest as

3

one stitches. Once the principles of this method are mastered, one can create clean tracking sequences for patterns taken from available blackwork sources. Many books do not provide numbered sequences of any sort. Frequently the shape that a pattern will be used in can make it more efficient to execute the pattern in a certain way. For example, a rectangular shape is usually filled faster and more efficiently if the sequence rows follow the direction of the longest side. Most allover patterns can be stitched in rows that are either horizontal, vertical or diagonal so an experienced embroiderer can alter a sequence to suit each need. The ogee pattern on page 74 is a good example of this versatility. It fits Sampler 1 best with a horizontal sequence, but in the *Winter Whimsy* design (Color Plate VII) it fits the shape of the large trees best with a diagonal sequence.

One can also learn to derive original patterns either from doodles or from pattern networks readily available in other styles of ornament (see the bibliography of pattern sources in the back of the book). It is usually easy to transpose a printed pattern to a grid. Sometimes exact angles and proportions must be slightly altered, but the essence of the pattern will remain the same. By studying the pattern, one can divide it into logical row sequences based on the pattern repeats and the general shapes of the motifs involved. Sometimes a busy pattern can be made simpler if the pattern can be broken down into two separate sequences rather than one complex one. Patterns 7 and 17 (pages 59 and 84) are good examples of complex patterns that can be simplified when the outlines are broken down into two separate sequences. Being able to analyze a pattern helps one to plan an efficient stitching strategy that builds the pattern in individual rows.

Stitching in rows also allows one to plan thread amounts so that one never runs out of thread in the middle of a row. It is much easier to start and end threads in the outline areas and to not clutter up the back of the blackwork with bulky thread tails. If one starts to run short, one can usually eliminate all side trips and travel directly to the pattern edge. The next thread can complete the omitted stitches, and no tails will have to be whipped around the stitches on the back side.

Having a planned row sequence also allows one to add compensation stitches accurately along the pattern edges as part of the regular sequence. Planning a sequence makes one study the pattern closely. Therefore it is easier to memorize the pattern flow sooner and to recognize what the partial stitches need to be when the regular sequence rhythm is interrupted.

The main shortcoming of the reversible technique is that naturalistic shading cannot be achieved with this method. Scattered stitches cannot be added or subtracted without breaking the continuous path so a more random approach is essential. It is possible to achieve some stylized shading by using some unbroken or uninterrupted patterns, and the mountain treatments in the *Coyote Chorus* design (Color Plate II) illustrate this point. Each tier of mountains uses a different scale pattern to suggest distance, and each composite pattern is a combination of two separate patterns (one superimposed on the other) that use two different values of the same color. The effect is interesting and effective, but it is not naturalistic.

A second shortcoming is that a double running stitch path leaves untidy threads in the sinking holes around every stitch unless previous and subsequent stitches angle away from the stitch as in a zigzag path. Running stitches are not snugly wrapped like back stitches so adding later stitches that must share the same cluttered holes is messy and can cause distortions in the patterns if certain principles are ignored. This is what I call the "inherent vice" of double running method, but its advantages outweigh its negative features.

Another disadvantage of the reversible method is that the first row of every pattern tends to be somewhat confusing since the broken line of the running stitch sequence leaves gaps. It is hard for the eye to compensate for this until the pattern is established and the rhythm is familiar. However, once a full repeat is completed, it is easier to follow the flow of the pattern from this frame of reference rather than from the chart. By studying the overall chart carefully before stitching, often certain clues about the pattern will emerge, and one can memorize the stitch sequence faster by seeing these obvious relationships. If one concentrates on the rhythm of the sequence rather than the numbers that mark the sequence, this pattern recognition will usually occur sooner too. Patterns with straight stitches are always easier to learn than those with oblique or slanted stitches so warm up on a few simple outlines before moving on to intricate patterns.

To further understand the basic differences between the three types of blackwork methods, some comparison charts are included in the segment that follows.

METHOD COMPARISON CHARTS

The following charts should be helpful in understanding the unique features of all three of the different methods of executing blackwork. The comparisons made explore three important characteristics that demonstrate why one method is more favorable than the other.

BACKING COMPARISON

1. **BACK STITCH ROW**

2. **DOUBLE RUNNING ROW**

3. **COMBINATION ROW –**
alternating running stitch
and back stitch sequence

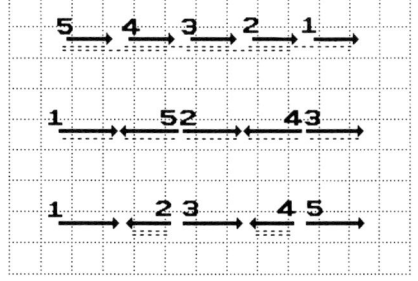

Back stitch rows have a double backing that is unnecessary. It could also create slight shadows around the stitches on the front side. The double backing is also less thrifty on thread use (a higher priority certainly when silk is used instead of cotton but a consideration worth noting). The combination rows do not have an ideal backing since there is no backing behind the running stitches and a double backing behind the back stitches. Should one need to end a thread in the middle of a row, the task would be more difficult with the "broken line" backing. The double running rows are reversible so they have the ideal backing with paths of equal density on both sides.

TIDINESS COMPARISON

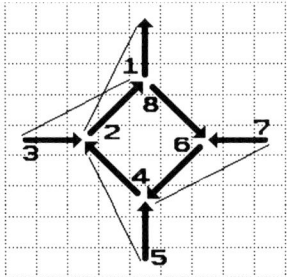

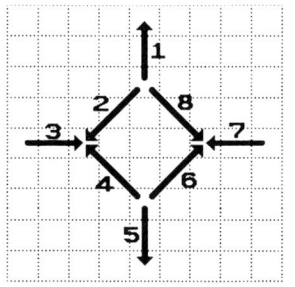

1. BACK STITCH SEQUENCE

2. ALTERNATING SEQUENCE
Back Stitch And Running Stitch Combination

The chart to the left demonstrates how untidy a back stitch sequence can be, especially when a pattern has a lot of turns (and most do!). These exposed traveling paths do not matter on a dense fabric like Aida cloth, but they are particularly offensive on porous fabrics like evenweave linen and canvas. A combination sequence like example 2, however, is tidy like the double running sequence. In this example the pattern is reversible because only one pattern repeat is illustrated. If additional repeats were added, or if the pattern had a lot of extensions away from the diamond core, however, the combination sequence would be more apt to meet with dead ends, and some backtracking would be needed to continue. A combination sequence can work when it is combined with double running to connect such extensions (dead ends are avoided) so there are some limited applications of this method in the patterns with isolated motifs (see Patterns 33 and 44 on pages 113 and 130).

STITCH LENGTH COMPARISON

1. BACK STITCH ROW

2. DOUBLE RUNNING ROW

3. COMBINATION ROW – alternating running stitch and back stitch sequence

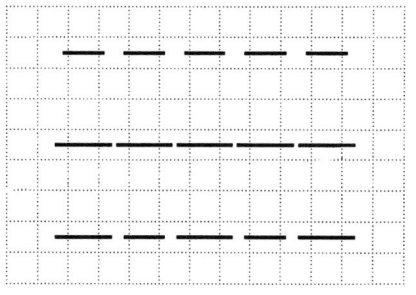

Back stitch rows have snugly wrapped stitches that have a taut tension on both ends of each stitch. The thread always comes from behind to wrap the stitch, and it exits forward, thus maximizing tension on the stitch itself. Back stitches nest nicely in straight rows because the double backing on the reverse side is not close to the front surface. The traveling paths are longer too so they move out of the way more readily when a new stitch is added. The needle tends to sink around the traveling path easily with minimal risk of piercing it. Therefore holes appear cleaner after the row is complete, and the stitches look straight and do not need "doctoring." These stitches will look smaller than stitches done in a double running sequence over the same path. Back stitches are the most consistent in size, as running stitches will vary when they turn corners. However, the fact that these stitches do not turn without leaving a dark path in an open area is a negative feature that outweighs the benefits listed.

Straight rows of running stitches do not wrap the canvas threads at all since the tension on the thread is away from the stitch itself. The stitch appears larger and always leaves a cluttered hole at both ends. However, careful manipulation of the needle on the return trip can correct distortions that would normally result so double running stitch method is still superior. By planning sequences that have "merged" stitches and that turn corners as much as possible to avoid having two or more straight stitches in a row, one can also minimize the negative "inherent vice" of the double running method. Stitches will vary in size depending on how much of an angle is created in traveling to the next stitch, but most pattern repeats are identical so this fact will not be that noticeable. Mirror image patterns can look distorted if executed casually too, but careful attention to balancing symmetrical motifs by planting the needle strategically on the return trip eliminates such discrepancies. Therefore my conclusion is that **ONCE UNDERSTOOD AND MASTERED, the reversible method is the most flexible method of all, and it will give optimum results!** The patterns that follow will expose you to some of the steps I have taken to improve results using the reversible technique, and the principles involved should prepare you well for all future blackwork dilemmas. You may find some of the solutions a bit nitpicky, but they do work. You may find another solution that is equally effective too so the goal is simply to awaken you to the fact that you can control the results in a way perhaps never realized before.

In presenting the various patterns, the general principles that have influenced the sequence provided will be discussed. In addition, certain individual "glitches" will be cited that need to be fixed on the return trip part of the sequence, and the appropriate solution will be given. These glitches are also more pronounced on a cotton canvas since the grid is more uniform – crooked stitches or patterns are more obvious against a straight even background. Linen tends to have irregular threads or slubs so the grid is somewhat less even, making slight discrepancies in stitch uniformity less obvious. Linen threads are usually thicker than cotton threads on the same size canvas so the actual holes on the cotton canvas are bigger. This means that stitches executed in a fine thread that does not fill the hole will lean or shift more readily from the tension exerted on the thread from the running stitch path. Therefore it is necessary to adjust them on the return trip to correct the crookedness. This is done with strategic planting of the needle on the return trip to "fix" them. The solutions developed to improve the appearance of blackwork patterns on canvas are equally applicable to blackwork on other fabrics in theory, but the smaller holes and the finer gauge sizes tend to reduce the conspicuousness of the same problems.

A few rare individuals are able to analyze a pattern instinctively and to stitch it in the reversible manner without the benefit of a numbered sequence. They are able to grasp the concepts of the double running method without the need for building a pattern with separated row segments. These same people usually have a natural gift for understanding mazes and other similar puzzles. This is an obvious advantage in doing any kind of blackwork outlines, but it is not a prerequisite for enjoying the reversible method. By learning a few useful terms and following simple guidelines, anyone can master the principles needed.

The following pages provide an outline of the basic techniques that are used in the execution of blackwork embroidery. All options are included where relevant, but the patterns provided for the stitched samples will utilize only the reversible method. The one exception is in chapter 6 where some isolated blackwork motifs are added in the negative spaces of some open composite patterns. These motifs do not touch to form an overall pattern so it was beneficial to alter the sequence to a combination of back stitch and running stitch with occasional double running rows. This allowed me to manipulate each motif so that it could be started and ended at a spot where traveling from area to area was limited to short distances and easily concealed.

Since good books already exist on the history and styles of traditional blackwork, this book will concentrate on ways to move beyond conventional concepts and to expand the application of these versatile linear outline patterns. It focuses on ways to improve and alter the appearance of what was historically considered a blackwork pattern. By using the patterns on canvas, it is possible to combine blackwork with other canvas techniques that can enhance it further. It had previously been combined with other surface embroidery techniques in English designs, but no layering or actual combination patterns existed to the best of my knowledge.

CONVENTIONAL VS. UNCONVENTIONAL STYLES

Unconventional Stitch Lengths

Traditional blackwork stitches span two threads for straight stitches and two intersections for diagonal stitches. On linen, stitches done over any less than two threads might slip through the weave of the fabric and be lost, so I presume this risk was a factor in determining the conventional stitch length. Sizing is minimal on linen fabric compared to stiffer canvas, however, so stitches have added support on canvas. Therefore I have successfully used the following unconventional stitch lengths on canvas:

1. Patterns can be done with stitches that cover only one thread or intersection on canvas if the canvas is filled with basketweave beforehand. The blackwork pattern is applied on top with a backstitch method for cleaner entries and exits. The usual pattern is reduced in scale by 50% since twice as many repeats fit the same area. This is a real advantage on canvas since 23-mesh is the smallest weave for practical application. Many traditional patterns were developed for much finer linen weaves so they do not adapt well to canvas use (too bold). By overstitching the blackwork, you still maintain 100% canvas coverage if it is desired – this is more appropriate for some designs, so why not? As long as the background stitch is compatible with the overlay so that no stitches are split when the blackwork is done, this approach can be tidy and effective.

An example of this use can be seen in the window treatment of the *Persian Fantasy* design (Color Plate XI). The window area was first filled with tent stitch, using Medici crewel, and the blackwork was added on top in back stitch method, using DMC fil d'or gold metallic.

2. Patterns can be done with stitches that cover one intersection on canvas. A tent stitch holds well on canvas whether it is executed with the traditional back stitch wrap or is done in a running stitch so traditional patterns can be altered this way to create greater density. I call this process "compressing" a pattern, and one example is shown on page 48 (Pattern 3-b).

3. Patterns can also be done with stitches that are longer than two threads or intersections. Stitches that cover three or four threads or intersections are stable on canvas so I have often merged two regular running stitches into one long stitch over four threads or intersections. Two or more stitches in a straight line can be unsightly even when consistent rules are followed. Therefore why not merge two stitches over two threads to one stitch over four threads? Similarly three stitches over two threads can be improved by making them two stitches over three threads. As long as other supplementary treatments or later reversible rows do not have to intersect these "split" stitches, they can be extended or merged. A single long stitch is always more attractive than a pair of smaller "less straight" stitches. The end result is that the overall pattern becomes more uniform when the stitches are merged so the cosmetic benefit certainly justifies the alteration.

A stitch that is longer than three or four threads, however, tends to be unstable without couching. Therefore if a straight line in a pattern is six threads or intersections long, it should be split into two stitches over three threads instead (see Pattern 5 on page 54; the sides of the heart are treated this way). A straight line that is twelve threads long could be divided into three stitches that are four threads long (see Pattern 5 again as the line that connects the hanging hearts is handled this way).

An unusual use of a longer thread length was needed in the *Mamadillo* design (Color Plate III). The mother and four baby armadillos are all outlined in tent stitch so the overall design had an unavoidable center thread rather than a center hole along the center axis or midpoint of the four babies. I could not properly center a conventional blackwork pattern in this situation but it occurred to me that I could center the pattern by working all the straight stitches over three threads while maintaining the traditional length of two threads for the diagonal stitches. Actually on 23-mesh Congress cloth a straight stitch over three threads is comparable in length to a diagonal stitch over two threads so an interesting change in the proportions of the pattern occurred that was attractive and appropriate in scale for the background effects desired. Since then I have referred to this type of adaptation from a traditional pattern as an "expanded" pattern – the opposite of a "compressed" one (study pages 42-45 to compare the specific changes discussed here).

4. Patterns can be done with stitches that are slanted rather than either straight or diagonal. Many star patterns, and those that utilize the hexagon, the ogee and the scale networks can be translated into blackwork when slanted stitches are used. The traditional slanted stitch was a simple gobelin stitch that was two threads tall and one thread wide. However, for unconventional treatments any size slanted stitch is acceptable.

Composite Networks with Secondary Fillings

Conventional blackwork patterns were usually single networks rather than composite networks. However, the dense patterns often left interesting negative spaces and shapes between the motifs that could be filled with the following treatments:

1. One or more secondary blackwork patterns – either running stitch or double running stitch sequences.

2. One or more exposed canvas patterns – not reversible but executed so that traveling threads are concealed as much as possible.

3. A pulled thread pattern.

4. A darning pattern.

Superimposed or Layered Patterns

Additional variations and composite patterns can be made by combining the following treatments that involve layering rather than alternating two compatible patterns in a single composite network:

1. A foundation of tramé, using the blackwork overlay as a means to secure the unstable laid threads.

2. Use of one or more tramé networks on top of a blackwork pattern – very three-dimensional effect here, especially when the blackwork is in a dark recessive color.

The right side of the small leaf design (Color Plate IX) uses this treatment. There are both a square trellis and a diagonal trellis pattern on top of the blackwork pattern. Couching stitches over the overlapping intersections also fall into the negative spaces of the blackwork pattern. This particular pattern is charted on page 104.

3. Use of a blackwork pattern to couch down a foundation layer of sheer fabric. The fabric is first secured in place with either a counted outline for a symmetrical shape or with basting stitches for a more free form shape that will be outlined later with a couched thread or a stitch like stem outline. The canvas holes will still be visible through the transparent fabric so the blackwork is then stitched through both fabrics. The excess fabric is trimmed away after the pattern is completed, and the basting stitches are covered by the outline.

The stomach area of the *Comely Catfish* (Color Plate XV) is done in this technique, and the couched Japanese gold outline is added last so that it does not snag any of the delicate threads used in the patterning.

4. Layering of one blackwork pattern on top of another foundation pattern. The chapter on superimposed blackwork patterns begins on page 80 and discusses a number of examples of composite networks that combine two compatible patterns.

Color and Thread Variations

Blackwork patterns were traditionally done in one color - usually a single dark thread on a light background. Variations on this concept would include:

1. Patterns that use a light thread on a dark background.

2. Patterns that use two or more colors or values within the same composite pattern. Make sure that contrasts are adequate so that the blackwork pattern is not diluted. Values that are too close create a "fuzzy" effect that is usually lost completely at viewing distance.

This concept can also be used to shade in a manner that does not require altering the structured sequence. In the *Rainy Winter Landscape* design (Color Plate VI) four different patterns were used in the bridge. Every pattern has a combination of gray values to suggest both dimension as well as detail in the wrought iron railings, the posts and the abutment. Close values were used rather than sharp contrasts since a clear view would be obstructed by the sleet and drizzle. It is unusual to use middle values in blackwork treatments since the pattern itself is somewhat diluted when contrasts are minimal – however, isn't it appropriate to this particular subject matter? For this reason, don't let rules inhibit your judgment. I prefer to call them guidelines rather than rules since rigid rules imply that exceptions are not invited.

3. Patterns that use two or more weights or types of thread within the same composite pattern. Traditional patterns use the same weight thread throughout the pattern except when shading or outlining; density is increased with a heavier thread – another strand of the same floss or silk thread is usually added for shading, and a heavier fiber like perle cotton is often used for outlining. Combining different weights of thread in a single composite pattern can create interesting textures as well as added density, and a different thread can be used for each separate sequence to produce unique effects.

4. Patterns that use overdyed or variegated threads. Today's elegant choices of hand dyed threads make them irresistible to use. I often use the ombré metallics in my tramé treatments, and I have successfully combined a foundation layer of pattern in blended colors with a top layer of solid pattern. However, a single outline in a variegated thread tends to dull or negate the pattern definition so be careful to choose a combination with high intensities and/or dark values to avoid this. Sometimes the pattern may appear clear at close range as it is stitched, but it will be lost or diluted at viewing distance. Therefore proceed cautiously when you use threads with mixed blended colors, and remember that blackwork depends on its strong linear outlines for its visual success. Be sure the pattern works both close up and far away before a final decision is made within a design.

When I am not stitching I frequently place my "in progress" piece on the mantle of the fireplace so that I notice any unsettling problems as they emerge. One can purchase a gadget called a reducing glass to simulate a distance view while seated close to an embroidery, but I prefer to walk by the piece and to evaluate it from varying distances and angles since the finished design will be viewed in a similar home setting.

Pattern Variations

The last category of ways to use blackwork in an unconventional manner is a broad one that deals more with methods to vary a specific pattern or blackwork motif. Historical patterns were generally either stripes (patterns with a one way thrust) or diaper patterns (patterns that form visual diagonals in both directions or which have a four-way repeat).

If one studies books about pattern in general, it is possible to apply a lot of the same mechanics used in pattern development to blackwork.

For example, one way to vary a pattern is to rotate it. If a stripe pattern is rotated and joined to an existing upright version of itself, an interesting zigzag or chevron stripe can result. In Color Plate X, the small heart is filled with such a stripe that is rotated along the center axis of the symmetrical shape. The mirror image or flip-flop pattern truly reinforces the shape in this case so the choice is most appropriate. This same pattern is also used in Sampler 1 (unmirrored and without step 3) and can be found on page 181. The core pattern is found on page 97.

A single blackwork motif can often be manipulated in the same way other pattern repeats are altered to form an interesting variation. Imagine the variety that can be produced if pattern terms such as half-stepping, overlapping, interlacing, interlocking, enlarging, or reducing are applied to a single figure or outline in blackwork. Another entire book could be written on this subject, but it is more appropriate to save this information until the chapter on pattern design.

TECHNIQUE

Now that ways of developing new blackwork treatments have been discussed, let's proceed to the technical points needed to execute such patterns. An outline format is used for this discussion since it is a "manual" on blackwork technique. First a brief overview of the three basic methods to execute these linear outline patterns:

I. Ways Of Doing Blackwork

A. Back stitch method. A random approach of just "walking around" in a pattern with no structured path or numerical sequence.

    1. Advantages

        a. Easier to memorize the pattern since the whole repeats can be stitched in a continuous solid path.

        b. More versatile method for adding naturalistic shading when desired.

        c. Stitches seat more easily since the traveling path does not interfere. The traveling path is not as close to the surface as it is in a double running stitch path – less apt to be pierced and moves aside readily.

        d. Stitches are snugly wrapped – shared holes stay clean.

    2. Disadvantages

        a. Not tidy on the back – no control over the traveling threads so they show in open areas whenever the line turns.

b. Traveling path is heavier since back stitch method has double coverage on the back side.

c. Harder to rip if mistakes are made, or to backtrack when sections or stitches are omitted – no organized path to follow.

B. Combination of alternating back stitches and running stitches. This method is used by several contemporary teachers in a consistent manner or just at corners to prevent the traveling thread from leaning in.

1. Advantages

a. Pattern fills in a solid line so less confusing at first.

b. This method does eliminate the visibility of the traveling threads since the alternating rhythm causes these to fall behind the back stitches. There is no path behind the running stitches but there is a double path behind each back stitch.

c. This method also combines well with the reversible technique in handling some outlines. In Color Plate XIV the blackwork areas are isolated and do not form an overall pattern so a combination routine allowed me to add these accents in an efficient manner to each pattern. One example of this technique is provided on page 30 in the step 2 sequence of Pattern 44.

2. Disadvantages

a. Less versatile for intricate paths with side trips since a detour would eventually become a "dead end." Must backtrack to a new starting point by weaving through or wrapping around the path on the back side. This creates unnecessary bulk that is avoided with the reversible method – double running paths automatically return to the original starting point.

b. Backing is not solid – there are double paths behind every back stitch and nothing behind the running stitches. This does not make it easy to secure threads within the outlines when it is necessary.

c. Stitches vary in size since the snugly wrapped back stitches are tighter and smaller than the running stitches (see the chart on page 6 that compares this feature).

C. Double running stitch method. Superior in every way, particularly for the advanced student who has no difficulty following intricate charts or mazes. Methodical structured approach creates the most attractive results, if controlled properly so that the inevitable glitches of its forward rhythm are handled consistently to form uniform repeats. Additional advantages and some minor disadvantages were discussed in depth on pages 5-7 so they are not repeated here.

II. Materials

A. Fabrics. Any evenweave material is suitable, but the count and density of the fabric will vary whether a linen, cotton, wool or synthetic fabric is chosen. The fineness or coarseness of the material should be appropriate to the design and comfortable for one's eyesight as well. In addition, the texture and color of the fabric should be suitable.

B. Threads. The appropriate thread is usually one of the same weight and thickness as the threads of the fabric selected. One that is too heavy will stretch the holes and appear strained and bulky. One that is too thin will appear skimpy. Silk and cotton floss are the most flexible threads to use since a single strand is so fine, but remember that silk is NOT colorfast so do not use it on table linens or other items that must be laundered. Other weights of cotton can also be used effectively, especially on canvas (perle cotton, broder, tatting thread, Danish flower thread, etc.). Some of these come in several weights but all are twisted and cannot be separated into single strands. Metallic threads and some rayon threads like Natesh can create lovely shiny patterns or glimmering accents when combined with other threads in a composite pattern. However, synthetic threads are somewhat harder to work with so always try a sample swatch first to see if a thread is suitable and not too tedious to use.

Heavier twisted threads like perle cotton are usually used for the outlines around the design shapes. They maneuver well on canvas, especially around curves using stem outline, which covers drawn outlines better than outline stitch or backstitch. The thicker look of the heavier thread is also a nice contrast to the flat blackwork pattern inside. In traditional designs, an outline tends to frame in or contain the pattern inside. It usually matches the color of the blackwork, and it also provides a place for securing starting and ending tails that is heavier than the delicate blackwork. Many contemporary treatments use free form shapes and scattered patterns with no defined outlines or contours, however, so anything goes.

The *Vase of Flowers* design shown in Color Plate VIII is an unusually large one that is done on a dense 22-count evenweave wool fabric using Appleton crewel yarns. The wool yarn was appropriate both to the design and to the count of the fabric. The design was adapted from an example of an 18th century woven bed rug that is in the Historic Deerfield collection. The small repeats in the dark darning patterns in the rug resembled blackwork so I couldn't resist adapting the floral design to a blackwork interpretation. This embroidery was also my first attempt at executing a blackwork design in more than one color. Several values of gold and green were used in the patterns so I was being somewhat "unconventional" over a decade ago even though the patterns used are all traditional published ones.

C. Needles. A blunt tapestry needle in an appropriate size is usually recommended for stitching the patterns. However, a chenille needle is sometimes helpful when securing traveling threads on the back side. My preferred method carefully avoids piercing or sinking into previously laid stitches as you reuse shared holes so the blunt needle is ideal until it is time to bury the tails. Most #24 or #26 tapestry needles are sharp enough to pierce threads and to draw blood, however, so beware!

D. Hoops or frames. These are recommended to keep the fabric taut as you stitch so that a uniform tension control can be maintained. A lined wooden hoop is preferable since it slips less and minimizes the ring from the crimping of the fabric. Do not leave a hoop on the fabric when you are not stitching, however, as it may stretch or distort the fabric beyond repair with repeated abuse. A stretcher frame is better for canvas and for large designs on linen. Use tacks rather than staples to mount the fabric so that it can be easily tightened as needed. If the frame is secured to a floor stand, or to a table with a squeeze clamp, both hands are left free to stitch. A hoop can also be stabilized or anchored with a weight such as a heavy book or a bag filled with sand or buck shot to leave both hands free.

III. Pattern Characteristics

Blackwork patterns vary greatly in both scale and density. When planning a design, it is important to consider these features and balance the elements accordingly. Playing with various densities of newspaper print within the design outlines is an excellent way to determine a good balance of contrasts before patterns are selected. Newspapers are cheap and readily available for cutouts, and the variations in the size and the spacing of the lettering in the various sections somewhat resembles pattern so they are a great tool.

Color-Aid papers in the assortment of "graduated grays" are another useful tool for planning density and scale distribution in a design. However, these papers are expensive and they are solid so they show only value contrasts without any suggestion of pattern. Squinting at actual pattern samples helps to determine their density at close range. Turn to the index of the patterns included in the back of the book. The patterns presented are all charted on computer graph paper that measures twelve squares to the inch so the patterns would appear the same size on a 12-mesh canvas. By seeing all of the patterns on the same size grid, it is easy to judge both the relative scale and density. A design must be effective both at viewing distance and close up, and careful planning can eliminate hours of unpleasant ripping later if things don't work out. A doodle cloth is essential, not only to test the sequence planned, but to see the scale of the pattern on the same size mesh selected for the final design. Thread weights can also alter the scale and density of a pattern so play with several options. Patterns with sharp oblique angles usually need a lighter weight thread to punctuate the sharp points so use a single strand of silk for these instead of two strands of floss on Congress cloth.

A. Scale. The scale of a pattern must always be appropriate to the size of the shape chosen. A large scale pattern looks overwhelming and uncomfortable in a doll house, and by the same token, a mini-repeat pattern tends to get lost in a large area or to blur when viewed at a distance. Therefore a good rule to use in selecting a pattern is that "a pattern must show a minimum of 3-4 repeats in at least one direction to be appropriate for the size and shape of an area." The essence of pattern is repetition, and it takes several repeats to establish the flow and make it comfortable to the viewer. This guideline is important, and careful placement of the pattern also adds to its viewing pleasure. By centering one repeat, the eye is drawn to this focal point so that compensation along the outer edges is less conspicuous. Directions within certain patterns can also be used to reinforce certain shapes – e.g. patterns with oblique rows would be ideal for a parallelogram.

15

There are two examples in the *Sailboat* design (Color Plate V) that illustrate how a pattern can reinforce rather than antagonize a shape. In the mainsail there are three divisions that are all tall triangles. The same elongated cross pattern (Pattern 4A, page 50) was used in the two side sections. Notice how the pattern was placed in a mirror image position so that the oblique rows of pattern repeats contour nicely to the slanted edge lines of the sail. Careful placement as well as selection of a pattern helps to reinforce a shape, and making such logical choices will make your designs that much more sophisticated.

The midsection of the rear sail teaches another lesson about applying the rules too rigidly in pattern. Earlier I said that a pattern should repeat at least 3-4 times within a shape to be effective. Since this area is narrow and tapered, a small repeat pattern was used first, but it had no "pizazz." It was removed, and a dramatic bold pattern was substituted that had a strong vertical thrust. Even though some areas have not even a single repeat of the pattern, careful centering of the tulip motif so that the vertical repeat was clear made the pattern effective. The end result was perfect and actually created some perspective that did not exist when the bland small repeat pattern was there (the headsail in front seems to billow out more against the present background). The lesson here is to never rule out any possibility when the usual solution does not work.

Incidentally this same bold pattern was used in the *Rainy Winter Landscape* design (Color Plate VI) in a horizontal position for the center bridge railing. Notice how much less obvious the tulip shape is in this two-value presentation with less contrast. Many variables can affect pattern so it is fun to experiment with the same pattern and see how much the outlines can change in their visual effect. The more doodling you do, the better you can anticipate the end result. Keep records on your experiments so that your observations and conclusions will remain useful to you when future planning is needed.

B. Density. Small scale patterns are usually more dense than bold large scale patterns, but there are also ways to make larger repeats heavier and denser.

1. Use a thicker thread, or more strands of a fine thread.

2. Add additional patterns within the shapes formed by the original pattern. Possibilities here are endless, and many were cited when the ways to vary traditional concepts were discussed. Plan these additions with a pencil on graph paper first to save time. You will often be surprised at how easily new combinations and networks are produced.

3. Random shading is particularly appropriate in naturalistic designs, but adding to or subtracting from a given pattern can usually be achieved only with scattered back stitches if a realistic effect is desired. More stylized variations can be achieved by maintaining the reversible rows but omitting some stitches or segments within the regulated sequence. Another possibility would be to complete a bold reversible pattern, but then fill negative spaces randomly with shading to achieve further density in desired areas.

IV. Starting and Ending Threads

A. Use an "away" knot or tail when a pattern is started along the edge of the shape. In reversible blackwork, all thread tails are secured in the outline area unless an outline is not planned. When this is done depends on whether the outline is added first or last. I prefer to work without a stitched outline in the way. Traveling is done with pivot stitches along the drawn outline, and entries and exits are cleaner with no outline to interfere. Compensation decisions are also easier to judge since visibility is clearer. If the stitched outline is already in place, however, thread tails can be buried immediately, and traveling is accomplished by weaving through the outline on the back side from one exit point to the next entry point.

B. It is always more graceful to center a pattern within a shape. The exact center can be measured in symmetrical shapes, but it can be eyeballed in other shapes by dividing the shape in half in opposing directions. The point where the lines intersect defines the center. In both cases, there is less counting or guesswork if the blackwork sequence is started at the center point. Adjust the first stitch so that the pattern motif will be positioned evenly around a center hole or thread. Then take a double length thread and come up into the starting hole with half of the thread length. Park the remaining half away from the direction of the first sequence, being careful to secure it on the front so that no dangling threads interfere with the working thread. Use the threaded end to execute the running stitch row towards the opposite side until it reaches the edge of the shape. Then park this thread on the front side, thread up the other end, and work the remaining running stitch step to the edge of the other side. Continue with this thread and complete the double running sequence to form a solid line for the first row. Thereafter one end will do the rows on one side of the middle row, and the other one will do the rows on the opposite side. Often small areas can be filled with a single double length thread, and half of the starting and ending threads are eliminated as a result.

The only shortcoming with this technique is that half of the thread is worked "against the direction" when natural threads are used. With threads like perle cotton that have a tight twist, the direction does not matter, and the thread wears well in either direction. However, with floss there is a slight difference in the sheen of the smooth thread when worked in opposing directions. With only 2 strands, however, the difference is minimal compared to solid satin stitches done in 4-6 strands. It is more important to minimize the number of starting and ending threads in open techniques. Outlines should not be overloaded with bulky thread tails and traveling paths so the usual guideline regarding thread direction with natural fibers is broken to honor this higher priority.

Since blackwork is an open technique, the thread seldom fills the hole so abrasion is minimal as you stitch. Therefore the risk of uneven wear is much lower than it is in solid canvas fillings where threads often rub both the canvas and the adjacent filled areas as they are seated.

C. There is another "trick" that can be used to minimize the number of starting and ending tails when 2 strands of floss are needed. A double length thread is again used, but this time it is folded, and the two cut ends are threaded into the eye of the needle. Enter along the side edge of the shape for the first row and come up from the back, leaving the loop dangling at least 2" on the back. As the needle sinks into the next hole to complete the first stitch, pass it through the loop and tighten it towards the direction of the next stitch. With this method, the thread will lock on the first stitch, and all starting tails are eliminated – an obvious advantage! Again this solution would not be acceptable when multiple strands are used, but for finer thread weights as in blackwork, the advantages far outweigh the disadvantages, so why not? You will have a double backing on the first stitch, but the reversibility is still maintained in spite of the additional density. To sum up, ONE CAN BEND OR EVEN BREAK A RULE TO SATISFY A HIGHER PRIORITY AS LONG AS THE CONSEQUENCES OF BREAKING THE RULE ARE NOT CONSPICUOUS ENOUGH TO OVERSHADOW THE POSITIVE RESULTS ACHIEVED.

NOTE. This method cannot be used when you need to start in the middle of a pattern to properly center it. **In addition, it is very important to tighten the looped thread towards the direction of the next stitch.** If it is tightened in the opposite direction, the loop may end up on the front surface where it is a definite eyesore!

D. Ending Threads. When outlines are available, all tails are secured in the backing of these edge contours. Use either a simple weaving motion for at least an inch, or combine the weaving with a locking back stitch halfway if the thread is slippery, or if the item will be laundered. These back stitches form loops rather than knots so they are acceptable since additional bulk is minimal. If the backing is pierced as one weaves, additional security is also attained with no additional bulk. If outline backings are scanty, as in the backstitch path of stem outline, a whipping or wrapping motion is easier. This forms a slight ridge but is very secure. Another alternative is to snake the tail in and out of the line of back stitches. Pivot after an inch and snake one quarter of the way back to lock this thread. This lacing is less bulky than the whipping, but both methods are acceptable procedures.

HINT: At the end of every row of stitching, check to make sure there is adequate thread to complete the next trip before it is started. Ending in the middle of a row is tedious and well worth avoiding. However, when necessary, tails can be secured within the blackwork rows, and they must be when there are no outlines available. To accomplish this, merely whip or wrap the tail around the pattern lines on the back side, following the same path so that no threads show in open areas. If you wrap 2-3 times over each back side stitch, and tug forward at the end of each series, the tail will be less likely to wiggle loose, and you will not have to have as long a path for each tail. These whipped rows will add density to the back side, needless to say, but it is usually not conspicuous enough to be noticeable on the front. When two plies are being used, one can separate these and run one tail in one direction and the other tail in the opposite direction to minimize excessive bulk.

When blackwork is used as a background pattern, try to start and end along the outer edge of the design so that tails can be secured in the bald canvas outside of the design area. This is particularly practical when a mat is planned for a framed piece since a wider selvage is added around the design. End the tails with either 1" rows of closely spaced split stitches or running stitches that start at least three threads beyond the mat edge (why risk any clutter in case the mat is not perfectly placed!).

IMPORTANT: After the design is completed and ready to mount, check the back side one more time before you present it to the framer or finisher. Clip any tails snugly that have wiggled loose. Even short ends can be unsightly in open areas, and only those that blend with the backing fabric are safe. Usually one chooses a backing fabric similar in color and shade to the dominant thread in the design, but the joy of the reversible technique is that you can use any color. This flexibility is particularly welcome in a multicolor mixed media design where this decision is best made after the design is completed.

V. Outlines

A number of line stitches are appropriate here depending on the weight desired. Chain stitch creates a dense outline if done with a medium to loose tension. Stitches like coral or pekinese are highly decorative but difficult to control on canvas. A back stitch outline tends to look too angular on canvas, but the lines can be softened by either whipping or lacing the outline after it is completed. A laid or couched thread, however, is easy to control since it maneuvers well around curves. The secret here is to come up and sink into the same canvas hole with the couching thread. Swing the laid thread out of the way to accomplish this easily – not only will the couched thread hug the outline better, but the couching stitches will automatically lay perpendicular to the laid thread the way they are supposed to. Using two different holes for the couching stitches does not tend to create an attractive uniform spacing.

Stem and outline produce a similar weight line, and both stitches are easy to control around intricate contours. Stem (which throws the loop of the thread _below_ the line as each stitch is taken) is particularly forgiving on canvas since it maneuvers well around curves even if there are unavoidable discrepancies in the stitch lengths when the holes of the canvas are used. Fabric threads can be pierced easily to control stitch lengths accurately, but it is unwise to risk breaking a canvas thread by doing this. Stem stitch produces a lovely rounded corded line that is attractive and that covers a drawn line well. Outline stitch (which throws the loop of the thread _above_ the line as each stitch is taken) is somewhat more angular and thinner so less attractive around difficult contours. Both of these stitches can also be whipped when wider coverage is needed.

Charts for all of these outline stitches are included in most embroidery stitch manuals, and many are included in other blackwork books too so they are not repeated here. Books do differ in how they label the stem and outline stitch, however. I prefer teacher Audrey Francini's labels, as she developed a clever way to remember the two stitches. Outline stitch begins with an "o" so the loop goes "over" the outline path as the stitch is executed. Stem begins with an "s" for subway so the loop goes "below" the line as the stitch is executed. The reason that the two stitches look different has to do with the direction of the twist of the thread as it is laid so an understanding of how the loop affects the stitch is more important than the name of the stitch.

To better clarify the difference between these two stitches, charts for both stem and outline are included below. The actual numbered sequence is the same for both stitches so notice the difference in the position of the loop. Both stitches must be worked from left to right, but the direction of the loop must also lean towards the arc of a curve to maintain a uniform appearance throughout. Therefore adjust the starting point and position of the frame to accommodate the dominate swell of each curved line. For best results keep the stitch length as even as possible, but shorter stitches maneuver better around tight curves so again adjust accordingly.

OUTLINE AND STEM STITCH CHART

OUTLINE STITCH   STEM STITCH

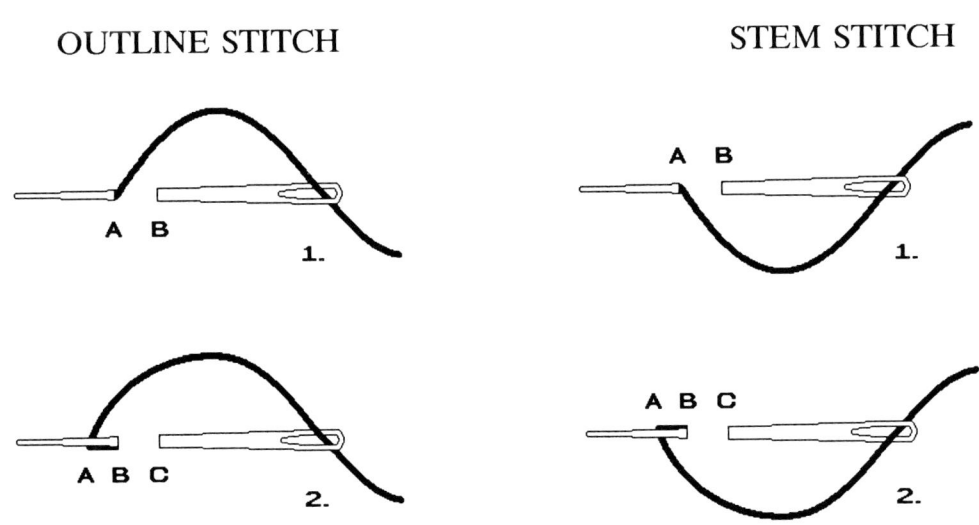

NOTE: In the diagrams above, stitch A-B is a compensation stitch that must be used to keep the line thickness uniform throughout. However, this should be eliminated when an outline tapers, as in the tip of a leaf.

Another trick to controlling both stem and outline stitch is to tighten each stitch by drawing the thread straight up perpendicular to the canvas. If you "swing" the thread as you tighten it, the tension is less even so the stitches will look less uniform. Slight variations in tension control are more obvious with both chain and outline so my preferred choice is usually stem, particularly when curved lines are being outlined. As stated earlier, if stem is worked on canvas, it is usually not necessary to pierce the canvas to control the stitch. There is a chart on the next page that illustrates an appropriate spacing for stem outline on 23-mesh Congress cloth, using the canvas holes to place the stitches. If a twisted thread like perle cotton is used for the outline, slight discrepancies in stitch lengths and placements will be even less conspicuous.

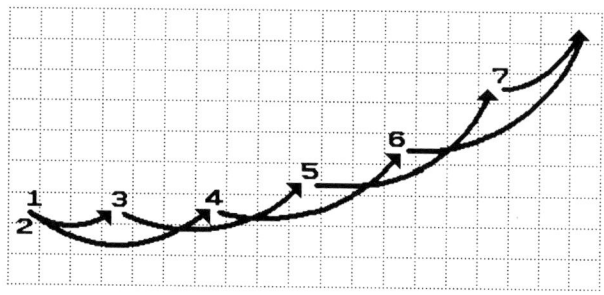

EXAMPLE OF STEM STITCH
AROUND A CURVE
ON CANVAS

One dilemma that occurs in using stem outline around a drawn curved line on canvas is confusion about the sinking hole. When the drawn line is over a hole, the decision is obvious – use the hole! However, when the drawn line covers a canvas thread rather than a hole, one must sink on one side or the other of this line mark (unless a sharp needle is used to pierce the thread, but I only recommend this for linen since canvas threads are stiff and hard to penetrate, especially with a thick thread like perle cotton). The needle should sink on the inside of the swell of the curve since the loop of the stitch will always lean out towards the arc of the curve and cover the drawn outline. Study the example drawn below to be sure you understand this concept.

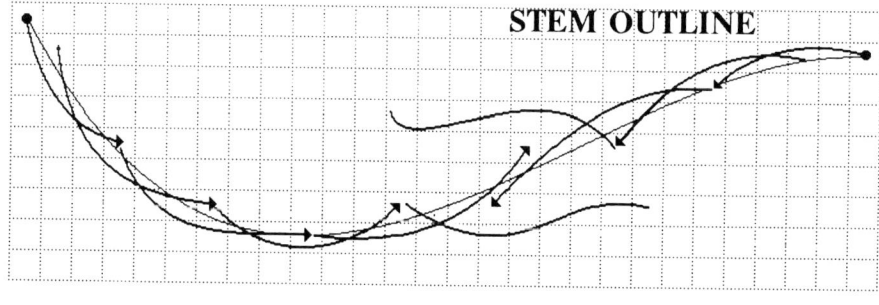

STEM OUTLINE

SINKING HOLES

The chart to the left shows a stem outline along an S-curve. One thread is worked left to right along the lower curve, and it uses the holes that are inside the arc (or above the line) since the braid leans outward as it is seated. The upper curve is worked from the opposite direction with the canvas rotated so that the direction is still left to right. Again the sinking holes are below the line (or inside the arc) since the braid swells outward as it is seated. The loose threads will meet in the middle and must be tucked around each other as they sink a final time to create an inconspicuous join.

Symmetrical shapes present special problems since they cannot be drawn on the canvas accurately. If a stem outline is planned, draw or baste only the right half of a symmetrical shape like a heart. Start in the middle along the center axis and fill the right side first on each row of pattern. Then add the left side sequence, using a mirror image compensation of the right side along the left edge. After the pattern is completed, both sides of the shape should match. The outline of the left edge will be accurately defined by the pattern, especially if it is dense. To remove any doubt, the sinking holes for the stem stitch sequence can be marked on the right side with enlarged poked holes and then repeated with mirror image placement on the left side. This will assure that the outlines of both sides match when the stem outline is completed, and the shape will appear symmetrical as long as the tension control is uniform on the stitches.

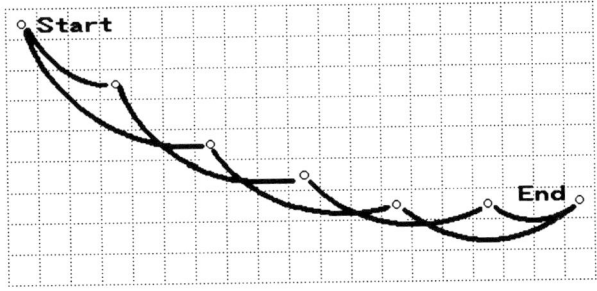

MIRROR IMAGE PATTERN
STEM OUTLINE

The pattern to the left is a mirror image of the one at the top of page 21. The circles mark the poked holes that set up the guidelines for the stem stitch. If joined to the right side pattern above, this outline would form an exact symmetrical left or mirror image side.

NOTE: This technique of outlining with stem was used in the sea gulls of the *Sailboat* design (Color Plate V). Only one wing was drawn on the canvas for each bird. The second wing merely repeated the same pattern of sinking holes as the first wing so the birds appear uniform and symmetrical. There are two rows of outline in each wing. The second row was added after the measured row was completed in each bird.

A more simple way to outline a symmetrical shape is to use a tent outline or a texture stitch. Draw half of the shape on a doodle cloth that has the same canvas mesh as the planned final design. Follow this line with the stitch chosen, being sure to center the first stitch along the center hole or thread. Once the outline is stitched accurately for one half, a chart can be drawn that shows the mirror image side next to the copy of the stitched side. If you are lazy, just make a transparency of the chart of the stitched half – turn it over and voila! You have an accurate chart of the other side. If charted outlines are used, they should be stitched first, and then no drawn lines have to be put on the final design at all. A tent outline is adequate for most simple blackwork fillings, but if intricate composite patterns are planned, create a bolder outline that will accommodate many thread tails of varying weights. Coarser outlines are usually more appropriate for large areas too (notice the heavy outlines used around the shapes in Color Plates VII, XIII, XIV, and XVI).

When a stitched outline is in place before a blackwork filling is added, it is used both to enter and exit each new row and to travel from row to row when needed. When it is necessary to enter or exit a row on an underneath stitch, it is important to secure the thread in the outline backing at the appropriate place that will keep the traveling path directly under the stitch that will be completed on top later. There is a tendency to forget this since the stitch on top of the canvas is already completed so turn the canvas over to pierce into the outline at the correct place each time. To travel correctly on the back of the outline, merely weave through the back side path or whip the working thread around the outline backing at strategic points to hold the traveling thread behind the outline edge until the new entry point is reached. All blackwork rows will start and end at the inner edge of the outline stitch, but be careful not to pierce it as you enter the edge hole.

When no preworked outline exists, it is easier to add the blackwork with no interference in the edge holes. However, another technique must be used to travel from row to row when no outline stitches exist. If a row ends with an underneath stitch, come up in the starting hole and take a pivot stitch to both secure the thread and to guide it to the entry point of the next row. This pivot stitch is usually taken over a single thread rather than an intersection, and I adopted the term "roll over" stitch for the maneuver from teacher Betty Bohannon – it will tend to recede and almost disappear when tightened, and an inconspicuous turn is favorable since it will not interfere with the outline when it is added. Carry the thread to the next entry point and study its path under the canvas. If it leans in and tends to show in the open area, take a back stitch at strategic intervals to hold the traveling path to the outline. This back stitch shows less if made over a single thread too, but an occasional tent stitch will be needed when the drawn line falls over an intersection rather than in an open channel or on a canvas thread. To enter the new row, determine what the count of the pattern should be and merely come up at the appropriate point. If it is necessary to start on an underneath stitch, take another pivot stitch to position the needle for the correct angle for the first stitch. Pattern 23 is an example of one pattern that lays better if the diagonal stitches of the running stitch row are always placed on top of the canvas (see pages 97 and 30 for a complete explanation of why this is true).

NOTE. Inconspicuous "roll over" stitches over a single thread rather than an intersection make the least conspicuous pivot stitches. However, both maneuvers will show less if they are executed with a "wrapped" back stitch pull. Avoid running stitches since they sit up higher on the canvas and will not recede.

When one ends a row on a down stitch, one can often carry to the next entry point without any pivot or holding stitches. This usually depends both on the contour of the shape as well as on the scale of the pattern (small repeats have less distance between the rows). It is important to enter and exit at all times along the outline edge to maintain the reversibility of the pattern so **NO SHORT CUTS PLEASE!**

VI. Compensation

This is a simple process since running stitches are usually straight stitches whether they are horizontal, vertical or diagonal. Merely foreshorten the stitch to the hole that falls closest to the drawn or stitched outline edge. If the nearest hole is on one side or the other of a drawn line, judge the placement by assessing the lean of the direction of the outline stitch planned (e.g. with stem or outline stitch the thread will lean with the curve so sink beyond the line when the curve swells out, and sink inside the line when the curve swells in). On fabric a sharp needle can be used to pierce the fabric at the exact point where the line touches it, but one has to be somewhat more creative to resolve problems on canvas. It is easier and safer to pierce a canvas thread with the finer weight of the blackwork thread than it would be to pierce it with the heavier outline thread, but be careful.

With patterns that have oblique lines, more "fudging" is needed to maintain a consistent appearance, but lay the thread across the fabric in the exact direction of the next normal sinking hole to determine which hole along the edge should be used for the foreshortened stitch. With prefilled outlines, the pattern always ends on the inner edge so no overlapping please. It is harder to count across the cluttered edge, but aim for accuracy, as slight changes in the pattern do attract attention. Careful centering of a pattern also draws the viewer's eye to the middle of the pattern so that the edges are less noticeable.

CAUTION: Some compensation stitches will straddle a single thread rather than an intersection so they can be vulnerable and slip between the fabric threads if too much tension is applied. A prefilled outline helps to hold these weak stitches in place sometimes, but be careful when they occur. A pivot stitch along the edge before traveling is also a good way to lock these weak stitches in place so that later pulls cannot affect them.

VII. The Stitches

A. Running Stitch. Traditional running stitch is a stitch that goes in and out of the fabric holes at either even or uneven intervals, forming a broken line. In conventional blackwork, these intervals were always over two threads for straight stitches or two intersections for diagonal stitches. If the stitches are any shorter, they can slip between the warp and weft threads of a woven canvas or fabric and move, but longer stitches can be used with no repercussions or risks. Some of the patterns will illustrate the advantages of using longer stitches for certain outlines, but it is definitely harder to memorize patterns that use varying stitch lengths. We all tend to be creatures of habit when it comes to breaking traditions, but the improved appearance is definitely worth the added concentration.

As discussed earlier on page 2, some blackwork patterns use only running stitch sequences. These patterns are not reversible, but like darning patterns, they tend to have another uniform pattern on the reverse side. Sometimes the reverse pattern is even nicer than the one on the front so always peek and anticipate a pleasant surprise. When executing these particular patterns you often enter and exit on an underneath stitch so it is even harder to maintain consistency on the reverse pattern. Remember to use pivot stitches or holding stitches both to change directions when you have to travel and to enter at the correct angle for a new row when an underneath stitch is first.

B. Double Running Stitch. This stitch is a two-step sequence that forms a solid or unbroken line. The first step is a simple running stitch row, and the second step is a return trip on the same path that will fill in the gaps left in the broken line of the first row.

Diagram 1 below shows a running stitch sequence, and Diagram 2 shows a double running stitch sequence back over the same path.

DIAGRAM 1	DIAGRAM 2
RUNNING STITCH	DOUBLE RUNNING STITCH
Step 1	Step 2 – Return Trip

Unfortunately a running stitch leaves a mess in a hole since it comes from behind and travels forward. There is minimal tension on the ends of these stitches whereas a backstitch wraps snugly and places a firm equal tension on both ends of each stitch. Therefore a running stitch will always look longer than a backstitch done over the same number of threads or intersections. When running stitch paths have a lot of straight lines, it is difficult to return on the same path without interference from the mess left in these holes.

Some embroiderers prefer to pierce the traveling threads of the first row on the return trip in order to keep the stitches and lines straight. However, this puncture can be unsightly and conspicuous, especially with thicker threads like perle cotton that do not split easily. It is also difficult to split each thread exactly in the middle, and an off center stab can shift the stitches enough so that uniformity is lost and distortions occur. On fine fabrics, piercing the smooth flat threads is more practical as well as less conspicuous. It is easier to pierce a thread since fine needles are sharper, and clean punctures are less visible. However, on coarser fabrics and porous canvasses, I prefer to sink "around" the traveling thread.

Strategic placements of these stitches can correct or prevent slight distortions within the pattern, and these solutions work equally well when linen is the ground fabric. To correct specific situations that occur often, I recommend certain formulas. Try the following exercises on a doodle cloth in order to see and feel the problems created by a double running stitch path. Experience both the incorrect and correct solutions in order to understand the recommended solutions.

    1. On return rows of straight lines, do not sink and come up on the same side of the traveling thread or else the line will appear crooked. In addition, a random approach can create wobbly lines. If, however, one consistently comes up on the same side of the traveling thread and sinks on the opposite side as the return trip is made, the finished line will appear straight and uniform (study Diagram 1 below).

INCORRECT   **CORRECT**

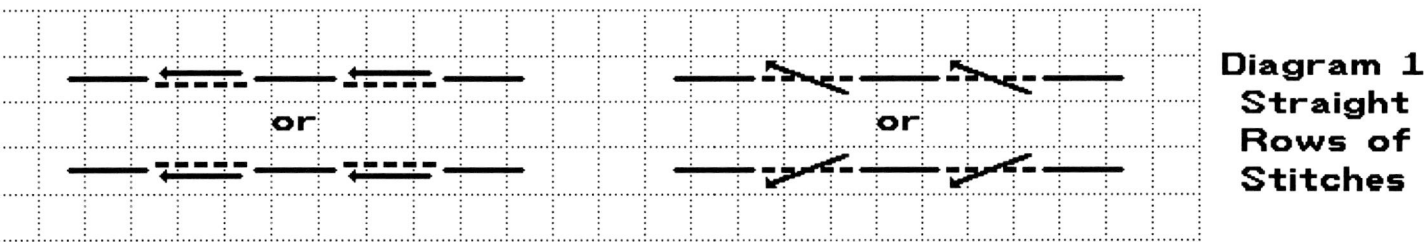

Diagram 1
Straight
Rows of
Stitches

NOTE: When there is a choice for the correct handling of the thread on a return trip, one must be careful to maintain consistency once the choice is made. Switching to the alternative correction tends to make the pattern look less uniform, and therefore wrong.

2. Zigzag rows of diagonal stitches stitch cleanly in double running stitch. However, zigzag rows of straight stitches do not tend to look straight and uniform unless the stitches are manipulated on the return trip. The stitches tend to lean because of the tension on the traveling thread. Unlike straight lines, a consistent rhythm on the return trip will not correct this, but an alternating rhythm will (study Diagram 2 below).

If one can assess the tension that the traveling thread is placing on the running stitches in the first step, it is easier to judge the appropriate solution to correct distortions on the return trip. Sharp angles naturally occur when two diagonal stitches follow each other in a zigzag path so sequences seldom need to be doctored on the return trip – the points or peaks will be maintained if the return stitch simply sinks or comes up on the outer side of the sharp corner or apex created. The hole is clear so there is no resistance or clutter in the way. Therefore I developed the phrase of taking the "line of least resistance" on the return trip when stitching these chevron paths. There is no need to force anything to happen since the natural flow creates optimum results.

INCORRECT   **CORRECT**

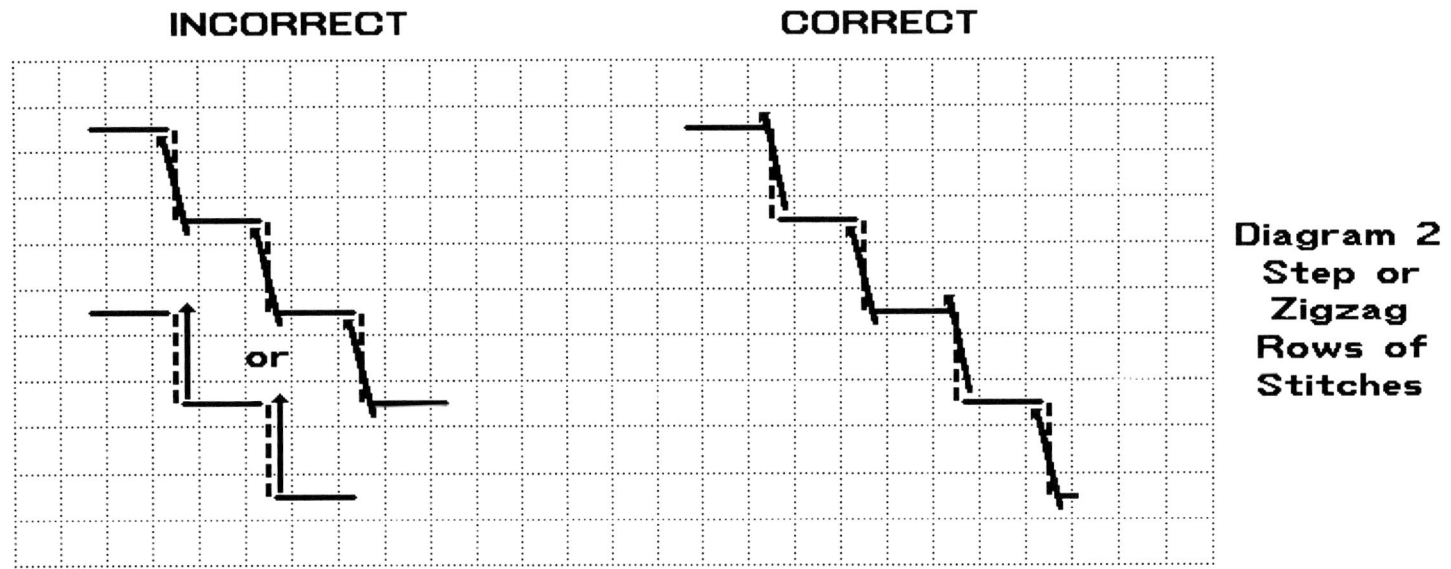

Diagram 2
Step or
Zigzag
Rows of
Stitches

3. When boxes or diamonds are formed from opposing rows of running stitches, they tend to look more like rectangles or parallelograms if the stitches are not placed on opposite sides of the traveling thread at the crossing junctures where opposing rows and stitches intersect to form the shapes (study Diagram 3 on the next page).

NOTE. The examples of running stitch patterns on page 2 both illustrate this point. Stitch a complete pattern of each example, and see if you can maintain an even appearance to the boxes and/or diamonds throughout both patterns. Again the units will appear more even if the same correct sequence is used throughout the pattern.

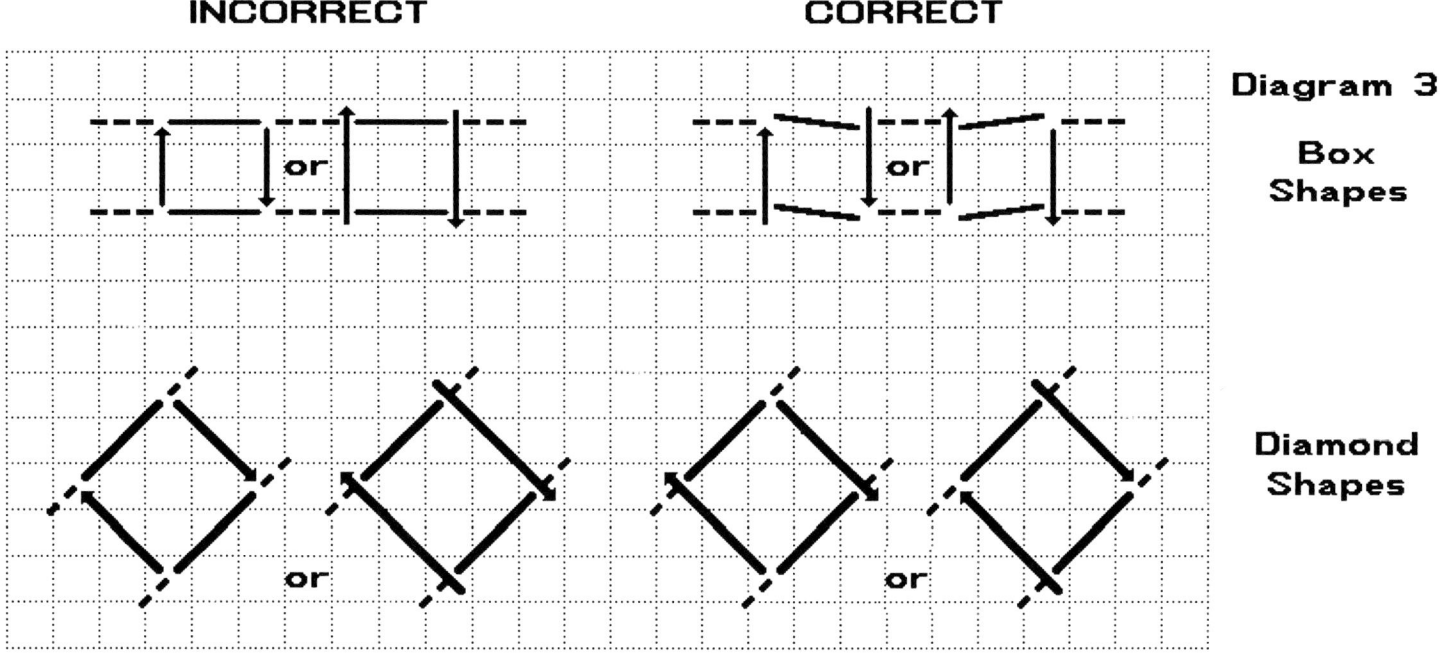

Diagram 3

Box Shapes

Diamond Shapes

4. When crossing a previously filled row of straight stitches, it looks nicer to sink a down stitch on the near side of the completed row. On the other hand, an up stitch should come up on the far side of the completed row. If this rule is followed consistently, the intersecting row of stitches will not straddle or lay on top of the stitches of the previous row so they will appear to be the same length. Stitches that cross existing stitches look longer since they extend beyond the midpoint of the shared hole. Therefore this should be avoided (study Diagram 4 below).

Diagram 4 – Intersections of Crossing Lines

INCORRECT   **CORRECT**

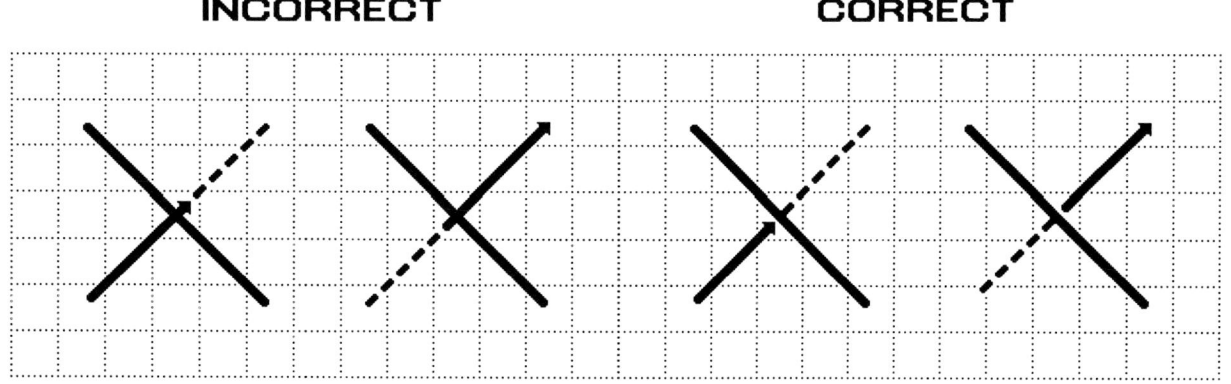

5. Wherever possible, try to avoid having two straight stitches together. For example, a single stitch over four threads is straighter and more attractive than a pair of back to back stitches over two threads that create a line of the same length. This alteration can be made as long as the hole between the split stitches does not need to be used again to complete the pattern. Therefore the merging of stitches is a logical solution to correct the tendency for two stitches in a straight row to appear crooked.

Further Stitch Refinements

Many times a side trip is taken on both sides of the main path. If done in sequential order, and both side trip stitches are horizontal, the two stitches will be executed with a running stitch path straight across the middle. The first one will appear straight and slightly longer, but the second one will turn the corner and travel south so it will appear slightly shorter and slanted compared to its counterpart on the other side. If one side trip is done on the running stitch row, and the other one is done off of the return trip, both straight stitches will have a sharp turn off of the main path so they will appear to be exactly the same length. The other threads of the vertical path will keep them from slanting in the direction of the pull since four threads should fill the shared hole (study the comparison below).

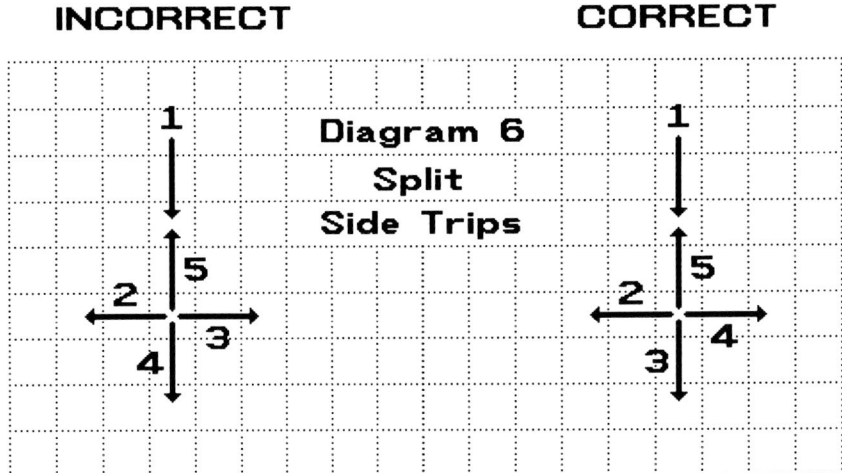

NOTE: The incorrect sequence has a cluttered hole between the side trips. The correct sequence has a clean hole between the side trips.

The previous situation is an exception to one of my general rules that recommends adding side trips on the running stitch row rather than on the return trip (read the section on side trips in the glossary on page 37 for clarification of this rule). There is one other situation where I recommend that some side trips be postponed until the return trip. When a single stitch side trip is added to a running stitch path, it is easier to add it when the needle is in the "on top of the canvas" position. In this case if the thread is held back by the left hand to keep the return hole open, the needle can make the side trip with an out and back stab motion while tightening the thread only once after the second stitch. This technique is similar to that used when stab stitching a stem stitch on canvas, and I personally use the fourth finger on my left hand to hold back the thread – my apologies to any left-handed stitchers for my method of describing the hand position for the technique described here. I am right handed so you may have a different "comfort zone" in executing your stem stitch. However, the point is that using this "out and in" method lessens the chances of piercing a thread in the return hole in addition to making the stitching more efficient. In applying this concept to side trips, **it is better to take single side trips when the needle is on top of the canvas. If the needle is underneath the canvas when it meets the entry point of a side trip on the running stitch row, ignore it and add it on the return trip when the needle is automatically on top of the canvas at the same juncture.**

Another corollary to this principle of adding side trips at a point when the comfort is optimum would be to add side trips off of the right side of the path rather than the left side when there is a choice. This would be more natural for a right handed person to do, and a left handed person would be more comfortable with side trips added off of the left side of a sequence. On the other hand most stitchers learn to be proficient in stitching in all directions on canvas since efficient stab stitching requires the use of both hands (one on top and one underneath the canvas). Therefore slight changes in the degree of comfort might go unnoticed. Some patterns like the one that follows offer a choice in the direction of the side trips.

IDENTICAL PATTERN
Sequence 1

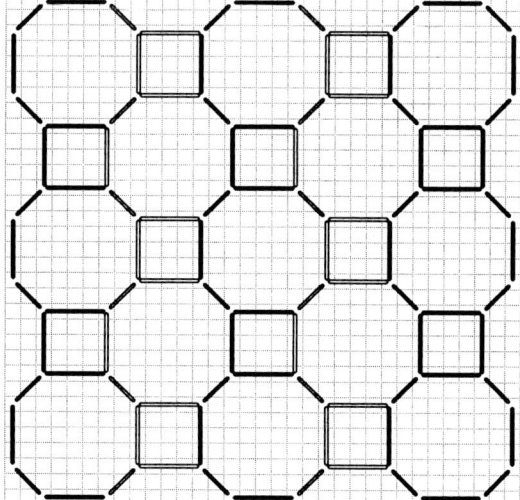

IDENTICAL PATTERN
Sequence 2

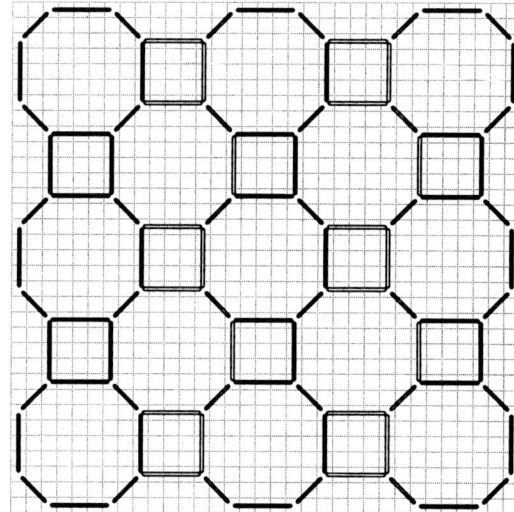

Try a row of each sequence and see if either one is more comfortable to execute. Sequence 1 adds the side trips to the right side of the main path. Sequence 2 adds the side trips to the left side of the path. Execute just one repeat of each sequence, and add the side trips along the way. When there is a difference in your degree of comfort in stitching in either direction, make this a priority when you chart a sequence – or alter an existing sequence to accommodate this benefit when it is feasible.

NOTE. Go back to page 29 again, and rotate the page 90°. The view of the pattern now shows horizontal paths for the sequence. If a particular area is wide and not very long, it would be smarter to use horizontal paths to fill it because there would be fewer full rows to execute. Since traveling from one row to another involves added steps, is it not wise to minimize the number of individual rows when executing a pattern? Stripe patterns can only be stitched in rows in one direction, but allover patterns can usually be stitched in either a horizontal or a vertical direction. Sometimes a diagonal direction is more practical too so all options must be considered before a final decision is made. If a horizontal sequence is less comfortable to stitch, one can always rotate the canvas 90° and place it as a vertical sequence instead. This versatility in allover patterns creates a lot of choices in planning sequences for a pattern so most published sequences are merely suggestions that can be adapted to specific needs and/or "comfort zones."

The degree of comfort in both executing side trips and in returning on a running stitch path is often determined by the lean of the stitches on the running stitch path. When following a zigzag line, it is usually easier to reenter a hole on the return trip with a minimum of interference if you come up or sink on the side of the traveling path that is open or away from the direction that the surrounding stitches lean. If you force the needle to sink on the opposite side, it is difficult to avoid piercing the traveling thread since it is leaning into this side of the hole. I usually recommend taking the line of least resistance. However, patterns will look different if you follow this principle unless the needle is kept in the same position on top of the canvas. The following example will demonstrate this fact.

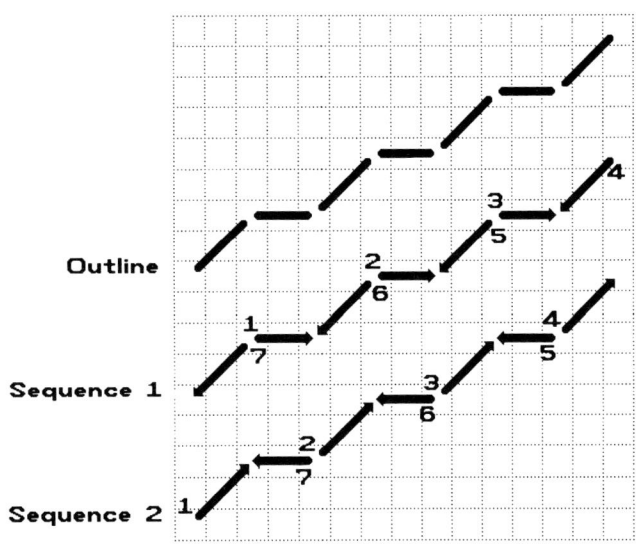

Execute the outline to the left twice. Use sequence 1 the first time, which lays all of the straight stitches on the running stitch row. On the return trip, notice how easily stitches 5 and 6 can come up "above" the traveling thread and sink "below" it since the running stitch path leans away from the holes in these positions. To reverse this would be uncomfortable since the needle would have to be forced to pass inside the lean of the traveling thread.

In sequence 2, the line of least resistance on the return trip would be to come up below the traveling thread with stitches 5-7 and to sink above the traveling thread with them. To reverse this process would be the equivalent of "swimming upstream or against the current".

30

Ideally one would always want to take the line of least resistance since it is easier, faster, and tidier. However, study the two completed stitched paths, and notice how different they appear. The diagonal stitches appear slightly longer in sequence 1 since they are laid on the return path. If you were filling an area with this pattern, would it not look more consistent to constantly use the same sequence rather than a combination of the two sequences? Since one usually starts each row along the edge with a stitch on top of the canvas regardless of whether it is a straight or a diagonal one, it would be necessary to use the uncomfortable return trip to force all of the paths to match. An easier way to assure consistency is to begin every running path row with either the diagonal stitches or the straight stitches on the top. It is a little more difficult to start on an underneath stitch when necessary since the underneath stitch must enter at the correct point to make the underneath path match the eventual "on top" stitch. However, the extra effort is most worthwhile since this single adjustment will make all of the return trips more consistent. In this particular pattern I prefer the look of sequence 2 with its less conspicuous diagonal stitches, but either sequence is acceptable as long as the uniformity is maintained.

NOTE. This point of refinement may seem nitpicky since subtle variations in the outlines are not visible at viewing distance. However, needlework is often studied at close range, and total consistency is a strong judging point in a competition or exhibit setting. Understanding the way double running paths work helps one to anticipate and to avoid unnecessary problems and to approach perfection in your work. If something puzzles you as you stitch, sit back and analyze it and I bet you can figure out a way to resolve the problem and to get optimum results.

The following example will demonstrate the advantage of taking a side trip when it is comfortable rather than when it is uncomfortable.

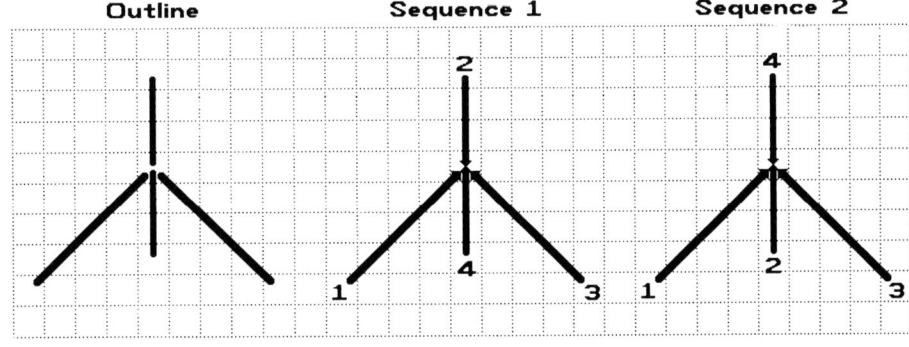

The outline to the left is a zigzag line (stitches 1 and 4) with a single side trip on both sides of the main path (stitches 2 and 3). In sequence 1 the side trip on the outside of the corner turn is taken on the running stitch row, and the side trip on the inside of the corner is taken on the return trip. The procedure is reversed in sequence 2. The shared hole stays a bit cleaner in sequence 2 since the angle is sharper when stitch 2 is the one below the apex of the main path rather than above it. However, the angles are adequate for either maneuver so interference is minimal in both sequences. On the other hand, if either sequence is started with stitch 1 as an underneath stitch, it is much easier to lay the next three stitches with the needle on top of the canvas since the thread can be held tightly aside as the needle goes down and up to complete each stitch in one motion. If this statement is ambiguous, review page 29, paragraph 1 again. Another alternative is to use sequence 2 but to reverse the order of stitches 3 and 4. This would be the equivalent of doing stitch 2 as a side trip on the running stitch row and stitch 3 on the return trip - the best option in my opinion since stitches 2 and 3 are not back to back so the shared hole remains clean.

31

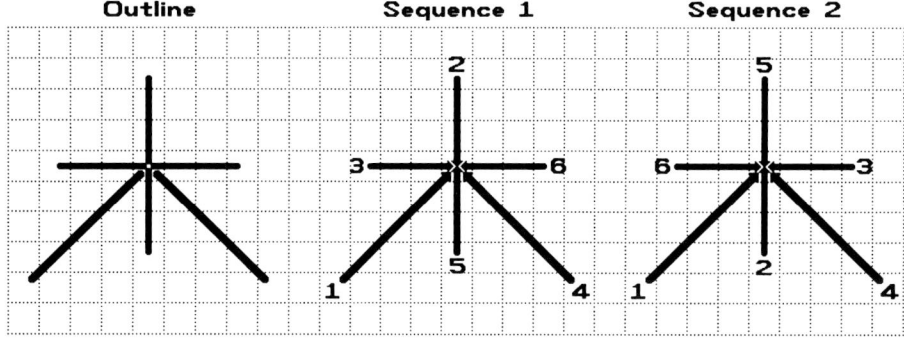

Outline   **Sequence 1**   **Sequence 2**

The next example uses the same outline as the previous one, but two additional side trips have been added to the path. In this example the key stitches are not stitch 2 and 5 and the order in which they are taken. The critical stitches are stitches 3 and 6. In sequence 1 stitch 3 exits "towards" stitch 4 and clutters the shared hole more than necessary. By reversing the order of the two horizontal side trips in sequence 2, the angle from stitch 3 to stitch 4 is much sharper so stitch 4 can now sink cleanly back into the shared hole. The path after stitch 6 will also angle sharply underneath stitch 1 to complete the reversible sequence. In sequence 1 stitch 6 exits towards stitch 1 so the traveling path back to the beginning of the sequence is not at a clean angle.

One could also take all four of the side trip stitches (stitches 2, 3, 5, and 6) in a radiating path after stitch 1 as long as the first side trip stitch is at a sharp angle from stitch 1 and the last stitch exits at a sharp angle to the second diagonal stitch. In this case the side trips form an eyelet stitch so it is important to maintain a back stitch pull on both ends of every stitch to keep the center hole clean.

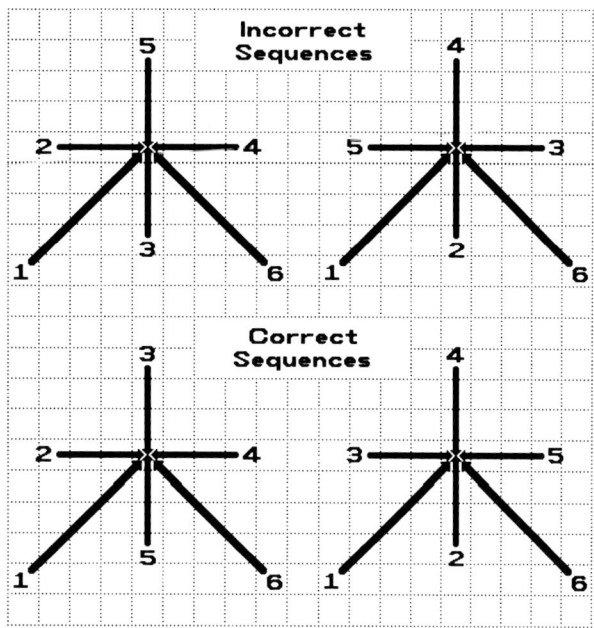

Study the four sequences shown to the left. In the incorrect sequences the counter clockwise path of the side trips ends on a stitch that lays towards stitch 6 so the exit will not be clean. In the correct sequences the clockwise paths both end on a stitch that sinks away from stitch 6 so the traveling path will angle cleanly away from the shared hole. All four sequences show a clean path from stitch 1 to stitch 2. If stitch 1 began as an underneath stitch in any of these sequences, the same radiating path of side trips would still be recommended, and the same two sequences would be correct. However, it is always better to sink into the center hole of an eyelet rather than to come up in it since there is less risk of piercing a thread with the needle on top of the canvas. Therefore I would try to maintain an "on top" position for the stitch that begins any sort of eyelet path in a blackwork pattern.

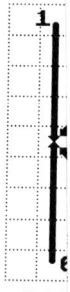
Other situations also create choices that affect the degree of comfort in executing the double running path. The stitch chart below is borrowed from Pattern 1 on page 43. Take a doodle cloth and execute three versions of the path shown.

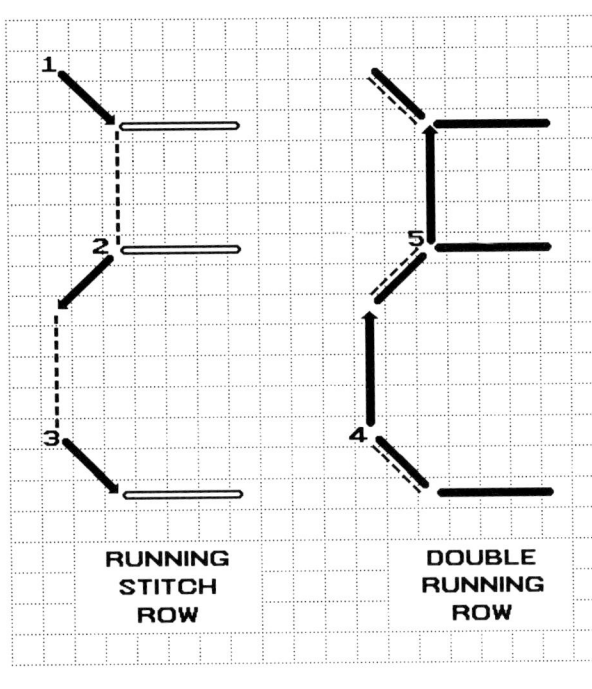

RUNNING
STITCH
ROW

DOUBLE
RUNNING
ROW

**STITCH SEQUENCE
PATTERN 1**

NOTE. In the previous sequences in this segment on stitch refinements, the side trips were numbered into the sequences rather than "highlighted" with the open stitch symbol. This illustration shows the way the side trips will be shown in the pattern sequences that start on page 44.

In version 1 add the side trips on the running stitch row as shown. The needle will be on top of the canvas for the side trip before stitch 2 but underneath when the side trips are taken after stitches 1 and 3. It is easy to take all the side trips on the running stitch row. However, it is not easy to reenter the holes with stitch 5 on the return trip with the side trips already in place. The traveling thread underneath stitch 5 is leaning to the right so there is less resistance if the needle stitch 5 is laid to the left of the traveling thread, but the holes are cluttered since two previous stitches have been taken in both holes.

In version 2, add the side trips when the needle is in the "on top of the canvas" position. On the return trip it will easy to come up on the right side of the traveling thread to start stitch 5 and to add the side trip at that juncture, but it will not be easy to end stitch 5 in the cluttered shared hole above. If you take the path of least resistance, you would come up to the left of the traveling thread to start stitch 5 and sink to the right of the traveling thread when you end it. The stitch is apt to look crooked especially after a second parallel stitch is added to the right side of these side trips from the adjacent row to complete the square box. To force the left vertical stitch to fall to the left side of traveling thread at both ends is tedious so it is not logical to choose to execute the side trips in this situation with the needle in an "on top" position.

In version 3, add both side trips on the return trip. There will be no interference since the traveling thread under stitch 5 is leaning to the left because of the tension from the angles of stitches 1 and 2 of the running stitch row. Both horizontal side trips can be added

sense must prevail when general formulas cannot be applied so when discrepancies occur in a pattern, try to think of a way to manipulate the sequence to eliminate these irregularities.

This completes the general information needed to understand blackwork technique. I have stressed tendencies and peculiarities that have occurred in my own experimentation on canvas since most of my recent growth has focused on developing blackwork variations for canvas use. Therefore some observations and suggestions may be less relevant to stitching on fabrics.

I have also focused exclusively on the reversible technique since other books have not covered this method as extensively as it needed to be explored. I have always stressed the "whys" of a technique as much as the "whats" in my teaching because a thorough understanding will foster more creativity as well as greater excellence in the technique. I hope my experimentation will inspire you to develop original patterns and styles of blackwork. By departing from restrictive traditional methods and concepts, I intend to broaden your horizons and plant some seeds for future growth.

I often use the term "blackwork variations" when referring to my unconventional patterns since every innovation begins with a linear outline pattern done in double running stitch method. However, only a few of the patterns presented were derived from or even inspired by available historical blackwork patterns so the term variations refers not to variations on traditional patterns but to variations on traditional concepts. The word suggests change or deviation from established methods, yet the common thread and essential feature of linear outlines is still maintained.

The chapters ahead will provide a variety of unconventional patterns for your pleasure and experimental use. I would like to encourage you to make several samples of the composite arrangements to see how the pattern changes with variations in color, value, varying weights of threads, etc. I have deliberately not provided specific guidelines on these variables in most cases because possibilities are endless.

After the chapters on specific categories of pattern, a brief chapter is included on how to derive blackwork patterns and variations from both printed and non-printed sources. In one class a student presented me with a catalogue of mattress styles as her inspiration for blackwork patterns so nothing is too mundane to be overlooked! Notice your surroundings, and make a habit of toting a small graph pad at all times so that you can jot down that blouse pattern in the airport, or that bridge abutment on the expressway. You usually need to record only two repeats of a simple pattern, but if the pattern is complex make sure you clarify all of the important details. A camera is always a handy tool for recording pattern too. Pattern is ubiquitous so be prepared!

In order to execute the patterns provided, and to understand the features used in the reversible sequences, one must learn the vocabulary developed by Ilse Altherr to identify the components of her pathfinders system. Her labels help to clarify types of patterns. They also identify the steps used to connect complex networks of linear outline patterns in an orderly workable manner that is a step beyond regular reversible methods.

is difficult to sink stitch 3 and stitch 5 cleanly without angling around the traveling thread in the way. In the correct path, only stitch 5 has any interference so changing the path of this side trip to a clockwise rather than a counterclockwise path does improve the comfort of the stitching. The sharp angle of stitch 2 in the correct sequence leaves the hole clean for stitch 3 to enter.

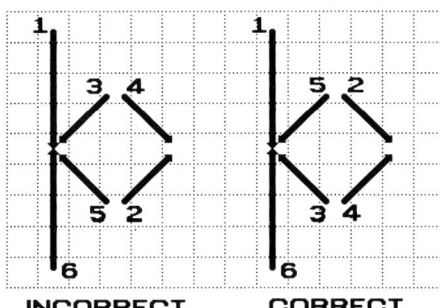

INCORRECT   CORRECT

NOTE. This side trip could also be executed at two separate intervals. It would be acceptable to take the upper pair of diagonal stitches after stitch 1 and to add the lower pair of diagonal stitches on the return trip. However, doing the complete diamond as a single side trip after stitch 1 is the most ideal sequence since there is no traveling thread to contend with in the shared hole between stitch 1 and stitch 6 until after the whole diamond is completed.

NOTE. Regardless of which sequence is used, stitch 5 should sink inside the angle of stitches 1 and 3, and stitch 6 should sink outside of the angle of stitches 1 and 3.

In summing up this section on the refinements in executing the double running stitch paths, I want to stress the importance of using what I call a zigzag method of doing the outlines wherever possible. In addition, choose the zigzag that provides the sharpest angle when there is a choice since this path will always leave the holes cleaner for the return trip. This concept is consistently applied in the arrangement of the sequences in the patterns provided in this book. In following the sequences provided, you will build further skills in planning your own original patterns and sequences.

Conclusions

Some basic guidelines are provided in the text, but new patterns will always present new challenges. If a stitch sequence feels awkward or is not generating optimum visual results, see if you can alter it in some way to both relieve the discomfort and to improve the appearance of the outlines. The solutions derived will expand your understanding of the double running stitch as well as enhance the appearance of the outlines created. The more blackwork you do, the more proficient you will become at both anticipating and eliminating problems. Analyze them in the same way that I have shown you, and don't be afraid to follow your instincts.

If one has difficulty handling the inherent glitches of certain patterns, it is better to use heavier threads – they will not shift or be affected by the tension on the traveling thread so patterns will appear consistent with minimal effort. However, part of the beauty of blackwork is its delicacy and laciness, and some of this is lost when coarse threads are used.

Hopefully these rules and formulas identify the most common problems that occur, but some problems are exclusive to specific patterns so they will be pointed out along with appropriate corrective measures when each individual sequence is explained. Common sense must prevail when general formulas cannot be applied so when discrepancies occur in a pattern, try to think of a way to manipulate the sequence to eliminate these irregularities.

This completes the general information needed to understand blackwork technique. I have stressed tendencies and peculiarities that have occurred in my own experimentation on canvas since most of my recent growth has focused on developing blackwork variations for canvas use. Therefore some observations and suggestions may be less relevant to stitching on fabrics.

I have also focused exclusively on the reversible technique since other books have not covered this method as extensively as it needed to be explored. I have always stressed the "whys" of a technique as much as the "whats" in my teaching because a thorough understanding will foster more creativity as well as greater excellence in the technique. I hope my experimentation will inspire you to develop original patterns and styles of blackwork. By departing from restrictive traditional methods and concepts, I intend to broaden your horizons and plant some seeds for future growth.

I often use the term "blackwork variations" when referring to my unconventional patterns since every innovation begins with a linear outline pattern done in double running stitch method. However, only a few of the patterns presented were derived from or even inspired by available historical blackwork patterns so the term variations refers not to variations on traditional patterns but to variations on traditional concepts. The word suggests change or deviation from established methods, yet the common thread and essential feature of linear outlines is still maintained.

The chapters ahead will provide a variety of unconventional patterns for your pleasure and experimental use. I would like to encourage you to make several samples of the composite arrangements to see how the pattern changes with variations in color, value, varying weights of threads, etc. I have deliberately not provided specific guidelines on these variables in most cases because possibilities are endless.

After the chapters on specific categories of pattern, a brief chapter is included on how to derive blackwork patterns and variations from both printed and non-printed sources. In one class a student presented me with a catalogue of mattress styles as her inspiration for blackwork patterns so nothing is too mundane to be overlooked! Notice your surroundings, and make a habit of toting a small graph pad at all times so that you can jot down that blouse pattern in the airport, or that bridge abutment on the expressway. You usually need to record only two repeats of a simple pattern, but if the pattern is complex make sure you clarify all of the important details. A camera is always a handy tool for recording pattern too. Pattern is ubiquitous so be prepared!

In order to execute the patterns provided, and to understand the features used in the reversible sequences, one must learn the vocabulary developed by Ilse Altherr to identify the components of her pathfinders system. Her labels help to clarify types of patterns. They also identify the steps used to connect complex networks of linear outline patterns in an orderly workable manner that is a step beyond regular reversible methods.

GLOSSARY OF TERMS FOR PATHFINDERS SYSTEM

One-Way Pattern - a pattern worked only in running stitch sequences (see page 2 for examples). When the running stitch sequences are worked in opposing rows, the intersecting lines will form a pattern. Patterns created with this technique will not be reversible, but a second pattern is formed on the reverse side by the traveling threads of the running stitch rows.

Two-Way Pattern - a pattern worked in double running sequences. Each row of pattern is outlined with a two-step trip. The first step is a running stitch row, and the second step is a return trip back over the same path to create a solid line. Patterns done with this technique will be reversible.

Trip-and-a-Half Pattern - A reversible pattern that has a two-way (ex. a heart) or four-way (ex. a diamond) motif that repeats at regulated intervals along the main path. Part of these units must become part of the main path. On the running stitch row, each unit is outlined completely with a dotted line. Then the sequence returns to the midpoint of the unit so that half of the motif is completed as part of the running stitch path. Subsequently, one returns over the remaining incomplete half on the return trip, using it as a bridge back to the starting point. These motifs actually interrupt the main path and block traffic unless one half becomes part of the main path. The other half becomes a side trip off the running stitch row, and its entire outline is completed before the running stitch sequence continues.

NOTE: Pattern 2 on page 45 is an example of a trip-and-a-half-pattern.

Main Path - the path travelled from one side of a shape to the other on the first running stitch sequence of each row. It is a dotted or broken line and excludes any side trips made as completed journeys off the main path. The return trip, or double running path, is usually an "express ride" home that fills in the dotted line of the main path.

Single Stitch Side Trip - a single stitch that is marked with a bold "open stitch" symbol as opposed to the solid stitches that identify the main path. The symbol identifies it as an individual side trip that should be completed with an in and out or an over and under journey of 2 stitches that makes a line on both sides of the canvas. These are not numbered into the regular sequence.

Side Trip - a stitch or series of stitches taken off of the main path in either direction. It is worked in double running sequence and the outline is completed before returning to the main path. Series of stitches are marked with the same bold symbol shown in the single side trip category above. These can be executed at any point where they connect with the main path, but the sooner the better since they can be forgotten or omitted.

I usually add them on the running stitch row – although occasional exceptions were noted earlier – because they add a solid path at regulated intervals in a maze of dotted lines. Their presence helps you to keep track of the pattern better until it is well established and familiar. Any discrepancies in stitch lengths or angles are usually noticed sooner when these clear solid areas do not line up properly.

Side trips often join adjacent rows in a pattern so they can be added as extensions of these rows if forgotten earlier. However, such stitches taken out of sequence can sometimes be spotted easily so do not make a habit of this!

NOTE: Complicated paths will always have separate "lettered" charts included for their suggested sequences. Since main path charts are always "numbered," the lettering will distinguish these paths as side trips. When you encounter a bold stitch, it is a "traffic signal" that says "Whoa! It's time to detour and leave the main path to add a side trip." Switch to the lettered sequence until you have memorized the whole routine.

The sequence charts will always include a return trip sequence that shows the side trips already in place. Here they will appear as solid stitches. Occasional exceptions that postpone the side trips until the return trip will be noted, when appropriate.

The fifty patterns that follow will have explicit step-by-step directions. However, certain "short cut" measures are taken in some of the later patterns to conserve on space. Since the concepts of the double running technique have been established in the earlier patterns, such "short cuts" merely eliminate the need for separate numbered charts on simple sequences. **However, it is advisable for less experienced readers to stitch each pattern in sequential order until all of the concepts are clear.**

COLOR PLATE I – SAMPLER 2

Bargello Diamond Geometric

(Instructions start on page 184)

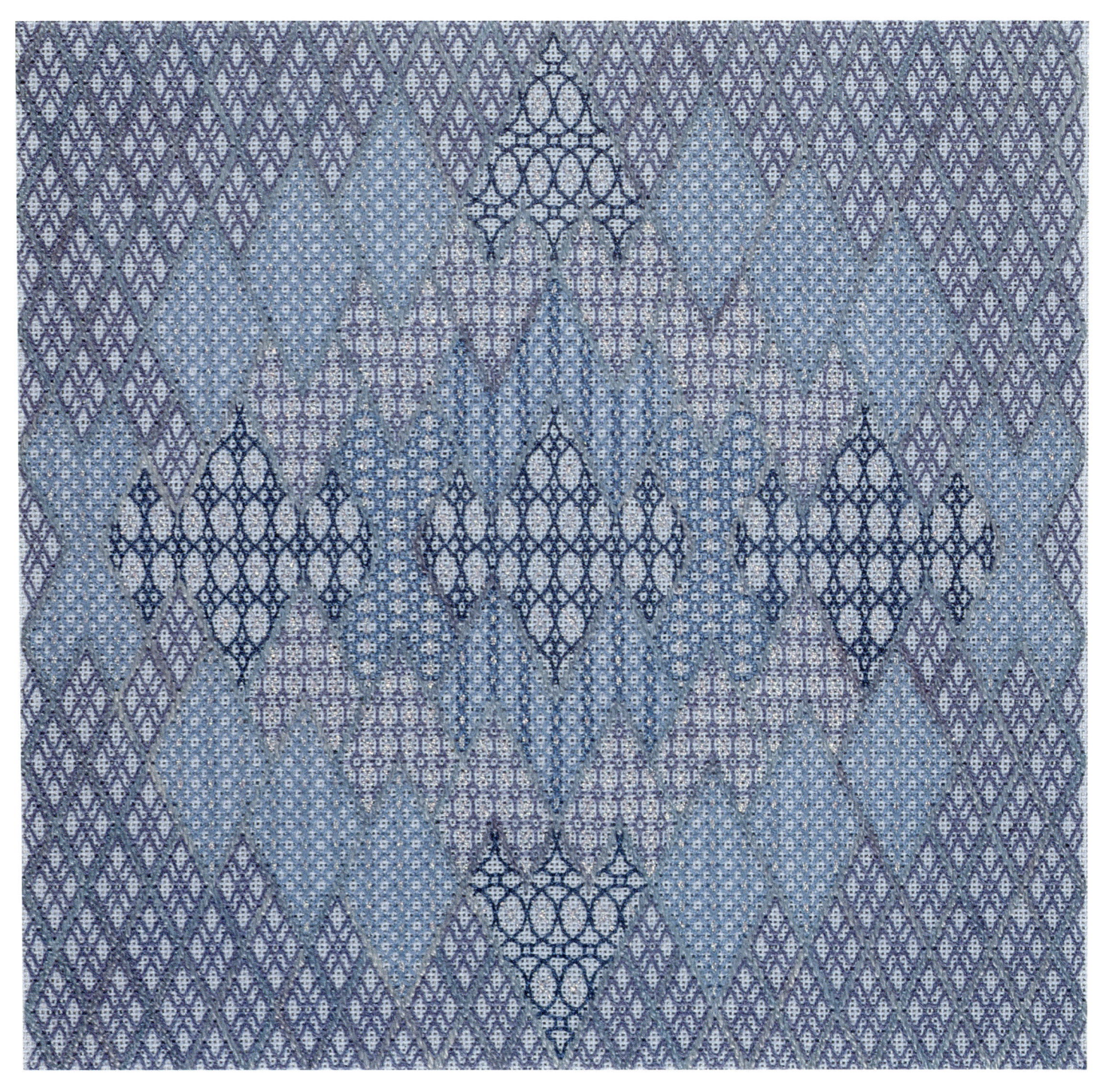

COLOR PLATE II
Coyote Chorus

COLOR PLATE III
Mamadillo

COLOR PLATE IV
Bunny Hop

COLOR PLATE V
Sailboat

COLOR PLATE VI
*Rainy Winter
Landscape*

COLOR PLATE VII
Winter Whimsy

COLOR PLATE VIII
Vase of Flowers

COLOR PLATE IX
Leaf Luster

COLOR PLATE X
Friendship Heart

COLOR PLATE XI
Persian Fantasy

COLOR PLATE XII
Tulip Fantasy

COLOR PLATE XIII
Vowlentine

COLOR PLATE XIV
Diaper Medallions

COLOR PLATE XV
Comely Catfish

COLOR PLATE XVI
Country Geese

CHAPTER 2 - PATTERNS WITH IRREGULAR STITCH LENGTHS

The patterns that follow are examples of original networks that use expanded or "merged" stitches that are longer than the traditional length of two threads or intersections. Some patterns have examples of "compressed" stitches, or stitches that straddle only one intersection rather than the conventional two. Some of the patterns use stitches that are slanted rather than straight. This is the only way to interpret patterns that have hexagonal or star contours, and patterns based on the scale or ogee networks require slanted stitches too. Formerly these stitches were always small gobelin stitches, but again I sometimes merge two short stitches in a row to one long stitch to create a smoother line.

For example, when a simple star shape is executed, it often looks distorted when the sides of a point are split into two stitches. If the needle is not planted consistently on the return trip, each point can look like this:

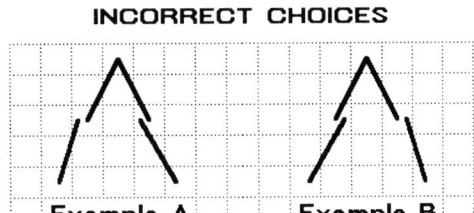

If the needle is planted consistently, either on the inside or the outside of the "peak stitches," the points will look more symmetrical or uniform like the following examples:

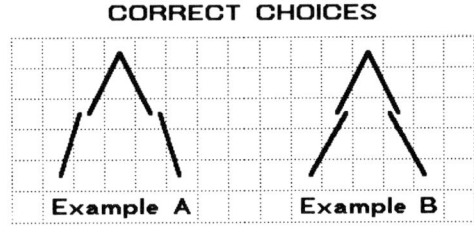

I usually prefer Example B because it tends to create a nicer taper to the points, but either of these choices is an improvement over the combination treatments shown earlier. If a shape is symmetrical, it always looks more comfortable if both sides match in a mirror image arrangement.

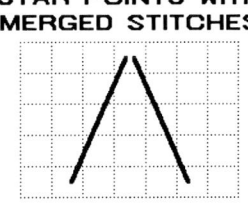

By merging the two stitches to one long stitch, the star point is even more graceful (see the example to the right), and only half the usual number of stitches are needed to form the shape. Since stars are usually four-way or five-sided shapes, think of how much easier and quicker it is to outline a whole figure this way!

39

When such refinements are needed in a pattern, an "inset" will show exactly how the stitches of each repeat should appear after the double running sequence is completed. It will be up to you to create this same position on the return trip by planting the needle strategically on the **correct side of the traveling thread** to keep an existing stitch on the desired side of the new stitch. Because the needle position sometimes changes from being on the top or bottom side of the fabric at the various junctures, an inset view is an easier way to show the ideal placement than trying to simulate the placement on the actual numbered chart. The stitcher can create the same view regardless of where the needle is.

When all else fails, remember that the essence of pattern is repetition. If you don't consistently repeat the manner in which the elements are formed, the pattern will look distorted even if the stitch lengths and angles are correct. Learning to adjust a sequence to keep it even and uniform is part of the challenge of the reversible method, but it is also one of the pleasures since the technique allows you to manipulate the patterns in a way that other methods do not permit.

Each pattern that is presented will begin with an overall view of at least 3-4 repeats. The grid used for the overall patterns is 13 threads to the inch so the scale of the patterns is the same as if they were stitched on a 13-mesh canvas. By keeping this scale constant throughout the book, readers can evaluate the density of each pattern and compare the patterns to each other in a meaningful way. Most of today's sophisticated canvas embroidery is stitched on either 18-mesh or 23-mesh canvas. Therefore an index of all the patterns is included in the back of the book (starting after page 202). Each pattern is shown there in a view that is half the size of that used in the overall pattern charts – or approximately the size it would appear if stitched on Congress cloth. The small examples will provide a good reference for selecting patterns for use in projects that are not part of this book.

The sequence charts will follow the overall charts for each pattern, and these show only a single repeat of a given row. If you are filling an area, or trying to do a sample that is the size of the overall chart or bigger, you must repeat this sequence a number of times to complete one row. The left chart will always show the running stitch row, or step 1 of the sequence. The right chart will always show the double running row, or the return trip, which is step 2. In the running stitch row, the last numbered stitch will always be the first stitch of the next repeat so until you memorize the sequence, go back to stitch 1 at this point and continue the same journey. Turn to page 44, and study the running stitch row of the sequence chart for Pattern 1. Stitch 3 is the beginning of a new repeat so it will become stitch 1 again as a second repeat is added.

After the first two rows of a pattern are completed, you should reach a point where you are less dependent on the numbers to execute the sequence. This "pattern recognition" usually occurs faster if you take a moment to study a pattern before you start stitching. In my notebook courses, I frequently suggest to students that they use a Hiliter pen to color in one row sequence on the overall chart before they start stitching. Once you are familiar with the double running sequence, this is all you need to execute most simple patterns.

In some of the composite patterns where two separate blackwork networks are combined, two different densities are used in the outlines to identify the separate patterns. This will help you to isolate the two patterns better and to stitch them in separate sequences. Once they are completed, they will look like a single complex pattern, but it is much easier to stitch them in two separate segments.

All of the patterns that follow will be listed by numbers rather than names. Unlike stitches, which are easily identified by names that reflect either their structure or an origin or some association that is commonly accepted, blackwork patterns tend to have shapes or geometric motifs that are repeated in more than one network so it is not feasible to identify them with a meaningful name. A few have names that have evolved from either a recognizable element in one of the sequences or from an association that it triggered – in this case, I will share both the name and the experience that prompted it.

NOTE: All sequences provided in the patterns that follow are merely suggestions. Most networks that are allover patterns could be executed in either a horizontal, vertical or diagonal path. Sometimes a particular shape makes it easier to execute a pattern in a different manner from my published sequence. A good example of this is the ogee pattern on page 74. In Sampler 1 (back cover of the book), the pattern (Area 2, page 172) is easier to stitch in horizontal rows since the middle row contours nicely to the wide part of the shape. Once the center horizontal row, which has no compensation, is established, surrounding rows with compensation can be added with a nice view of full repeats to assist you. This same pattern is also used in the largest trees of the *Winter Whimsy* design (Color Plate VII). The formula developed for the outline of the trees contours exactly to the diagonal flow of the ogee pattern so a diagonal sequence was used in this instance.

CONCLUSION: The published sequence is only one possibility. Hopefully I have chosen the least complicated in every case, but other options can always be used. Therefore do not hesitate to adapt the patterns to your own needs. As you grow more familiar with the concepts involved, see if you can plan a sequence before you peek at my suggestions. You will grow more this way, and prepare yourself for a wonderful adventure as you adapt and create your own original patterns!

SYMBOLS USED IN CHARTS

1. Arrow - a stitch on the right side of the canvas worked in the direction the arrow points. Only one number is needed to clarify the up and down movements of the stitch when this symbol is used so it is superior to the usual manner of marking both the up and down movements separately. With only half the numbers, charts are less cluttered and easier to follow.

2. Dotted line - indicates the travelling threads on the back side of the canvas.

3. Blunt stitch - indicates a partial or a compensated stitch. Regular stitches will be rounded on both ends. Some of the composite patterns will have compensation along the edges since the overall chart generally crops the pattern to form a square or rectangle. However, most individual patterns will be shown without compensation. There will always be some compensation within a freely drawn shape so it is important to learn to do the patterns with an understanding of what a foreshortened or partial stitch is.

41

PATTERN 1. The first pattern is a simple bold double running stitch pattern with single side trips. It is actually the foundation pattern of a superimposed pattern in chapter 2, but it is included here to introduce the double running stitch method to readers who have never been exposed to it before. This pattern is an expanded version of a traditional pattern that alternates simple octagon shapes with squares. Below is an overall chart of both patterns. The traditional pattern has stitches that straddle only two threads or intersections whereas the expanded version has straight stitches that straddle four threads. Notice how much larger the scale of the expanded version is.

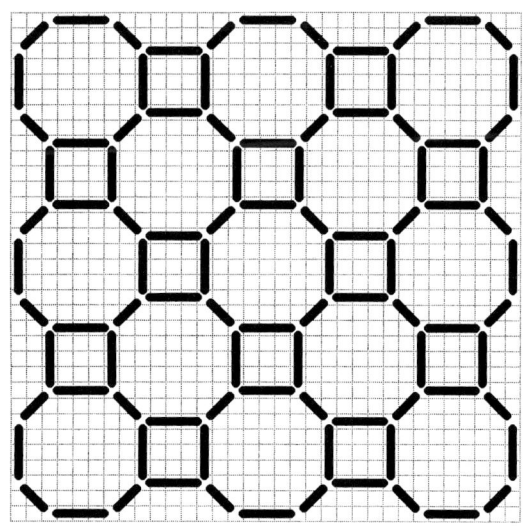

PATTERN 1 OVERALL CHART

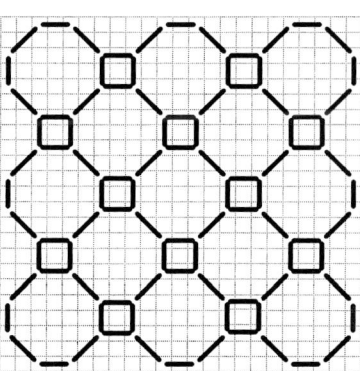

TRADITIONAL PATTERN

NOTE. The chart to the right shows the above pattern without "merged" stitches. Conventional blackwork patterns used only stitches that straddled two threads or intersections so the longer lines would have had two stitches instead of one. These are merged in the unconventional patterns because lines are straighter if they are not split into two stitches.

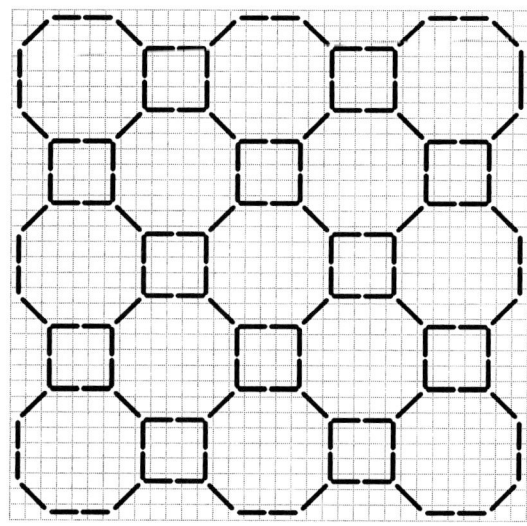

TRADITIONAL VERSION OF THE EXPANDED PATTERN

42

The next chart shows isolated rows of the planned double running stitch sequence that will create this pattern. The open stitches identify two individual rows with identical placement within the pattern. To the left of these rows are two solid rows that have an identical flow. However, the placement of these in-between rows is shifted to a half-drop position. The sequence chart provided on the next page shows the sequence for the open stitch rows. The in-between rows start on stitch 2 of the sequence.

PATTERN 1 SEQUENCE FLOW

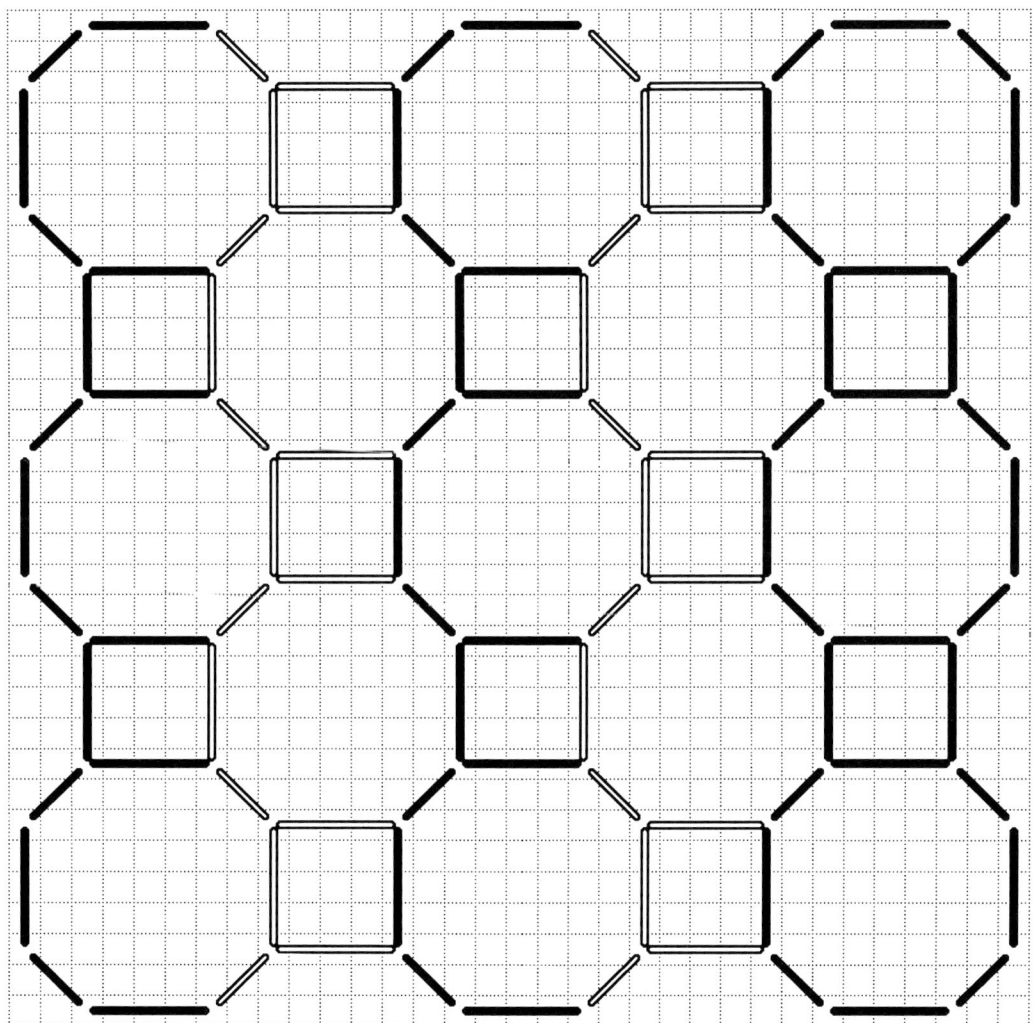

To build the complete pattern within an area, these two sequence rows will alternate to form the hexagons and squares. Each row is completed from one side of an area to another before the next row is started. However, would it not be possible to execute the entire pattern with "side trips" off of a single row if a long enough thread could be used? A double running sequence is merely a convenience that allows you to build an overall pattern in a logical sequence of pieces.

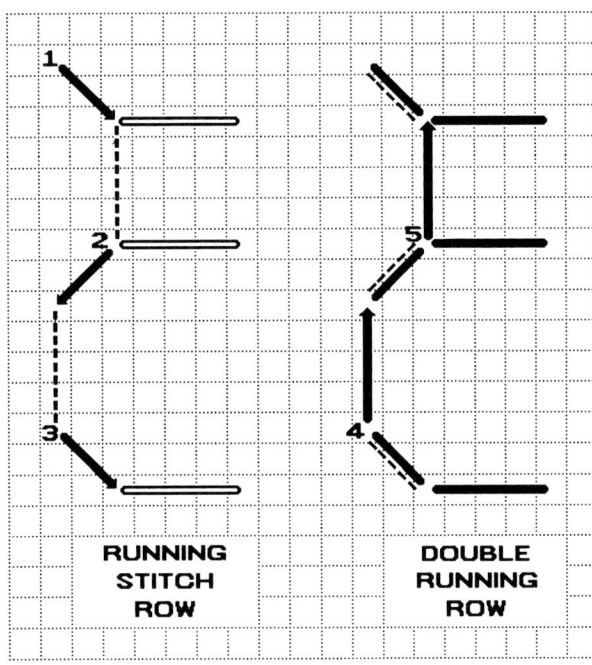

RUNNING STITCH ROW

DOUBLE RUNNING ROW

PATTERN 1 SEQUENCE

The numbered path is a vertical row of undulating curves. The rhythm of the sequence is a constant "over two intersections and under four threads" as the running stitches are laid. All of the diagonal stitches straddle two intersections, and the straight stitches straddle four threads. Stitch 3 is the repeat point and becomes stitch 1 of the second repeat. Two side trips are shown as horizontal stitches off the right side of the path after stitch 1. However, as discussed earlier on page 33, the sequence is smoother if these side trips are added on the return trip after stitches 4 and 5. Therefore ignore them on the running stitch row and add them on the return trip or double running row instead.

This pattern sequence is a simple double running stitch path with single stitch side trips to connect all of the lines. Refer back to the overall pattern on the previous page for placement of the successive rows. Unless the "maze" technique is used whereby all of the pattern is connected as side trips off of one main row, it will be necessary to travel on the back from one completed row to the starting point for the next row. Methods to use when no background is provided are described on pages 22-23. However, if beginners wish to execute the patterns as samples, I would recommend that a simple square outline be executed first that would create a border around each sample. This can then be used not only to travel from row to row but to bury thread tails in as well.

OVERALL CHART
ENLARGED TENT OUTLINE

The enlarged tent stitch outline shown to the left is easy to stitch and wide enough to provide an attractive frame or outline around the pattern. This square will fit the overall pattern for Pattern 1. If a wider frame is desired, merely enlarge the stitch length to cover three intersections instead of the two that are shown. Use a circular path to outline the square and use a #8 perle cotton if the sample is on 23-mesh Congress cloth. Use a #5 perle cotton if the sample is on 18-mesh canvas. Unless otherwise stated, the blackwork is done in two strands of floss on either size canvas.

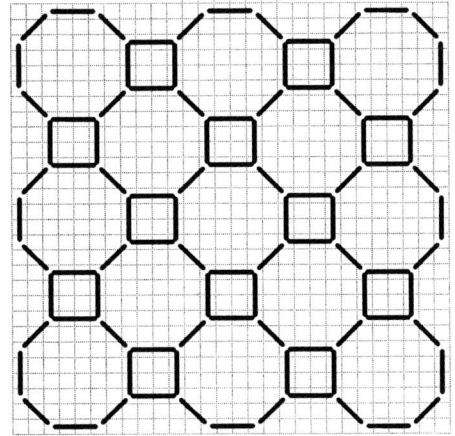

PATTERN 1 VARIATION

Pattern 1 is an expanded version of the traditional pattern shown next to it on page 42. On page 9, paragraph 3, a situation was described whereby a traditional pattern was expanded to three threads rather than two. The pattern used for the background in the *Mamadillo* design is the same as Pattern 1 except that all of the straight stitches straddle three threads rather than four. The pattern to the left shows this particular version of the pattern. The scale of this pattern is larger than the traditional version but smaller than Pattern 1, as expected.

PATTERN 2. This pattern was developed as one that would serve as a "compatible" pattern with Pattern 1. It is used as a superimposed second layer on top of Pattern 1 in the left side of the leaf design in Color Plate IX, and this "combined" pattern is shown to the right of the overall chart for Pattern 2 below. Pattern 2 is included here as a separate pattern because it is a simple example of a trip-and-a-half pattern.

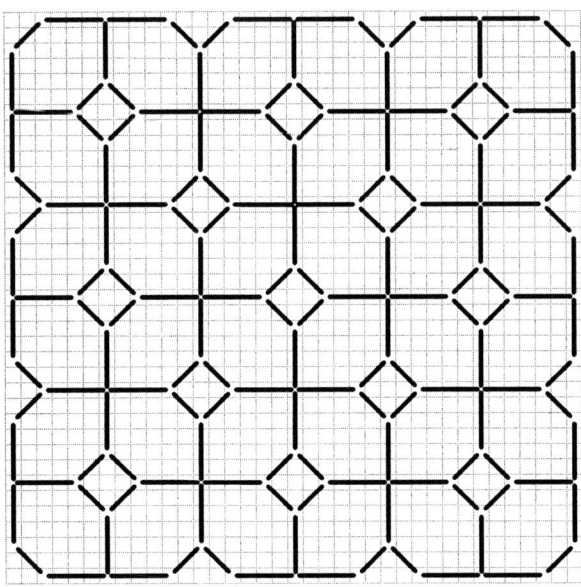

PATTERN 2 OVERALL CHART

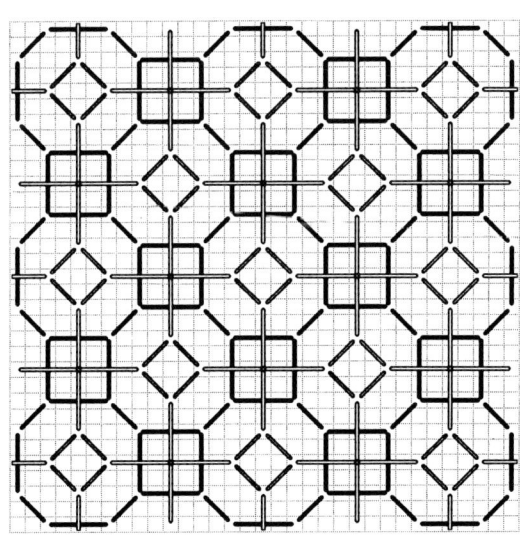

PATTERN 2 SUPERIMPOSED ON PATTERN 1

The next chart shows isolated rows of the planned double running sequence that will create Pattern 2. Notice that a small diamond interrupts the flow of the vertical rows. Because of this the running stitch row of the sequence will outline the entire diamond and then return halfway to continue to the next repeat. There is a side trip off the left side of the diamond and another side trip at the point where the two vertical straight stitches meet. Add both of these on the double running path as there is no advantage to postponing it this time.

PATTERN 2 SEQUENCE FLOW

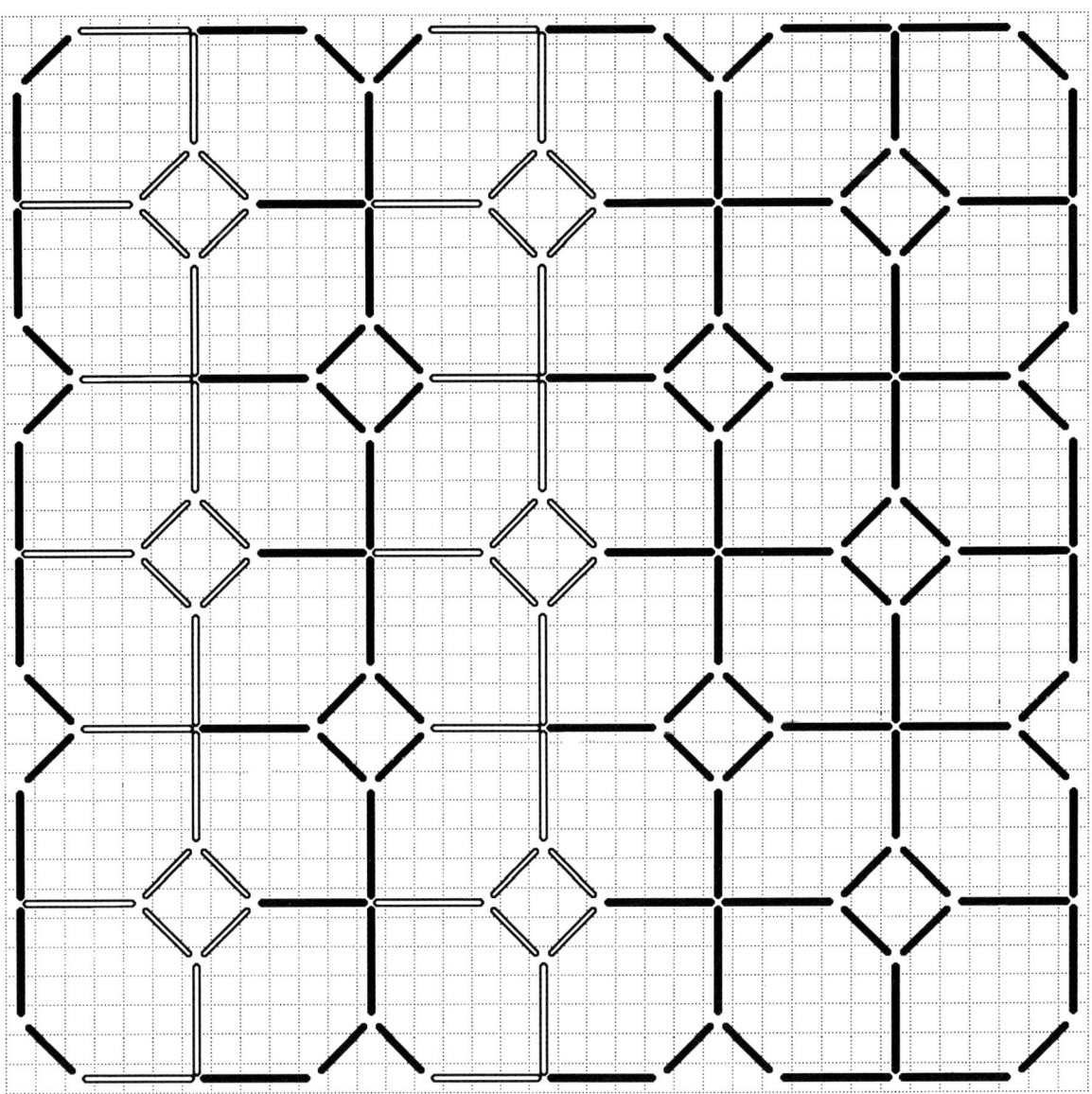

The diagonal stitches in this pattern straddle two intersections, and the straight stitches straddle four threads – exactly like Pattern 1. This pattern is also another example of one that has staggered rows – notice how the position of the diamonds shift halfway in the row between the highlighted rows. Therefore the pattern will build with the same sequence in each row, but the placement will shift in alternating rows.

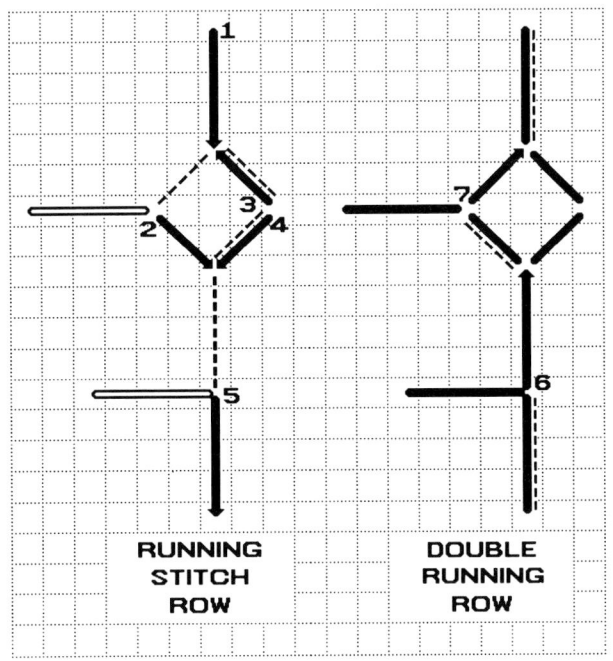

RUNNING STITCH ROW

DOUBLE RUNNING ROW

PATTERN 2 SEQUENCE

Step 1. Running Stitch Row. Add the first side trip after stitch 1. Stitches 3 and 4 fill in the whole right side of the diamond and are actually a full side trip after stitch 2. However, when a motif like the diamond interrupts the main path, it will be included in the numbered sequence to identify it as a "trip-and-a-half" unit. The right half of the unit is completed on the running stitch row. The left half of the unit remains a dotted line and becomes part of the main path. Stitch 5 is the repeat point and becomes stitch 1.

Step 2. On the return trip this time, all side trips are already completed so the path is an "express ride" back over the main path. After stitch 7, come up in the starting hole of stitch 1, and add the side trip to the left that is not shown here but is shown on the overall chart. This side trip is postponed since it will place the needle on the reverse side of the canvas if it is executed on the return trip instead of the running stitch row. It is now convenient to travel to the next row from this position.

There is no need to have a stitch behind this side trip unless a totally reversible pattern is desired. In a "judged" situation, it may be better to have it, but I personally feel it is unnecessary. The main reason to do blackwork in a reversible method is not to have a reversible pattern but to eliminate clutter in open areas. Having a void area along the edge on the back side is equally "clean," and once a piece is mounted, the reverse side is not visible.

I hope these first two simple patterns have served as a good introduction to the double running stitch method of doing blackwork. Since there are already many books available that include a variety of patterns, the patterns that follow have been carefully selected to illustrate various points about the reversible method. The intent of this book is to stress concepts so that readers will be able to create a double running stitch sequence for any pattern of their choice. By focusing on fewer patterns in a more in-depth manner, I hope to expose stitchers to many facets of reversible blackwork that have never been explored before. The patterns are grouped into specific "unconventional" categories or families so that readers can better understand how they differ from traditional patterns and from each other.

The samplers illustrate how the various types of patterns can be used together successfully within an overall design on canvas. Unconventional patterns can also combine well with traditional patterns. It is important to stitch the patterns to develop a thorough understanding of the technique so I want to encourage you to stitch them either as part of the samplers provided or as separate samples in a reference notebook. Once "fluid" in the technique, one can consider the ultimate goal – the development of original patterns and some designs that incorporate them.

PATTERN 3. This pattern is a geometric arrangement that I "doodled" and stitched in the conventional manner the first time I did it. Because the scale of it was too bold for the purpose intended, I restitched it, compressing the diagonal stitches to shorter stitches. The traditional proportions to this pattern are shown in the example on the left side below. The modified pattern is shown on the right side. **Notice that diagonal stitches over two threads have been compressed to a single tent stitch, and the pairs of diagonal stitches that form the arrow ends are reduced to a single stitch that straddles three intersections.** The straight stitches are not merged because there are side trip stitches that join along these rows of straight stitches.

PATTERNS 3A AND 3B - OVERALL CHARTS

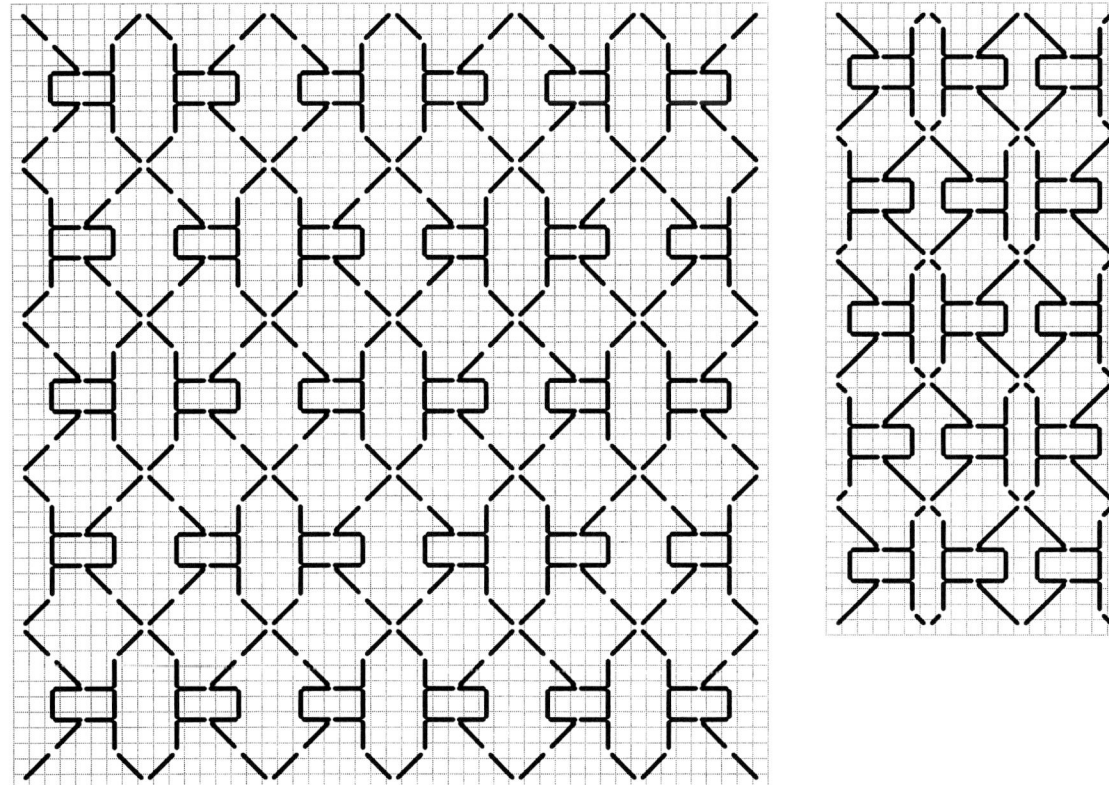
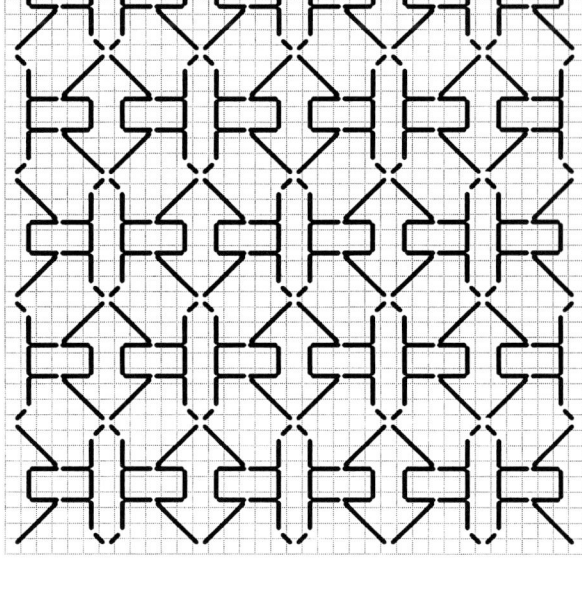

PATTERN - TRADITIONAL PROPORTIONS   **PATTERN - MODIFIED PROPORTIONS**

These two patterns are so similar that I provided only the sequence for the modified version. The rhythm is identical in both patterns so the same sequence can be used to stitch the traditional version of the pattern – only an adjustment in stitch length is needed, and this should be easy after the sample for the modified version is completed.

Both patterns have alternating repeats of arrows and what I might describe as "tabs with hinges." These repeats are shifted in the alternating rows so the pattern is classified as a "half drop" pattern. When such a pattern has uniform repeats that form visual diagonals in both directions, it is also called a diaper pattern. These terms are important when one starts

48

to create original patterns so I will identify such characteristics when they are relevant to the specific patterns being discussed.

PATTERN 3 SEQUENCE

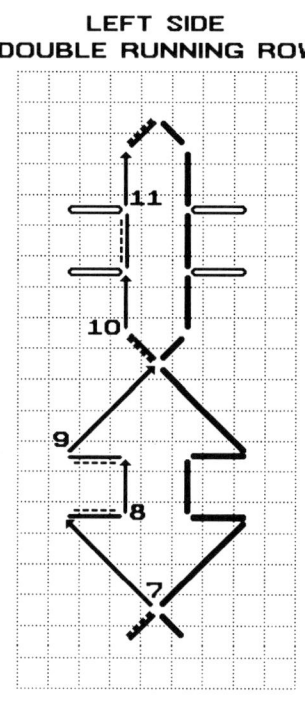

LEFT SIDE RUNNING STITCH ROW

LEFT SIDE DOUBLE RUNNING ROW

The sequence for the modified pattern is worked in vertical rows since the pattern rows divide evenly in this direction. The sequence chart to the left shows the numbered sequence for only the left side of each motif. However, this sequence is shown next to a completed right side so that you can see the other half of one full vertical repeat. Once the left side is completed, add the right side, using the same rhythm with a mirror image placement. The single side trips should be added after stitch 1 and again after stitch 2. These sharp turns to add the side trips will keep the three straight lines in a row from appearing crooked.

NOTE: When the second full vertical row is added, it will begin with an arrow rather than a tab. At this point the numbered sequence will be useless, so go back to the overall pattern chart and add the next row, using it to guide you. The first stitch of the arrow will now be an on top stitch so the needle position is merely reversed from the row 1 sequence. The third row is identical to the first row so the sequence chart will again match the needle position. Notice too that the left side of the overall charts both end with a right half row, and the right edges end with a left half row. No compensation is needed, and these half rows could be left out, but I added them to make you more aware of the way that patterns can be split gracefully.

If you were going to use this pattern in a geometric design, notice that the traditional pattern is almost a square, as shown. The same number of repeats in the compressed pattern, however, creates a rectangle. For this reason I often let my patterns determine the sizes of my shapes in designs rather than vice versa. An example of this is obvious in *Persian Fantasy* (Color Plate XI). The size of the windows here was determined by the blackwork pattern. I chose an outline stitch for the window frames that could create a space that would accommodate the blackwork patterns with no undesirable compensation. **This kind of careful planning can greatly enhance a needlework design, but such perfection usually goes unnoticed. However, an unbalanced placement is always an eyesore so aim for this sort of subtle refinement.**

NOTE. WHILE SEVERAL VERSIONS OF A PATTERN ARE PRESENTED IN THE TEXT, ONLY ONE VERSION WILL APPEAR IN THE INDEX - THE UNCONVENTIONAL ONE. In this case the modified pattern will appear as Pattern 3.

PATTERN 4. This pattern was selected because it shows how a new pattern can be derived from a traditional pattern by elongating it. On the right side below is a traditional pattern. Each line in this pattern straddles two intersections. In the modified version on the left side, each line has a gobelin slant, and the crosses have been stretched or elongated. The pattern on the right is a St. Andrews cross, and each cross is placed in an offset position against the previous one so that the flow of the pattern is a slanted zigzag rather than a diagonal flow. This sort of "rick-rack" edge can be attractive in a geometric design so I have presented it in an uncompensated shape to display this feature. The elongated version of Pattern 4 is similar, but the slope of the pattern is steeper since the stitches themselves are slanted.

PATTERNS 4A AND 4B

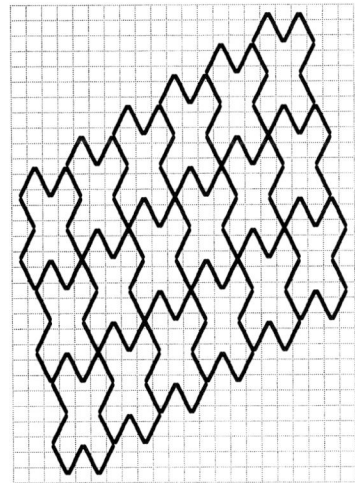

ELONGATED VERSION

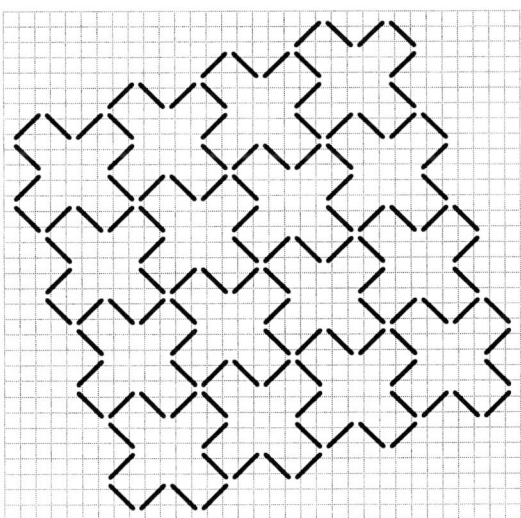

TRADITIONAL VERSION

Notice the difference in the scale and density of these two patterns. The elongated one is denser. Even though it is stretched vertically, it is also squeezed horizontally so there are more repeats in this direction for the same amount of space.

These two patterns are stitched somewhat differently than the previous patterns. The sequence that connects the lines in the easiest way is one that has a pair of sequences rather than one. On the next page there is an enlarged chart that shows two rows of stitches for the traditional pattern. The vertical zigzag rows are shown in dark lines, and the horizontal zigzag rows are shown in highlighted open stitches. In building the pattern, stitch the vertical rows first, and then add the horizontal rows second – or vice versa.

Since each row is an isolated row of double running stitch with no side trips, no numbered sequence is provided – merely follow the lines in a running stitch path and return on it to complete the row. Notice that there are two straight lines in a row in the pattern repeat, and the rhythm of both rows is the same – every pair of diagonal stitches in one direction is followed by a single stitch that is perpendicular to them in the other direction. This zigzag rhythm is easy to follow, and the same rhythm will apply to the elongated pattern – only the slant of the stitch will change.

50

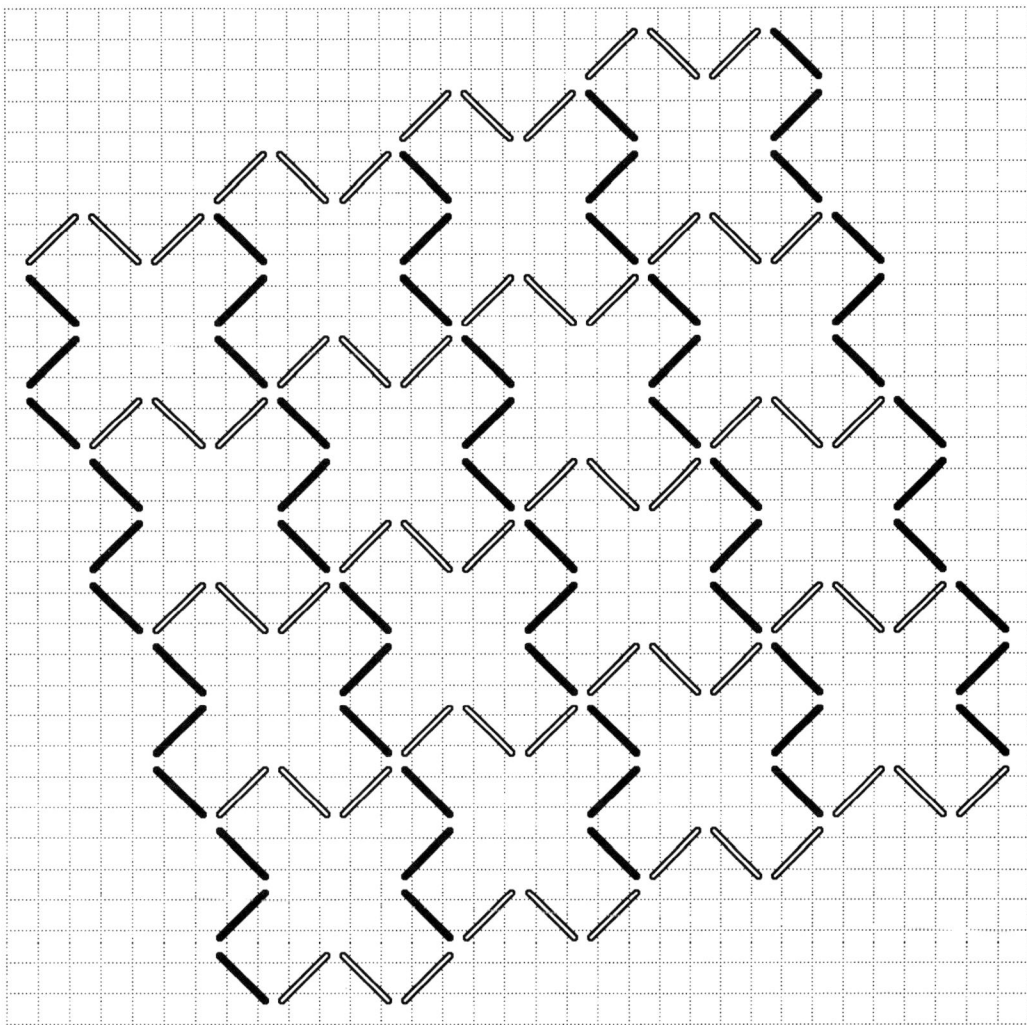

When fitting this pattern into an asymmetrical shape such as the sail of the sailboat design (Color Plate V), it is easier to stitch several horizontal rows, and then add a few vertical rows rather than doing all of the rows in one direction before starting the rows in the opposite direction. Any placement errors will be caught sooner if this is done, and compensation dilemmas are more readily resolved when the cross shapes are visible.

It is also easier to execute this pattern within a shape by starting new rows in the middle and working the thread in both directions to the edge to set up the running stitch row – again placement is easier with no compensation to deal with at the beginning of each row. Because of the offset placement of the crosses in both patterns, the parallel rows do not line up visually. Notice, however, that it is easy to read the four open threads in the middle of each cross in both patterns. If later rows are started four threads below the center point for one of the new crosses somewhere in the middle of the new running stitch row, a placement error is less likely to occur. This is crucial with the elongated pattern since the angles of the gobelin stitches make it harder to maintain accuracy as the rows are added.

NOTE. The alternative to the prescribed sequence is to execute the pattern with only the horizontal sequence and taking the stitches of the vertical rows as side trips off of the horizontal paths. This is certainly a viable option, but for the elongated version in particular the separate paths are much easier. The main advantage of the side trip choice is that the pairs of straight lines would be interrupted by the zigzag side trip so they would remain straight. However, as long as the rules of Diagram 1 on page 25 and Diagram 4 on page 27 are applied to the separate running stitch rows, the lines will remain straight. Therefore either choice is good and will produce optimum results.

PATTERN 4A SEQUENCE

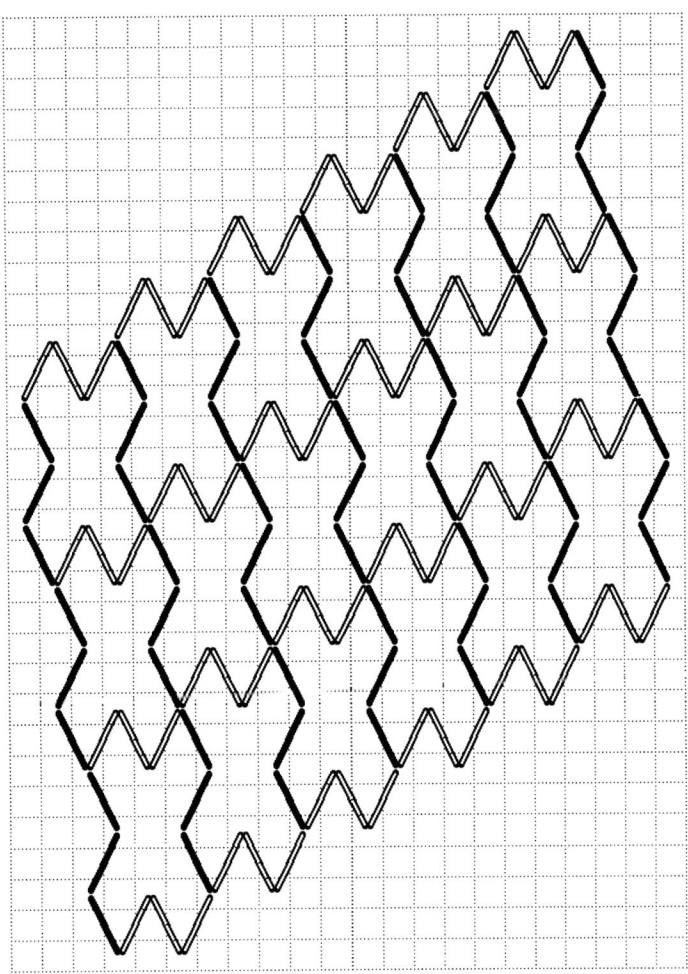

The sequence chart for the unconventional version is shown to the left. As in the traditional pattern, the horizontal rows are open highlighted stitches, and the vertical rows are solid stitches.

This particular pattern was discussed earlier as being ideal for the narrow background sail in the sailboat design (Color Plate V) so reread the section regarding this on page 16, paragraphs 1 and 2. When patterns have natural slants like this, they rotate effectively to create interesting mirror image patterns. Stripe patterns do too, and an example of one of these appears on page 106.

NOTE. Many of my geometric designs are inspired by quilt patterns. The ones with squares and rectangles are easily adapted to canvas interpretation. However, the examples with star shapes and slanted angles are somewhat more challenging. This sort of elongation of a pattern can create a natural angle that could be useful for these shapes so this process of converting a pattern can be useful for such designs. There will be more discussion about taking advantage of the natural lines in a pattern in the chapter on pattern design that starts on page 150.

Since Pattern 4B is a more open and large scale pattern than Pattern 4A, I wanted to suggest a way of adding density to such a pattern. On the next page there are two overall charts of the same pattern, but in the example on the left (Pattern 4C), a straight line has been added to each St. Andrews cross. In the pattern on the right (Pattern 4D), an upright cross has been added to each St. Andrews cross. The crosses themselves no longer stand out in the latter pattern, but the small repeats would show up well in a small area so adding stitches to a bold pattern can add density and make it more useful as a small scale pattern.

PATTERNS 4C AND 4D - VARIATIONS OF PATTERN 4B

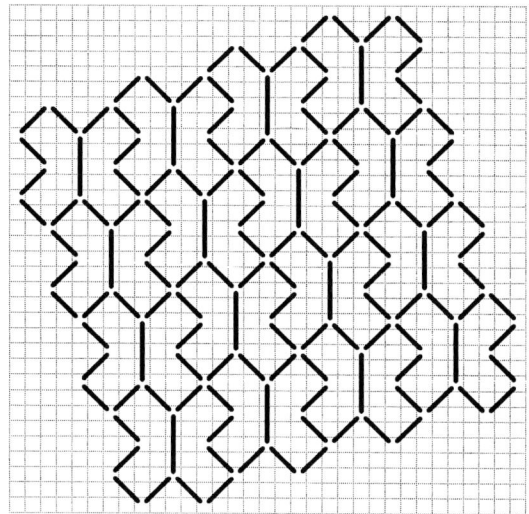
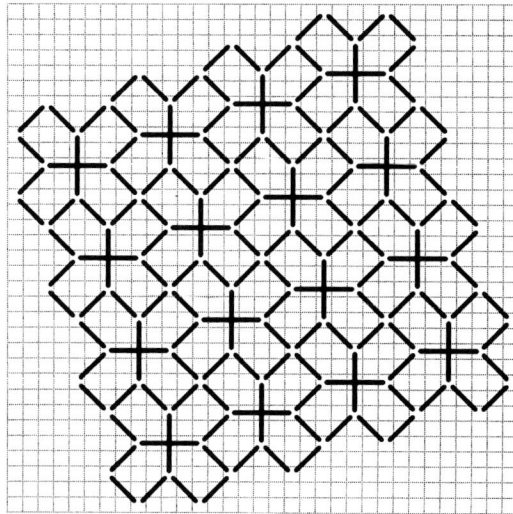

PATTERN 4C SEQUENCE - RUNNING STITCH ROWS

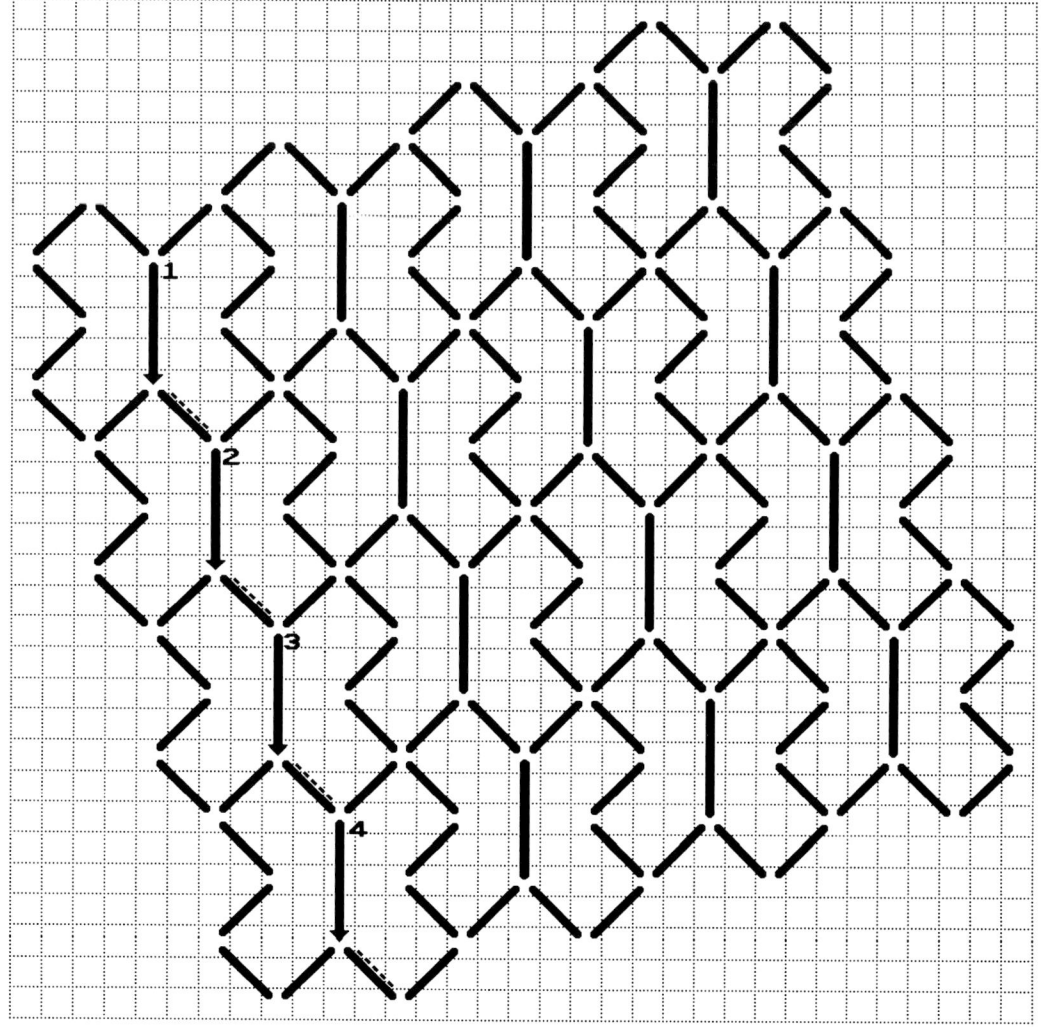

Simple running stitch rows are used to add the vertical stitches in Pattern 4C. Notice that the traveling thread will fall behind a previously laid thread so it will not show in an open area. To add the additional horizontal stitches in Pattern 4D, merely rotate the chart for the vertical sequence in Pattern 4C and use it. The stitches will cross the vertical ones so should be added second to resemble an upright cross. These additional stitches could be added in the same weight thread – or consider a finer thread like cordonnet or tatting thread for a contrasting effect. The finer threads will shift in the holes more, but they will always shift at the same angle so will still look uniform. If consistent straight stitches are desired, use the same weight thread (and one that fills the holes of the canvas size chosen).

PATTERN 5. This pattern is one of several that were developed using hearts as the pattern motifs. This pattern is called Dangling Hearts because the hearts appear to be hanging on strings. The hearts are evenly spaced on each string, and the separate rows are staggered in placement to form a half drop pattern. Unlike the previous patterns this one is a stripe rather than an allover repeat. However, each row of the pattern can be executed in the double running stitch method since it has a continuous flow.

OVERALL CHART - PATTERN 5

This pattern is used in both the *Heart of Blackwork* design on the cover of the book and the *Vowlentine* design (Color Plate XIII). Both of the shapes where it is used have a strong vertical thrust so the vertical flow of the pattern reinforces the shapes nicely. The pattern motif of the heart is certainly appropriate for both designs too.

The heart in this pattern is actually a "double heart." Inside the bold heart is a smaller heart detail. This detail is added as a side trip off of the main path in the sequence. Since it is a complex side trip a lettered sequence is provided on page 57.

NOTE. Since the overall heart motif interrupts the vertical lines of the main path, this pattern is an example of a trip-and-a-half pattern. Notice also that the bottom part of the large heart shape is six intersections long so it is divided into two stitches that straddle three intersections. Similarly the straight line that joins each heart spans twelve threads. It is broken into three stitches that span four threads so use the glitch fixer shown in Diagram

54

1 on page 25 to keep these lines uniform (an inset is also provided of the suggested final view).

NOTE. Read all of the instructions for the sequence before you begin this pattern. Stitches 9 and 10 need special attention as do stitches 19-21.

PATTERN 5 - STEP 1 RUNNING STITCH SEQUENCE

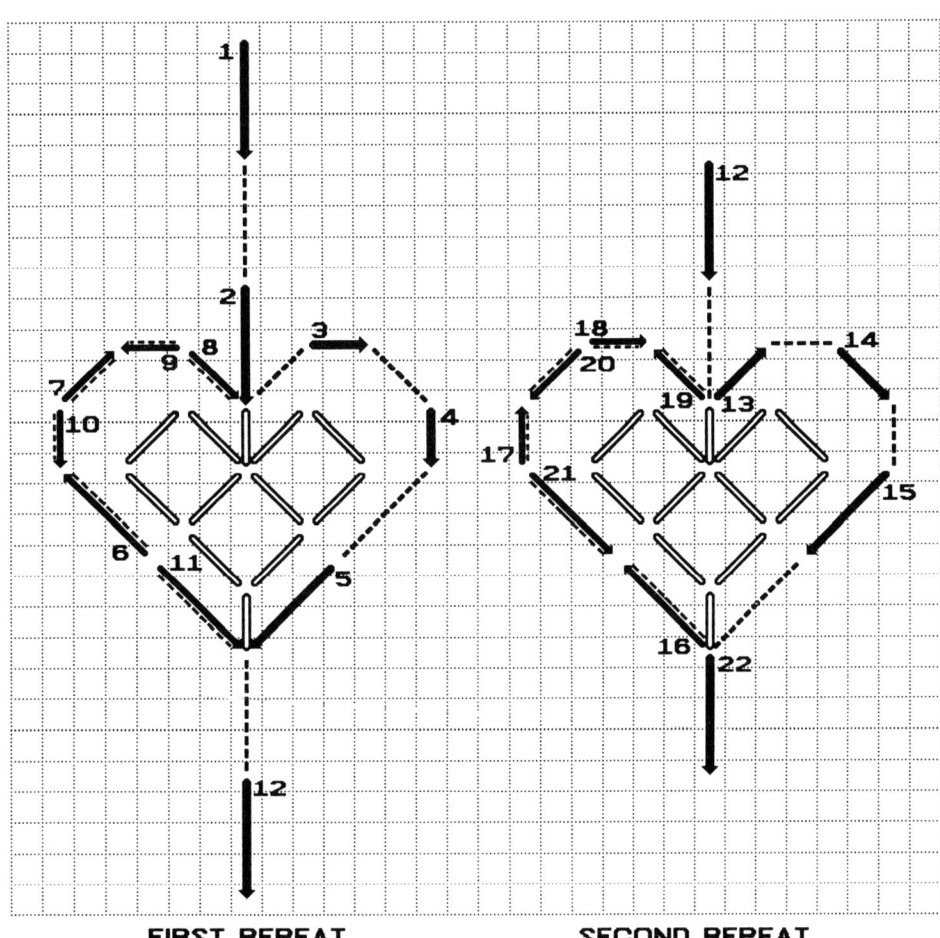

FIRST REPEAT   **SECOND REPEAT**

Two repeats of the running stitch sequence are shown for this pattern since the repeat point does not occur until stitch 22. Because there are three straight stitches joining the hearts instead of two or four, the odd number of stitches makes the "on top of the canvas" stitches reverse in the second heart. The sequence for the third heart will be like that of the first one (stitches 1-12) so the thread placement is the same for every other heart rather than every heart throughout the rows. This kind of sequence reversal occurs in blackwork patterns with odd counts in their repeats, and it usually doesn't cause any trouble. However, in this pattern there are several times on the return trip when stitches have to be placed accurately so the needle position may be confusing. **Do not focus on whether the needle is on top or underneath the canvas on the return trip when you place the strategic stitches – concentrate on the final view as the stitch is laid and match the pattern to this view in the inset on page 57).**

55

PATTERN 5 - STEP 2 RETURN TRIP SEQUENCE

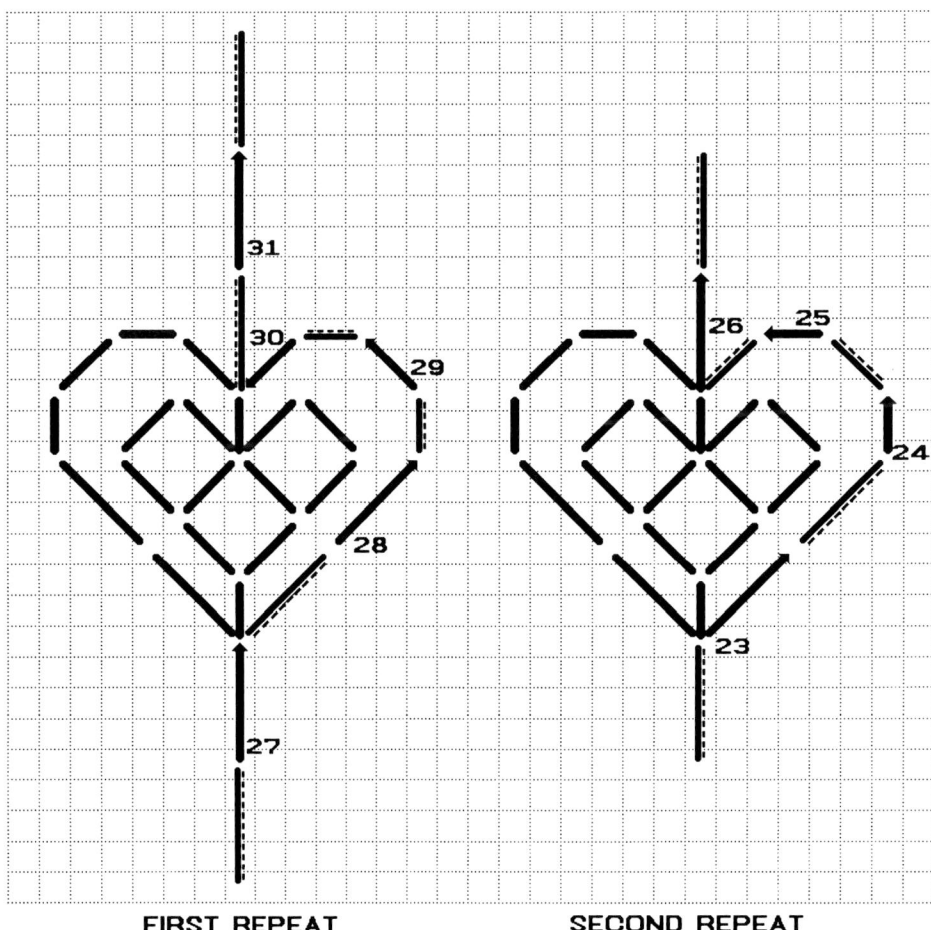

FIRST REPEAT　　　　**SECOND REPEAT**

NOTE. Hereafter the double running stitch path will be referred to as the return trip. It is easier to use this short label on the charts, and the words are interchangeable.

The side trip will be taken after stitch 8 in this pattern since that is a good angle from which to enter. The lettered sequence on the next page was also discussed on page 34 of the text as an example of "zigzagging" a sequence to keep it clean. A vertical stitch is added after stitch c in this path, and it is one where the thread should be held back so that the stitch can be completed cleanly and at the same time on the underneath side (reread paragraph 1 on page 29 if this is unclear). The needle is on top of the canvas for this stitch, and it is a single side trip. In essence this whole sequence is a side trip with 3 "single side trips off of the main side trip." A view of this is also provided on the next page.

Stitches 9 and 18, 10 and 17, 4 and 24, 3 and 25, and 12 and 31 need special attention on the return trip. The first four pairs of stitches are all of the short straight stitches in both repeats. These should remain <u>outside</u> of the traveling thread underneath. This will be easy to accomplish on stitches 9, 10, 24 and 25 since the stitches before and after these stitches angle away so the correct placement is the "line of least resistance." However, the other stitches are already on top on the return trip so the stitches before and after must be planted strategically to keep these stitches <u>outside</u> of the traveling thread. Since the straight stitches are shorter than the diagonal stitches the proportions of the pattern look better when these are outside – they appear longer, and the contours are nicer. More important, the lines on the opposite side of a symmetrical shape look more uniform if they match in a mirror image placement – hence the effort to refine the lines is worth it!

LETTERED SIDE TRIP SEQUENCE

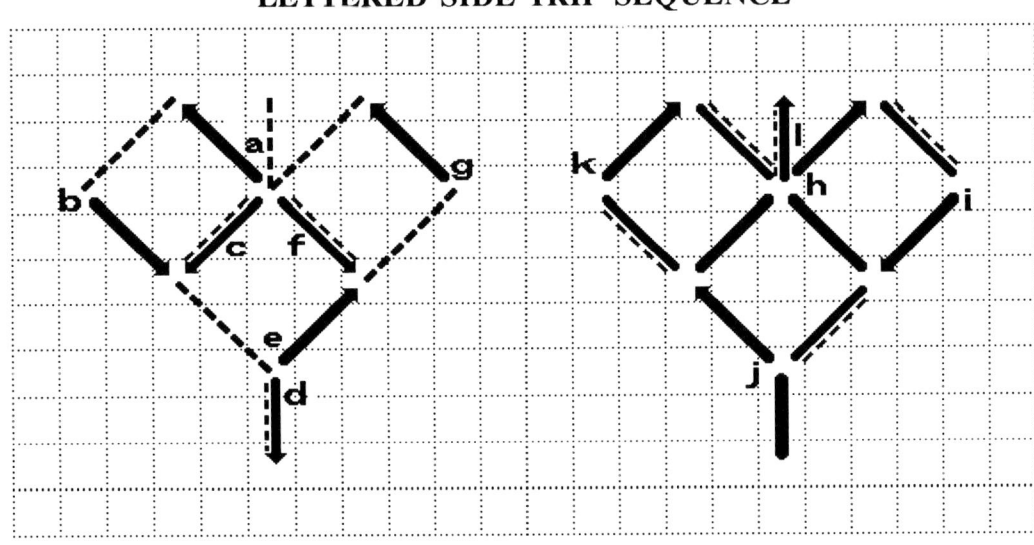

RUNNING ST. ROW   **RETURN TRIP**

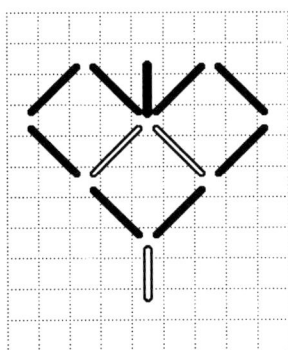

**OVERALL PATTERN
SIDE TRIP**

**VIEW OF SIDE
TRIP WITH "SIDE
TRIPS OFF OF
THE MAIN SIDE
TRIPS"**

INSET (RIGHT)

The chart to the right shows the final view of the middle stitch of each series of straight lines in Pattern 5. If a consistent stitch is planted here each time, the straight line will appear straight and uniform throughout the pattern. It is impossible to create a perfect straight line, but such consistency will create the illusion of one.

Use this solution for stitches 12 and 31.

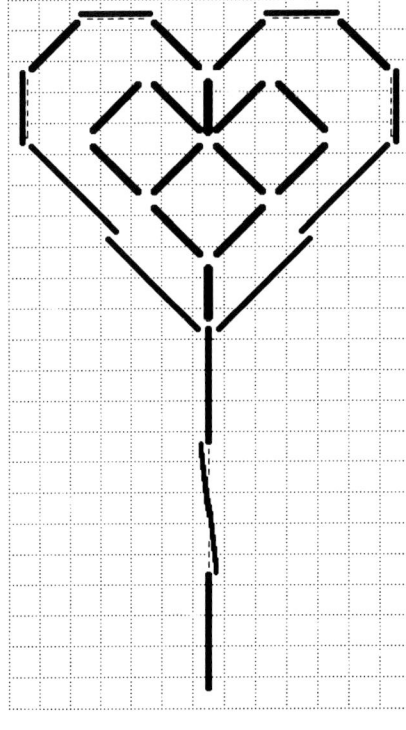

57

The inset chart on the previous page also shows the suggested placement of the small straight stitches in the heart outline and the long diagonal stitches along the base. An exact mirror image placement of these stitches greatly enhances the view of the heart.

PATTERN 6. This pattern is a symmetrical one with a strong horizontal thrust. The same unusual motif repeats and interlocks to form the pattern. The repeat unit is formed from a reflection of half of it. Therefore, the sequence of the pattern will consist of two double running paths – one of the left side vertical path and one of the right side vertical path. There are two side trips off of one side of the motif and one side trip off of the other side.

**OVERALL CHART
PATTERN 6**

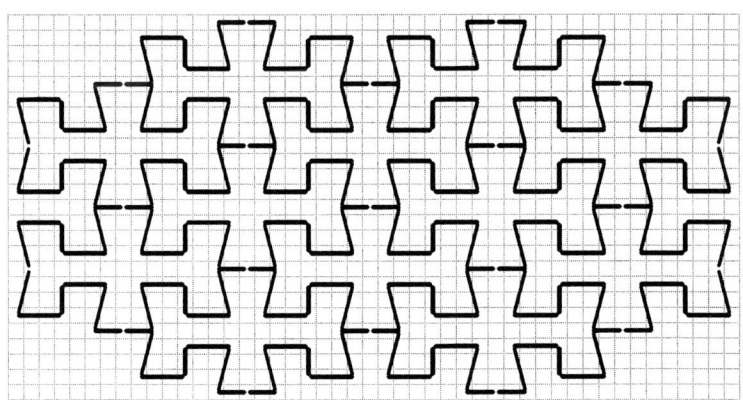

PATTERN 6 SEQUENCE

No numbered sequence is provided this time since the path is a clear simple outline. However, a bold overall chart is provided on the next page that has dotted lines that show the divisions between the row repeats. Use these two charts together with the overall chart above to build the segments of double running paths.

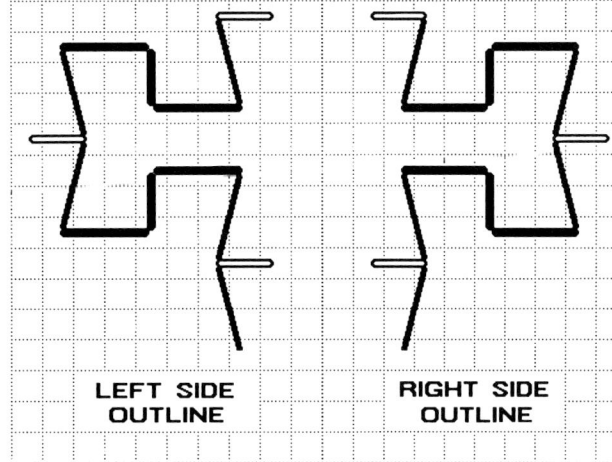

LEFT SIDE
OUTLINE

RIGHT SIDE
OUTLINE

Notice how the in between rows are automatically defined by the outlines of the surrounding rows since the shapes interlock. The short stitches that form the side trips could actually be one long stitch over four threads. If this stitch length is chosen, however, the side trips are added on every other row rather than every row, as shown above. Either option is acceptable, but it is always easier to memorize an unchanging sequence.

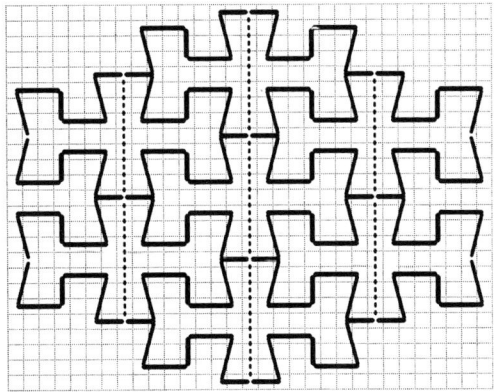

PATTERN 6
BOLD
OVERALL
VIEW

PATTERN 7. This pattern is an example of another interlocking pattern. However, this time the units rotate as they repeat, and the extensions of one motif fit into the recesses of the next one. As a result the pattern resembles a jigsaw puzzle so it received that name.

OVERALL CHART - PATTERN 7

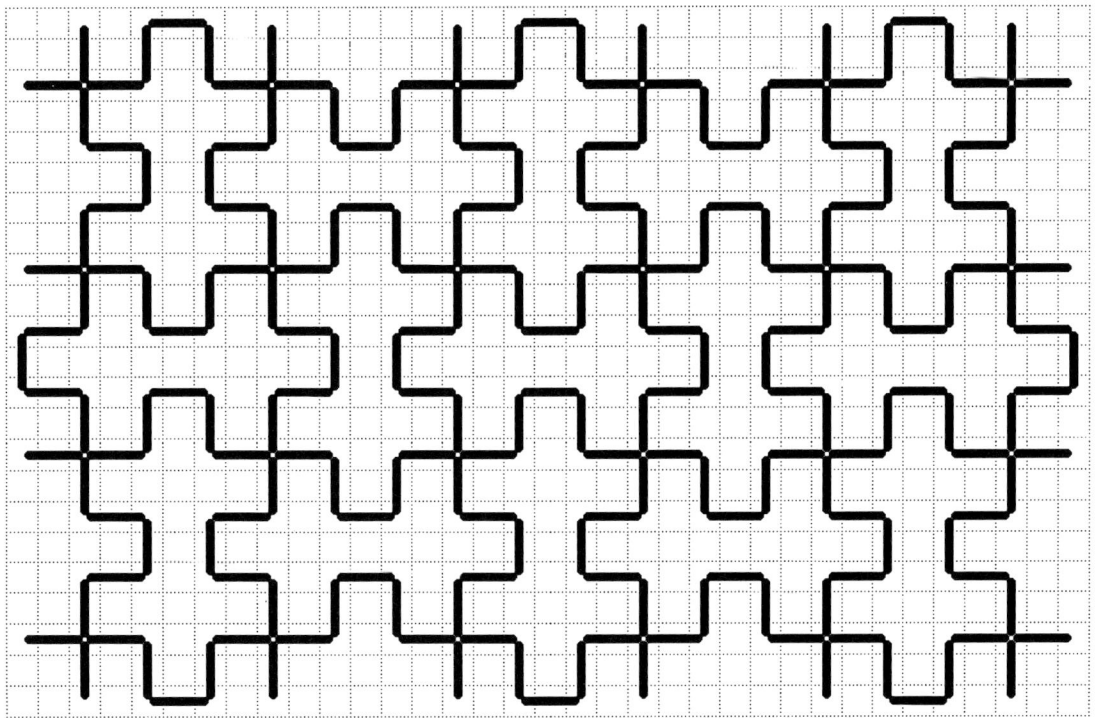

This pattern can be executed in several ways, but the simplest sequence is one that uses a pair of horizontal rows and a pair of vertical rows. Below is a second overall chart that isolates these rows. Notice that the two rows of each pair are a mirror image outline.

PATTERN 7 SEQUENCE ROWS

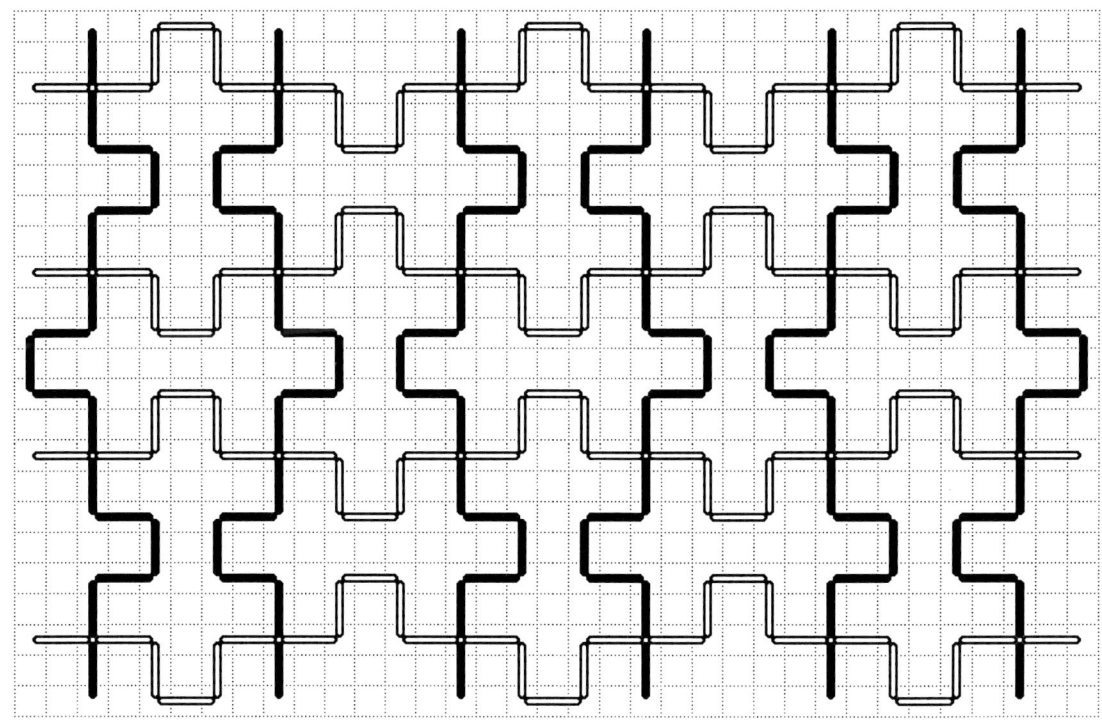

PATTERN 7
ISOLATED VERTICAL ROWS

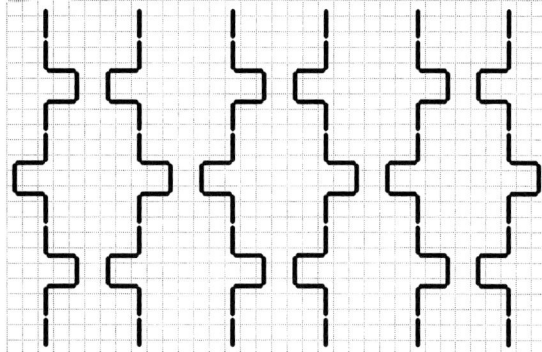

PATTERN 7 SEQUENCE
VERTICAL ROWS
Double Running Paths

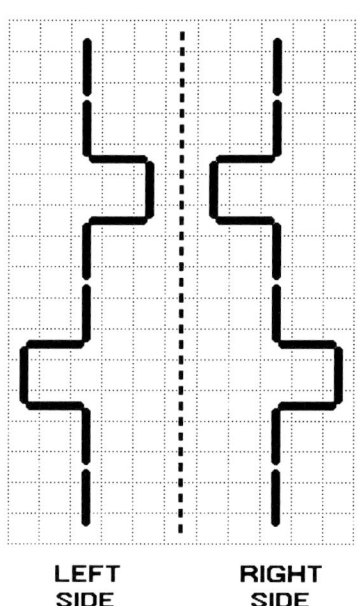

Rotate the sequence chart to the right 90° to add the horizontal rows of double running stitch. Use the large overall chart above for placement guidance. No numbers are needed for these simple outlines.

LEFT
SIDE

RIGHT
SIDE

Pattern 7 could also be executed by using only vertical rows of double running stitch. At the appropriate junctures the horizontal segments would be added as side trips. This option is more efficient since the use of side trips eliminates half of the traveling paths from row to row. It is somewhat more difficult to establish the pattern this way since the side trips are confusing at first with the flip-flop shapes. However, after two full rows are completed the alternating sequences are easy to follow.

PATTERN 8. This pattern is very intricate. Like the previous one, the pattern motifs alternate in a flip-flop arrangement, and the shapes interlock with each other. This pattern is so complex, however, that both a horizontal sequence and a vertical sequence are definitely recommended.

**OVERALL CHART
PATTERN 8**

Like pattern 7, this pattern can be divided into two separate sequences. Half of the pattern is formed with two alternating vertical outlines, and the other half is created with two alternating horizontal outlines. However, this time the rows are not just simple double running paths. Side trips are needed to connect the extra elements.

It is impossible to see the separate sequences in the overall chart above, but an enlarged chart on the next page clearly shows the two separate patterns that are combined. On page 63, there are four additional charts that show the separate patterns along with dotted lines that delineate the separate row sequences. The pattern formed by the vertical rows is a half-drop arrangement, and the pattern formed by the horizontal rows is a brick arrangement. Both patterns are identical, and each can form the other if it is rotated 90°.

It is important to learn to see these relationships within a pattern in order to analyze it and create sensible sequences for stitching it. This pattern could be stitched with either a vertical or a horizontal sequence, but it is less complicated to break it down into isolated paths that are easy to follow. Flip-flop patterns can usually be charted in this way so study them until the visual separations are clear. I often print several copies of a pattern so that I can outline various paths in color to determine an appropriate sequence. Use Hiliter pens for these outlines since they do not obscure the printed line underneath.

ENLARGED OVERALL CHART - PATTERN 8
(Shows two separate patterns that are combined)

62

PATTERN 8
ISOLATED VERTICAL ROWS

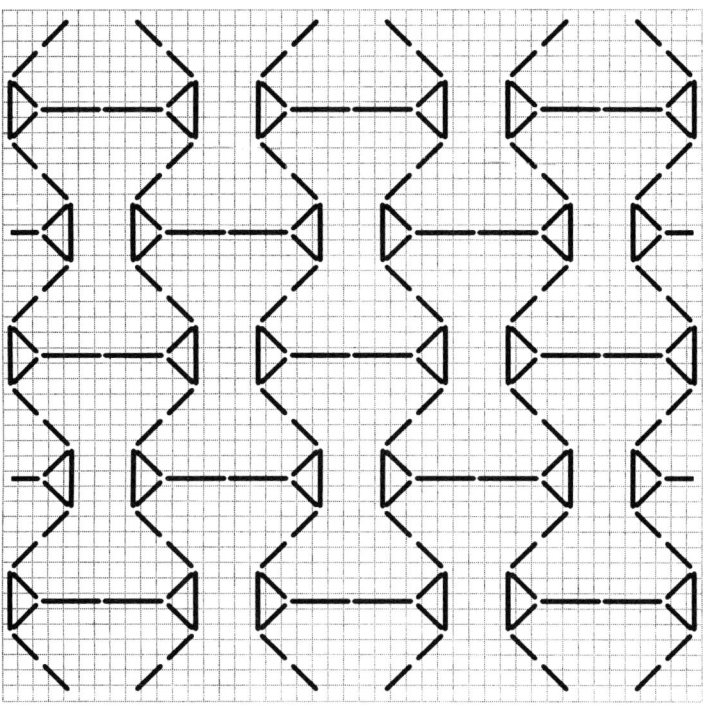

PATTERN 8 SEQUENCE
VERTICAL ROWS
Left and Right Sides

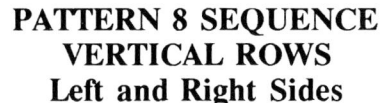
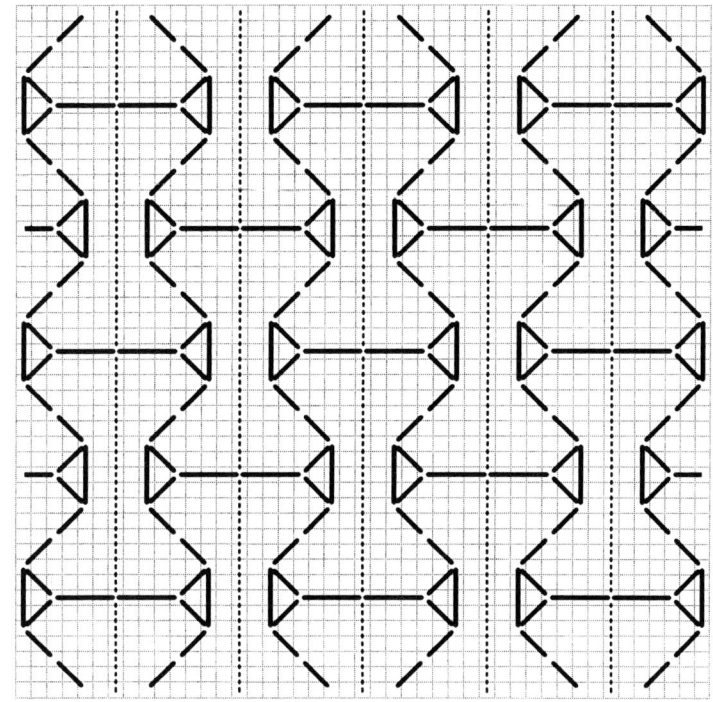

PATTERN 8
ISOLATED HORIZONTAL ROWS

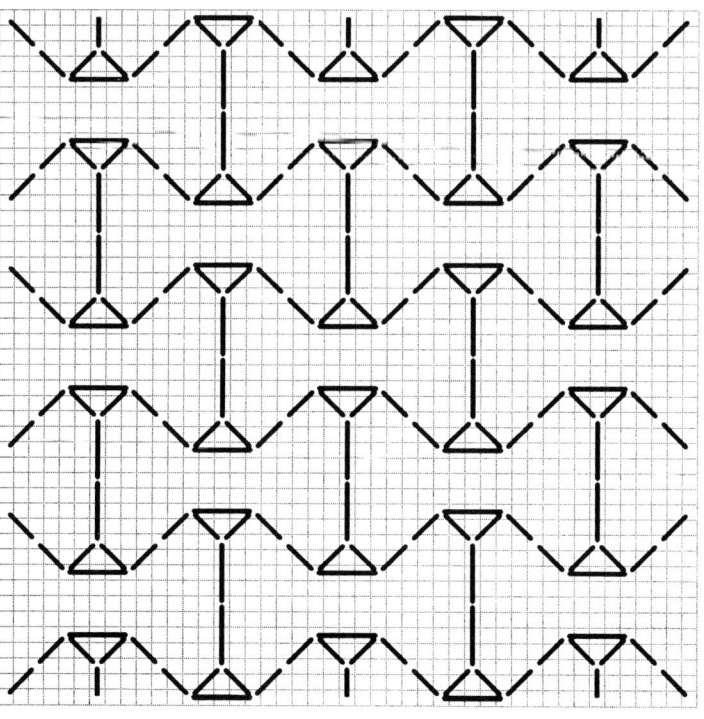

PATTERN 8 SEQUENCE
HORIZONTAL ROWS
Upper and Lower Sides

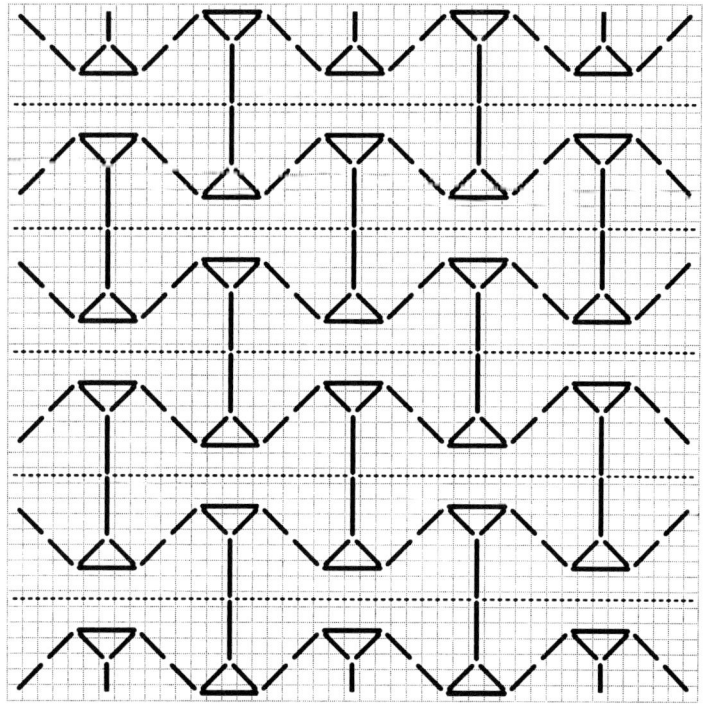

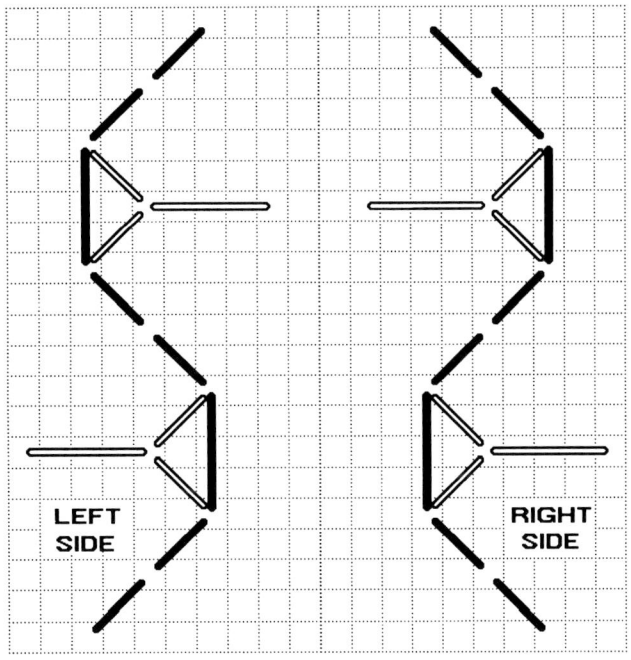

PATTERN 8 SEQUENCE
VERTICAL ROWS
Double Running Paths

The chart to the left shows the double running paths for the vertical rows. Notice that the left and right sides form a mirror image of each other. Execute each row in a double running sequence, and add the side trips where they join the long vertical stitch. Each side trip can be added in one step. However, I find it somewhat tidier to add part of it at the beginning of the long vertical stitch and part of it at the end of the long vertical stitch. Below is a numbered chart for each method, showing the vertical rows. Choose one method and use it consistently throughout the pattern.

VERTICAL ROWS
NUMBERED SEQUENCES

The left side sequence shows the complete side trip taken after stitch 1 and after stitch 6. This method is cleanest when the long stitch (number 4) is taken after the two diagonal stitches (numbers 2-3) are outlined. The sharp angle automatically leaves the hole more open for the straight stitch to sink into, but use one hand to hold back the traveling thread from stitch 3 underneath the canvas as you reenter the hole. Since the needle position is reversed in the lower side trip, stitch 8 can be held back on top of the canvas as the hole is reentered for stitch 9.

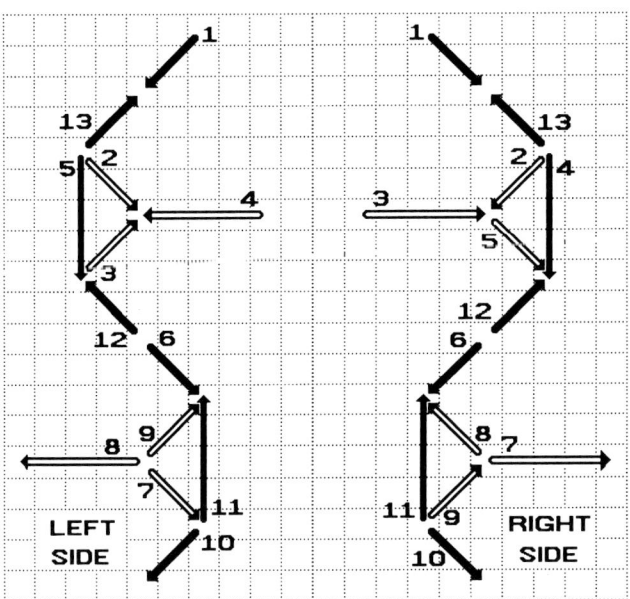

The right side sequence splits the diagonal stitches of the side trip into separate steps, thus keeping the shared hole for stitches 2,3, and 5 even cleaner. No threads have to be held back in order to reenter the hole.

Try both of these methods on a doodle cloth first to see which one is more comfortable. Both present an attractive pattern, but choose one and stick with it as a mix and match approach may produce "telltale signs."

64

Complete the vertical row pattern before adding any of the horizontal rows to the pattern. Rotate the charts on the previous page 90° to add the horizontal rows.

Note. The pairs of consecutive diagonal stitches in this pattern would normally have to be manipulated carefully on the return trip in order to create an illusion of straightness. However, since the horizontal paths will intersect these pairs of stitches there is no need to use a particular strategy on the return trip of the vertical rows. **However, when the horizontal rows intersect the vertical rows, it is important to observe rule 4 on page 27 in order to maintain an attractive consistent appearance.**

NOTE TO ADVANCED STUDENTS. The pattern of horizontal rows can be superimposed on to the pattern of vertical rows, if desired. In order to do this, the pairs of diagonal stitches that straddle two intersections must be merged into a single stitch that straddles 4 threads. This will make each long diagonal stitch lay comfortably on top of the dimple or "ditch" between the two short diagonal stitches underneath. If a flat thread is used for the bottom layer, the pairs of diagonal stitches could actually be merged in both layers, but I find that the top layer is usually more stable when the "ditch" is underneath to hold the thread. When a dark floss is used for the foundation pattern and a slightly lighter value #8 perle is used for the top layer, the pattern will appear even more three dimensional.

PATTERN 8 ALTERNATIVE TREATMENT

(Showing the horizontal row pattern as a superimposed layer with merged pairs of consecutive diagonal stitches).

PATTERN 9. This pattern uses another heart motif as its core, and it was named Smiling Hearts because each heart appears to be a face with "ears" covering the eyes and a smile at the base. This is a complicated arrangement since the hearts have been rotated 180° to form a mirror image joined at the "ears." Each pair of rows is followed by another row that flip-flops and is placed in a staggered position to fit. In spite of this complexity, however, the pattern can be outlined with just two alternating sequence rows.

OVERALL CHART
PATTERN 9

The scale of this pattern is so large that the view here is not symmetrical. Enough is shown, however, to indicate a clear-cut repeat at the bottom of the pattern.

If a symmetrical sample is desired, either reduce or enlarge this view accordingly.

This pattern is used in the *Heart of Blackwork* design featured on the cover of the book. It is also used in *Vowlentine* (Color Plate XIII).

The sequences for this pattern are divided into two distinct segments. These divisions are shown in the overall chart on the next page that has dotted lines between the rows. One segment outlines the alternating star and diamond shapes, and the second segment outlines the bases of the hearts. The star sequence is a trip-and-a-half path with side trips on both sides of some of the diamonds. The sequence that outlines the base of the heart is a zigzag row with side trips on both sides of the path at the point where the zigzag pivots.

The straight lines that join the star shapes to the heart rows are part of the star sequence. **These lines straddle four threads, but the straight lines in the zigzag rows straddle only three threads.** There is a tendency to make both sets of straight lines the same length so beware! The proportions are better if executed as shown. Notice too that the diagonal lines of the zigzag rows straddle three intersections to form a heart outline that is the same size as those in the Dangling Hearts pattern on page 54. It is important to make the lines on both sides of the heart shape match on the return trip in this pattern the same way they did in Pattern 5 (study the inset chart on page 57 again). However, the rotation in this pattern makes the final presentation more complicated. A view of one segment of the pattern in the chart below to the right shows my preferred final appearance. Plant the needle strategically on the return trip to achieve this view, and maintain the same consistency throughout the pattern.

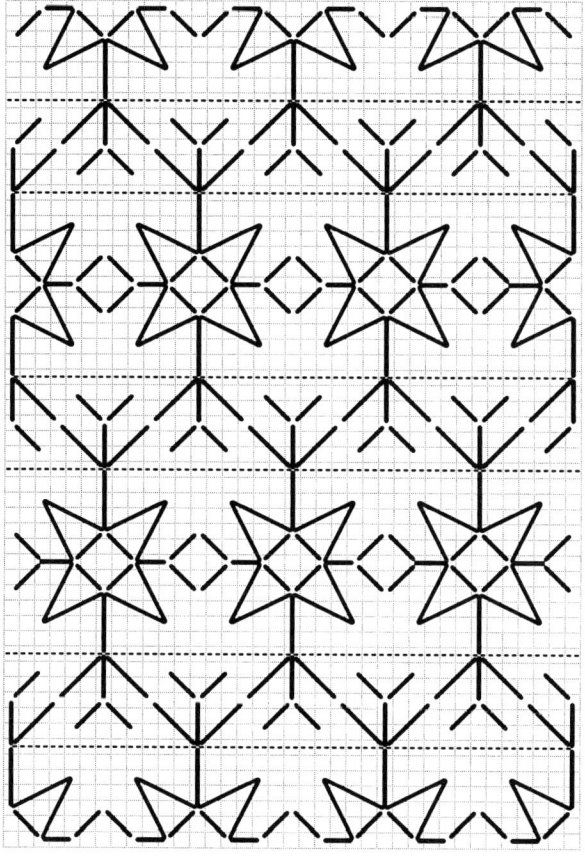

The chart above shows the divisions between the two row sequences of the double running stitch outlines for this pattern.

The sequence charts for the two double running stitch sequences that build this pattern follow on the next page. Begin with the zigzag row since it is less complicated. It also provides a good reference for placing the angled stitches of the star and diamond row. Instead of counting the angle of these stitches, merely sink the tips of the stars three threads above or below the ends of the angled stitches of the side trips of the zigzag rows. **Seeing such relationships within a pattern can make the placement of difficult stitches**

67

much easier so learn to look for such clues when analyzing a pattern that does not have a prescribed sequence.

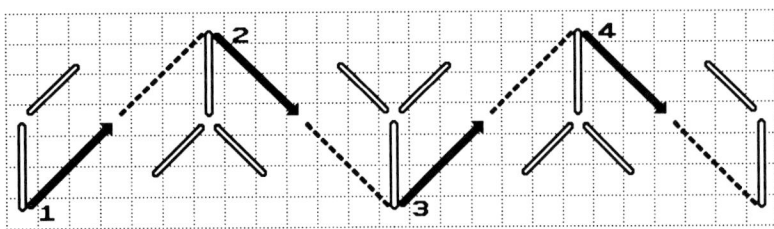

ZIGZAG ROW SEQUENCE
STEP 1
Running Stitch Row

To execute the rows in the opposite position, merely rotate this chart 180°, and follow the same sequence.

SIDE TRIPS FOR THE RUNNING STITCH ROW

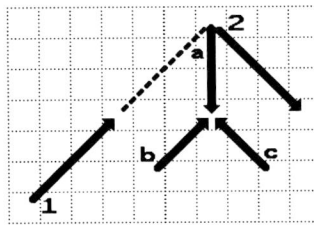

These side trips alternate since the base of the heart flip-flops along the path. As the path is worked from left to right on this row, it is slightly cleaner to execute the left side of the angled stitches (stitch b) at the tip of the side trip first. The tension on stitches 1, a, and b leans in towards the same void

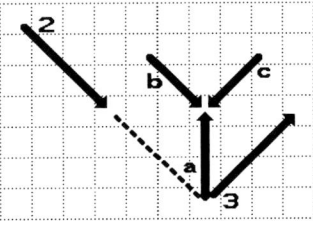

area so the shared hole for stitches a,b, and c stays more open when the running stitch path follows this outline. Therefore it is easier to sink stitch c to the right of stitch b with less chance of piercing any of the traveling threads underneath.

NOTE. If the side trips were added on the return trip, the path would be worked right to left so it would be cleaner to add stitch c first. The side edges of these rows show only partial side trips since the pattern units are only half units. Add these partial side trip stitches either at the beginning or at the end of the double running sequences. There is a tendency to forget these so the sooner, the better!

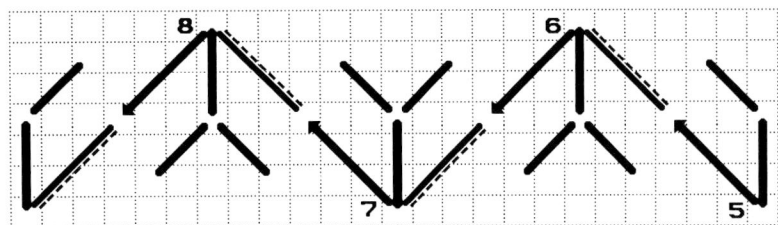

ZIGZAG SEQUENCE
Return Trip

Reminder. Sink stitches 5 and 7 on the inside of the already placed stitch. Sink stitches 6 and 8 on the outside of the already placed stitch.

The star and diamond sequence is shown on the next page. Add these rows between the zigzag rows to complete the pattern. A suggested lettered sequence for the side trips in this sequence follows the running stitch row sequence. Sharper points can be obtained when each star outline is divided into two separate steps. It is more difficult to memorize the sequence at first, but the results are worthwhile as a point of refinement.

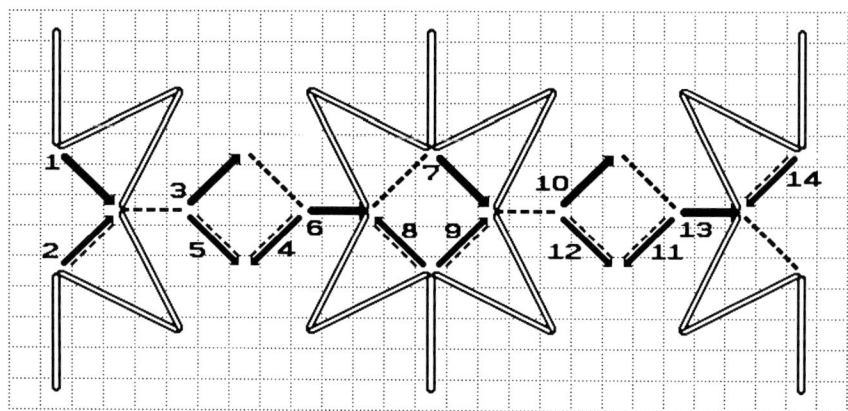

**STAR AND
DIAMOND
SEQUENCE
STEP 2
Running Stitch Row**

The main path of this sequence is a series of diamonds followed by a single connecting straight stitch. All of these stitches straddle either two threads or intersections. Every other diamond is the center of a star, which is added as a side trip. Use the lettered chart on the left side below to add the star outlines. Stitch a is added after stitch 6. Stitches b-d are added before stitch 7. Stitches e and f are added after stitch 7. Stitches g-i are added before stitch 8. Stitch j is added after stitch 8. Add the partial side trip stitches along the row edges at the same placement point along the main path as that of the whole units.

STAR SIDE TRIPS

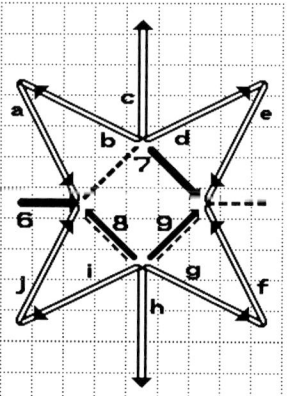

**STAR AND DIAMOND SEQUENCE
Return Trip**

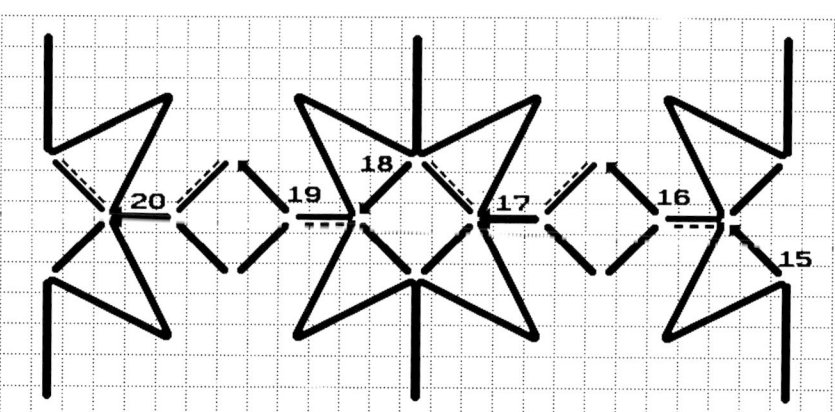

The return trip in this sequence travels only on the upper half of the diamonds. The lower half is completed as part of the trip-and-a-half segment of step 1.

This pattern is a large scale pattern that should be used only in a bold area. However, it makes a handsome horizontal or vertical stripe if an area is created to fit its proportions gracefully.

PATTERN 10. This pattern is a simple one based on an arrow shape. The alternating rows of the pattern are staggered with a half-drop placement of the repeats. The main path of the outline forms the arrows and the zigzag lines that connect them. Inside the bold zigzag lines is a hexagon motif that is added as a side trip. The overall pattern is shown in the chart below on the left side. The chart on the right side shows the pattern without any side trips. The bold "open" diamond shape between the opposing arrow shapes is large enough that it invites further embellishment. In this pattern a simple blackwork addition is added, but in Pattern 35 on page 116 an open canvas filler is added.

OVERALL CHART - PATTERN 10

PATTERN 10 - OVERALL VIEW WITH NO SIDE TRIPS

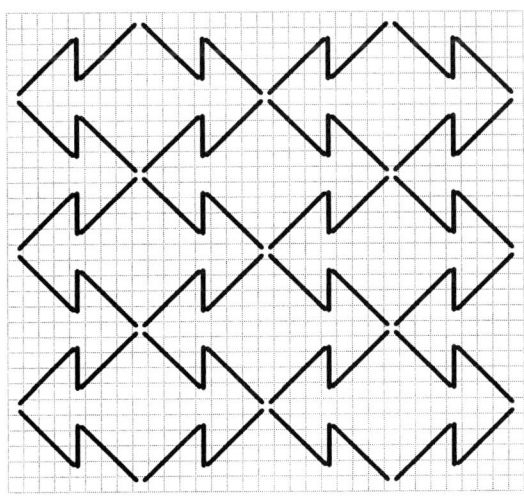

**PATTERN 10 SEQUENCE
Running Stitch Row**

The sequence for this pattern is executed in horizontal rows. The shapes divide nicely in half so the top side paths and the bottom side paths are mirror images of each other. The side trip is added either before stitch 2 or before stitch 3, and it is added in a tidy zigzag sequence so there is no benefit from splitting it. The running stitch row sequence is shown to the left, and the return trip row sequence follows on the next page. In addition, there is also an enlarged view of the overall pattern on the next page that has dotted lines that show the center division of each row. Actually the double running sequence is only used on half of the visible rows – the in-between rows are created by the negative spaces that form when the other rows are added.

70

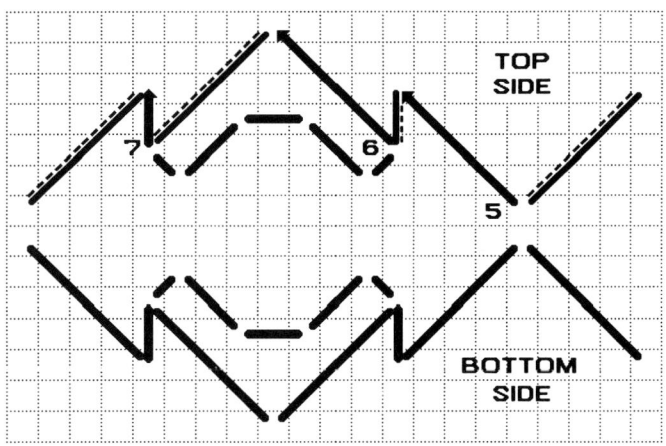

PATTERN 10 SEQUENCE
Return Trip

No fixing is needed on this return trip. However, it is important for the straight stitch to be outside of the traveling path of the surrounding diagonal stitches, as shown in the inset below. This will happen automatically, however, since it is the "line of least resistance."

SIDE TRIP - PREFERRED FINAL VIEW

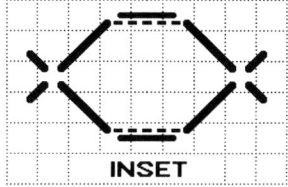

INSET

PATTERN 10 - OVERALL VIEW WITH DIVIDING LINES

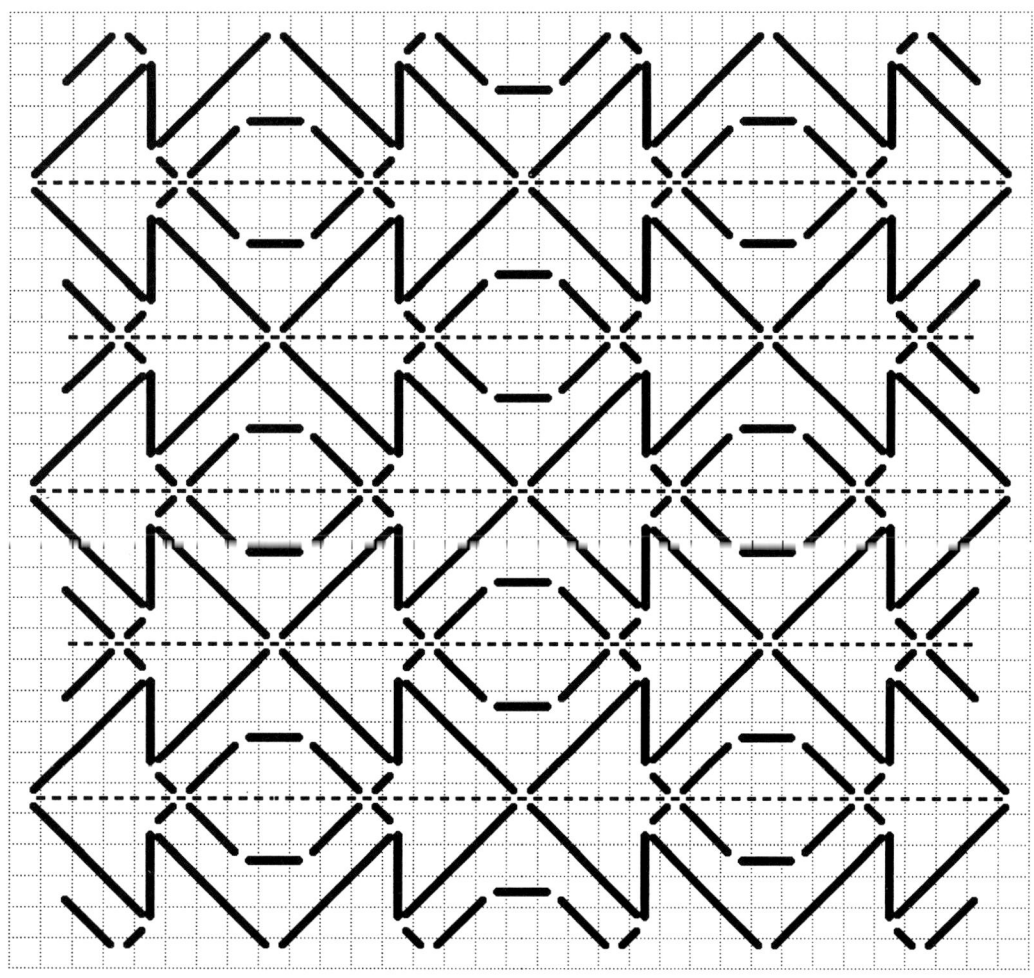

NOTE. No sequence chart is provided for the bottom sides of the horizontal rows of Pattern 10. Simply repeat the numbered sequence used for the top sides, being sure to mirror image the stitches. Use the overall charts to assist with the placement.

PATTERN 11. This pattern is another simple outline that combines two sizes of diamonds in an alternating flow. The bold chart to the right of the overall chart below shows the alternating pattern repeats.

OVERALL CHART - PATTERN 11

**PATTERN 11
ALTERNATING
DIAMONDS**

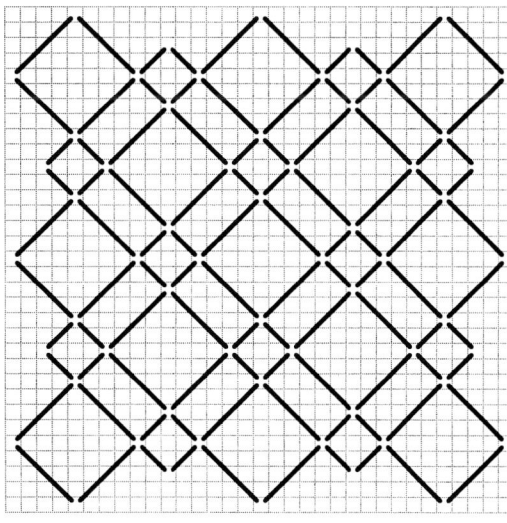

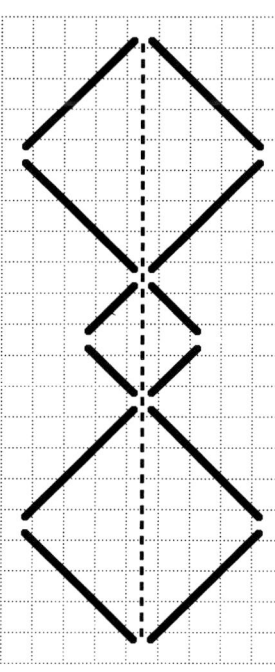

The enlarged chart to the right shows the alternating large and small diamonds that form the repeat of Pattern 11. The in-between rows of the pattern are placed in a half-drop position to form a diaper pattern. The large diamonds have sides that straddle four intersections in this pattern, and the small diamonds have sides that straddle two intersections.

The sequence for Pattern 11 is a simple double running outline with no side trips. Therefore no numbered sequence is needed to execute the pattern. The left side zigzag row is placed first for each row, and the right side is added in a mirror image position to complete the row. On the next page there is a large overall chart that shows the divisions between the left and right sides of the pattern in each vertical row. This pattern could also be executed in horizontal rows (and should be if the shape chosen for it is more horizontal than vertical). However, the detailed views here are shown with divisions that display vertical rows. Merely rotate the charts 90° if a horizontal path is preferred.

There are also two other versions of this pattern on the next page. They combine diamonds of a different size. Having a pattern that is flexible in size and scale can be very useful, and such variations can also be embellished further. Pattern 30 and Pattern 36 on pages 107 and 117 are examples of variations of this pattern. Both variations are composite patterns that have couching or open canvas fillers in the negative spaces formed by the blackwork.

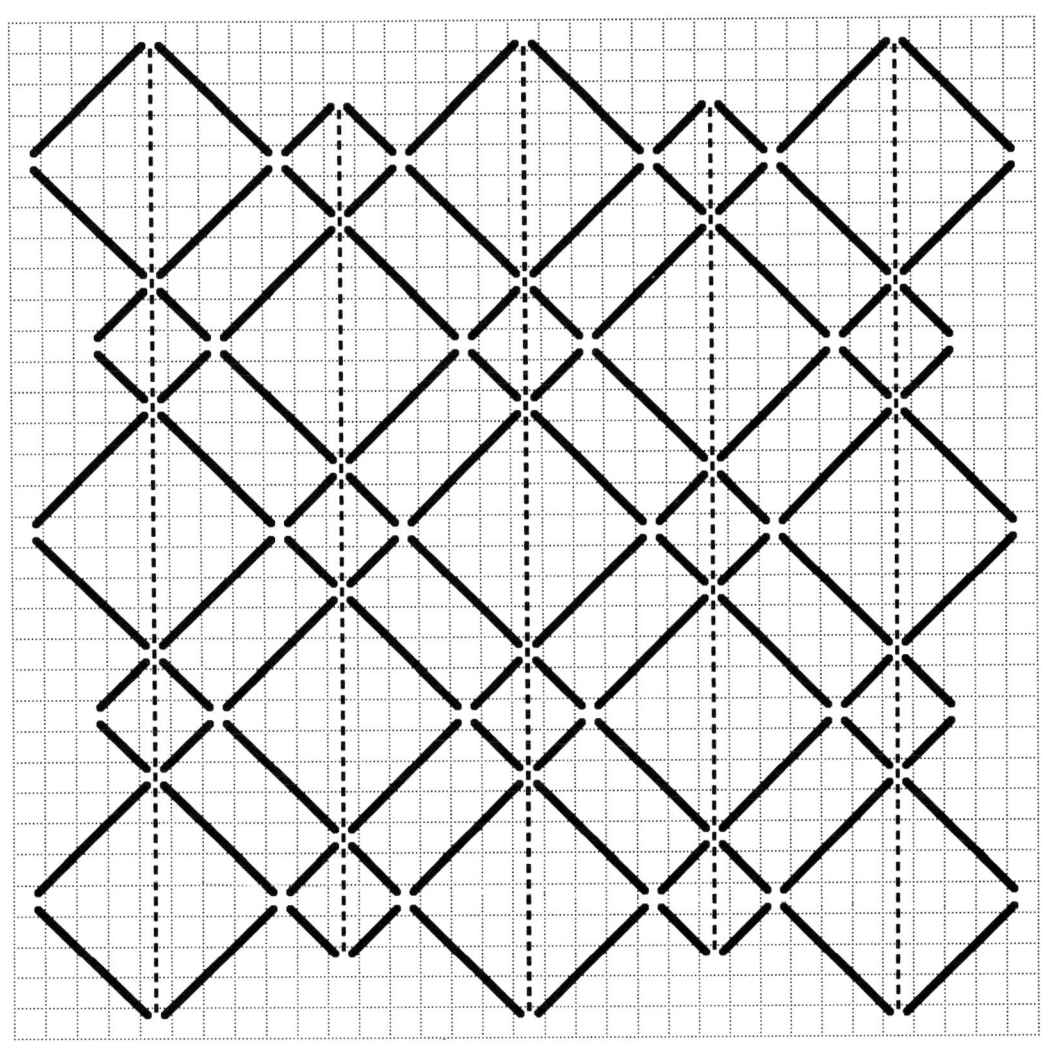

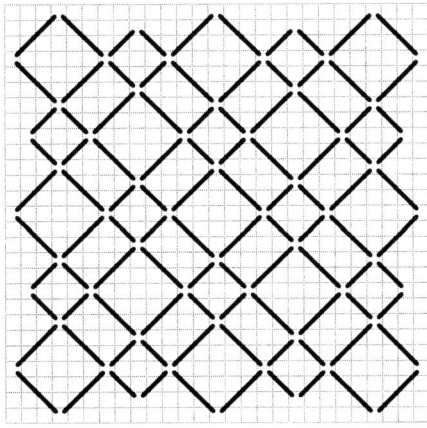

PATTERN VARIATIONS

The small chart on the left shows a pattern that combines diamonds with sides that straddle three intersections with diamonds of sides that straddle two intersections. The chart on

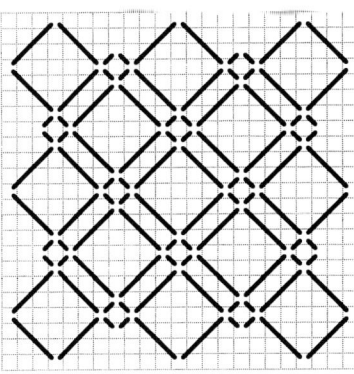

the right shows a pattern that combines diamonds with sides that straddle three intersections with diamonds of sides that straddle just one intersection.

These two patterns can be executed in either a vertical or a horizontal sequence just like Pattern 11. The rhythm of the sequence and the alternating placement of the diamonds are identical – only the length of the stitches has to be adjusted.

PATTERN 12. This pattern is an ogee pattern that features staggered rows of elongated ogee shapes. It is used in Sampler 1 on the back cover in the four prominent ogee shapes that form Area 2. The pattern is bold, and shows up well in the dark red thread. Because the ogee shape is a horizontal ogee, it is easier to execute the pattern with horizontal sequences in this design.

However, in the *Winter Whimsy* design (Color Plate VII) a "formula" outline was created for the trees that allowed this same ogee pattern to fit gracefully inside the two largest trees with minimal compensation. Because the pattern outline contours to the tree outline so perfectly, a diagonal path was used for the sequence in this situation.

Both sequences will be shown here to illustrate how a pattern can be stitched efficiently in more than one way. The shape of the area where a pattern is being used should influence the final choice. A wide area generally accommodates horizontal rows best, making fewer whole rows necessary to fill the space. Less traveling is needed between rows when the number of total rows is minimized too. A long area would naturally accomodate vertical rows best for the same reasons. However, a vertical path is not practical in this pattern. Because the single straight stitch that connects each separate ogee in the vertical rows is also the side stitch of a unit in the adjacent row, the path is blocked in this direction. The necessary detours or side trips to connect the repeats in a vertical route would be complex and tedious, and other directions offer a better sequence flow. The diagonal path is not blocked or interrupted so it is the best choice for a long narrow area like the trees.

OVERALL CHART - PATTERN 12

The interior section of the ogee outline is a large area that could be embellished in a variety of ways. I have presented one attractive option, but doodle some others to create appealing alternatives or variations. Each center section will be added as a side trip, and the main outlines will be used as the main path for the first sequence.

OVERALL CHART - PATTERN 12
Shows Horizontal Main Paths

The heavy lines isolate the outlines of the ogee shapes when a horizontal sequence is used. Notice that it takes two rows to complete a whole ogee outline. There is a top row and a bottom row. All other lines in the chart show the side trips that must be added to these main path rows to build a complete pattern.

Notice that the bottom row of one outline is also the top row of an in-between row that is in a half-step position.

NOTE. The straight side stitches of every ogee are added as side trips off of the main path. These side trips will be added on the sequences of the top rows – unless, of course, one is forgotten. Then it may be added from the bottom row that follows.

OVERALL CHART - PATTERN 12
Shows Diagonal Main Paths

The heavy lines here isolate the outlines of the ogee shapes when a diagonal sequence is used to form the pattern. It also takes two rows to complete a whole ogee outline. One row completes the upper right sides of the ogees in that row and the lower left sides of those of the adjacent row. The interior embellishments and the upper left and lower right sides of each ogee are added as side trips off of the diagonal main path.

PATTERN 12 HORIZONTAL SEQUENCE Top Half

The chart to the left shows one repeat of a horizontal path. The interior side trips should be added after stitch 1. The exterior side trips should be added on the return trip. A lettered chart of the side trip sequence follows on page 76.

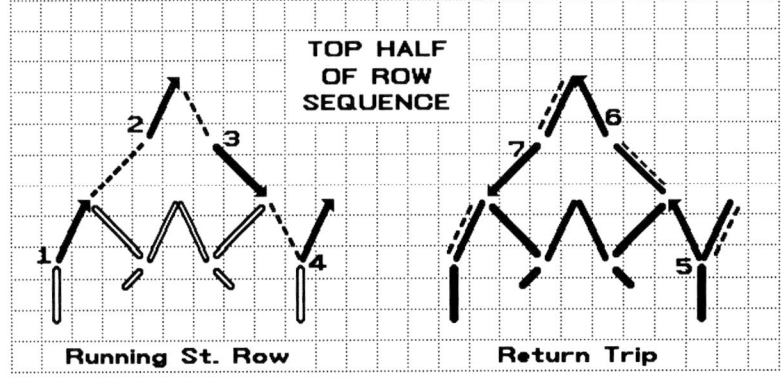

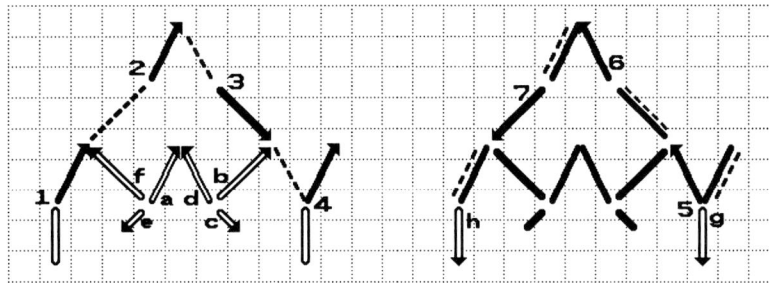

Take stitches a-f after stitch 1. Take stitch g after stitch 4. Take stitch h after stitch 7 on the return trip.

Stitches g and h are cleaner when they are added on the return trip. If they are added before stitch 1 or before stitch 4, the shared hole does not stay as clean as it does when they are added later. The sharp angle of stitches 4-5 keeps the traveling thread leaning away from stitch g so that it can reenter the shared hole comfortably. Since stitch h is an edge stitch it is added at the same juncture in the sequence even though there is no stitch to the left of stitch 1.

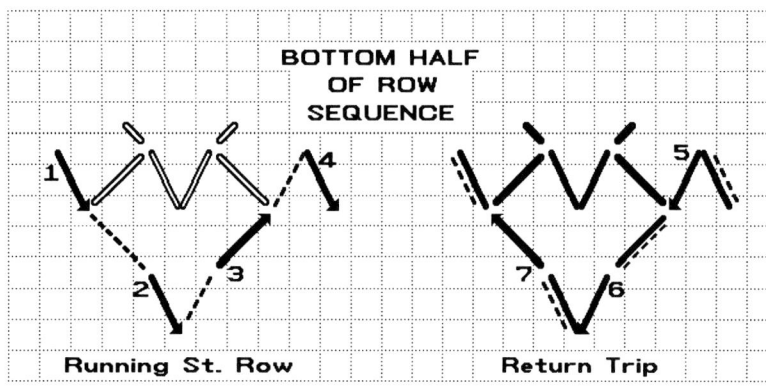

BOTTOM HALF
OF ROW
SEQUENCE

Running St. Row   Return Trip

PATTERN 12
HORIZONTAL
SEQUENCE
Bottom Half

The bottom half sequence is a mirror image of the top half sequence except for the fact that there are no vertical side trips (stitches g-h on the chart above). Add the interior side trip after stitch 1 again. Do the "M" outline in running stitch first, and add the small tent stitches on the return trip. This is the same rhythm that was used for the top half sequence. There the "W" outline was done in running stitch first, and the tent stitches were added on the return trip.

Alternate these two rows until the pattern is complete. Use the overall chart on page 75 for placement assistance, if needed.

The diagonal row sequence is somewhat more complex since the side trip sequence combines the lower right side of each ogee with the entire interior filling. The sequence charts for both the main path and the side trip follow on the next page. Study the main path chart for the running stitch row. Notice that the interior segment could be added after either stitch 3 or stitch 4. I chose stitch 4 because it makes the journey from stitch 4-5 cleaner to detour here. It also seemed logical to use the missing side of the ogee outline as the appropriate entry point. However, when compensation needs require alternative solutions, side trips can be added after stitch 3.

NOTE. There is no need to "fix" any of the stitches of the main path in this sequence. A single row will tend to wobble by itself, but once the interior fillings are added, the lines will become clearly defined. The important thing in this pattern is to make sure that the long diagonal stitches of the interior filling sink "inside" the exterior ogee outline and "outside" of the outline of the small star motif in the center. The pressure from these opposing stitches will automatically correct any irregularities in the outlines around them so keep them "between" the two outlines.

PATTERN 12 - DIAGONAL SEQUENCE
Running Stitch Row

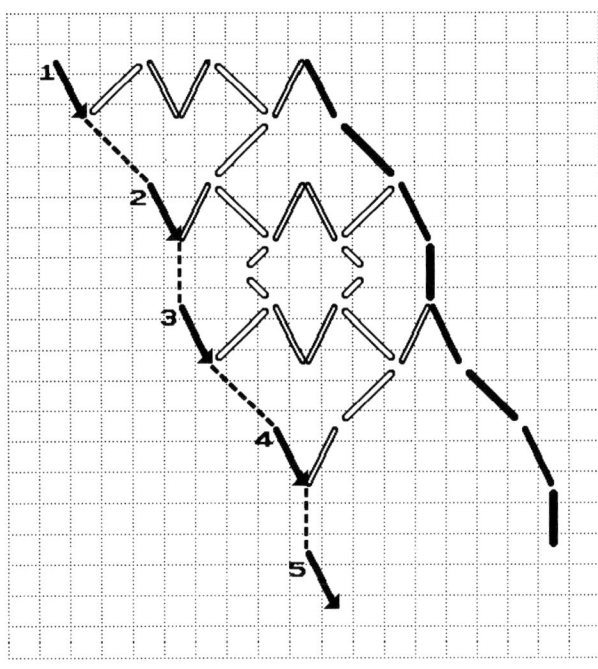

PATTERN 12
DIAGONAL SEQUENCE
Return Trip

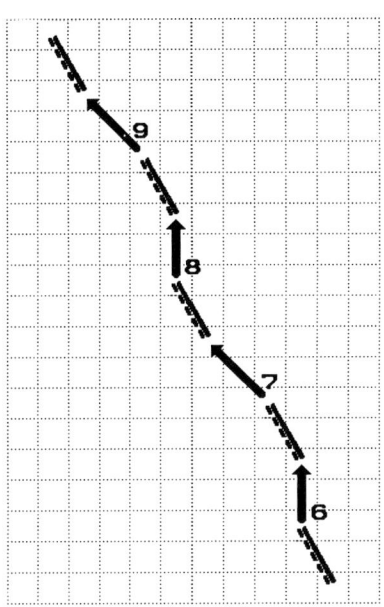

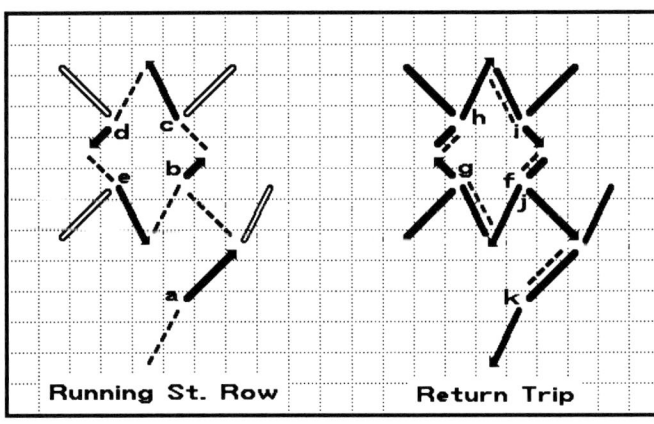

PATTERN 12
DIAGONAL SEQUENCE
Lettered Side Trip Sequence

The side trip sequence actually has four side trip stitches that are "side trips off of the side trip." Add these unlettered stitches on the running stitch path.

PATTERN 13. The following pattern is actually not a continuous pattern, but it appears to be at viewing distance. It is called the PacMan pattern because the core pattern motif resembles the icon or figure that was the "star" of the computer game of the same name that was popular in the early 1980's. The figures are repeated in horizontal rows of staggered "paper doll" chains. Each row encroaches on the row above it and below it. The "appendages" appear to interlock or join, but they do not touch. Therefore the pattern is technically a stripe, or series of isolated rows, but the lines merge at viewing distance and create what seems like an allover pattern. This pattern is used in the *Rainy Winter Landscape* (Color Plate VI) as the filling for the bridge abutment. It seems to suggest stone masonry as depicted here, and two weights of thread are used in the same value of gray to provide the texture desired. The ground fabric of this design is a 24-count gray Congress cloth, and two strands of medium gray floss are combined with a matching #8 perle cotton.

**OVERALL CHART
PATTERN 13**

**OVERALL CHART
PATTERN 13
(Shows top, bottom and middle
rows with no compensation
or in between rows)**

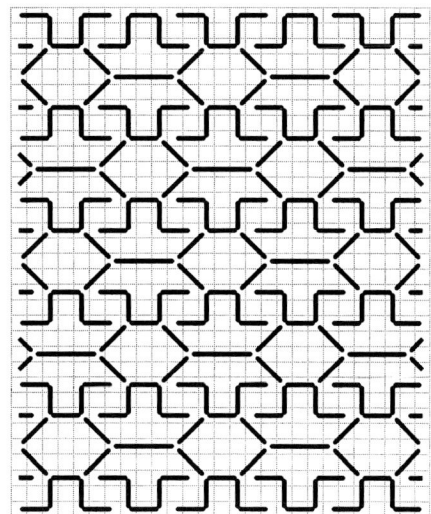

---- Row 1 ----

---- Row 3 ----

---- Row 5 ----

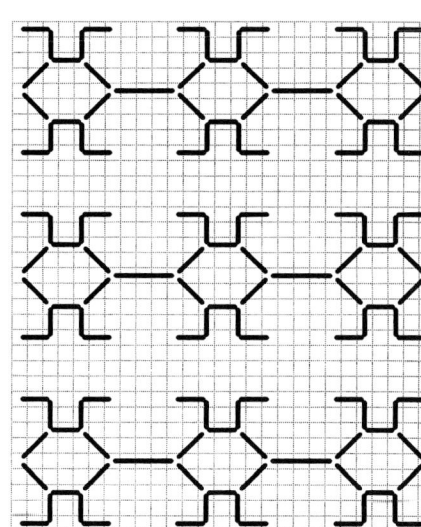

The overall chart above on the left shows the complete pattern with all the required compensation to fit a rectangle. The chart on the right shows only rows 1,3, and 5 without the in between rows 2 and 4 or any of the compensation stitches along the edge of the shape. Since the pattern is confusing, it should help to have this "partial" pattern.

On the next page there is another overall chart that is enlarged. Take a Hiliter pen and mark rows 1, 3 and 5. They will now stand out in color so the placement of the remaining rows will be clear. If you prefer not to soil the book, merely make a copy of the enlarged chart and mark it instead.

The in-between rows can be executed in another thread weight and\or a slightly different value of the same color to produce a different effect. Notice that there is one open thread between the "antennae" and the "hip" of the PacMan figure and those of the figures of the in-between rows. These rows are shifted to a half-step position, thus creating the illusion of a diaper or a continuous allover repeat.

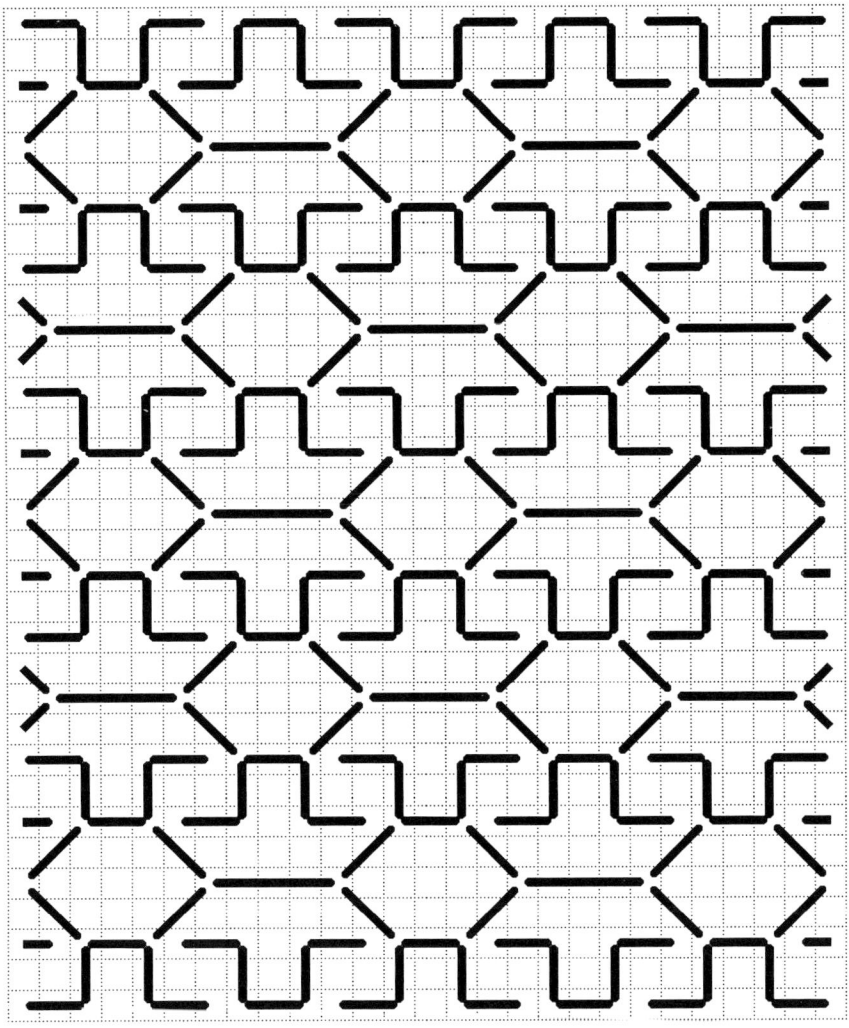

Sequence Instructions (chart below). The main path of the sequence is the hexagons which are joined with one long stitch that straddles four threads. The side trips in the pattern are the "antennae" and the "legs" of the PacMan figure. These are added to the running stitch row, and this row sequence is a trip-and-a-half path.

NOTE. This is a good pattern to consider working from the center out as each new row is placed. The compensation is hard to anticipate along the edges, but the correct placement of additional rows is easy to figure out in the middle of the area.

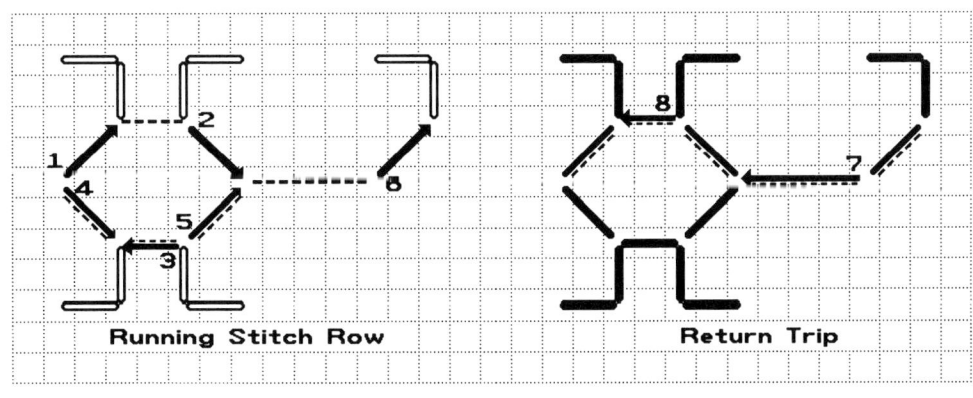

Running Stitch Row   Return Trip

**PATTERN 13
SEQUENCE
CHART**

This completes the chapter of patterns with irregular stitch lengths and angles. By now the reader should be well acquainted with the double running method of executing blackwork patterns. The chapters that follow will be composite patterns that combine blackwork with other canvas treatments or that superimpose one blackwork pattern on top of another compatible outline.

CHAPTER 3 - **SUPERIMPOSED BLACKWORK PATTERNS**

This chapter will present patterns that combine two blackwork networks into a single composite pattern that is layered. Occasionally the patterns will use the same network, but the second layer will have been shifted or rotated to fit attractively on top of the foundation layer. More often a different but compatible network will be added that fits gracefully on top of the foundation layer. There are no shared holes between the two patterns – one is clearly superimposed on top of the other.

Because there are two layers and two separate sequences in these patterns, one can combine two different thread weights, two different values, or two different textures. Two different colors are another possibility, but I tend to prefer monochromatic treatments that combine different values instead. I usually use the darker value for the foundation layer and the lighter value for the top layer since this adds dimension – dark colors tend to recede, and light colors tend to advance. However, anything goes when a special effect is desired so these suggestions are just that – merely guidelines.

PATTERN 14. This pattern is the first of three that are used in the mountain treatments of the *Coyote Chorus* (Color Plate II). It is executed in two light values since it embellishes the most distant mountain peaks. When doing a landscape, perspective is best achieved when the patterns are lighter and "fade" as the mountains recede.

OVERALL CHART - PATTERN 14

The chart to the left shows the overall impression of this pattern but it does not clearly delineate the two separate patterns. On the next page there is an enlarged view of this chart that shows the superimposed layer clearly on top of the foundation layer. It also shows three rows of the foundation layer without a second layer on top in the middle section.

SEQUENCE. Do all of the step 1 foundation layer before the second layer is added. There is no need to provide a numbered sequence for this simple zigzag outline. The path is a bold zigzag line that straddles four intersections. Each row is placed 4 threads apart. Use a double running stitch sequence to execute each row. Use the large chart on page 81 to assist with placement.

The step 2 top layer is shown in bold open stitches on the next page. This is also a zigzag row, but chevron lines that straddle three intersections alternate with a steep slanted zigzag that uses a stitch that steps up four threads and sinks one thread to the right of this point. Use a double running stitch sequence to execute each row. Use the large chart found below to place the stitches accurately. The side edges accommodate only a single slanted stitch, but no compensation is needed. The steep slanted stitches in this pattern provide an upward thrust to this pattern – certainly appropriate to reinforce the shape of a mountain peak.

OVERALL CHART - PATTERN 14 - ENLARGED VIEW

PATTERN 15. This pattern is used in the two mountain peaks that form the middle range in *Coyote Chorus* (Color Plate II). It is not quite as dense as Pattern 14, and it is executed in two middle values of coral to make this range appear closer than the peaks behind it. In this pattern the same zigzag line is used in both layers, but it is shifted so that the top layer overlaps the bottom layer in an attractive way.

OVERALL CHART - PATTERN 15

SEQUENCE. The zigzag outline features chevron lines that straddle two intersections which alternate with chevron lines that straddle four intersections. Again the outline is so simple for these rows that no numbered sequence is needed for either step. Use the enlarged chart below to place the rows accurately. Complete the first layer before the second layer is added. Notice that there are compensation stitches along the side edges of the second layer.

OVERALL CHART PATTERN 15 Enlarged View

PATTERN 16. This pattern is used in the foreground mountains of *Coyote Chorus* (Color Plate II). A sharp focus is created by combining a dark value floss with a medium value floss. and the pattern is larger in scale than the previous two patterns to further create the illusion of being closer to the viewer.

This pattern repeats the same network in alternating rows, but the placement is shifted in the two row sequences. Unlike the previous pattern where one layer was completed before the second layer was added, this pattern builds in rows starting from the top down. One row of step 1 (the dark stitches) is completed, and then one row of step 2 (the open stitches) is added, and this alternating sequence is used to fill the area. Each row overlaps the previous row so if all of step 1 were completed first it would be necessary to duck under step 1 at strategic points when step 2 was added – a tedious task that is avoided by doing an alternating sequence. When filling an irregular area some compensation may have to be added by tucking stitches behind previously laid stitches so make sure consistency is maintained.

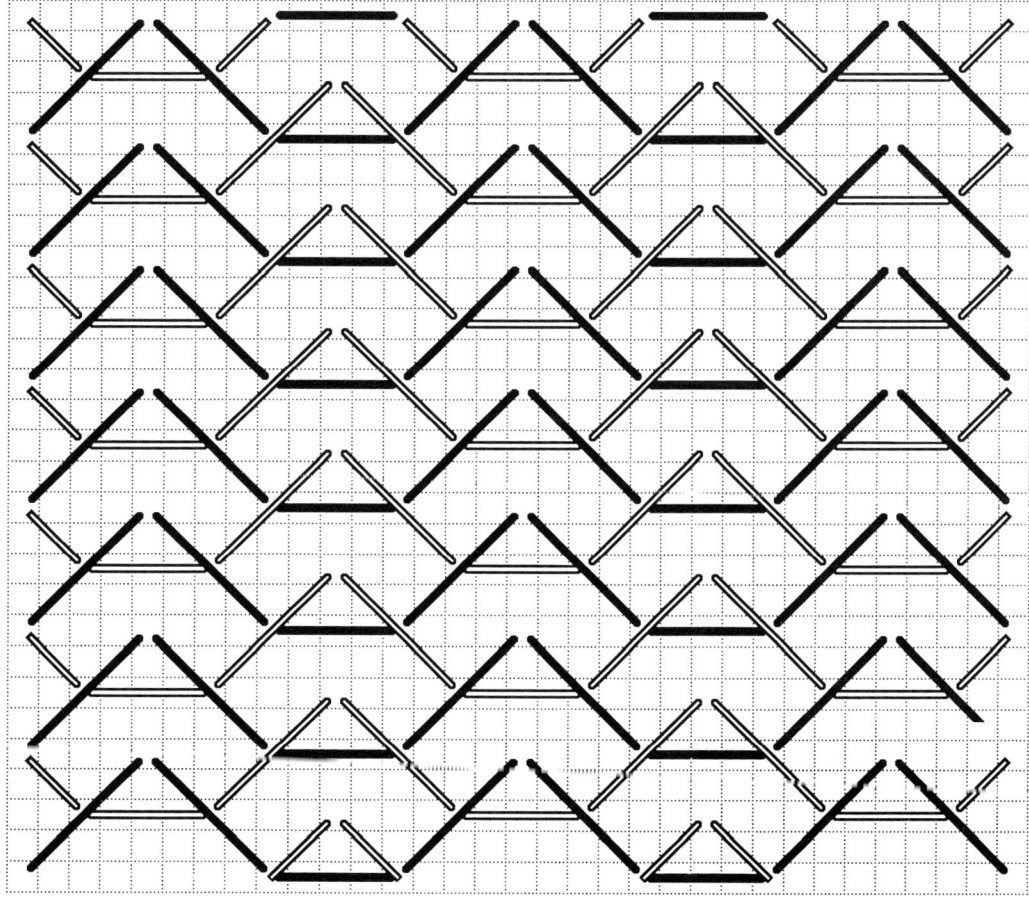

OVERALL CHART PATTERN 16

The enlarged view to the left shows the pattern clearly so a numbered sequence is not needed for this pattern. Every zigzag straddles four intersections, and it is always followed by a horizontal stitch that straddles four threads. Notice that the "peak" stitches of each row overlap the straight stitches of the previous row. This clue will make memorizing the pattern easy.

The chart below shows a single isolated row of the sequence for both step 1 and 2 of Pattern 16.

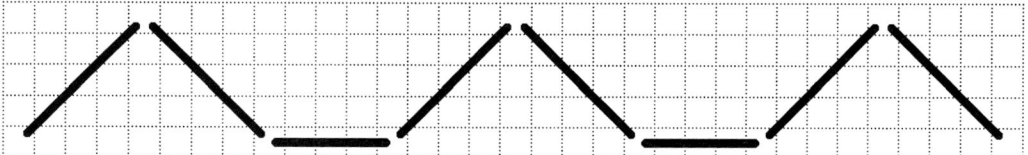

83

PATTERN 17. This pattern is a popular one in Oriental art. In order to create it in blackwork two separate sequences are needed. Step 1 is shown in the black lines below. Step 2 is shown in the open stitches. Step 2 is actually identical to step 1 but the pattern has been rotated 90° and placed on top of step 1. The only alteration made is that the long diagonal lines in step 1 are formed by two stitches that straddle two intersections. In step 2 these two stitches are merged into one stitch that straddles four intersections so that it lays on top of the pattern underneath. When a heavy thread like perle cotton is used for this pattern, this combination is preferred since the pair of stitches forms a ditch for the merged thread to lay comfortably in. In a flat thread like floss both layers could either have separate slanted stitches or merged ones.

OVERALL CHART - PATTERN 17

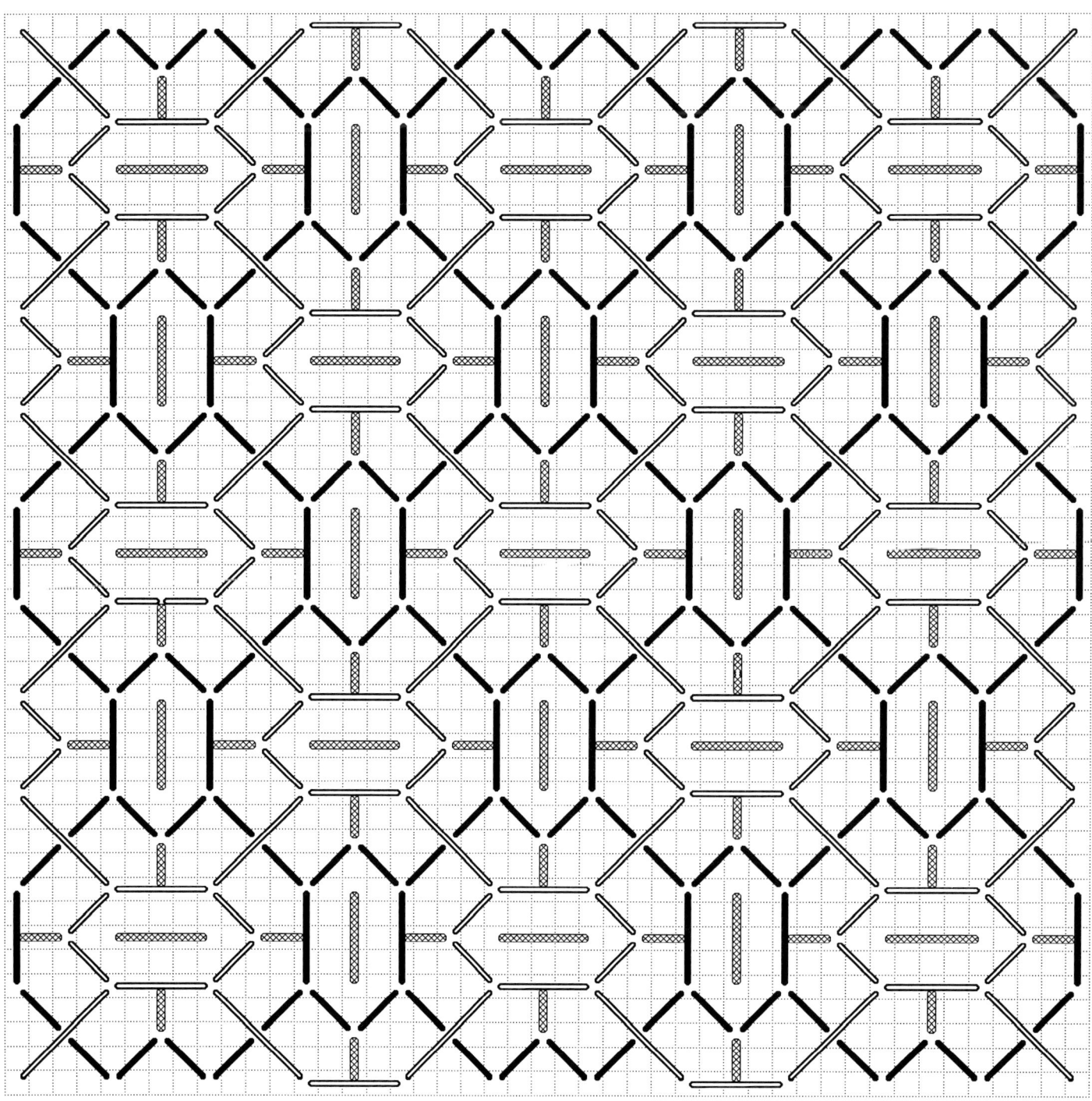

PATTERN 17 SEQUENCE CHART
Running Stitch Rows
Step 3

A cropped view of the overall chart is shown to the left. The "filled" stitches in this pattern are executed as step 3, and doing these in a metallic thread makes the pattern appear more Oriental. This step is executed after steps 1 and 2 are completed, and the dotted lines show the traveling threads of the stitches when they are connected in a running stitch path. Do all of the rows in one direction before starting the rows in the opposing direction. Be sure to slant the needle as you sink behind previously laid stitches, and do not pierce any threads.

NOTE. This step is not reversible, but the glimmer of metallic that shows in the open areas will be evenly distributed.

PATTERN 17 - VIEW OF STEP 1

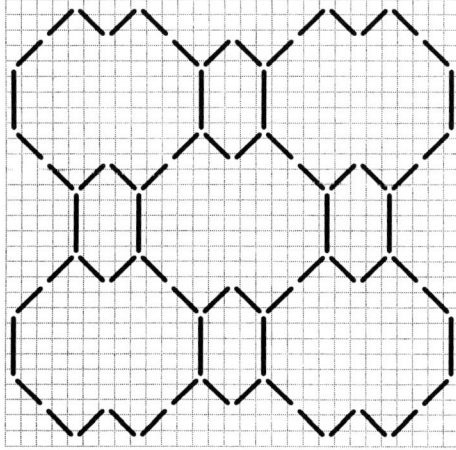

Use these two charts along with the overall chart on the previous page to execute the step 1 foundation pattern. It is cleaner to add the side trips after stitches 1, 3, 4, 6 and 7 since the sharp zigzag turn keeps the shared holes open.

PATTERN 17 - SEQUENCE CHART
Step 1 - Right Side

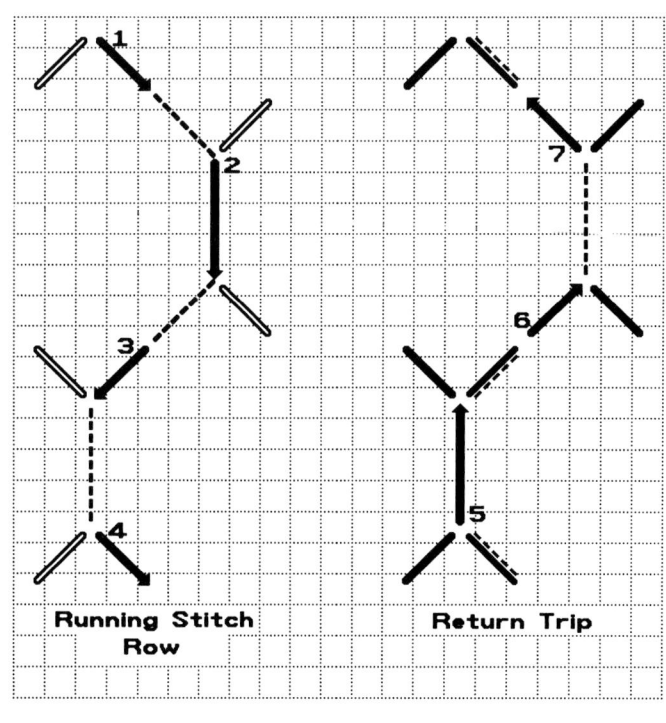

Running Stitch Row   Return Trip

85

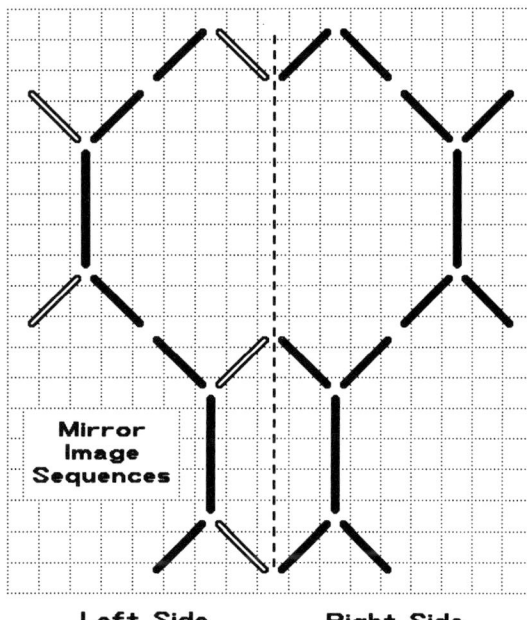

Mirror Image Sequences

Left Side   **Right Side**

PATTERN 17 SEQUENCE
View of Mirror Image Side of Sequence Row

It takes two complete rows to create one pattern repeat. Use the chart to the left to add the left side. Since the sequence is merely a mirror image trail of the right side, no numbered sequence is provided.

The Step 2 pattern is added by using the same two mirror image sequences. However, this time the two diagonal stitches in the main path will be merged into one long stitch. Some side trip stitches are eliminated along the side edges when this pattern is rotated and superimposed as shown. Since the pattern is familiar now, no adjusted numbered sequence is needed. Use the enlarged view of step 2 below along with the overall chart on page 84 to place step 2.

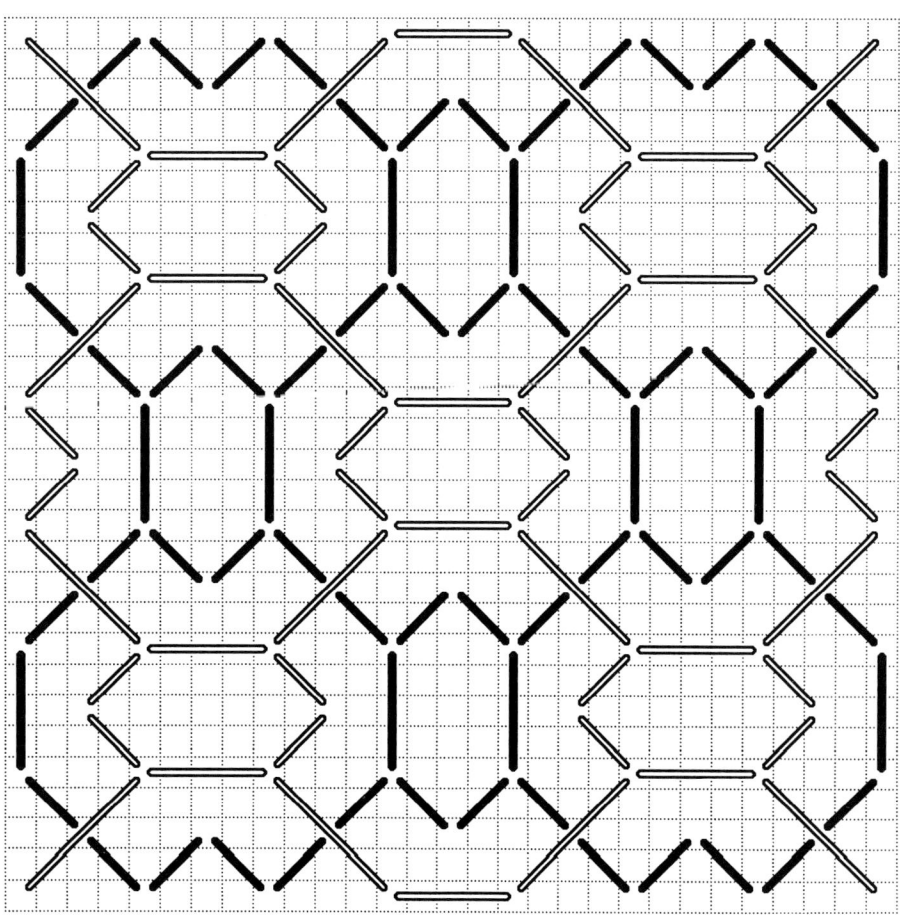

PATTERN 17 VIEW OF STEPS 1 AND 2

Rotate this chart and the overall chart on page 84 90° to make step 2 appear to be in the same upright position as the sequence chart on page 85.

Add step 3 to complete the pattern. The chart is located on page 85. When patterns have metallic accents, I frequently use a matching lamé backing fabric behind the piece when it is mounted. The added sheen further enhances the elegance of the design.

PATTERN 18. This layered pattern is used in the bridge railing of the *Rainy Winter Landscape* (Color Plate VI). It was created to suggest wrought iron, and #8 perle was used for both layers since the pattern is bold.

OVERALL CHART- PATTERN 18

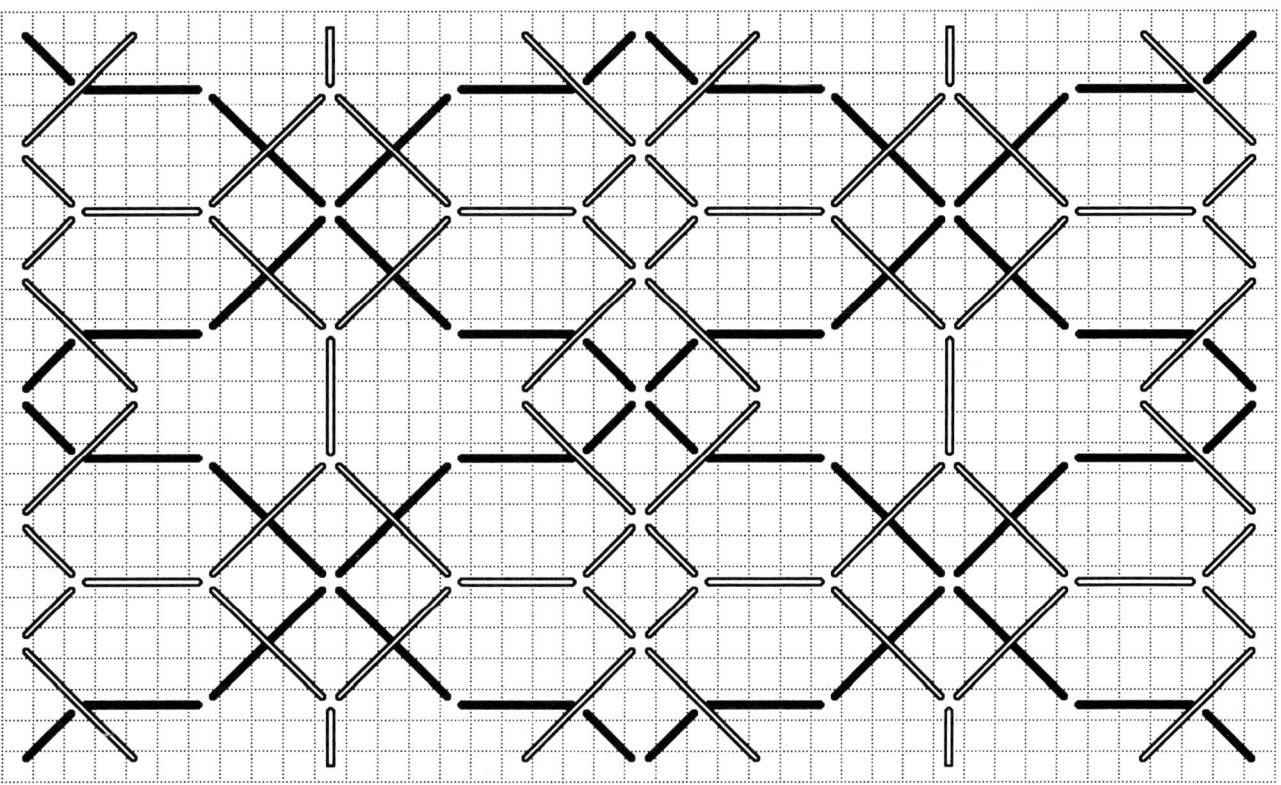

PATTERN 18
VIEW OF STEP 1

The foundation pattern, or step 1, is shown in the dark solid lines of the composite pattern. It is also shown separately in the chart to the right. Dotted lines are used to separate the repeats, and the center vertical line divides the left and right sides of the symmetrical units. No side trips are needed, and the outlines are simple so no numbered sequence is provided for this layer.

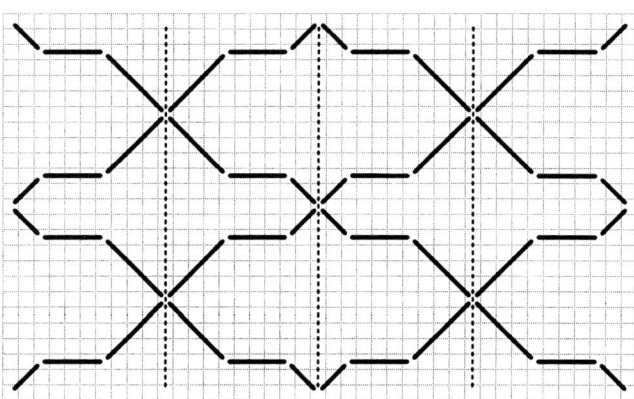

The top layer, or step 2 of the pattern, is an alternating sequence of rows. One row is a vertical arrangement of large and small diamonds. The other row is a vertical arrangement of large diamonds that are connected by straight lines that straddle four threads. The sides of the large diamonds also join the adjacent rows at the sides of the small diamonds. The row of alternating diamonds is the main path of the sequence used to execute this pattern, and the other row is added as a side trip off of the left and right sides of this row. Use the

87

sequence chart below to add this layer. Notice that the straight vertical stitches of the side trip are added <u>only</u> to the right side.

PATTERN 18 - STEP 2 SEQUENCE

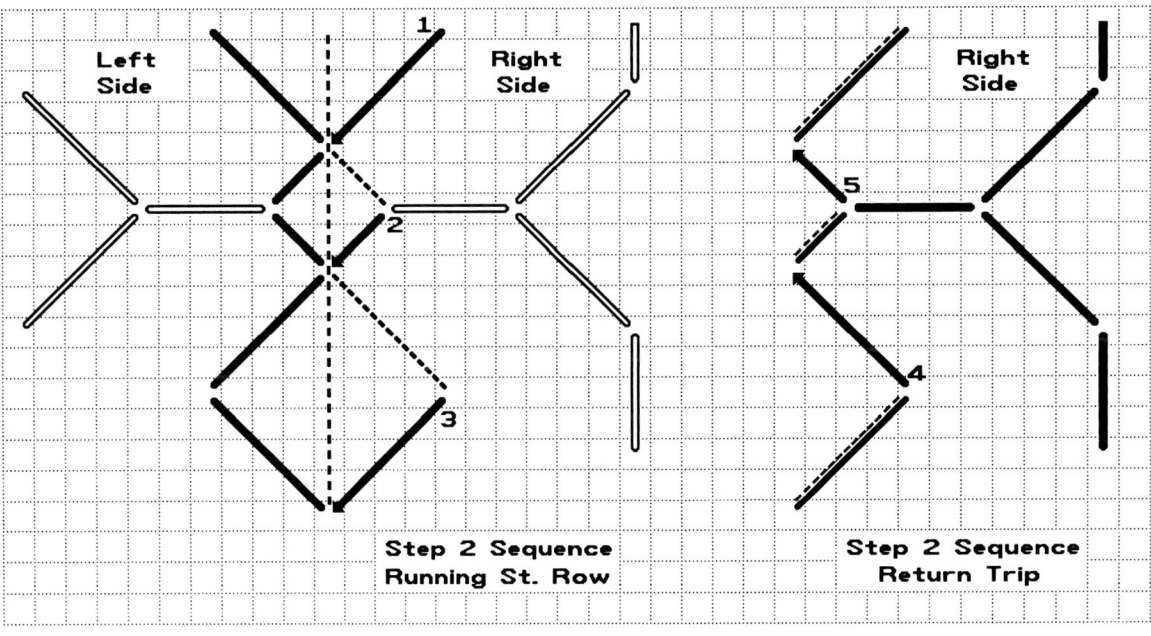

Left Side

Right Side

Right Side

Step 2 Sequence
Running St. Row

Step 2 Sequence
Return Trip

OVERALL CHART - VARIATION OF PATTERN 18

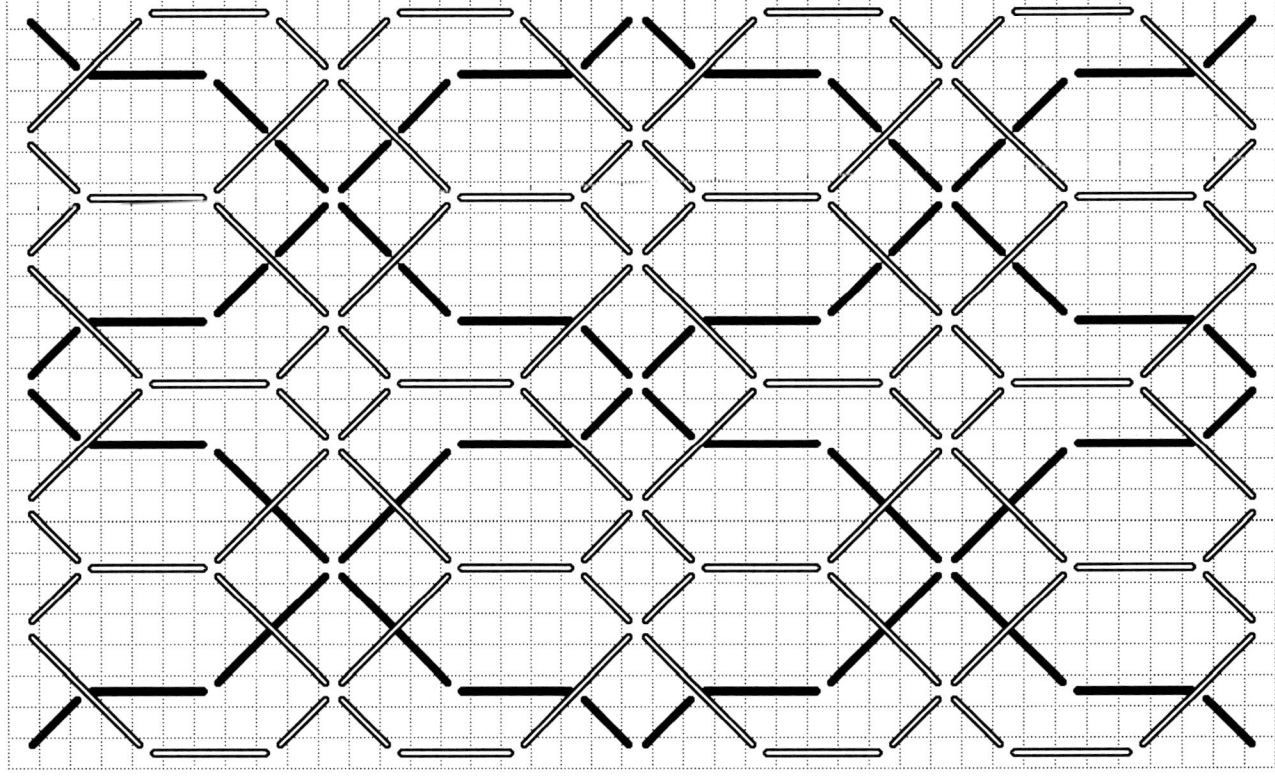

The variation of Pattern 18 shown on the previous page is used in the *Sailboat* design (Color Plate V). It is in the middle section of the rear sail, and it is also rotated 90° to fit better in the long narrow shape. It is unusual to use such a bold pattern in a narrow tapering shape, but no small scale patterns worked well so this dramatic pattern with a strong thrust was tried instead. Because the "tulip" motif is carefully centered and continues to repeat as the mast tapers, the pattern "works" and the eye is not distracted by the other compensated elements.

In this instance the pattern is not superimposed either – all of the long stitches over four intersections are divided into two stitches that straddle two intersections, and two weights of thread are used for the two steps. Step 1 is the same as that for Pattern 18. The step 2 sequence is shown for the layered version below. Any adjustments for a nonlayered pattern can be made easily from this chart.

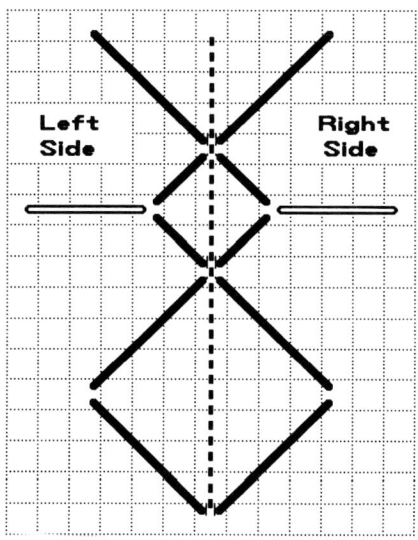

PATTERN 18 VARIATION
SEQUENCE CHART - STEP 2

This sequence outlines an arrangement of alternating small and large diamonds. There are side trips off of the side midpoint of each small diamond, and these connect this row to the neighboring paths. Notice the staggered placement of the sequence in alternating rows on the overall chart. This pattern is slightly denser than the original Pattern 18.

PATTERN 19. This pattern is used in the left gold bunny in the *Bunny Hop* design (Color Plate IV). The same pattern is used in both layers, and it combines octagons and diamonds. By shifting the pattern in the second layer, a denser arrangement is formed that has the diamonds of the second layer centered inside the octagons of the first layer. The straight stitches of the second pattern also cross the straight stitches of the foundation layer.

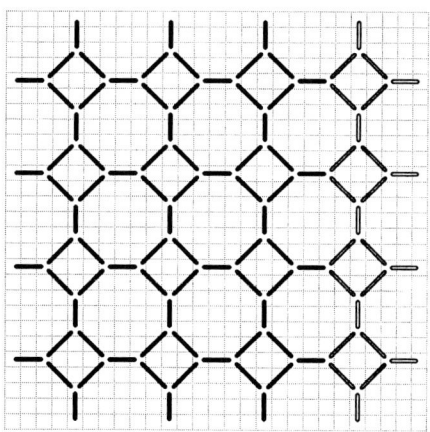

PATTERN 19 - CORE PATTERN

The basic pattern for this superimposed combination is shown in the chart to the left (the open stitches in the right vertical row outline a single row sequence). The overall chart for the combined layers is found on the next page. This pattern is particularly pretty when the foundation layer is done in a dark value thread and the top layer is executed in a medium dark value. The basic pattern is also similar to Pattern 2, but it is much smaller in scale.

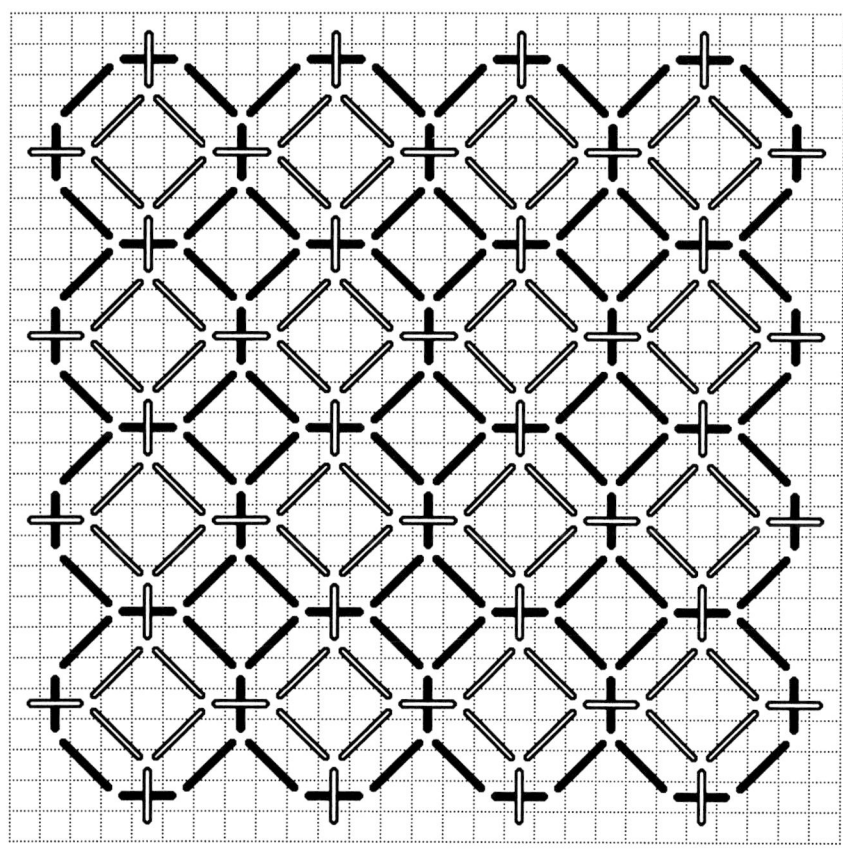

PATTERN 19 SEQUENCE

OVERALL CHART
PATTERN 19

Use the sequence chart on the left side below to build the pattern. On the right side below, an isolated pattern of the bottom layer is provided to clarify its outline. The bold open stitches show how the sequence fits the foundation shape.

NOTE. The sequence for both layers is a trip-and-a-half path that is worked in vertical rows. A single side trip is added to the right side of each small diamond. Two repeats are shown since the "on top-underneath" stitch position reverses in the second repeat.

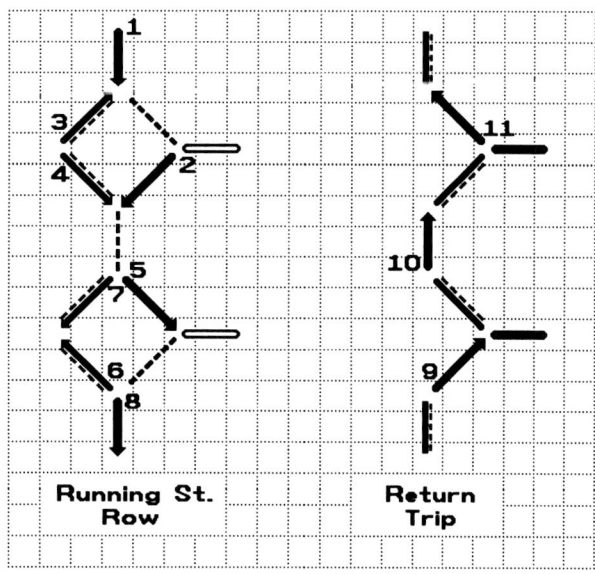

Running St. Row   Return Trip

PATTERN 19
FOUNDATION LAYER

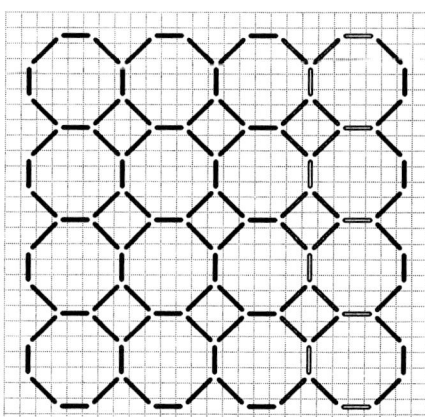

NOTE. A beaded version of this pattern is used in Sampler 1 (see page 183).

PATTERN 20. The last pattern in this chapter is unusual in that the second layer is not only superimposed but it criss-crosses itself as it is laid. At a first glance one might assume that the top layer is a simple herringbone stitch done in horizontal rows – and it could be. However, I decided to execute the same outline in a double running stitch so that no traveling threads would show in open areas. The top pattern is worked in vertical rows, and the right sides of the diamonds form one path and the left sides of the diamonds form the second path.

OVERALL CHART - PATTERN 20

PATTERN 20 SEQUENCE
STEP 1

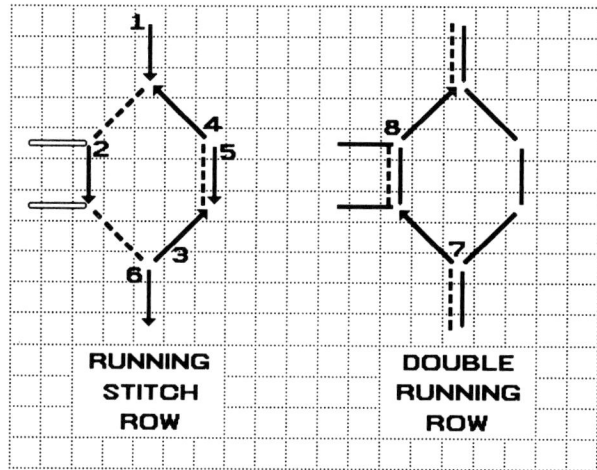

Sequences. The foundation layer in this composite pattern is a combination of small squares, hexagons and octagons. The most efficient way to build the pattern is to use the trip-and-a-half path that is shown in the Step 1 chart above. It outlines the elongated hexagons, and the squares are added as side trips in the vertical rows. The octagons are formed in the remaining negative space.

Step 2. Use the sequence chart on the next page in combination with the overall chart above to place the second pattern on top of the completed step 1 layer. Each zigzag row is outlined in a double running path, and each odd numbered row must be completed before the even numbered row that crosses it is added.

Having the rows of a blackwork pattern overlap is an unusual concept, but it is attractive and can be done in the reversible technique. We often get "tunnel vision" when we look at a familiar outline like herringbone so consider a double running path as a suitable alternative. Most canvas stitches build in units rather than in lines, but double running can be used for any linear outline that is continuous.

91

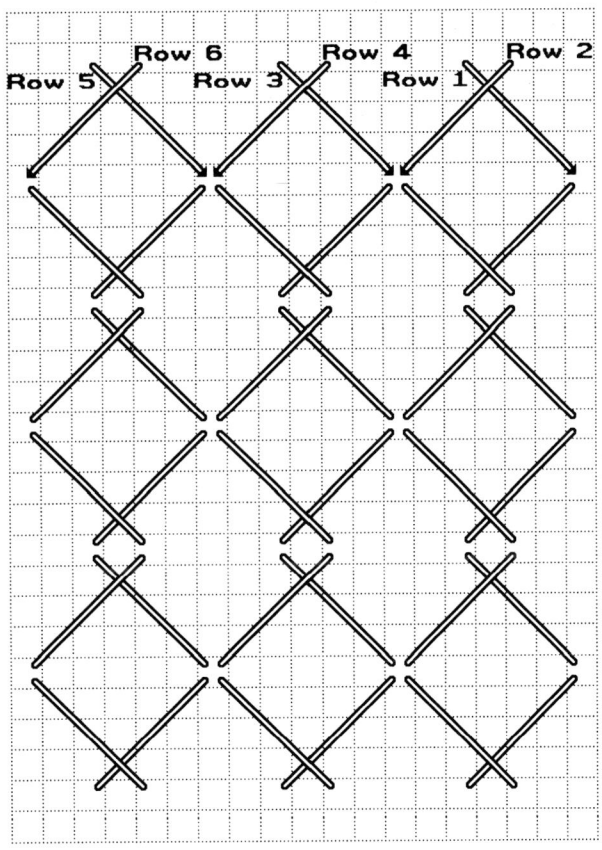

Row 6   Row 4   Row 2
Row 5   Row 3   Row 1

PATTERN 20 SEQUENCE
STEP 2

No numbered sequence is provided here since the rows are simple zigzag outlines.

This pattern could also make a lovely foundation pattern. On the right side below is a variation which shows an alternative treatment that uses this pattern as step 1. The sequence chart for step 2 is shown to the left.

The open spaces in this bold outline would also be attractive with additions of canvas stitches. See if you can design such a pattern and plan the appropriate stitch sequences.

NOTE. Another variation could be created by reversing the order of steps 1 and 2. This combination is stunning in two colors.

OVERALL CHART
PATTERN 20 VARIATION

PATTERN 20 VARIATION
SEQUENCE CHART
STEP 2

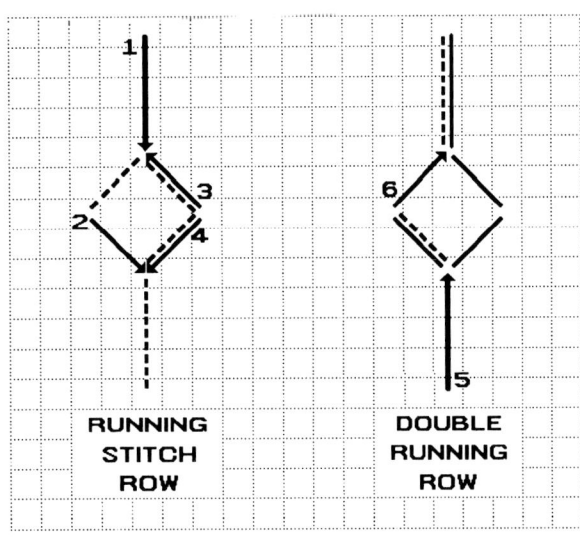

RUNNING
STITCH
ROW

DOUBLE
RUNNING
ROW

92

Another type of superimposed pattern is one that combines blackwork with tramé. A tramé is a laid thread that stretches from one side of a pattern to the other at regular intervals. Sometimes the laid threads are arranged in parallel rows in one direction only (see example 1 below). Other times these threads are laid in two directions to form a lattice or trellis arrangement (see example 2 below). A square trellis can also be combined with a diamond trellis to form a double or four-way lattice (see example 3 on page 94).

EXAMPLE 1 - ONE-WAY TRAME PATTERNS

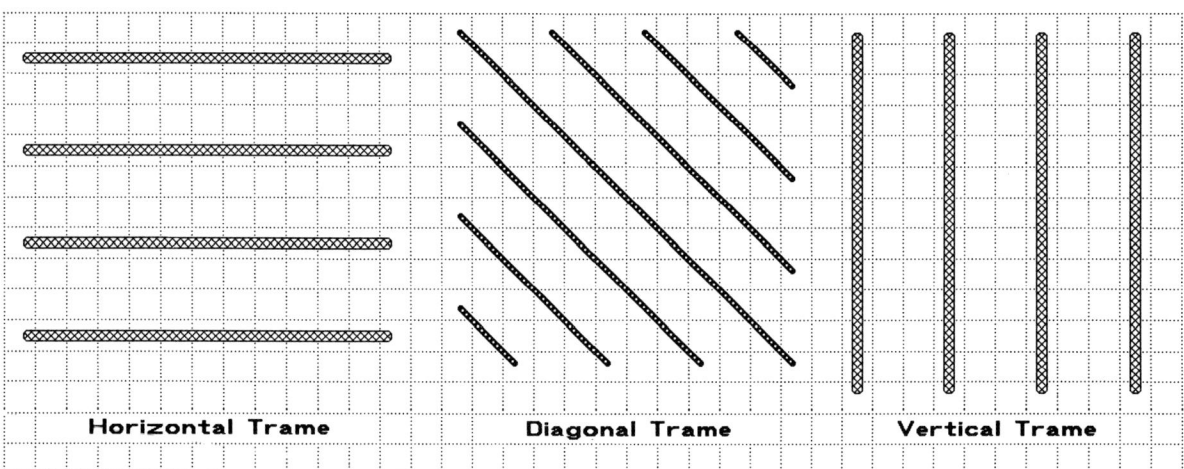

Horizontal Trame   **Diagonal Trame**   **Vertical Trame**

EXAMPLE 2 - TWO-WAY TRAME PATTERNS

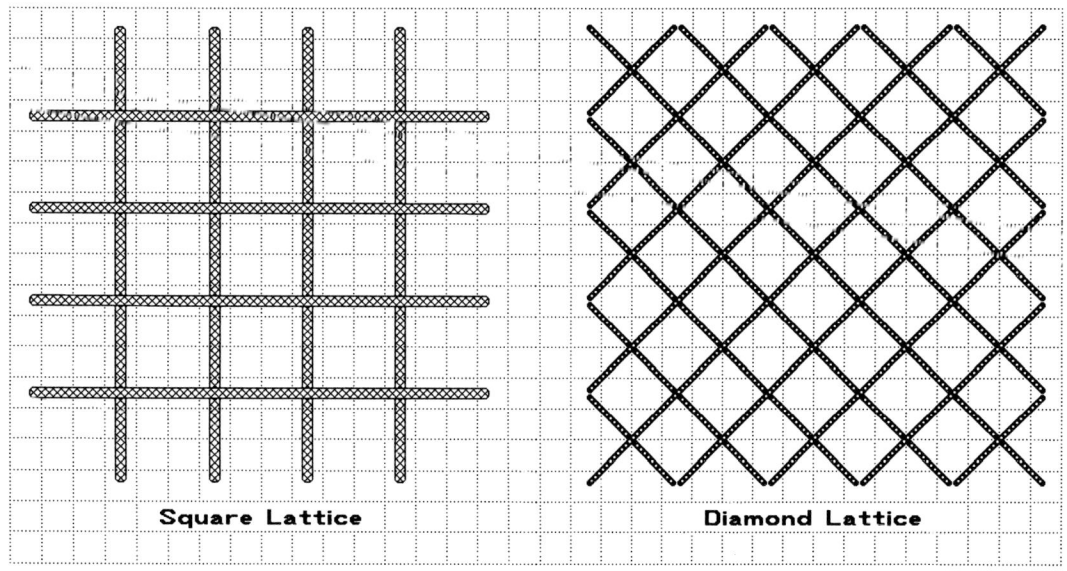

Square Lattice   **Diamond Lattice**

93

When long unstable threads are laid on top of the canvas they must be secured or stabilized with couching stitches. Usually these are simple stitches that are spaced regularly as part of the pattern. When a tramé is laid in two directions these holding stitches are placed at the overlapping intersections. However, it is possible to use a blackwork pattern to secure these threads, and such combination patterns are particularly elegant when a metallic is used for the tramé.

It is also possible to use a blackwork pattern behind a trellis pattern, and such patterns are quite three-dimensional. Pattern 28 on page 104 is an example of such a pattern, and it is used both in the center area of the *Heart of Blackwork* design on the cover and in the right side of the small leaf shown in Color Plate IX.

When a tramé pattern is laid, the backing should be minimal especially when an open network is to be added on top of it. Therefore the rows are laid back and forth rather than being wrapped like a satin stitch (see the numbered chart on the right side below). Thread tails are usually parked until the holding stitches are completed – their backing will usually provide enough density in which to secure the tramé tails. If the pattern is surrounded by a durable outline, tails could also be parked on the back side of these rows. If the tramé is too heavy to be buried in either of these places, merely fold each tail back behind the laid thread and use a sharp needle and sewing thread to fasten it to the back of the canvas.

EXAMPLE 3 - FOUR-WAY TRAME

TRAME SEQUENCE

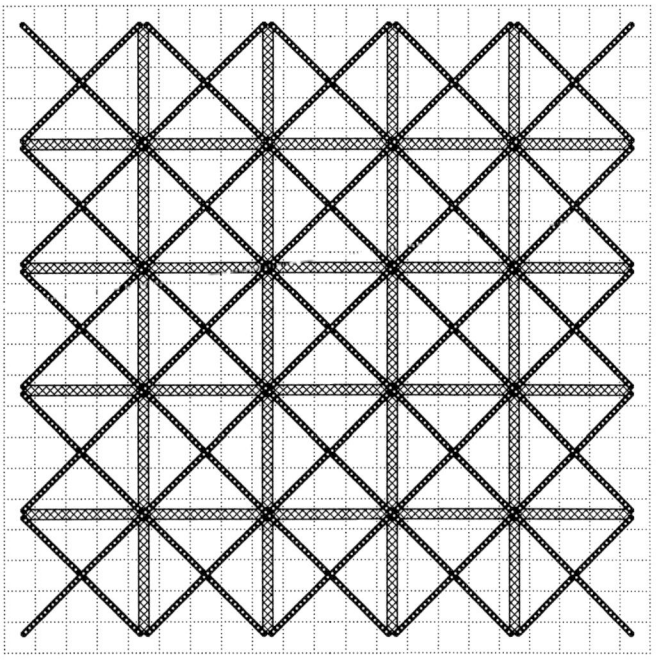

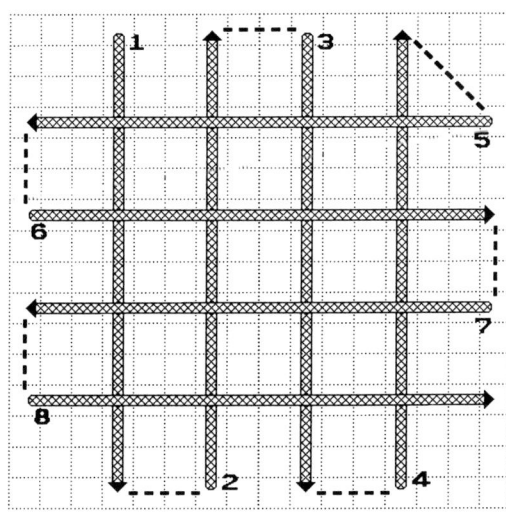

NOTE. The traveling threads lay along the edge of the pattern. They are usually concealed by an outline.

The patterns that follow will all have tramé foundations or overlays. The same straight and diagonal lines will be used in each pattern to designate a straight and/or diagonal tramé. No numerical sequence will be provided for these rows since the technique has been thoroughly discussed in this introduction. Only the blackwork segments of the patterns will have numbered sequences.

94

PATTERN 21. The first pattern in this chapter is a simple chevron zigzag blackwork pattern that is laid in horizontal rows on top of a vertical tramé. The pattern is used twice in the lower section of the front sail of the *Sailboat* design (Color Plate V). The tramé rows are laid in pairs that are two threads apart. Each pair is six threads from the next pair.

The blackwork rows are also two threads apart. Notice that the diagonal stitches are not "merged" from two stitches over two intersections into a single stitch over four threads. This time the blackwork is functional as well as decorative. It must tie down the tramé thread, and the short stitch holds it more securely than a longer stitch would. Because the stitches are split these zigzag lines will look crooked if consistency is not maintained on the return trip. The most attractive appearance will show the "peak" stitches of the chevron sinking on the outside of the ones below them – sort of like a roof shingle overlapping the one below it. The inset on the right side below shows this preferred final view clearly.

OVERALL CHART - PATTERN 21

**PATTERN 21 - INSET
PREFERRED VIEW OF EACH
BLACKWORK REPEAT**

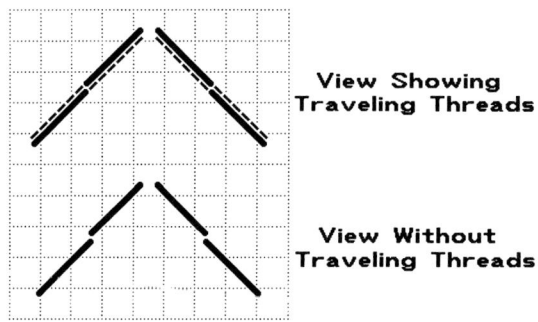

View Showing
Traveling Threads

View Without
Traveling Threads

NOTE. This view is tricky to establish since the needle is in a different position for the stitches on opposite sides of the center axis. Go slowly on the first row to create an accurate sample row.

PATTERN 22. This pattern is similar to Pattern 21. The tramé is laid in vertical rows, but the spacing is a single tramé placed six threads apart (step 1). Instead of a chevron zigzag, this pattern has a wave outline, and it is placed perpendicular to the tramé rows. The wave rows are also placed two threads apart (step 2).

There is a third step to this pattern which is a vertical row of brick stitches between each of the tramé rows. These are added after steps 1 and 2 are completed, and either a running stitch or a back stitch sequence may be used. The running stitches will show up more so let this be the determining factor. It is also important to place these stitches so that the top of every brick stitch sinks below the wave line that it touches and that the

95

bottom of each brick stitch sinks below the wave line that it "crosses." Both ends share holes with the wave rows, but the stitches are shown on the chart in the correct position and should be consistent throughout the pattern.

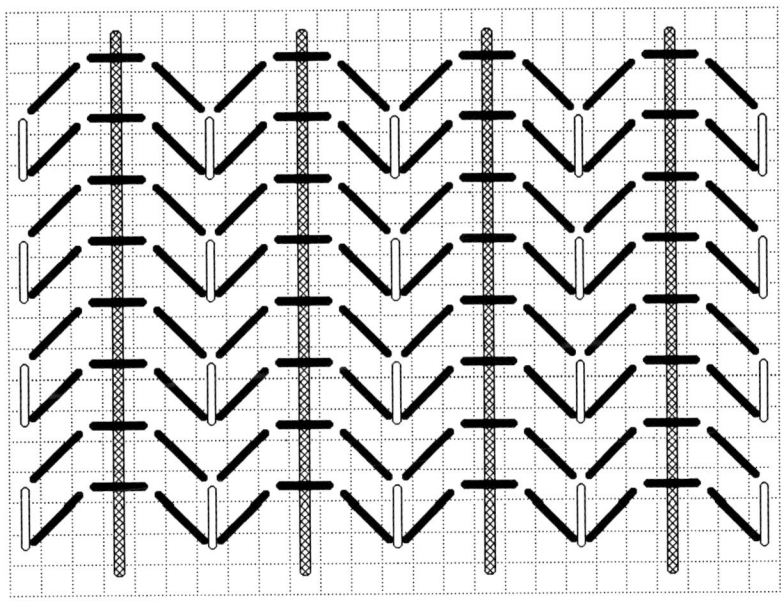

OVERALL CHART PATTERN 22

This pattern is used in the lower part of the stump in *Bunny Hop* (Color Plate IV). The pattern is also used in Sampler 1 for Area 5, and it is repeated twice. It contours nicely to the wavy lines of the Florentine outline and reinforces the shape well. It also centers gracefully.

INSET

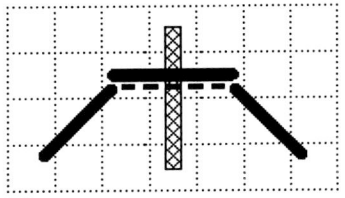

PATTERN 22 WITHOUT STEP 3

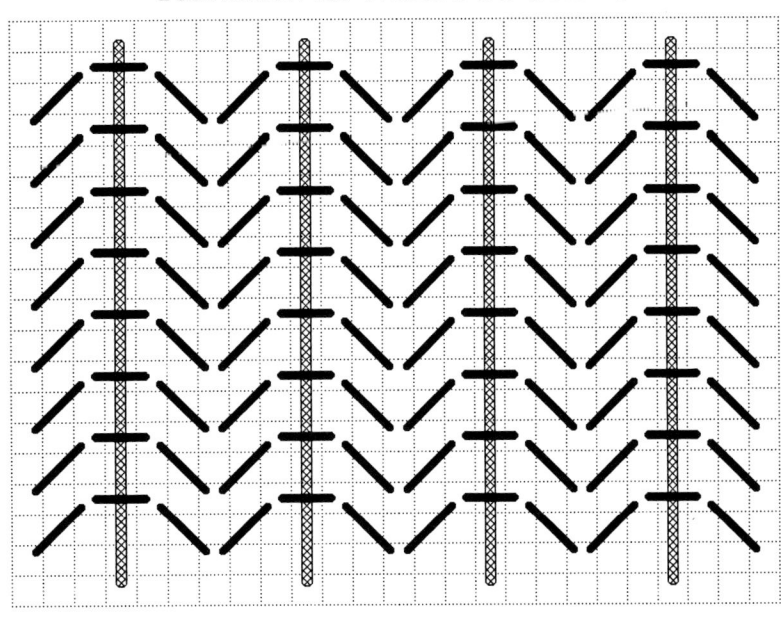

Step 2 Sequence. The overall chart to the left shows the placement of the blackwork rows without step 3 in place. Work these horizontal rows in double running stitch. On the return trip place or keep the horizontal stitches "above" the diagonal stitches (or on the outside of the wave swell). This position is shown clearly in the inset chart above and makes the straight stitches more prominent. Maintain this consistency throughout the pattern.

PATTERN 23. This pattern has a horizontal tramé that is spaced two threads apart (step 1). The blackwork overlay is divided into two segments. The solid dark stitches are worked in diagonal zigzag rows of double running stitches as step 2. The open diagonal stitches are step 3, and these can be worked in either diagonal paths or in vertical zigzag paths of running stitch rows. Either direction will force the traveling thread to fall behind a previously laid step 2 stitch.

**OVERALL CHART
PATTERN 23**

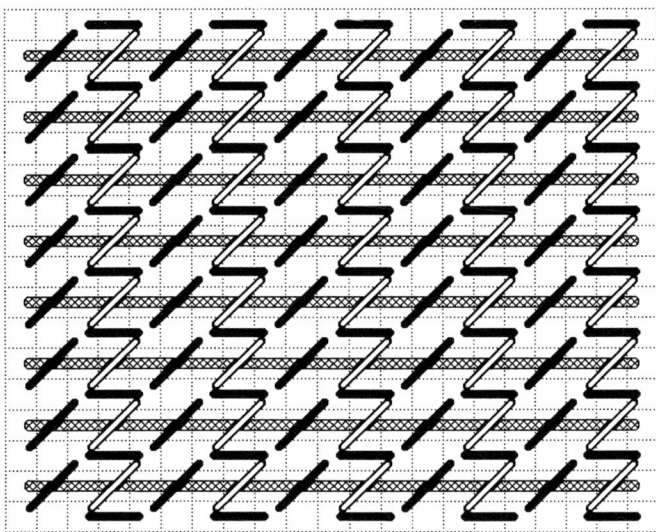

This pattern is used in the tail of the mother armadillo in *Mamadillo* (Color Plate III). It is also used in Sampler 1 for Area 6 which is repeated four times. Study the instructions on pages 30 and 180 for some helpful hints regarding the execution of this pattern. The pattern forms an interesting diagonal stripe when step 3 is left out. It also fits gracefully into narrow shapes without awkward compensation since it is a dense pattern with small stitches.

PATTERN 23 WITHOUT STEP 3

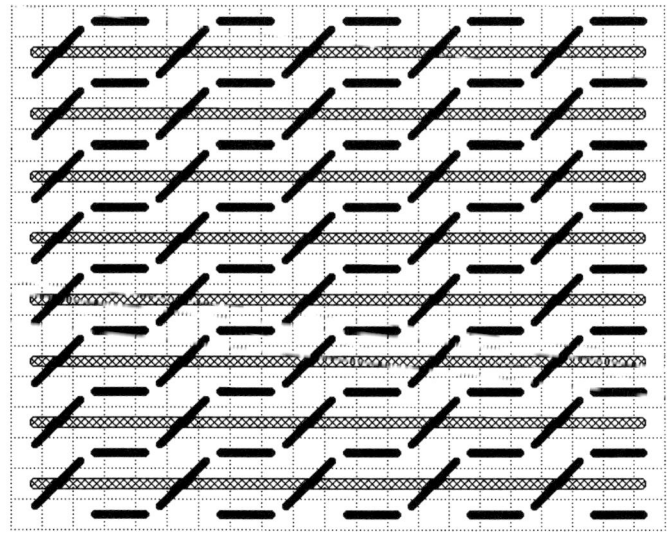

INSET

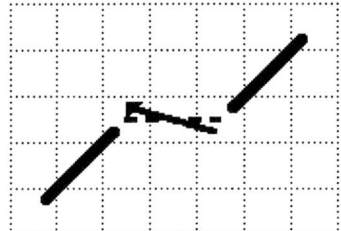

Step 2 Sequence. These zigzag rows lay more smoothly if the diagonal stitches of the running stitch row are always on top of the canvas. If the rows are executed this way, the straight stitches of the return trip will lay smoothly in the position shown in the inset above. If a reverse position takes place, the "easy" return trip placement will be the opposite of the one shown.

NOTE. The paths will appear somewhat different if the return trip rows do not all match so aim for total consistency. Steps 2 and 3 are particularly attractive when done in two close values of one color. I usually use the darker value for step 3.

On the next page is a variation of this pattern that has a different step 3 treatment. Since the rows added form crosses, a lighter value is suggested for the final step. Layered stitches appear more embossed when light values are used since light shades tend to advance visually.

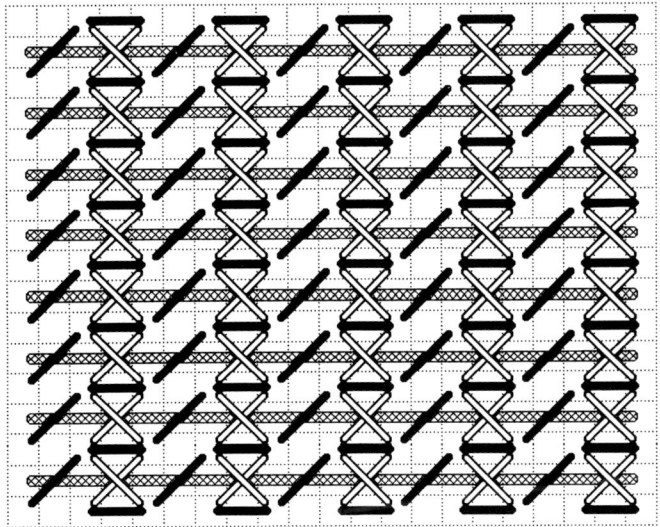

PATTERN 23 - VARIATION 1

Step 3 Sequence. The crosses are added with vertical running stitch rows. Do a running stitch row in one direction to add the underneath stitches. Then use another row of running stitches to add the top stitches. This would be the "blackwork way" of executing this step. However, since the area behind the crosses has a tramé, no traveling threads will show if the crosses are added the "canvas way" by working in vertical rows and completing each cross unit before traveling to the next unit. The traveling threads would also be concealed if the crosses were added the "canvas way" in horizontal rows as long as the tramé thread is thick enough.

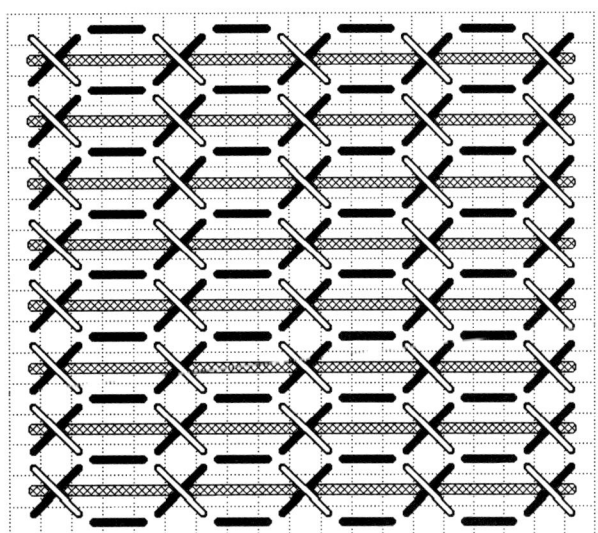

PATTERN 23 - VARIATION 2

Another variation of this pattern is used in Area 4 of Sampler 1. In this case step 3 is a vertical zigzag row of running stitches that cross the diagonal stitches of step 2. The same thread should be used in this pattern for both steps 2 and 3.

This pattern is repeated twice in the sampler, and it is used with a mirror image placement since each Area 4 section mirrors from the center axis of the design. The overall chart to the left corresponds to the view of the right half of the area on page 177. The entire tramé is added as step 1 in this pattern. Steps 1 and 2 are then executed separately for the left and right halves of the area.

PATTERN 24. This pattern is unusual in that the tramé is tied down with a row of oblong crosses rather than by the blackwork pattern (steps 1 and 2). The blackwork pattern is placed between the couched rows of tramé as step 3. The blackwork motifs are further embellished by brick stitches, which are added in vertical running stitch rows as step 4.

This pattern is used in Sampler 1 for Area 3 (the heart shapes), and it is repeated 4 times. No step 4 brick stitches were added, however, in the original model. I wanted this pattern to be the same density and color as the beaded border area so they were omitted.

OVERALL CHART
PATTERN 24

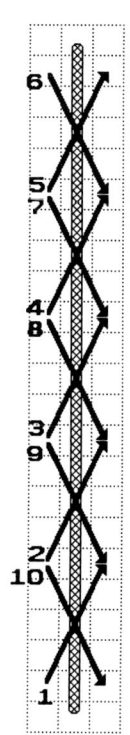

PATTERN 24
STEP 2 SEQUENCE

The sequence for the oblong cross holding stitches is shown to the right. The traveling threads are concealed behind the tramé if these units are added in two steps (an "up" row and a "down" row rather than completing each whole unit one at a time).

PATTERN 24 BLACKWORK SEQUENCE - STEP 3

The chart to the left shows the numbered sequence for the double running paths of the left side row in the pattern. Add the side trips on the return trip in this pattern as the undulating lines will leave the shared holes open and easy to reenter. The sequence for the right side row is merely a mirror image path so use the overall chart to place this segment in each row.

NOTE. If the oblong cross couching is done in the same color as the blackwork in this pattern it will look like an allover pattern. However, a strong vertical stripe will result if contrasting values are used.

PATTERN 25. This pattern is a dense one that is used in the middle bunny of *Bunny Hop* (Color Plate IV). Vertical rows of tramé are laid two threads apart as step 1. Then a blackwork overlay is added that is composed of staggered rows of elongated hexagons (step 2). This step is added in a double running sequence. Then brick stitches are added in running stitch rows to the centers of each hexagon (step 3).

NOTE. Because the bunny shapes have intricate curves and recesses that create compensation challenges, the patterns created for the shapes are deliberately easy to maneuver within the difficult contours. No long slanted stitches are used, and small repeats are needed to look graceful in the narrow areas. Nevertheless the patterns still look sophisticated and elegant so "simple" does not have to be "dull."

**OVERALL CHART
PATTERN 25**

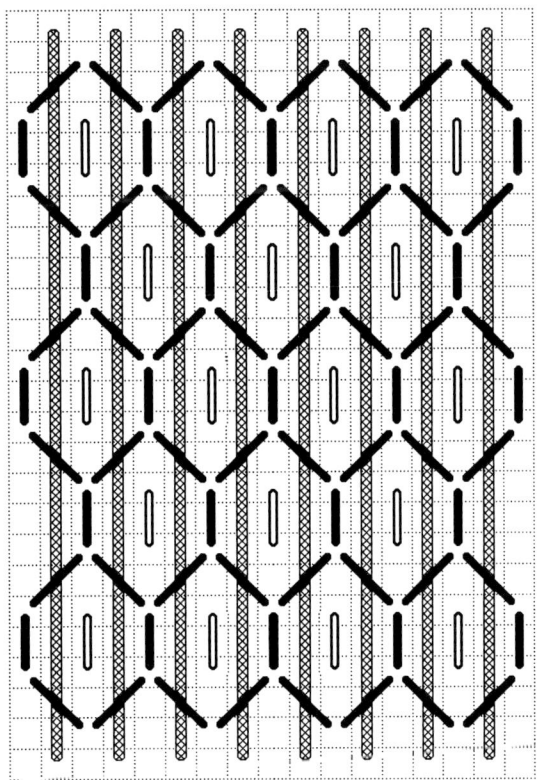

**PATTERN 25 SEQUENCE
STEP 2**

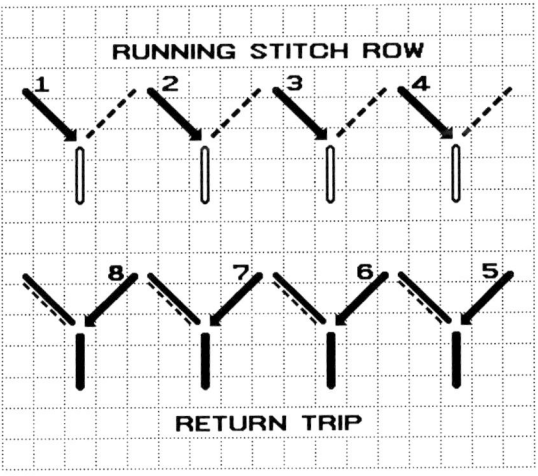

The sequence charted outlines the bottom sides of the hexagons. The pattern shifts to outline the top sides of the hexagons so adjust accordingly. The straight sides of the hexagons are added as vertical side trips. It is somewhat easier to add these on the return trip, but they can be added on either path. However, be consistent once the choice is made.

PATTERN 26. This pattern is a personal favorite since I am fond of parallelograms. The pattern is formed in three steps. First vertical rows of tramé are laid six threads apart (step 1). Then rows of wavy outlines are added in double running stitch (step 2). The final step is a series of running stitch rows that add slanted stitches between the blackwork rows of step 2. These are worked in zigzag vertical rows, and the sequence chart on the next page shows one full repeat in a lettered sequence.

This pattern is used in the right bunny in *Bunny Hop* (Color Plate IV). However, only the wavy lines of step 2 show up in the photograph since the stitches of the third step are in a light value. The pattern fits gracefully in spite of the angled stitches since a partial gobelin stitch is always a tent stitch so it compensates easily. However, the choice of the light value thread was to minimize the conspicuousness of any of the compensation distortions. The thread is a medium value taupe that blends with the airbrushed background so its presence is subtle. The step 2 thread is darker, and it is the dominant outline.

OVERALL CHART - PATTERN 26

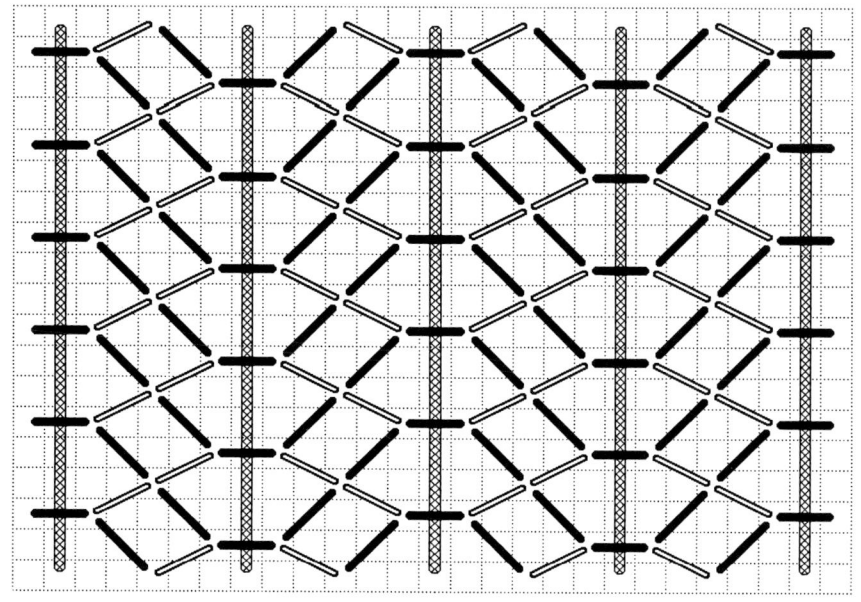

NOTE. By having the step 2 pattern in place when the angled stitches are added, one does not have to "count" the angles. Merely place the stitches in the shared holes of the earlier pattern. There is also no need to "fix" any of the pairs of straight stitches in the step 2 sequence. The step 3 stitches intersect these lines so any irregularities will be corrected automatically (review rule 4 on page 27, if needed).

PATTERN 26 WITHOUT STEP 3 ROWS

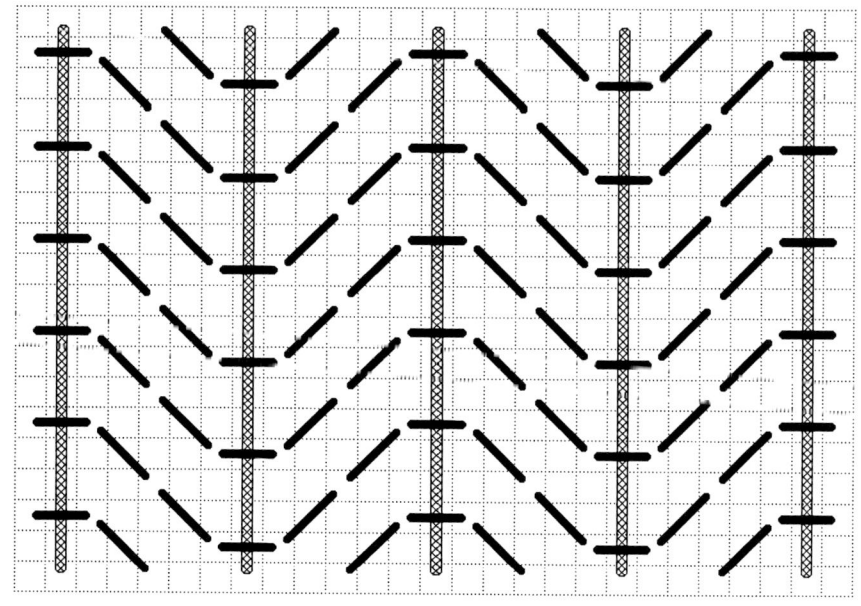

PATTERN 26
STEP 3 SEQUENCE
Running Stitch Rows

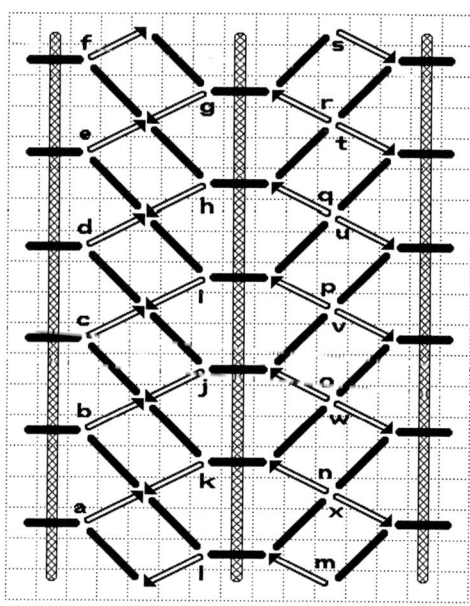

PATTERN 27. This pattern is a variation of the previous pattern, and it is somewhat more difficult to execute since the blackwork sequence is a double running stitch row with flip-

flop side trips. The step 2 wave path of Pattern 26 is the "main path" of this pattern. The "S" shape motifs are formed by the side trips which are always a straight stitch followed by a diagonal stitch (both over two threads or intersections). The placement of these stitches is tricky since the two different side trips alternate along the path. However, they are always added at the point where the two diagonal stitches join so this clue should be a useful reminder. The side trips will stitch "cleaner" if they are added on the running stitch row – they angle sharply from the main path and one can avoid having two stitches in a straight line if the "detour" is made here.

This pattern is used in the brown bunny on the right side in *Bunny Hop* (Color Plate IV). A variation here seems appropriate since it helps to unify and balance the design to have the two rabbits on the ends have similar patterns. Both are also wearing jackets for the same reason.

OVERALL CHART - PATTERN 27

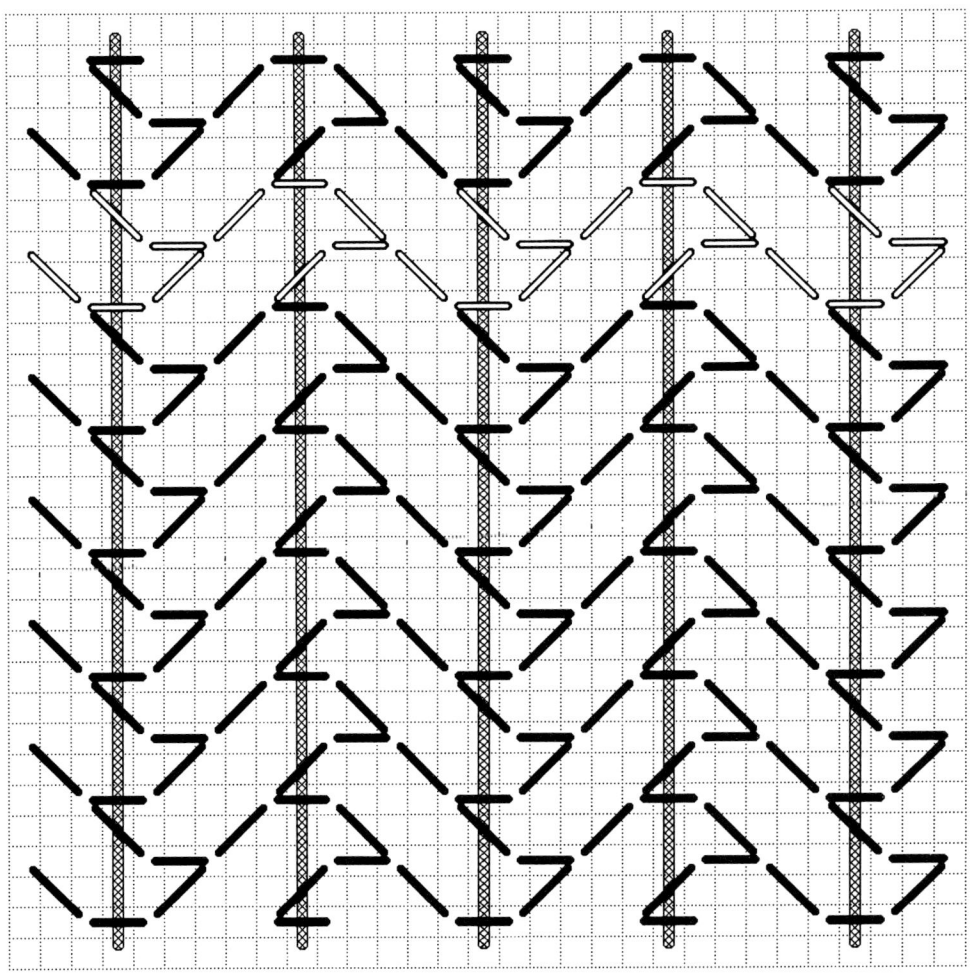

NOTE. The open stitches in the overall chart above outline one row sequence for the pattern, including the side trips. This isolated row should be helpful in starting the pattern along with the sequence on the next page.

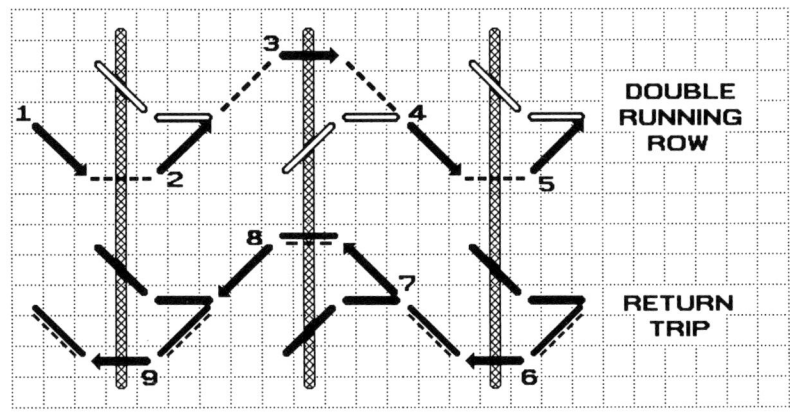

DOUBLE RUNNING ROW

RETURN TRIP

PATTERN 27
STEP 2 SEQUENCE

The wave rows are worked horizontally as in Pattern 26. The composition of each side trip alternates, but the straight stitch will always angle to the left of the main path. Each side trip will always match the one directly above it also.

If a denser pattern is desired, a diagonal stitch that straddles two threads may be added to divide each "S" motif in half. The overall chart for this variation is below and the numbered running stitch path needed to add this step 3 accent is incorporated into this chart.

PATTERN 27 VARIATION WITH STEP 3 NUMBERING

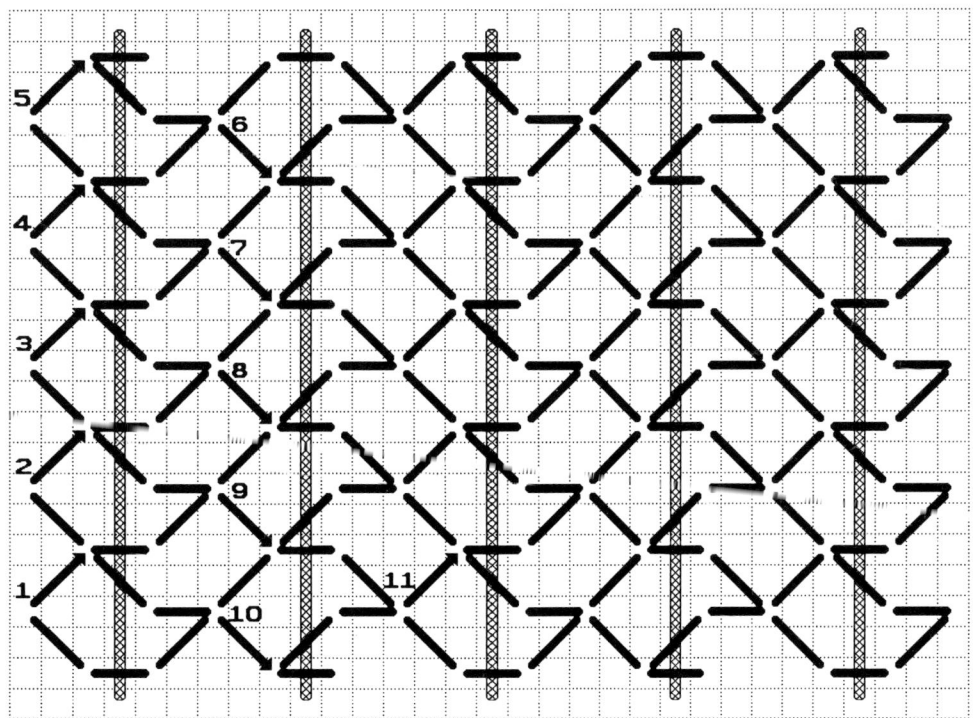

NOTE. The step 3 stitches are added in vertical rows of zigzag running stitch paths. Notice that the traveling threads fall behind the stitches of the step 2 path so they will not show.

103

PATTERN 28. This pattern is a variation of Pattern 1, and it is used in the right half of the small leaf design (Color Plate IX). A double trellis is added as an overlay to the blackwork background. Therefore the blackwork outline is worked as step 1 (use the directions on pages 42-44). Then a square lattice or two-way tramé is added as step 2. Lay all of the vertical tramé rows first and then add the horizontal rows. Step 3 will tie down these laid threads with a regular cross stitch at ONLY the overlapping intersections that are INSIDE the squares of the blackwork pattern. If these crosses are worked in horizontal rows, and each unit is completed before traveling to the next one, the traveling threads will be concealed behind the tramé threads. An enlarged view of steps 1-3 without the remaining layers is shown on the next page.

The last two steps in the pattern include a two-way diagonal tramé (step 4) that is secured with a double oblong cross. Notice that the overlapping intersections of the diagonal tramé also fall at the same place where the "uncouched" straight tramé rows overlap. Therefore the double oblong cross will tie down both sets of laid threads (step 5).

OVERALL CHART - PATTERN 28

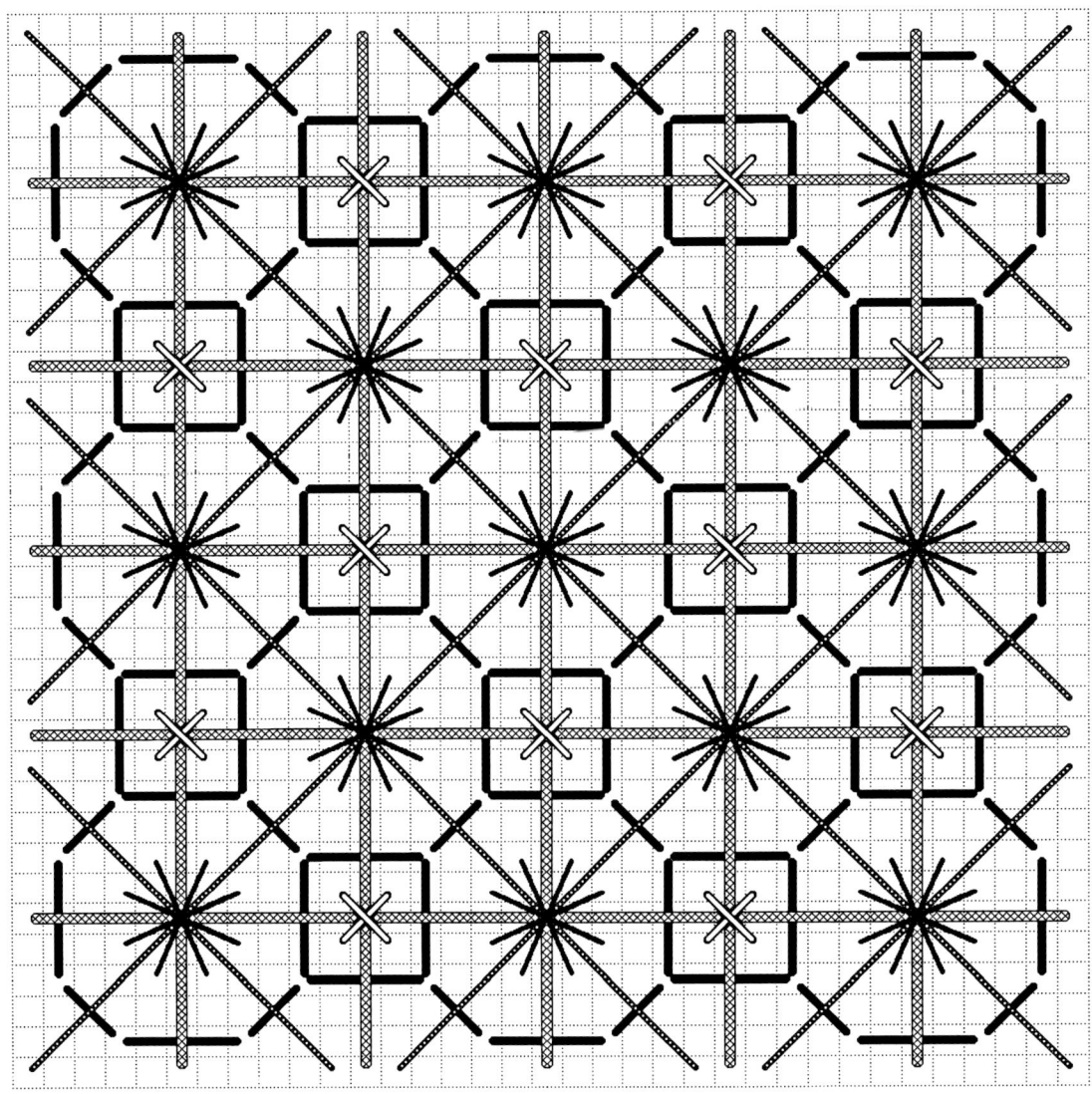

PATTERN 28 - VIEW WITHOUT STEPS 4 AND 5

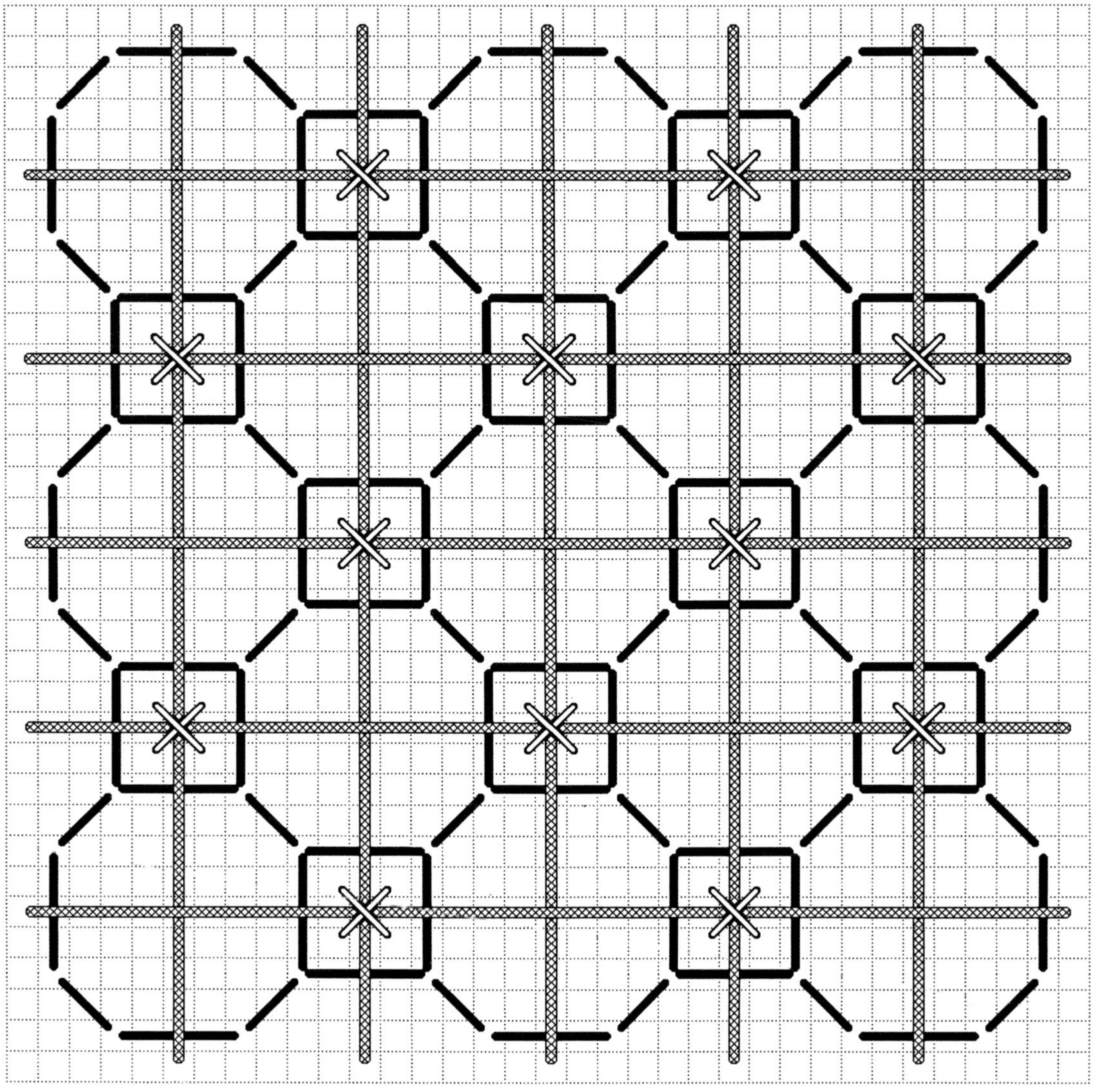

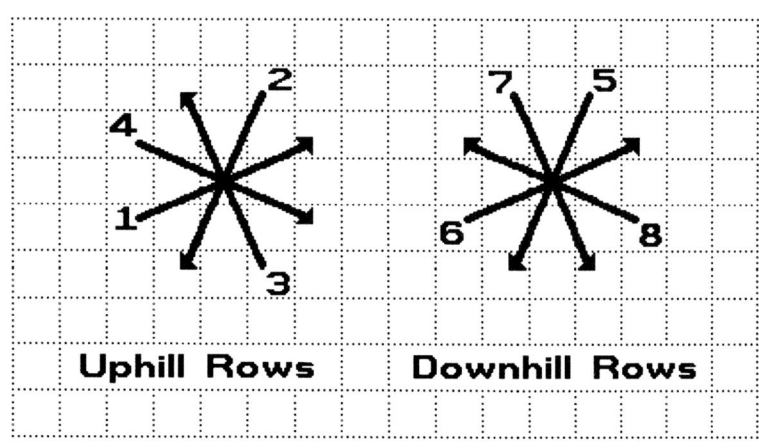

PATTERN 28
STEP 5 SEQUENCE
DOUBLE OBLONG CROSS

Start in the upper left corner, and work these tiedown stitches in diagonal rows. Use the right side sequence for the downhill rows and the left side sequence for the uphill rows. This will assure that each stitch is snugly wrapped and that the top cross will be the same throughout the sequence. Traveling threads will usually be concealed behind the diagonal tramé as long as it is thick enough. Some density in open areas, however, is unavoidable in this step.

PATTERN 29. This pattern is a very bold one, but it can be altered to a denser pattern by rearranging the spacing of the blackwork rows. Each row is what I call an alternating "M-W" wave. The undulating waves were conceived as an adaptation from a Florentine embroidery outline to a blackwork interpretation. As shown, the tramé rows are laid vertically, and they are spaced thirteen threads apart. The blackwork rows are laid in pairs that are two threads apart, and each pair is spaced six threads from the adjacent pair.

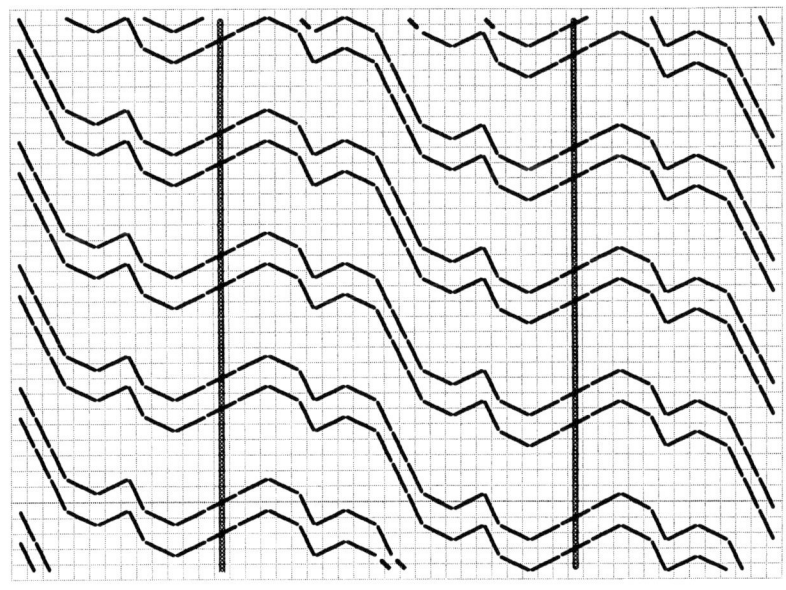

OVERALL CHART PATTERN 29

This pattern is used in the background of the *Comely Catfish* design (Color Plate XV). It is a perfect way to suggest water around the fish.

Each pair of outlines is executed in double running stitch paths. An enlarged view of one pair of rows is provided below to clarify the paths.

PATTERN 29 SEQUENCE ROWS

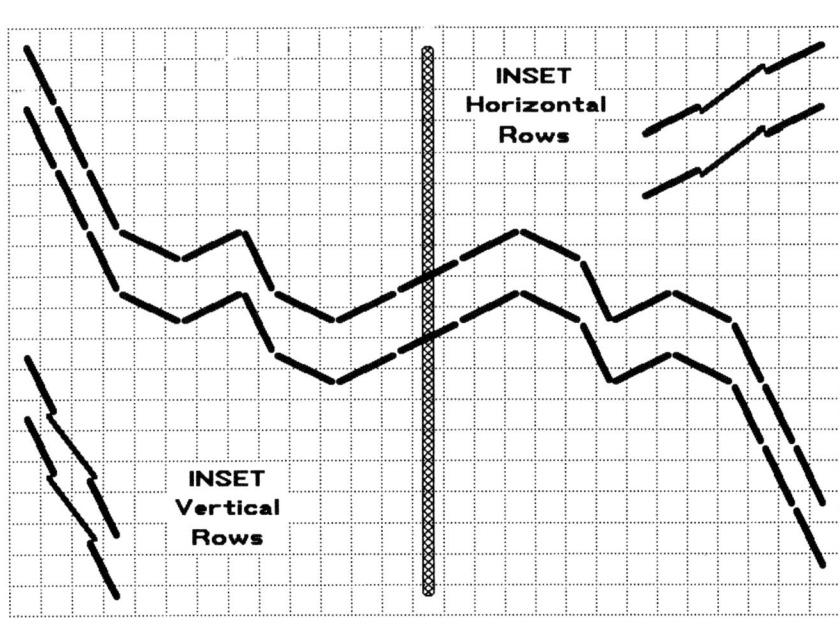

INSET
Horizontal
Rows

INSET
Vertical
Rows

NOTE. All of the stitches in the outlines have a gobelin slant. Some are horizontal and some are vertical. However, when there are three stitches in a row with the same slant, the middle stitch must be carefully adjusted on the return trip to maintain the illusion of straightness. The two inset views provide suggested placements for the middle stitches of the horizontal and vertical rows.

106

PATTERN 30. This pattern is a very simple blackwork network that has a diagonal lattice foundation. Diagonal tramés are laid in both directions and the parallel rows are twelve threads (or six intersections) apart (step 1). The blackwork will help to secure the unstable tramé threads, but further tiedown stitches are added inside both the medium diamond motifs and the larger St. Andrews cross shapes. An upright cross is used inside the medium diamonds and a double oblong cross is used inside the St. Andrews crosses. Add these alternating units in diagonal rows as step 2. The blackwork sequence is added last as step 3. The sequence charts are found on the next page.

OVERALL CHART - PATTERN 30

PATTERN 30 - ISOLATED VIEW
STEP 1 TRAME

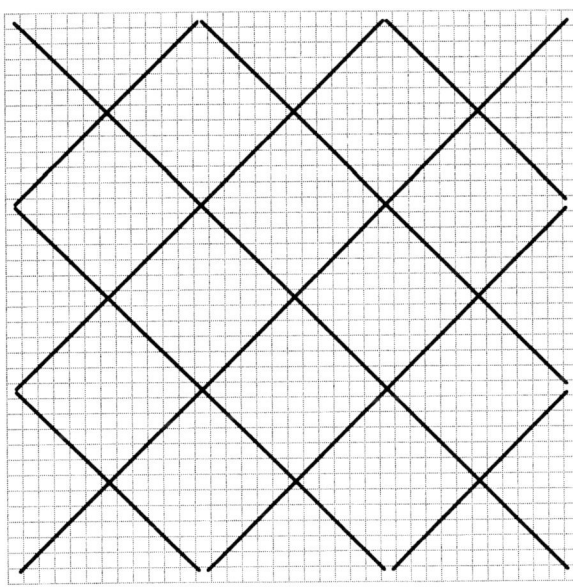

PATTERN 30 - ISOLATED VIEW
TRAME WITH TIEDOWNS (STEP 2)

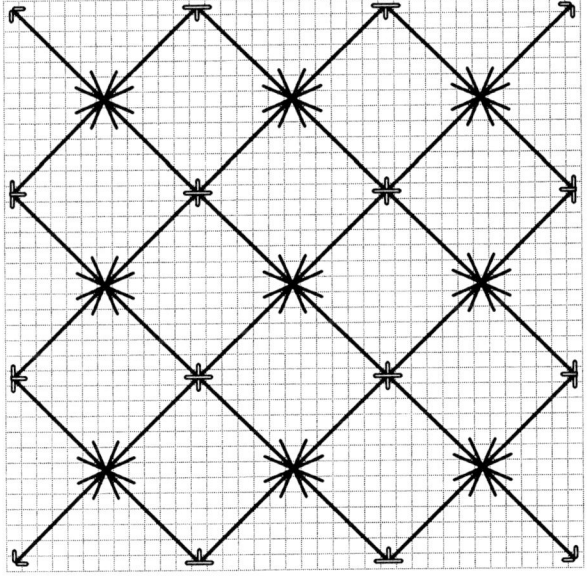

PATTERN 30
STEP 2 SEQUENCE
UPRIGHT CROSS

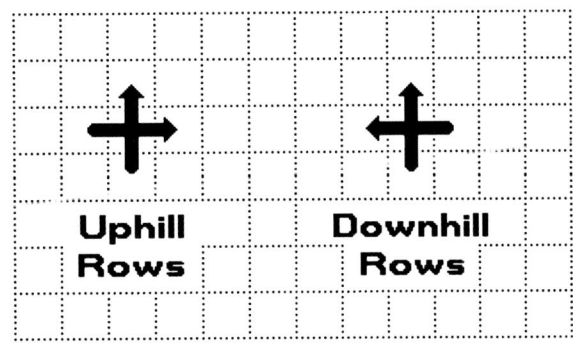

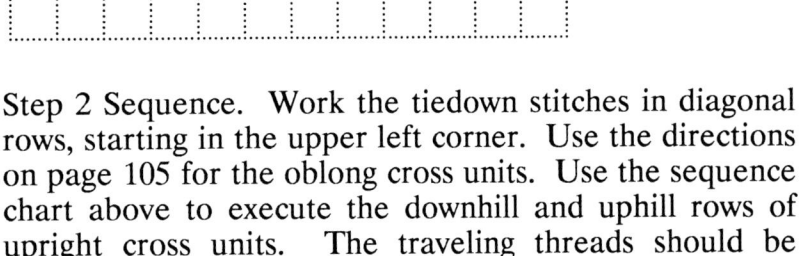

PATTERN 30
BLACKWORK ROWS
STEP 3

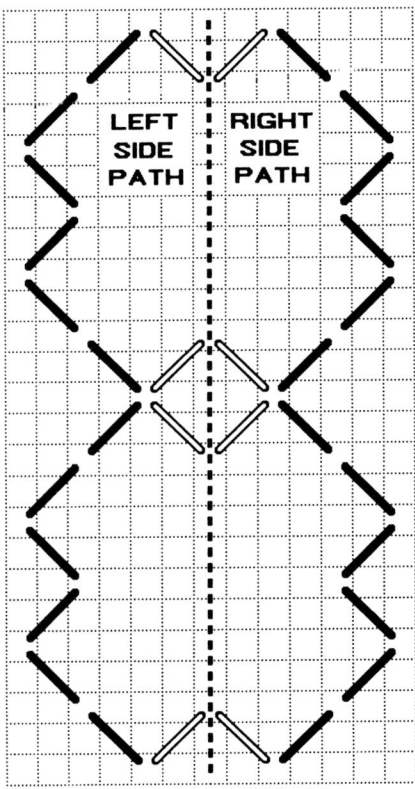

Step 2 Sequence. Work the tiedown stitches in diagonal rows, starting in the upper left corner. Use the directions on page 105 for the oblong cross units. Use the sequence chart above to execute the downhill and uphill rows of upright cross units. The traveling threads should be concealed behind the tramé rows if they are wide enough.

Step 3 Sequence. The blackwork sequence is a simple outline of left side and right side double running stitch paths with a single side trip at strategic points. Therefore no numbered sequence is needed. Two repeats of the vertical path outlines are shown to the right.

108

PATTERN 31. This pattern appears twice in Sampler 2 for Area 2 and Area 6. Both shapes are somewhat elongated so the vertical thrust of the pattern reinforces the shapes well. The same tramé with an oblong cross tiedown that is used in Pattern 24 on page 99 forms steps 1 and 2 of this pattern. The vertical rows are again placed six threads apart, but a different blackwork pattern is placed between the rows. This one is a simple diamond outline that shares holes with the oblong cross units so if the thread color is the same for both steps, the combined patterns look like a single blackwork pattern at viewing distance. If the colors or values used for both steps are different, the patterns no longer merge visually, and a strong vertical stripe will result.

OVERALL CHART
PATTERN 31

Step 1. Lay the vertical tramé rows six threads apart,

Step 2. Secure the tramé rows with a top layer of oblong cross rows. The chart for this step can be found on page 99.

Step 3. Add the blackwork pattern in between the tramé rows. A sequence chart is provided below for this step.

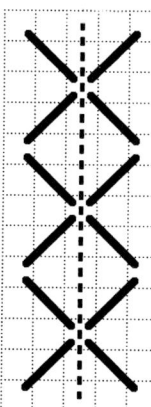

PATTERN 31 - STEP 3 BLACKWORK SEQUENCE

This simple outline of small diamonds can be executed in two separate rows of double running stitch. The chart to the left shows three repeats of the pattern, and it is divided in half to mark the left and right sides. Use a double running path to execute the left side zigzag of the pattern. Then add the right side zigzag with a second double running row. No side trips are needed, and the outline is so clear that no numbered sequence is needed.

NOTE. The oblong cross sequence in this pattern looks particularly nice in a perle cotton. The blackwork should be done in either a matching or contrasting floss. The flatness of this step tends to elevate the texture of the couched tramé even more to produce an attractive combination.

109

PATTERN 32. This pattern also appears in Sampler 2 and decorates Area 3. Again the shape is elongated so the choice of a vertical stripe is appropriate. Even though the shape is narrow and angular, the pattern maneuvers well and the compensation edges look graceful. The vertical tramé rows are laid six threads apart again as step 1. This time, however, the blackwork pattern secures the unstable threads as step 2. Additional canvas stitches are then used to further embellish the pattern as step 3.

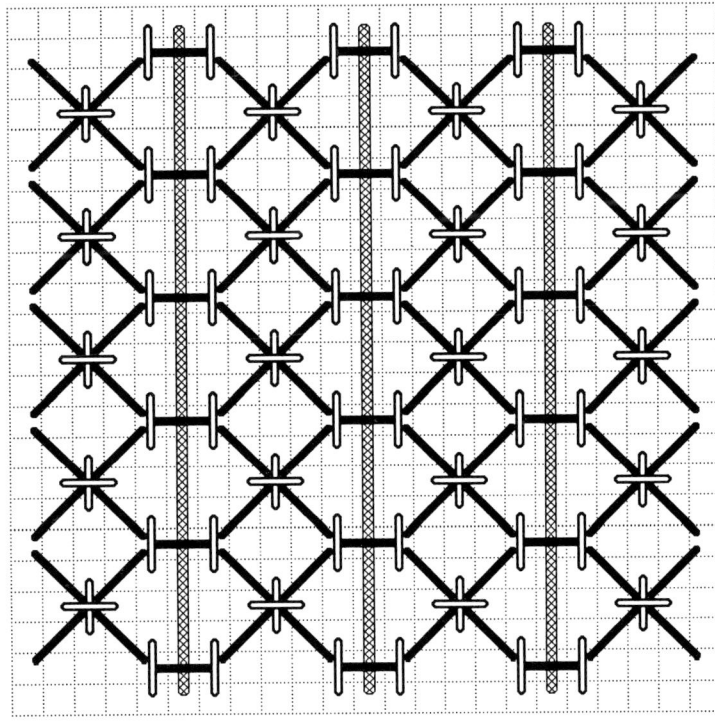

OVERALL CHART
PATTERN 32

Step 1. Lay the vertical rows of tramé six threads apart.

Step 2. Add the blackwork rows, using the horizontal paths of double running stitch shown below in Diagram 1. In a narrow shape like Area 3 in Sampler 2 it might be easier to use the same vertical diamond sequence shown in Pattern 31 for this step and to add the horizontal stitches that straddle the tramé as side trips off of the main path. However, in a square shape like Pattern 32, there are no compensation challenges so it is easier to execute the pattern in horizontal rows.

Step 3. Add the pairs of brick stitches and the upright cross units in a diagonal path starting along the upper right edge (see Diagram 2 below).

DIAGRAM 1
BLACKWORK
SEQUENCE

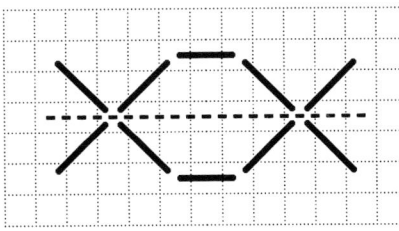

Diagram 2. The numbered sequence shows the downhill path, and the lettered sequence shows the uphill path. All traveling threads will fall behind the blackwork outlines so none will show in open areas.

DIAGRAM 2
STEP 3 SEQUENCE

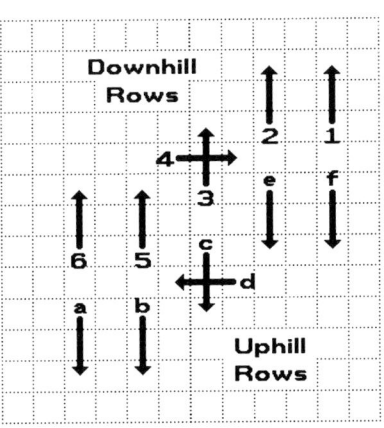

PATTERN 33. This pattern is an unusual one since it has a slanted tramé that is tied down with a cluster of three brick stitches. Each diamond formed by the tramé is filled with a blackwork "bow tie" motif, but the blackwork shapes are isolated and there is no continuous path. The bow ties are completed one at a time, and the sequence used is a combination of a double running path and one final back stitch. There are two ways to execute steps 1-2 of this pattern so read all of the directions thoroughly before proceeding.

OVERALL CHART - PATTERN 33

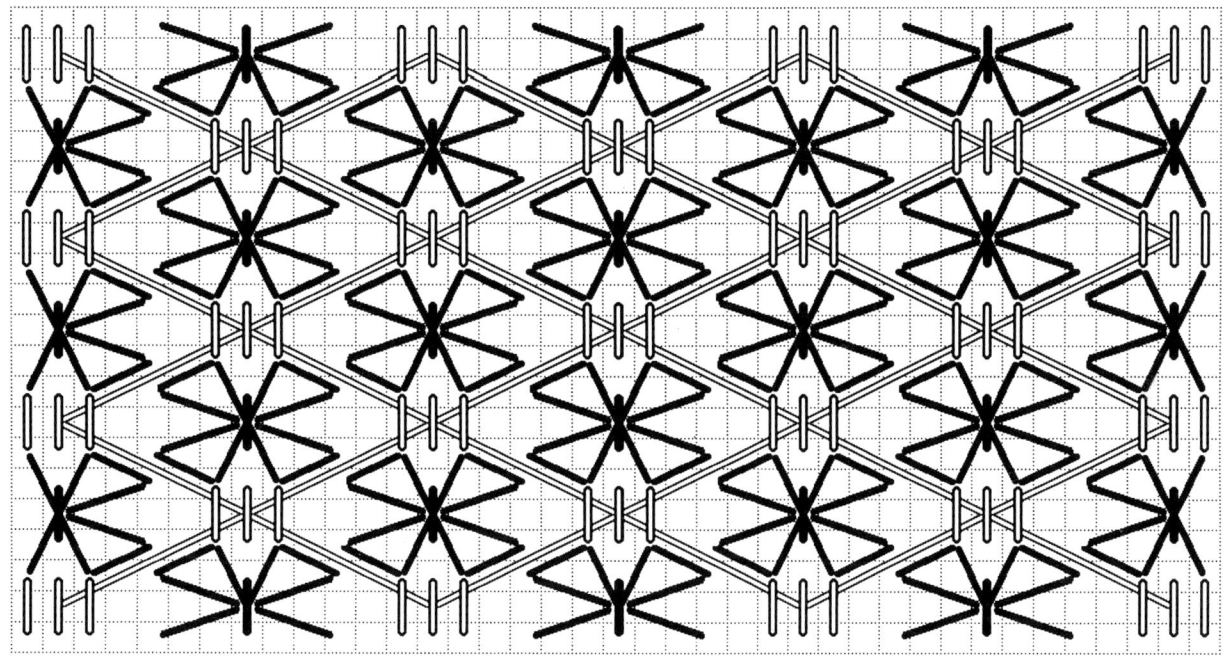

PATTERN 33 - STEP 1 TRAME

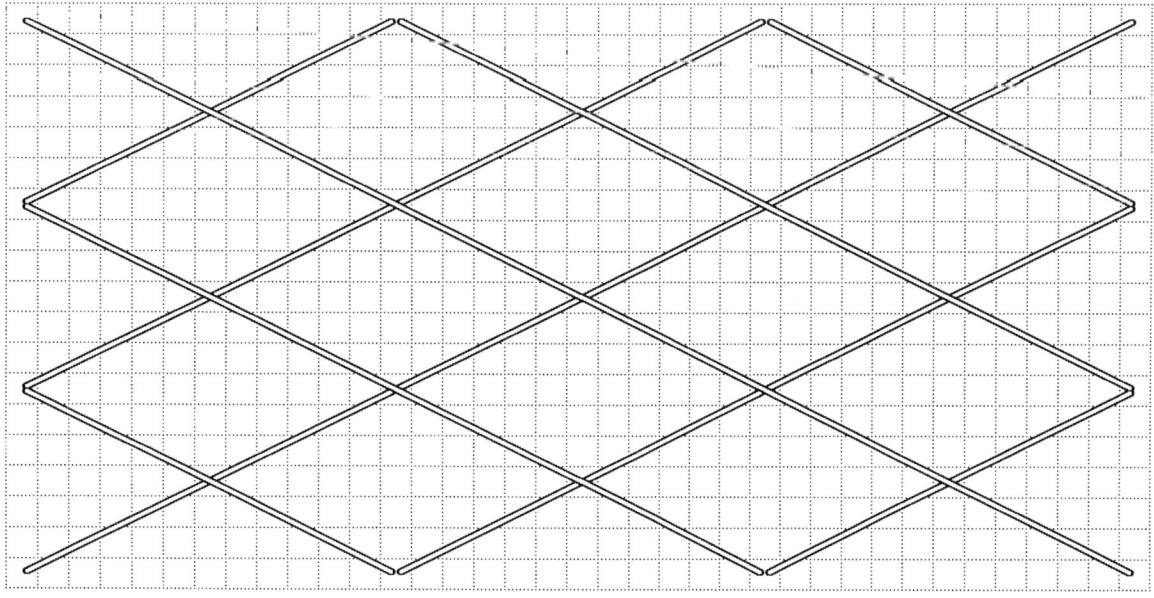

111

Tramé Sequence. Lay all of the slanted rows in one direction and then lay all the slanted rows in the other direction, as shown in the tramé chart on the previous page. To make the counting less difficult, notice that each "crossed" grouping measures six threads wide by three threads long. When laying the long rows, count this combination each time and poke a hole in the final hole with an awl to mark it for the next count. These enlarged holes will be covered by the brick clusters later so they will not show.

NOTE. Since the brick clusters will cover these overlapping intersections, the tramé could also be executed in a combination "back stitch-running stitch" outline or maze path. Start in the upper left corner and lay the first running stitch across six threads and down three threads. Work in a vertical zigzag path, and add the next stitch below it in a back stitch. Alternate this sequence until the row is completed, and then use the same sequence to work the adjacent row in an upward path. Although the concept of doing step 1 this way is "advanced," it is actually easier to stitch, and mistakes in placement are less likely. The outline will look like a tramé, but it is actually "faked" in a clever way.

PATTERN 33 - STEP 2 TIEDOWNS

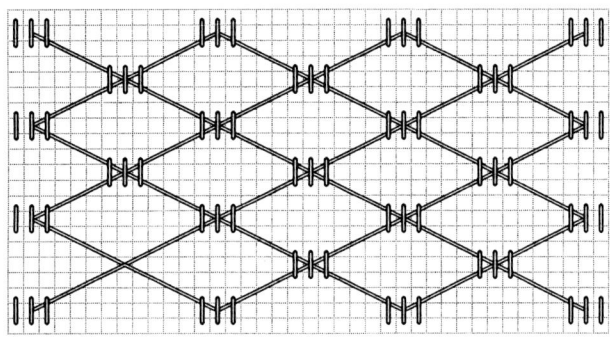

Step 2 Sequence. The brick stitch clusters should be worked in diagonal rows to conceal the traveling thread. Begin in the upper left corner and work the stitches left to right in sequential order. At the end of the row, rotate the frame 180° and work the uphill rows in the same "downhill" sequence.

NOTE. If the long tramé sequence is used for step 1, a combined sequence could be considered to eliminate traveling from one row to another twice (as long as the same thread is used for steps 1-2). Lay all of the tramé rows in one direction first. Each time a row in the opposing direction is laid, however, use a "return trip" to add the tiedowns. This is efficient and allows you to secure each row immediately so that the tension on each top tramé thread stays taut. If the holes are poked first, as suggested earlier, the "hole" will be behind the center brick stitch so use it to place the tiedown stitches accurately.

Blackwork Sequence. All of steps 1 and 2 must be completed before step 3 is added. Use the sequence chart on the next page in conjunction with the overall chart on page 111 to add each blackwork motif. These should be worked in vertical rows from top to bottom.

A double running stitch is used to outline each "bow tie." The shape is symmetrical, but the lines are slanted so work carefully until you have memorized the outline. Notice that stitch 12 also has no backing. It is used as a "bridge stitch" to put the needle in an ideal position for taking the final stitch, which is a brick stitch that wraps the middle of the motif. By manipulating the sequence in this way, no traveling threads will show, and the angle from stitch 13 to the entry point in the next diamond will force the "exposed" thread to fall behind a canvas thread rather than a hole.

Conclusion. One can alter or break the rhythm of a double running sequence when it benefits the pattern in a positive way. The reason for doing blackwork in a reversible method is not to create a reversible pattern but to conceal any paths on the back of the design. Some "unorthodox" treatments can be useful in making sequences more efficient

on canvas so consider such options when problems occur. An adjustment was needed in this pattern because of the isolated motifs, and the brick stitch was actually added to create a graceful exit from one diamond to another. The sequence could have ended after stitch 12, but the center hole would look less even if the stitch traveled forward. The brick stitch hides any breaks in the rhythm so its presence is quite functional, but it is attractive as well and the "fix" is not obvious!

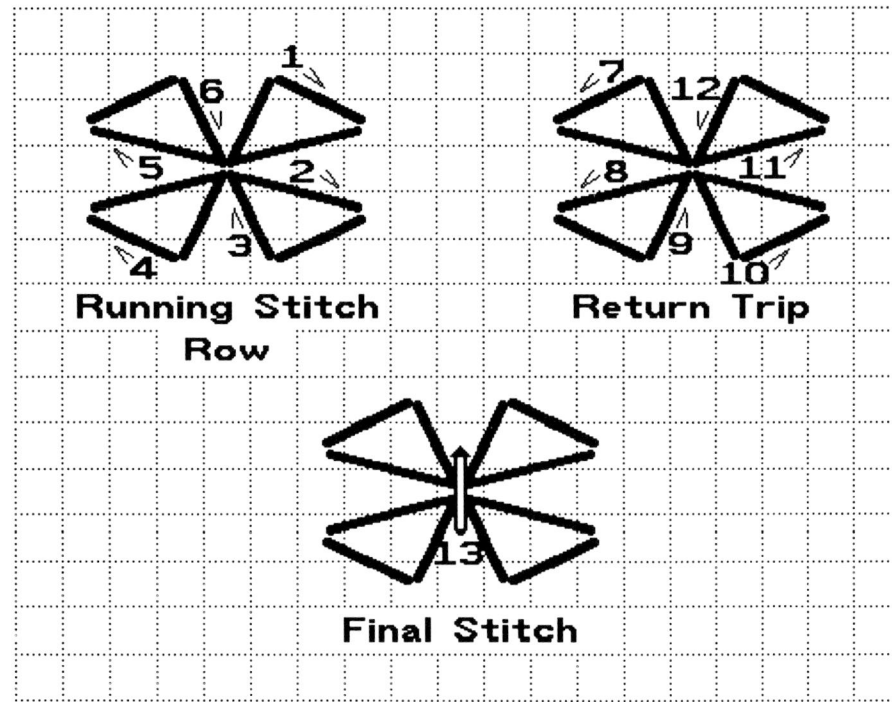

Running Stitch Row

Return Trip

Final Stitch

**PATTERN 33
BLACKWORK
SEQUENCE
STEP 3**

NOTE. An unusual method was used to chart this sequence since the stitches were too crowded to add arrows to the tips of the stitches. A separate arrow accompanies each number to indicate the direction of the stitch. Only stitch 13 uses the conventional "arrow" construction.

The usual "dotted lines" to indicate the traveling threads in the sequences were also eliminated this time in order to free the crowded area of excess clutter.

PATTERN 34. The last pattern in this chapter is a combination pattern that uses tramé and blackwork as accents in an open canvas filler. The previous pattern illustrated how blackwork can be used as an isolated filling rather than as a continuous pattern. In this pattern a diagonal tramé is laid in one direction only (step 1). Then Milanese blocks are added to stabilize the tramé rows. The remaining open diamonds are then filled with a diagonal row of Smyrna crosses that alternate with elongated tent stitches that straddle two intersections (step 3). The remaining parallelogram shapes are filled with a blackwork row (step 4). Steps 3 and 4 also tie down the tramé threads since the rows cross them in a perpendicular direction.

The blackwork outline is a stripe just like the step 3 canvas filling. The resulting pattern forms a lovely diagonal ribbon. Expand the pattern provided to form a wider band if desired. This ribbon is stunning in a multicolor combination so try using the following combination in coordinated colors on an 18-mesh canvas:

Step 1. Use a 1/16" ribbon (metallic or double face satin) in a medium dark value.
Step 2. Use a pastel Watercolours hand dyed thread or a #5 solid perle cotton in a medium value.
Step 3. Use a #8 Balger metallic braid in a light value.
Step 4. Use a dark floss, 2 strands.

113

In spite of the complexity of this pattern it would maneuver gracefully as an overall pattern since each step uses stitches that compensate easily.

OVERALL CHART - PATTERN 34

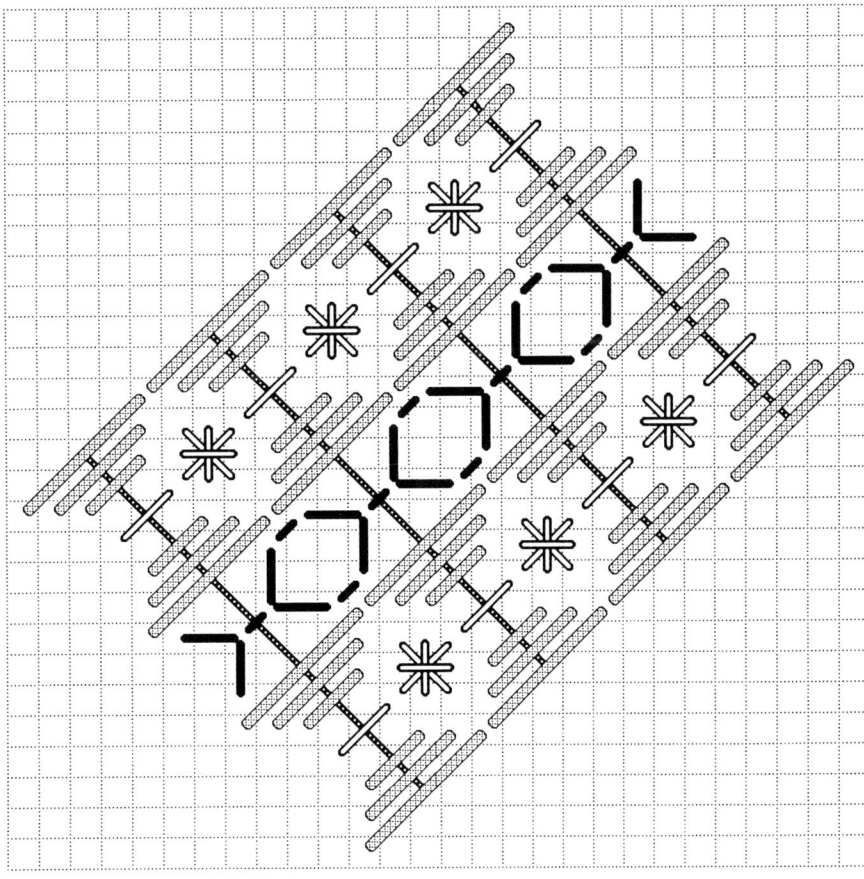

Step 1. Lay diagonal rows of tramé in rows that straddle eleven threads. Place the rows four intersections apart.

Step 2. Lay diagonal rows of Milanese blocks back and forth until the tramé is covered (see the diagram 1 sequence chart below).

Step 3. Add the rows of alternating elongated tent and Smyrna cross in the reverse diagonal direction (see the diagram 2 sequence chart below).

Step 4. Add the blackwork rows, as numbered in diagram 3 below.

DIAGRAM 1
MILANESE STEP 2
SEQUENCE

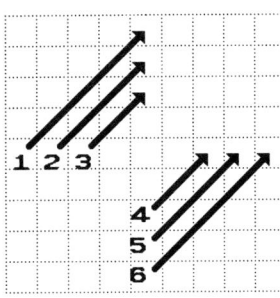

DIAGRAM 2
STEP 3
SEQUENCE

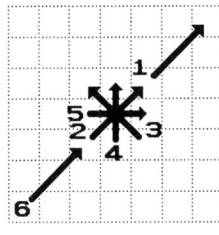

DIAGRAM 3
BLACKWORK SEQUENCE
STEP 4

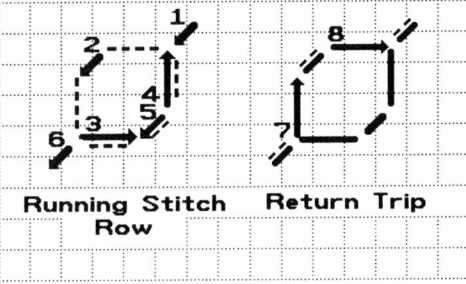

This chapter may have opened your eyes to the many possibilities of combining blackwork with couching treatments. In developing such patterns, I usually create the blackwork pattern and then add the laid threads in areas where they will fit. Patterns 31 and 32 are examples of planning such patterns in reverse. An interesting tramé was created, and blackwork doodles were developed to fit the remaining negative spaces. I hope the ideas presented become a catalyst for further experiments.

CHAPTER 5 - **BLACKWORK PATTERNS WITH OPEN CANVAS FILLINGS**

This chapter will explore composite patterns that combine blackwork networks with open canvas treatments. Blackwork patterns that have large negative spaces between their repeat units can be filled with interesting canvas stitches that add textural highlights and solid masses that compliment the delicate linear outlines of the blackwork. Since blackwork is usually one color in a medium-to-dark value, the canvas additions can add further contrasts with additional colors and\or values.

Since the blackwork is usually stitched with either silk or cotton floss, or other fine threads like #8 perle or Natesh rayon, it can be fun to use different threads for the canvas accents. The effect varies with the choice of thread, and one must decide whether light or full coverage is desired for the canvas stitches. Let me caution you about using threads that do not fill the holes, however. If the thread is fine, it will be affected by the tension on the traveling thread and may lean in an awkward manner. It is not possible to "fix" these crooked stitches in the same way one does on the return trip in blackwork so beware!

I usually avoid variegated threads too since they tend to "dilute" the pattern. However, some of the more subtle blended threads can be quite successful since soft muted contrasts do not detract from the "flow" of the pattern repeats.

After I create a pattern I then decide whether it is easier to do the blackwork or the canvas segment first. Sometimes the choice does not matter, but often some tedious counting can be avoided if the pattern network is "set up" by the sequence that is easiest to establish. Then other stitches fit comfortably in the open spaces without further counting since placements can be judged from the way they fit into already established surroundings.

When planning appropriate exposed canvas patterns, one must arrange the stitches so that they form square or diamond lattice networks that provide convenient solid paths for the stitch sequences. Some stripe patterns will have one-way rows, but allover patterns will need two-way intersecting paths. Sequences are usually either straight or diagonal rows that are continuous; if so, the stitches can usually be manipulated in such a way that the traveling threads are concealed behind the density of the stitches themselves.

To eliminate excessive traveling from one completed row to the entry point of a new row, I sometimes add side trips to a one-way sequence to add the elements that would eventually be added with secondary perpendicular row sequences. This blackwork concept adapts well to canvas sequences and not only minimizes the traveling threads needed but it saves time and economizes on thread usage as well. The techniques described in planning these patterns will be illustrated in the patterns that follow.

PATTERN 35. The first pattern is actually an adaptation from Pattern 10 on pages 70-71. By leaving out the hexagon in the side trips, a nice open shape remains that is filled with an elongated variation of the pavillion stitch (which is an enlarged Hungarian stitch). To connect these units, a brick stitch is added between them that also straddles the blackwork. The blackwork pattern is executed as step 1. The canvas filling is added in vertical rows as step 2. Even though the canvas rows are separated, the overall visual effect of this pattern is still a diaper pattern since the blackwork pattern is a diaper.

OVERALL CHART - PATTERN 35

Step 1 Blackwork Sequence. Use the sequence charts on pages 70-71 to outline the blackwork pattern. However, this time eliminate the hexagon side trips and add only the tent stitches that appear in the pattern above. Complete all of the blackwork rows before adding any step 2 fillings.

Step 2 Canvas Pattern. This addition is worked in vertical rows in the numbered sequence charted on the next page. Notice that all of the stitches lean "up" since the row direction is "down." If this rule is observed all of the stitches will be snugly wrapped, and they will also appear uniform in size if tension control is consistent.

STEP 2 CANVAS SEQUENCE

NOTE. The sequence is manipulated here to force the traveling threads to lay behind the stitches so that no paths show in the open areas. A circular path is followed to allow the open hole in the center of the modified pavillion unit to remain uncluttered. On the lower left side the row direction is uphill briefly, but since the traveling direction from stitch 7 to stitch 8 is still "down," stitches 7 and 8 are both snugly wrapped.

At the end of each vertical row, rotate the canvas 180° and use the same sequence to lay the adjacent row.

PATTERN 36. This pattern is a variation of Pattern 30 on page 107. The same blackwork network is executed first as step 1. Then the canvas filler is added in vertical rows. The pavillion variation here fills the St. Andrews cross outline, and each small diamond outline is filled with an upright cross.

OVERALL CHART - PATTERN 36

STEP 2 SEQUENCE

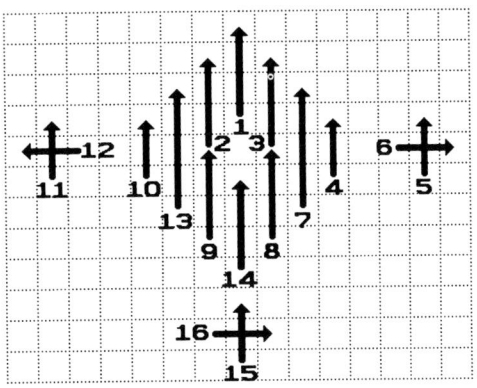

Like Pattern 35, the canvas sequence is worked in vertical rows. However, this time there are side trips so travel off the "main path" to add the upright cross units inside the small diamonds to the right and left of the enlarged pavillion units.

The sequence is again adjusted to force the traveling threads to fall in an inconspicuous place. They will trail either behind the pavillion unit or behind the blackwork lines so will not show.

NOTE. Not every row will have a stitch 5-6 or a stitch 11-12 side trip so just skip them when they are not needed.

PATTERN 37. This pattern is used in Sampler 2 for Area 4. It is a delicate pattern that combines diamond and octagon motifs in the blackwork outline (step 1.) Tied oblong cross stitches are added to the octagon shapes as step 2.

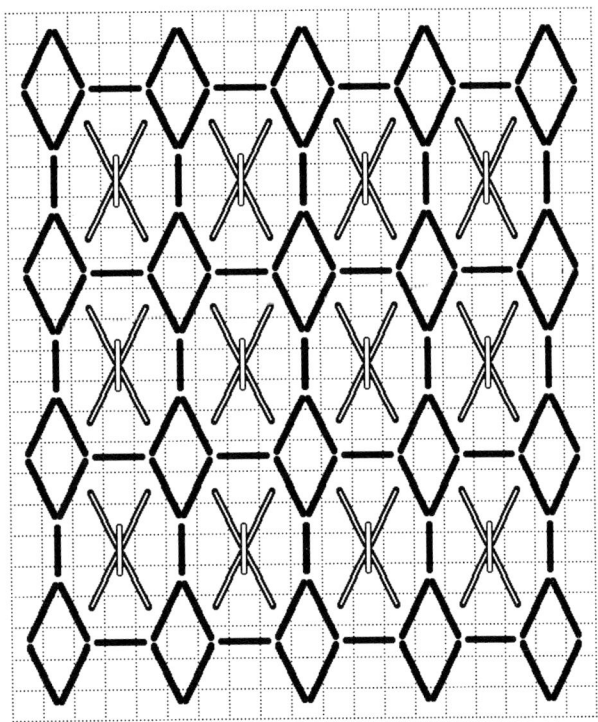

OVERALL CHART - PATTERN 37

Step 1 Sequence. The blackwork outlines could be worked in either horizontal or vertical rows. Since the pattern fits the Area 4 shape better if vertical rows are used, it is charted this way in diagram 1 on page 119. The double running sequence is a trip-and-a-half path, and the side trips go in a bit easier if they are done on the return trip.

REMINDER. Patterns with angled stitches and star points often look nicer if a single strand of silk is used rather than two strands of floss. The points look sharper without the added density.

Two repeats of the sequence are provided since the thread takes two repeats to reappear in the same position.

Step 2 Sequence. The tied oblong crosses are worked in horizontal rows, as numbered in diagram 2. It is impossible to conceal the traveling threads in this filling so choose a thread that will not be conspicuous.

118

DIAGRAM 1
BLACKWORK SEQUENCE

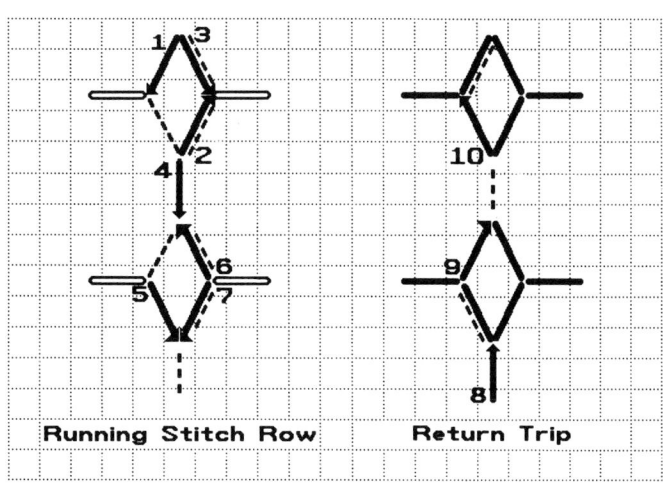

Running Stitch Row   Return Trip

DIAGRAM 2
TIED OBLONG CROSS SEQUENCE

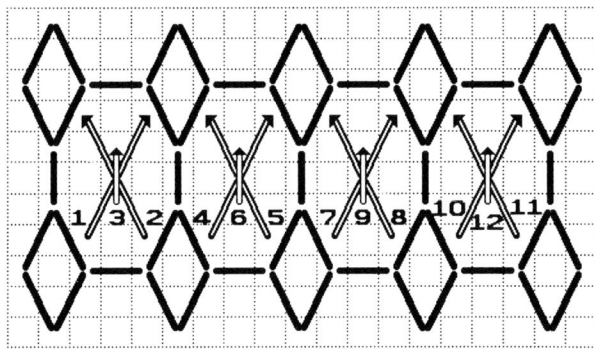

NOTE. Keep the canvas upright and use the same sequence in both horizontal directions.

PATTERN 38. This pattern is used in Sampler 2 for Area 5. In spite of the complexity of the shape the pattern looks comfortable, and it reinforces the shape nicely. The boldness of the pattern makes it particularly dramatic especially in a dark color.

OVERALL CHART - PATTERN 38

PATTERN 38 CORE PATTERN

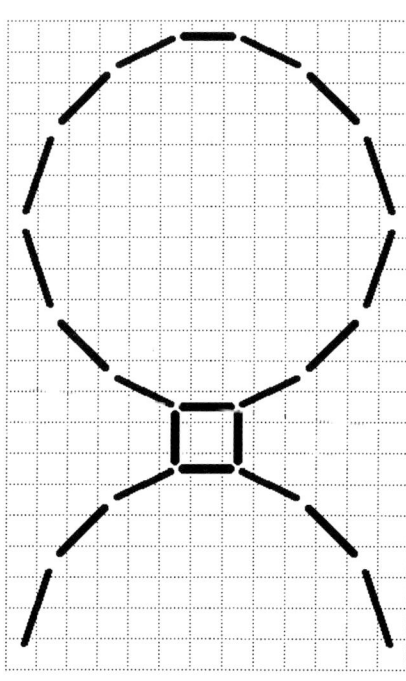

NOTE. The outline above shows the core or "root" pattern of this complex arrangement. The round Christmas ornament shapes are

119

formed from overlapping outlines of the circle pattern shown above. The pattern could be stitched in two separate sequences, using the network above. However, a combined network sequence is easier to use in the Sampler 2 shape so this is what is provided. There is an interesting discussion in the pattern design chapter about patterns and shapes made with overlapping circles so read pages 159 for further information.

PATTERN 38 BLACKWORK SEQUENCE

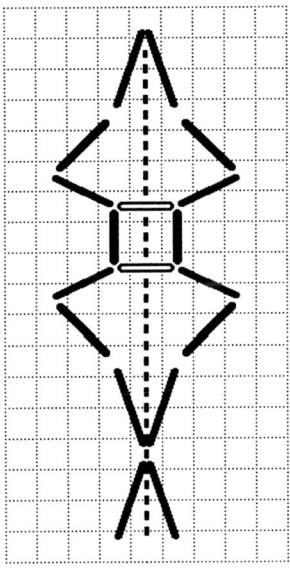

Step 1. The blackwork sequence selected is surprisingly simple considering the intricacy of the overall pattern. The flip-flop scale motif is joined by a square as a single repeat. Since the scale units are symmetrical the pattern can be executed with a left and right side double running stitch sequence. On ONE of these rows ONLY, add the straight horizontal stitches as side trips off of the main path. The dotted line on the chart to the left divides the left and right paths.

Step 2. The canvas filling in this pattern is merely an enlarged version of the tied oblong cross in Pattern 37. Therefore use the same sequence suggested on page 119 to add these units. The stitches line up well in the same horizontal rows, so only an adjustment in the lengths of the oblong crosses is needed. Again the traveling threads cannot be concealed so choose an inconspicuous thread for this step.

PATTERN 39. This star pattern is used in Area 1 of Sampler 2. The pattern motifs are similar to those in Pattern 38, and both patterns add a dramatic contrast to the other delicate pastel patterns in Sampler 2 since they are bold and dramatic in the dark blue used.

**OVERALL CHART
PATTERN 39**

The blackwork sequence is executed in horizontal rows this time, but it could have been a vertical path instead. However, the top and bottom points of the star stay sharper if the outline is done in horizontal paths, using one row for the top half of the stars and another row for the bottom half of the stars (step 1).

The negative space left between the star outlines is identical to that in Area 38. Therefore the same oblong cross filling is used to make the two patterns relate well within the same design. However, other interesting stitches also fit this shape so numbered charts are provided on the next page for two possible substitutes. No numbered sequence is provided for the oblong cross since the chart on page 119 for a smaller oblong cross unit can be used again for this one with a simple adjustment in the size of the oblong stitches. Similarly it is impossible to conceal the traveling threads so use an inconspicuous thread for this step.

PATTERN 39 - STEP 1
OUTLINE

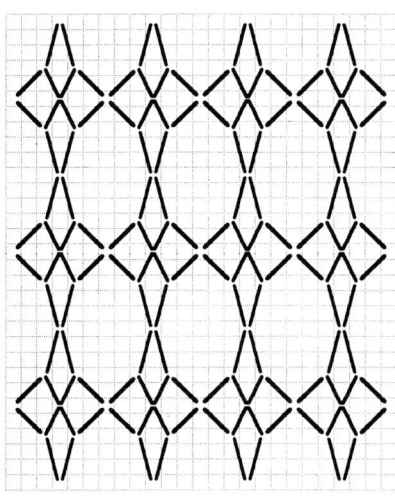

BLACKWORK SEQUENCE CHART

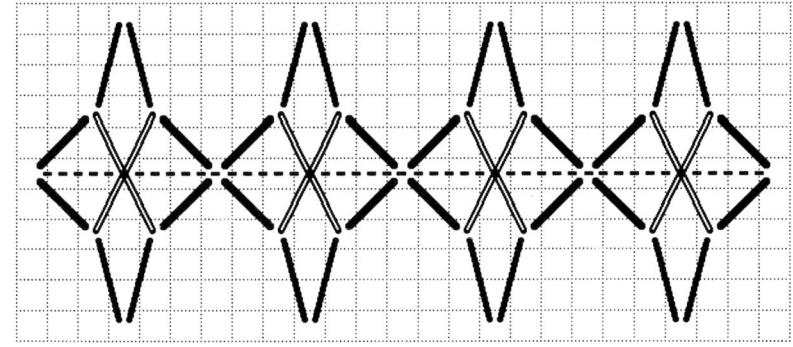

The dotted lines indicate the divisions between the top and bottom rows of the double running sequences. Each row has two side trips that fill the centers of the stars, and these should be added on the running stitch row.

OVERALL CHART
ALTERNATIVE CANVAS FILLINGS

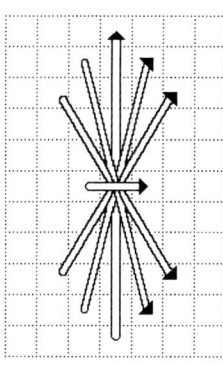

TIED WHEAT VARIATION 1

SEQUENCE CHARTS
ALTERNATIVE FILLINGS

TIED WHEAT VARIATION 2

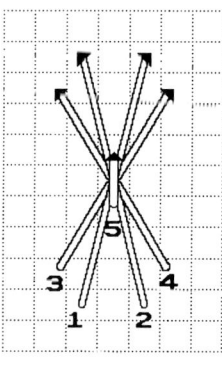

Work these units in horizontal rows. Reverse the direction of the top cross in Variation 1 when the row direction is left to right.

PATTERN 40. This pattern is the first one that uses an allover open canvas pattern as step 1 instead of the blackwork pattern. The canvas pattern is a diamond network that combines four-way units of Diagonal Hungarian with centers of Smyrna Cross. The blackwork pattern (step 2) has stars that surround the Smyrna crosses, and each star is connected by straight lines that meet in the middle of the open diamond shapes created by the canvas pattern.

OVERALL CHART - PATTERN 40

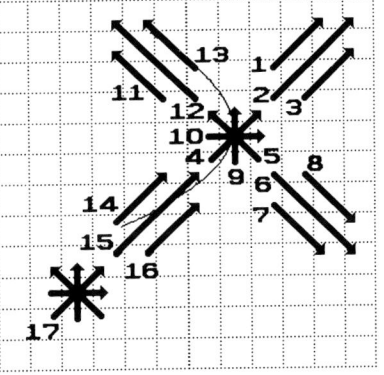

STEP 1 CANVAS SEQUENCE

SEQUENCE CHARTS

STEP 2 BLACKWORK SEQUENCE

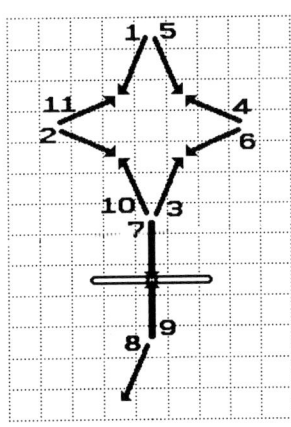

OVERALL CHART STEP 1 VIEW ONLY

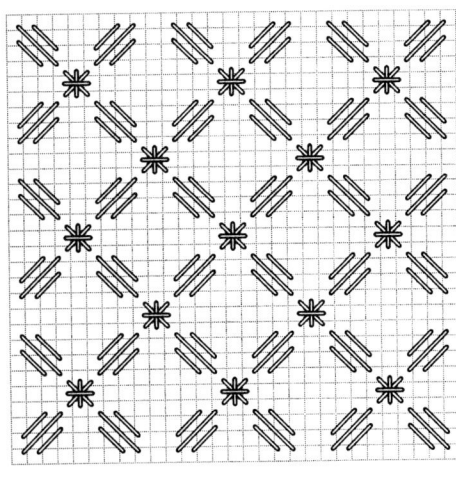

Step 1 Sequence. This pattern is worked in diagonal rows starting in the upper right corner. Normally one would work all the rows in one direction and then complete the remaining elements with rows in the opposing direction. To minimize the traveling from row to row and to eliminate the need for opposing rows, the concept of a side trip is applied to this sequence – stitches 6-8 and 11-13 are both "side trips off of the main path." The sequence is also numbered to automatically force the traveling threads to fall behind the stitched areas. Stitch 13, however, is an unavoidable "dead end." It is impossible to travel to stitch 14 cleanly without taking a tuck stitch on the back of the Smyrna cross to hold the thread behind the cross unit as it travels to the next cluster. The completed pattern forms a diamond lattice, and it is an attractive background pattern by itself.

122

NOTE. Some rows will have a side trip on both sides of the main path, but others will have no side trips so skip them and do the sequence with no further adjustments.

Step 2 Blackwork Sequence. The blackwork is added in vertical rows, and the sequence is a trip-and-a-half double running stitch path. The numbered sequence on page 122 is not broken down into two separate rows to indicate the running stitch rows and the return trip, but it is in essence the same thing. Take the left side trip after stitch 7 and the right side trip after stitch 9 to honor the principle discussed on page 28.

This pattern is used in the *Sailboat* design (Color Plate V) in the lower part of the front sail. The canvas filling is done in perle cotton, and the blackwork is done in floss.

PATTERN 41. This diamond pattern is used as the background in Sampler 2 (Area 7). The diamond outline is executed in zigzag rows of flame stitch, which are discussed on page 185 (step 1). This canvas framework is then embellished with an attractive blackwork pattern inside each diamond. The blackwork repeats are not continuous, but a sequence was developed that allows one to move efficiently from unit to unit.

**OVERALL CHART
PATTERN 41**

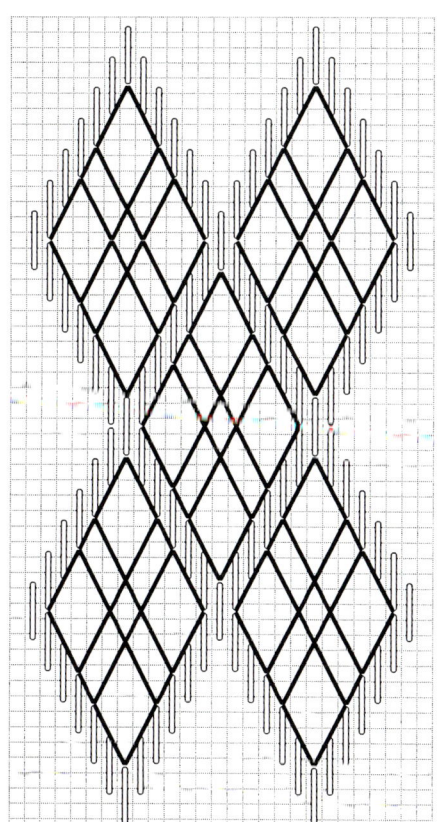

Step 2 Blackwork Sequence. The blackwork is executed in a combination of double running paths with some segments that use an alternating back stitch and running stitch sequence. By manipulating the sequence in this way, one can gracefully move from one diamond center to another without long journeys. The alternating rhythm is particularly useful for isolated blackwork motifs because it allows you to start and end in two different places within an outline.

STEP 2 SEQUENCE

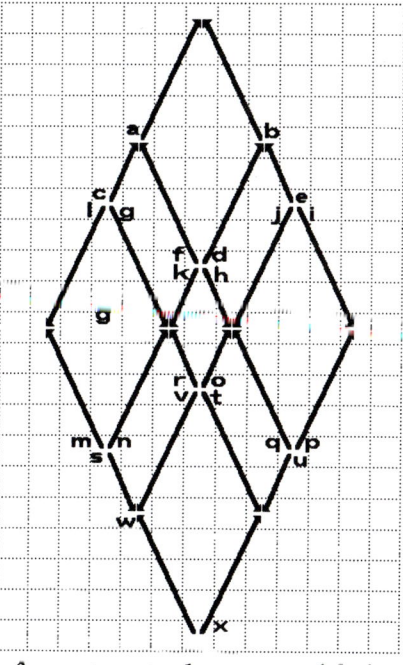

A lettered sequence is used here to minimize clutter. The sequence is planned so that the diamonds are connected with diagonal rows, starting in the upper left corner of the pattern. Each diamond outline begins at the top and ends on stitch "x" along the midpoint of the right edge to set up a short journey to entry point "a" of the next diamond. There is no formula for this kind of maze path. One merely figures out an efficient path and forces it to happen. Notice that there is a consistent rhythm to the sequence, however, in that the zigzag "tiers" are more or less outlined in horizontal rows from top to bottom with just an occasional necessary pivot stitch or break in the rhythm. If too random a sequence is used, it becomes impossible to memorize.

PATTERN 42. This pattern is quite similar to Pattern 41. However, this time the diamond lattice is created with an "offset" diagonal Hungarian outline as step 1. The diamonds are then filled with a similar blackwork filling, but the proportions are altered to fit the different shape, and the center diamond in the blackwork pattern is eliminated so that there is an open "x" shape instead.

OVERALL CHART PATTERN 42

Step 1 Sequence. Offset Diagonal Hungarian. The offset placement of the diagonal Hungarian units creates a "bumpy" slanted line that is unusual and attractive. To execute the outline, start at the top on the left side and work a vertical zigzag row of the Diagonal Hungarian, using a left to right sequence for the top left half of the diamond outline. Switch to a right to left sequence for the outline of the bottom left half, and continue to alternate the two sequences until the row is completed. Then rotate the canvas 180° and add the right side of the diamond outline in another vertical row.

The traveling path will be concealed if the alternating sequence is used consistently. This type of bold outline is ideal since it creates a dense backing that accommodates traveling paths and thread tails well. This feature is what makes combining blackwork with exposed canvas networks an ideal "marriage," and the use of a heavier weight thread for the canvaswork not only creates nice contrasts between the two types of patterns, but it makes the backing even stronger. Exciting geometric designs can be created with interesting

124

elongated shapes that depart from the usual arrangements that are considered for a canvas grid. By using a diagonal stitch in an offset manner, one can avoid the compensation dilemmas of a slanted stitch but still produce a slanted line.

**PATTERN 42
STEP 1 OUTLINE**

**PATTERN 42
STEP 2 SEQUENCE**

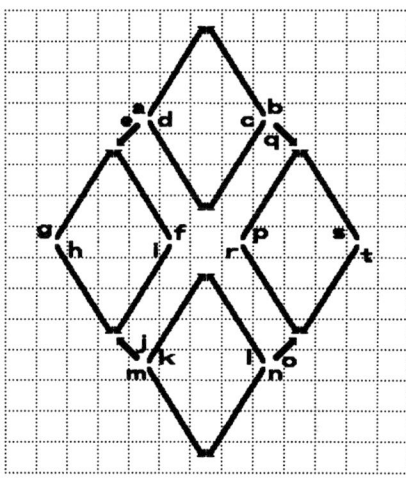

Complete all of step 1 before adding any step 2 fillings. End all thread tails in the open canvas outline. It is dense and continuous so it accommodates tails readily.

NOTE. The diagonal Hungarian units meet in a conventional four-way cluster in the corners where the diamonds join adjacent diamonds – only the side rows are offset.

Step 2 Blackwork Sequence. Add this sequence in diagonal rows, starting in the upper left corner of the pattern. The flow of this outline is different from that of the diamond filling in Pattern 41 since the gap in the center interrupts any horizontal path. The four small diamonds are more or less worked in a counter clockwise direction, doing the top and bottom halves in sequential order. The last diamond is manipulated to force the path to end on stitch "t" to create a short journey to entry point "a" of the next sequence. A combination of both double running stitch and alternating back stitch-running stitch method is used to create this efficient sequence.

PATTERN 43. This pattern is an interesting square network that is created with a diagonal Hungarian variation. Flip-flop units of diagonal Hungarian alternate to form a sort of rickrack outline. Inside the rows are arranged so that they create an attractive cross shape in the negative space, and it can be filled with a myriad of options. One possibility is presented here, using a blackwork pinwheel motif. A second possibility combines the blackwork pinwheel with a variation of tied oblong cross in an alternating checkerboard arrangement that forms a pretty diaper pattern. The open flip-flop Hungarian pattern is pretty by itself but the additional embellishments make it even more dramatic and ornate.

Step 1 Sequence. Use the Step 1 outline and sequence charts provided on the next page to create the exposed canvas network. Each cross space is outlined separately in building this pattern, and the sequence chart shows how to adjust the stitch direction when the row direction changes.

Each diagonal Hungarian unit is marked with a single number to identify the cluster. The number is in front of the first stitch of each cluster, and this stitch is marked with a dark arrow. Stitch each unit in sequential order, doing the long middle stitch second and the last short stitch last. Notice how the direction of the next cluster will always shift to provide clean turns and snugly wrapped stitches. Occasional adjustments are made when row directions change. Complete all of step 1 before adding the step 2 blackwork filling.

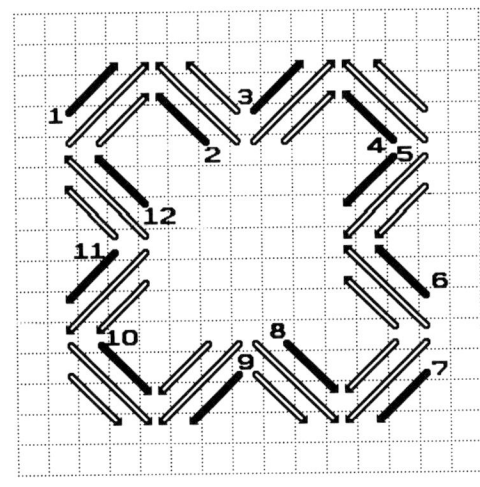

NOTE. Traveling threads are automatically concealed with this sequence. However, to add new segments it is necessary to weave through the established outline to get to new starting points. Once the rhythm is memorized, one can outline this pattern somewhat more randomly, if preferred, but be careful to make the appropriate adjustments when row directions change.

PATTERN 43 - STEP 2 SEQUENCE

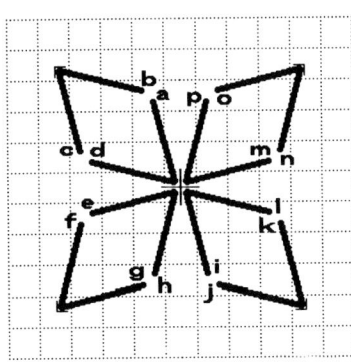

A back stitch-running stitch combination is used to execute this outline. Start in the upper left corner and execute the unit sequences in diagonal rows. The last stitch "p" will <u>not</u> exit cleanly behind stitch "l" to travel to the entry point "a" of the next unit. Therefore use a tuck stitch in the flip-flop Hungarian outline to hold the thread behind stitch "l."

NOTE. The extra fine lines in the chart indicate the direction of the arrow points of the blackwork stitches. Since two or four stitches come together in a shared hole, it was not possible to draw the points in the usual way.

This sequence completes each pinwheel separately, and the sequence progresses in a clockwise path in each unit. At the end of each row of units, rotate the canvas 180°, and execute the same sequence for the row in the opposite direction.

PATTERN 43 VARIATION. The overall chart on the next page shows an alternative treatment for this pattern. A tied oblong cross variation is placed in alternating positions with the blackwork units to form a fancy diaper pattern. However, the crosses in this composite stitch are not executed in the usual way. They are worked as eyelets to both eliminate excess bulk, and to allow one to exit in the desired direction. It is possible to work this stitch in 1-3 threads and/or sequences so the charts must be adapted to the intended choice. The original sample for this combination was on 18-mesh canvas, using Watercolours for the diagonal Hungarian outline and two strands of cotton floss for the blackwork. Use #8 perle for the step 3 oblong cross variation for a more delicate effect. A metallic accent could also be considered for part of this composite stitch.

OVERALL CHART - PATTERN 43 VARIATION

Step 3 Sequence. The numbered charts for what appears to be an oblong cross and a regular cross in this composite stitch use a radiating "eyelet" sequence which is hidden under the final upright cross. The second and third steps of this composite stitch will lay better if the stitches of steps 1-2 share the center hole. No actual layering is used until step 3 is added. Another advantage of this approach is that one can start and end on any spoke of

128

the wheel in an eyelet sequence so use this feature to create efficient transitions as the units are connected. This concept of "manipulating stitches, or the order of stitches," has been discussed and illustrated in earlier patterns so no specific directions are included here. Just remember that the main goal is to conceal the traveling threads so accomplish this in whatever way will work. Maintain a "back stitch" pull or snug wrap on every stitch also and adjust the stitch direction, as needed, to accomplish this. For example, stitch six is shown leaning from right to left in sequence chart a. This is ideal if the next unit requires traveling to the right. However, if the next unit is to the left, simply reverse the direction of stitch 6 to create a snugly wrapped stitch. **A stitch should always lean away from the direction towards which the thread must travel afterwards.**

PATTERN 43
VARIATION
STEP 3a
SEQUENCE

PATTERN 43
VARIATION
STEP 3b
SEQUENCE

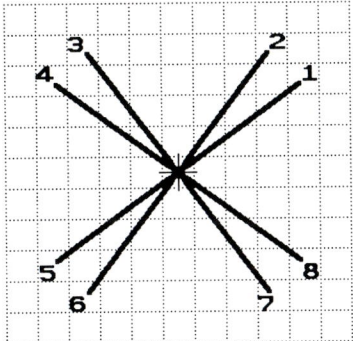

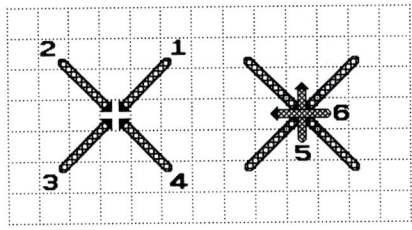

NOTE. Step 1 of this composite stitch is shown to the left. Steps 2-3 are combined in the chart above.

PATTERN 44. This pattern combines a satin stitch outline with a blackwork pattern. This outline is formed by units of upright Milanese stitches since the "bow tie" shape of each satin cluster suggests two triangles that face each other. The bow tie shapes are arranged in such a way that the outlines form "stars" with an open diamond in the negative space. A variety of fillings could be used to embellish these diamonds, but a blackwork pinwheel is used in this example.

Step 1 Sequence. The star outline or open canvas network is executed in diagonal rows, as shown in the sequence chart on the next page. Work the rows from left to right. At the end of each row, rotate the canvas 180° and add the next row, using the same sequence. Notice that each cluster of satin stitches overlaps the previous cluster by two threads as the row progresses. Connect adjoining rows by weaving back through existing rows until a convenient starting point is reached. This kind of "maze traveling" is necessary with stitch samples to avoid unsightly pivot stitches along the outside edges. One would normally travel within a design along an existing or planned outline.

129

OVERALL CHART - PATTERN 44

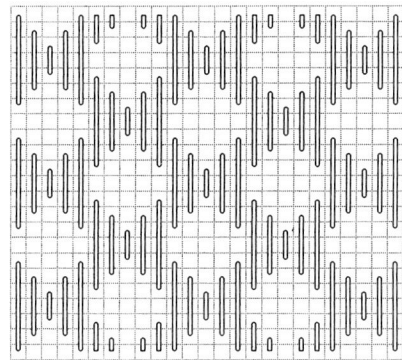

PATTERN 44
STEP 2 SEQUENCE

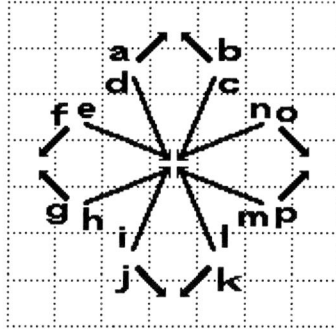

Use the open canvas network that shows step 1 alone to plan some other interesting fillings on your own. The diamond shape is easy to work with.

Step 2 Sequence. Add the blackwork pinwheels, starting in the upper left diamond. Work each motif in a counter clockwise path, as lettered in the sequence chart above, starting at the top. The distance from one unit to the next one is minimal so no need to weave through the bow tie outline to get to the starting point inside the next diamond. At the end of each row, rotate the canvas 180°. Weave through the back side of the bow tie outline to position the needle for an ideal entry for the first blackwork filling of the next row, and work the rows in the opposite direction, using the same lettered sequence. Since each pinwheel motif is isolated, a combination of running stitch and back stitch method is again used to execute the blackwork to allow one to start and end at an ideal place.

PATTERN 45. This pattern combines a four-way Milanese and an enlarged scotch stitch network with a star blackwork motif. The open canvas pattern is very dense, and the star blackwork outline actually shares holes with the edges of the canvas outline. The interior or center of the star is further embellished with a tied cross stitch. This is actually a layered canvas stitch, but since it is done in the same blackwork thread, it is lettered into the blackwork sequence.

Step 1 Sequence. Work the parallel units of Milanese and enlarged scotch stitches in diagonal rows. Use a maze path to connect the opposing rows, and weave through the back side of the previously laid rows to get to the entry point of the next opposing row. The pattern is dense and can accommodate both traveling threads and starting and ending threads comfortably.

**PATTERN 45
STEP 1 OUTLINE**

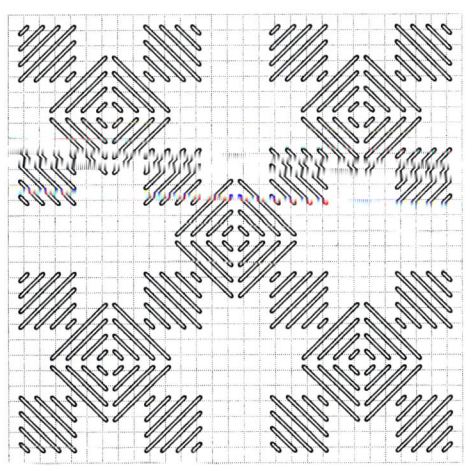

**PATTERN 45
STEP 2 SEQUENCE**

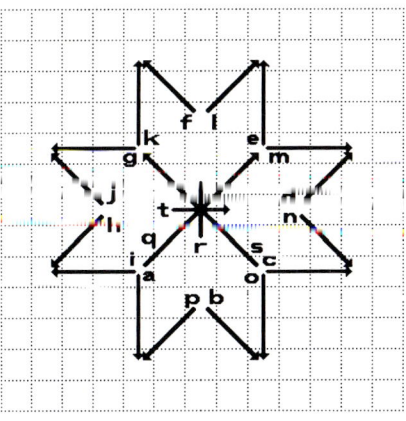

Step 2 Sequence. Follow the alternating running stitch and back stitch sequence that is shown in the lettered chart above on the right. Notice that the last 4 stitches (q-t) outline a tied cross in a somewhat unconventional way. Normally the regular cross foundation is completed before the top upright cross is added. However, by manipulating the sequence

131

in the way shown, there are no visible traveling threads behind the outline. Since the top cross hides the reversed order of stitches "r" and "s," one cannot tell that the stitches were not executed in the normal order.

PATTERN 46. This pattern has a dense open canvas network that does not create enough large negative space to accommodate a large blackwork motif. However, an attractive blackwork outline can be added around each of the stitch clusters that form the canvas network. As shown, the blackwork outline is added to only every other row of canvas stitches in a vertical path so a stripe is formed. However, the same pattern could be added to every row to form an allover pattern (see Pattern 46 Variation on page 134).

This pattern is used as the background pattern in *The Heart of Blackwork* design on the cover of the book. The exposed canvas pattern is also beaded as it is stitched in this design. A #10 crewel needle is used to lay the strands of floss, and a bead is added to the middle brick stitch of every pavillion variation. The beaded stitch is shown in the overall pattern chart below, but this is an optional addition.

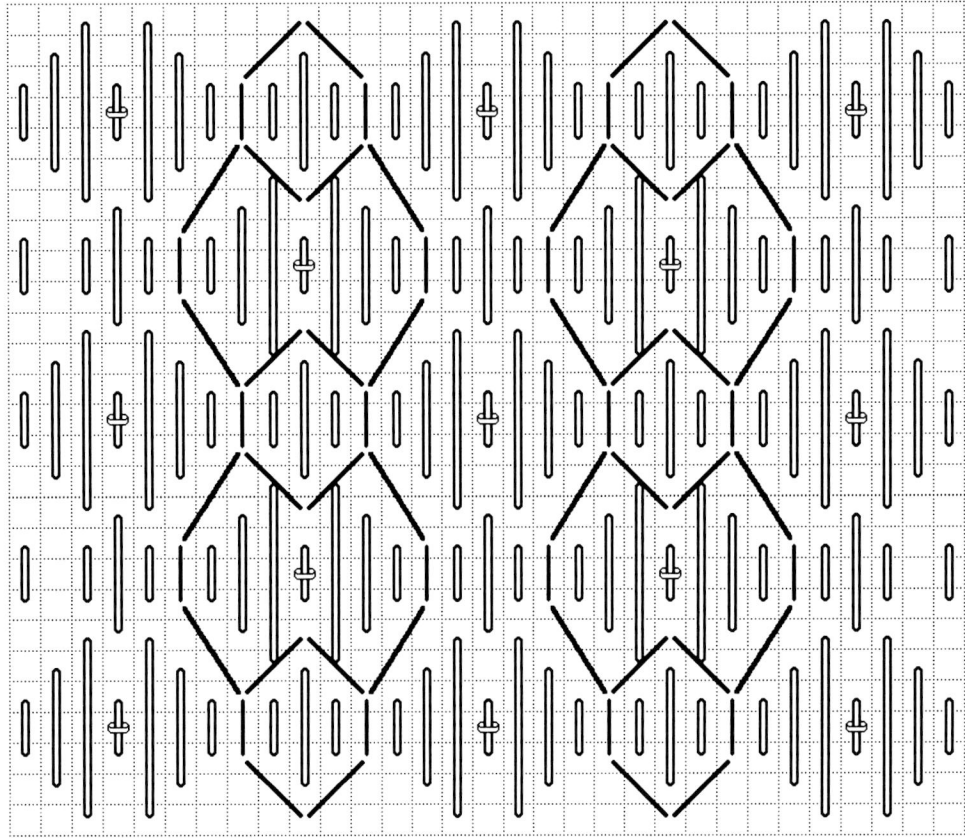

**OVERALL
CHART
PATTERN 46**

NOTE. None of the canvas stitches in this pattern share holes. Be careful to lay the stitches in the early rows accurately, as there is a tendency to crowd or overlap the horizontal rows. This would create an interesting variation to the pattern but it is not the one presented.

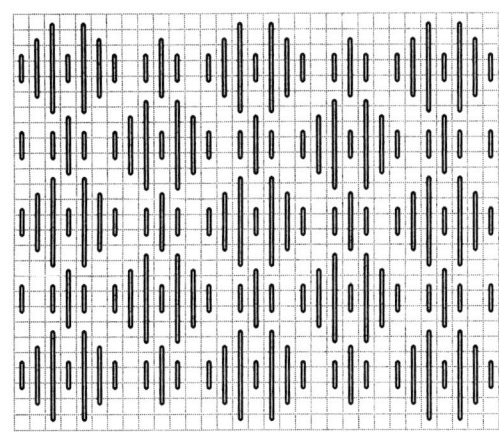

PATTERN 46 - STEP 1 OUTLINE

The open canvas network is composed of staggered horizontal rows of alternating Hungarian and pavillion variation. Pavillion stitch is usually an enlarged Hungarian or diamond shaped unit, but a brick stitch is substituted in this variation for the usual long center stitch. There is an open hole between the alternating units so they are separated and do not touch.

NOTE. The step 1 outline above does not show any beaded stitches. Notice the pretty open diamond pattern created in the negative spaces with just step 1 by itself.

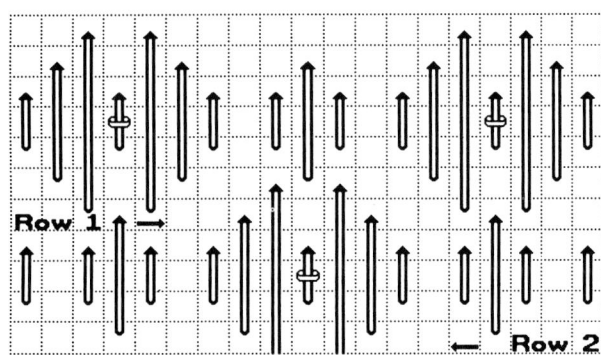

PATTERN 46
STEP 1 SEQUENCE

This sequence includes the beads on the center brick stitches of the pavillion variation units. Work these rows in a horizontal direction back and forth. If beads are added, be sure to tighten them securely on the stitch that follows so that they don't droop when the design is mounted.

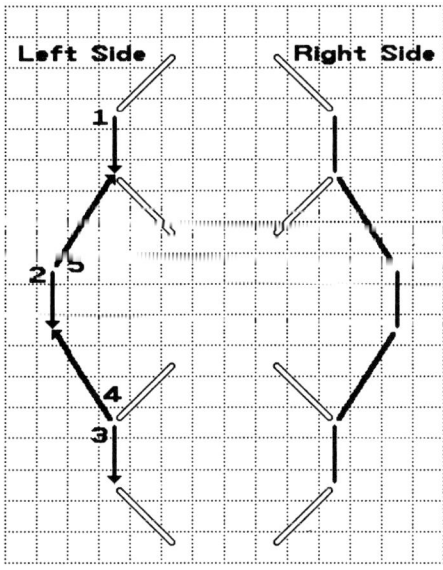

PATTERN 46 - STEP 2 SEQUENCE

Blackwork sequence. The blackwork outline is worked in vertical rows, using the numbered sequence to the left. Work one double running stitch path with side trips for the left side and one double running stitch path with side trips for the right side of the symmetrical outline. The side trips of the right and left paths share holes along the center axis of the vertical rows.

Use the overall chart on page 132 to assist with the placement of these rows.

IMPORTANT. Add the side trips after stitches 1, 2, 3 and 5. On the return trip keep the side brick stitches on the outside of the traveling threads of stitches 4 and 5. This makes the rounded turn swell out. However, stitches 1 and 3 should appear to swell in the opposite direction since the row undulates. The left and right sides of each row should also present mirror image views for total consistency.

A pattern variation is shown below that uses an allover blackwork pattern around the open canvas segment of the Pattern 47 network. The blackwork sequence for this version is the same as that of the original pattern except there are additional side trips immediately before and after stitch 2 on both the left and right sides. These diagonal stitches complete the blackwork outline in the "in between" canvas rows so that the pattern is no longer a stripe.

OVERALL CHART
PATTERN 46
VARIATION

PATTERN 46
VARIATION
STEP 2
SEQUENCE

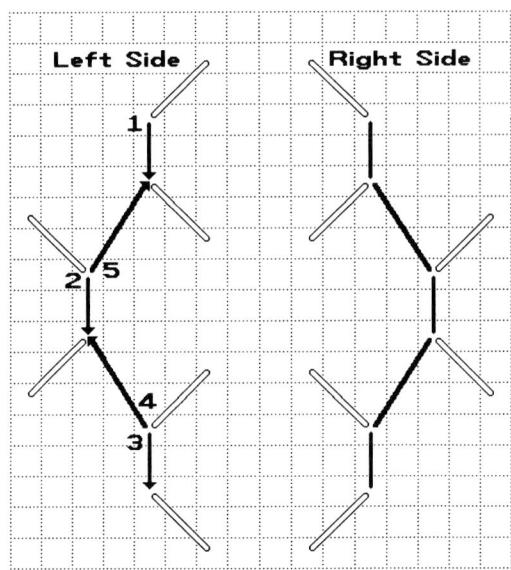

PATTERN 47. This pattern was adapted from a fabric that was printed in a black and white counterchange treatment. The canvas outline is a series of four-way clusters of elongated cashmere stitches. These are arranged in an offset placement so that the row directions are slanted rather than diagonal. The canvas stitches form an attractive open pattern by themselves but I decided to embellish the negative spaces with a blackwork pattern to form a composite treatment. The blackwork motif is an upright cross outline with rectangular shapes to fill the leftover spaces in each corner. The blackwork sequence is a double running sequence with side trips that connect the rectangles. Each separate blackwork section is completed as an individual unit, however, and the thread must travel in the canvas outlines to get to the entry point of the next unit.

The overall chart for this pattern and the blackwork sequence chart are found on the next page. A chart for the step 1 canvas pattern follows on page 136. The graphs fit the pages better this way since the pattern is a large scale one.

OVERALL CHART - PATTERN 47

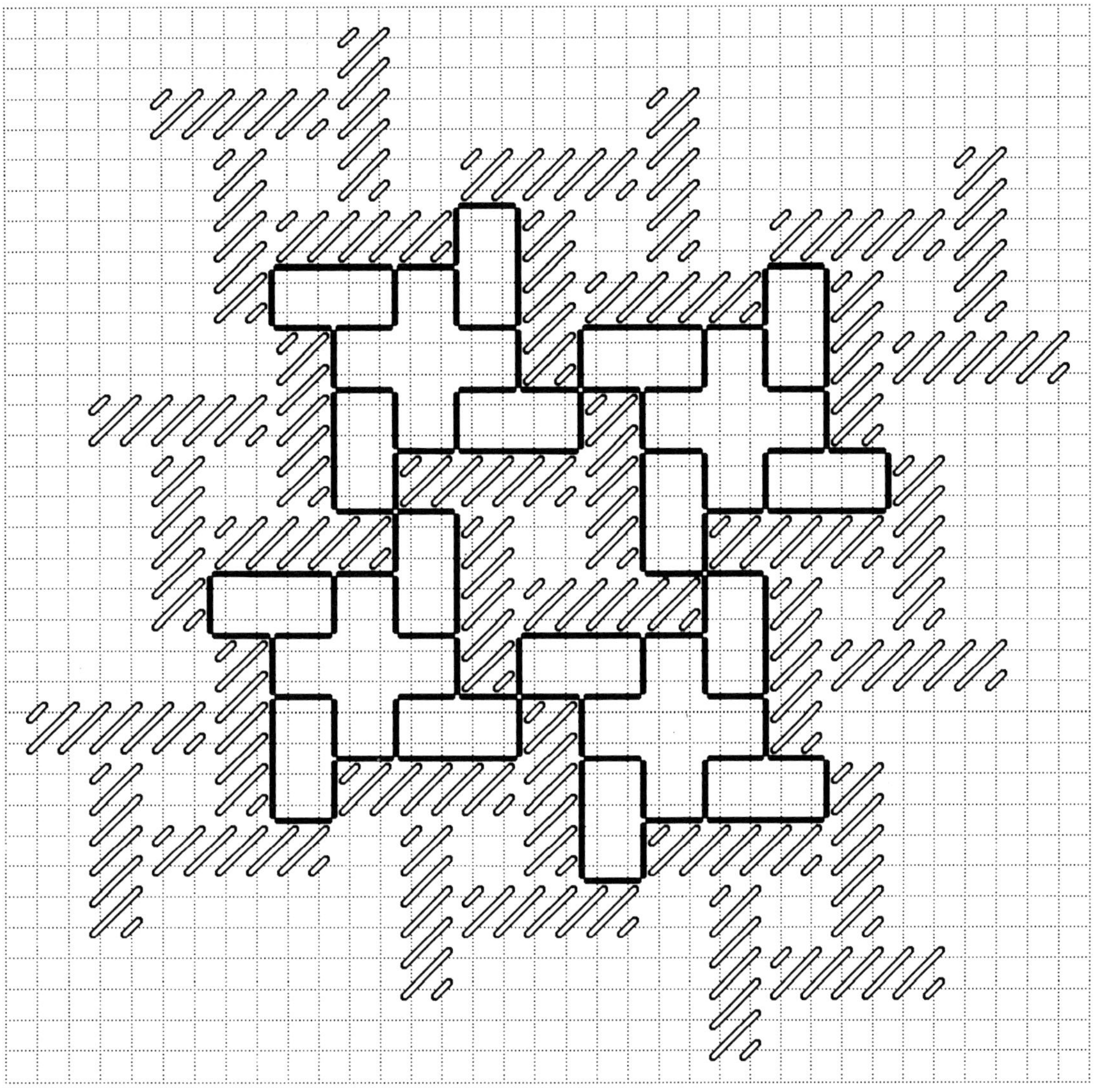

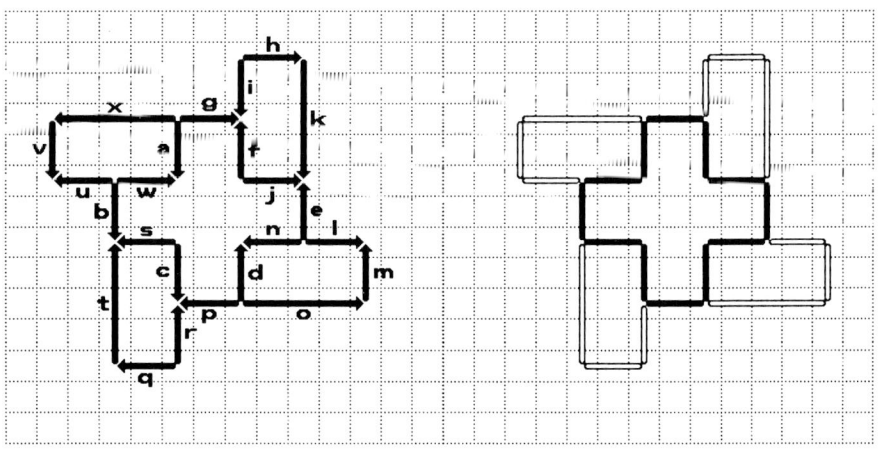

PATTERN 47
STEP 2
BLACKWORK
SEQUENCE

The left side of the chart shows the lettered sequence which uses a double running path. The right side of the chart shows the main path as dark outlines and the side trips as open stitches.

PATTERN 47 - STEP 1 OVERALL CHART AND SEQUENCE

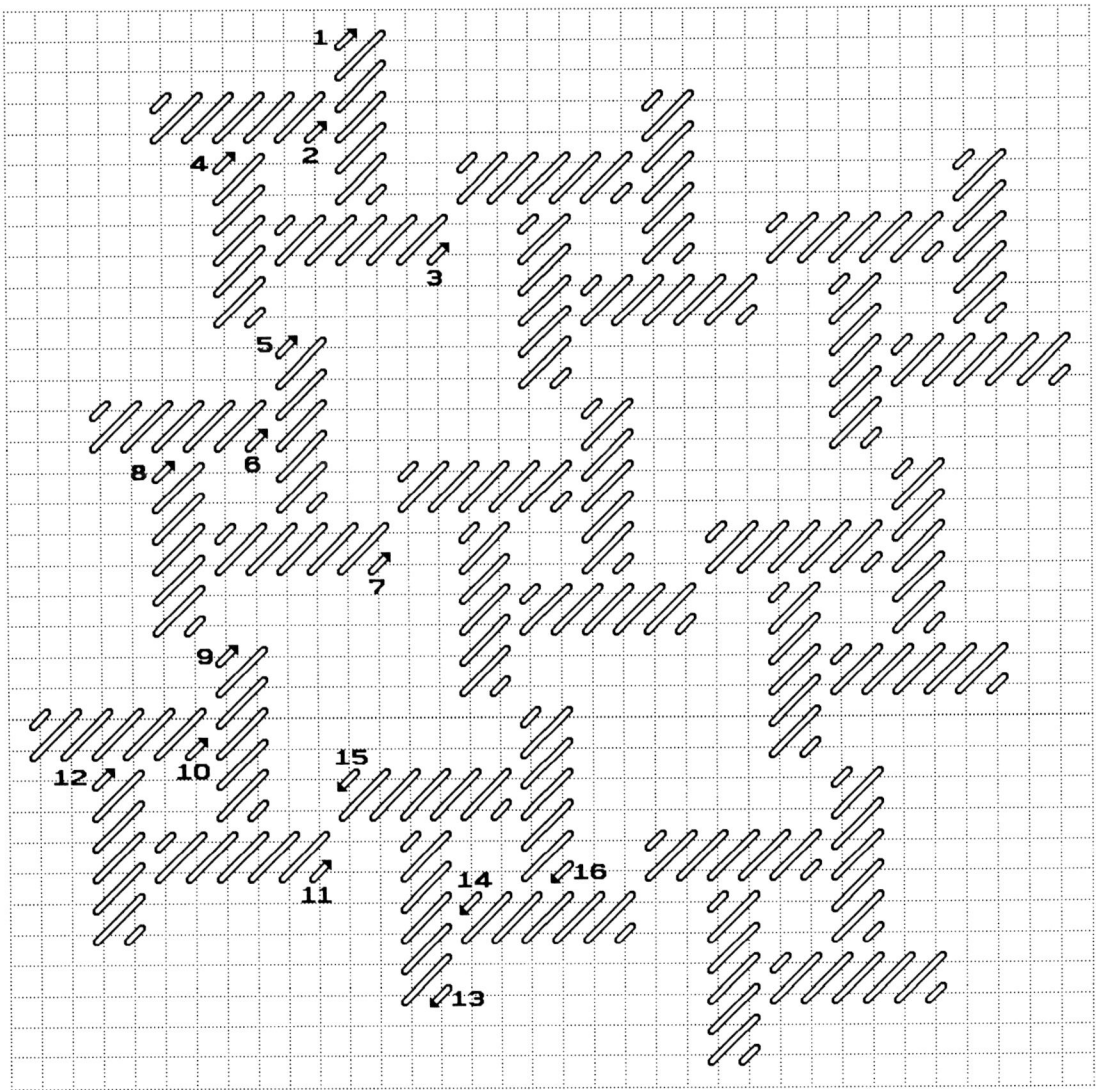

Step 1 Sequence. Use the chart above to place the canvas pattern. Work the clusters of elongated cashmere units in vertical rows, as numbered above. Each number shows the stitch direction and first stitch of each unit, and each unit is stitched in sequential order before going to the next one. After units 2, 6, 10, and 14, weave the thread back through to the bottom of units 1, 5, 9, and 13 to travel neatly to the next unit.

Step 2 Sequence. After the canvas filling is completed, use the sequence chart at the bottom of page 135 to add the step 2 blackwork pattern. Even though the blackwork pattern is continuous, it is easier to execute each separate motif individually since the pattern is complex, and the "main path" crosses do not connect. It is also cleaner to add all of the side trips on the return trip since the path zigzags better when they are added here. Weave through the canvas pattern to get to the entry points of adjacent blackwork motifs and add them in the same sequence.

PATTERN 48. The last pattern in this chapter is a combination of two compatible patterns. The exposed canvas pattern is a square network that combines a double straight cross and an enlarged double straight cross in an alternating repeat. It is stitched as step 1. The blackwork pattern is also a square network that combines a star motif and a hexagon in an alternating repeat. It is stitched as step 2.

OVERALL CHART - PATTERN 48

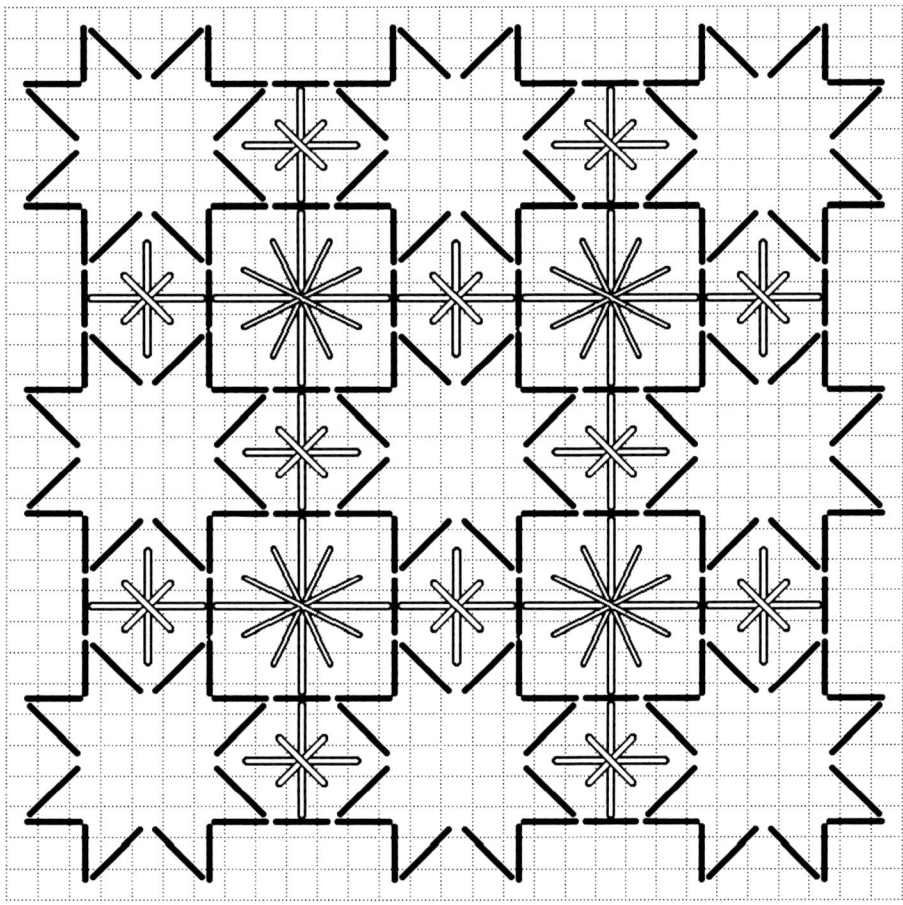

Step 1 Sequence. Use the overall chart on the next page to stitch the step 1 canvas pattern. It shows a lettered sequence to execute this pattern in vertical rows. The traveling threads are automatically concealed if this sequence is used, and stitch s is the repeat point so return to a to continue the next repeat. Notice that the double straight cross units to the left and right of the enlarged double straight cross are lettered in as "side trips" off of the vertical path. This concept in blackwork can be applied to a canvas sequence as well, and it was done earlier in Pattern 40, which was a diagonal path. This allows you to add adjacent units without additional horizontal paths so it minimizes the number of rows needed to complete the pattern.

Notice that stitches g-h and m-n are taken in the reverse order from stitches a-b of the first unit. This alteration allowed the traveling thread to be concealed, and since the top cross hides this change in the order of the layers, the inconsistency does not matter. Such efficiency measures are acceptable when they do not alter the appearance of the stitches in an obvious way.

137

To add the remaining row to the right of row 1, use the same vertical sequence, but eliminate the g-j part of the first row since it is not needed.

Step 2 Blackwork Sequence. Use the isolated overall chart and sequence chart below along with the chart on page 137 to add this segment. The blackwork sequence is done in vertical rows, using one double running path with side trips for the left side of the repeat and another double running path for the right side. The paths are mirror images of each other and easy to follow.

**PATTERN 48
STEP 2 OVERALL
CHART AND SEQUENCE**

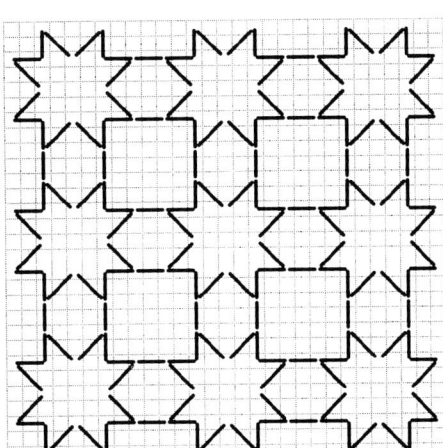

STEP 2 SEQUENCE

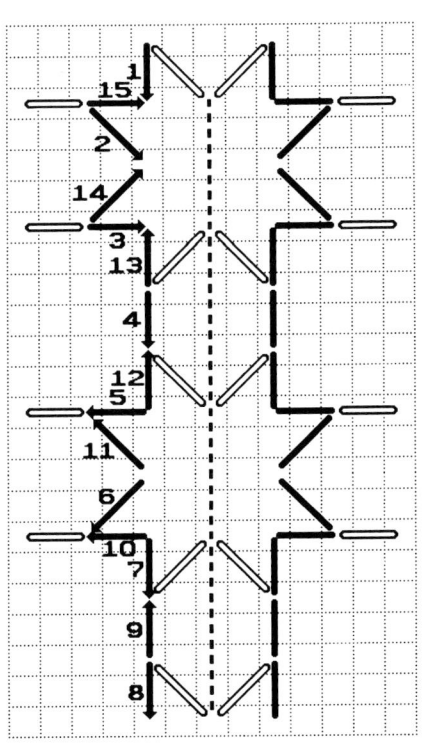

NOTE. Take the side trips after stitches 3, 4, two after 7, 10, 11, 13, 14, and 15 to get the optimum angle for each single side trip. The straight ones will be tricky to seat but will still lay straighter when added on the return trip.

138

If the straight side trips are added to both sides of the middle row, no side trips will be needed in the adjacent vertical rows. Try to keep the three straight stitches in a row as uniform as possible. The vertical groups will be easier since the diagonal side trips allow you to detour with a clean zigzag on both the running stitch row and the return trip.

This concludes the chapter on blackwork patterns that are combined with exposed canvas networks. Some examples were presented that used continuous blackwork patterns with continuous open canvas patterns. Other examples used continuous open canvas patterns with isolated blackwork motifs. Still other examples used continuous blackwork outlines with isolated canvas accents inside the negative spaces formed by the blackwork. Some composite patterns used blackwork outlines to punctuate or reinforce the shapes left by the exposed pattern networks whereas other composite patterns used different but compatible blackwork motifs inside the negative shapes formed by the open canvas networks.

As illustrated, this concept of combining the two types of patterns in an exciting way is quite versatile, and it is fun to analyze a single pattern of either type and see what additional accents could be added to create an original composite pattern.

CHAPTER 6 - MISCELLANEOUS BLACKWORK TREATMENTS

This chapter will explore additional ideas for blackwork, but there is only one example of each technique since these are not major categories of pattern. Instead additional ways to use blackwork within a design will be discussed. In some cases black and white photographs will be used to illustrate certain treatments.

Blackwork as a Background Treatment

Blackwork is used as an overall background in both *The Heart of Blackwork* design on the cover of the book and in *Mamadillo* (Color Plate III). A more specialized background treatment is used in the two Japanese lantern designs below, however. Each lantern is surrounded by a mat that is stitched in blackwork. Both the mat outlines and the patterns selected for the interior fillings are very oriental in feeling, and the stitched mats are an integral part of the overall design.

Notice how there is another blackwork pattern included in the actual lanterns themselves to "echo" the mat use. This use of repetition as a device serves to unify both designs and keeps them from looking like samplers of techniques. All of the blackwork patterns in these lanterns are traditional patterns except for the interior pattern of the round lantern which is Pattern 17.

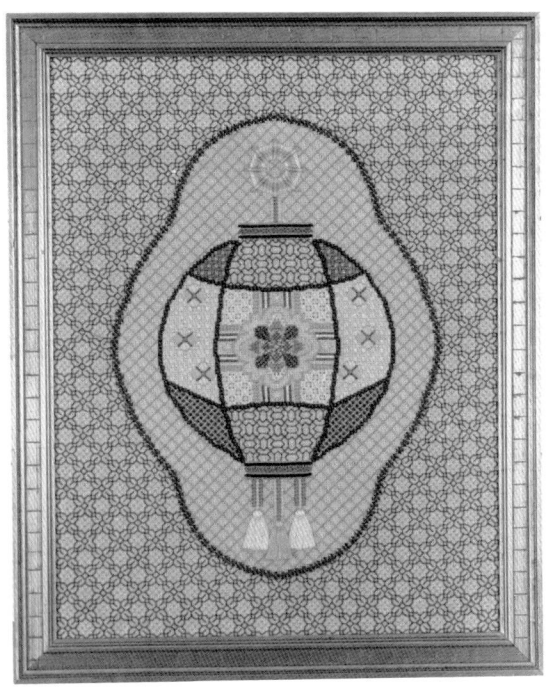
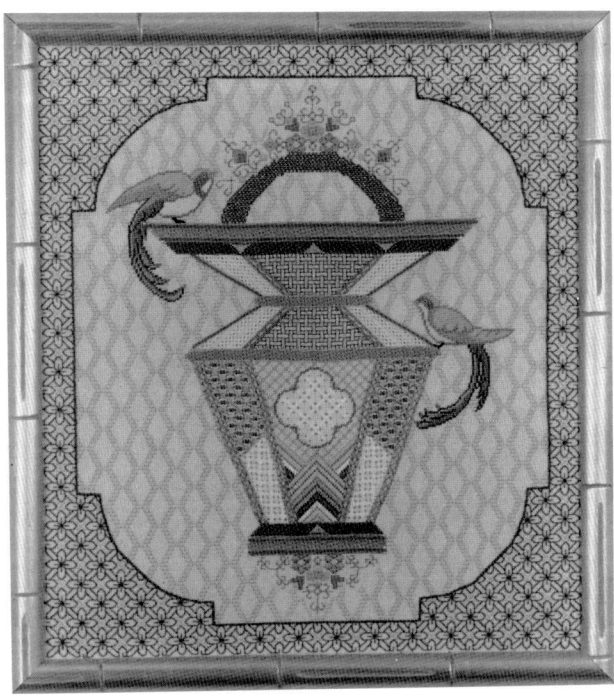

Blackwork as a Border Treatment

Blackwork can also be an effective accent in a border treatment, or a blackwork pattern can be an attractive border by itself. In the Assisi Angel design below, a double running border was developed that uses appropriate Christmas motifs that compliment the design. The design is mounted on a band box top so the border was planned to reinforce this circular shape. Although this design is done on Aida cloth there is no reason why a similar circular border could not be planned for a canvas design.

The mixed media pattern on the right below is a natural stripe that would make an attractive border. It could be combined nicely with either of the two small Diaper Medallions that are shown in Color Plate XIV. Such four-way patterns make ideal corner motifs. Stripe patterns make particularly effective borders since borders are "ribbons" or narrow strips around the edge of an overall design.

Assisi Angel

Border Stripe

Sometimes an overall pattern can be converted to a stripe by either changing an interior segment or by modifying it in some way to create a linear thrust. Pattern 49 on the next page is a pattern that could make an attractive border or stripe.

PATTERN 49. The foundation of this composite pattern uses an interesting sort of leaf motif. It is arranged in rows of flip-flop units that make it unusual and dramatic.

OVERALL CHART - PATTERN 49

The in-between rows are also staggered in placement, and the negative spaces created form the same flip-flop pattern in a horizontal direction. The leaves appear to be facing in four directions at once, and this kind of pattern is called a "quartered counterchange." It appears complex, but in actuality it is easy to isolate them into simple vertical or horizontal outlines.

PATTERN 49
OVERALL CHART
STEP 1

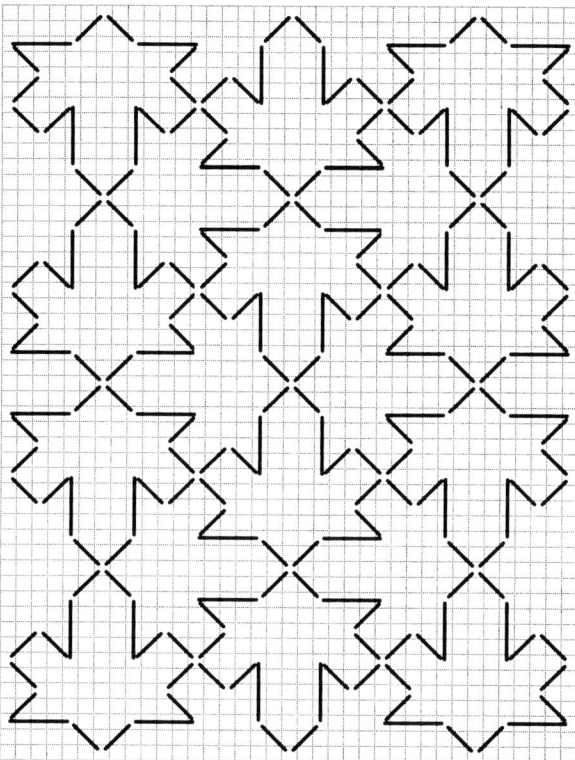

STEP 1 SEQUENCE

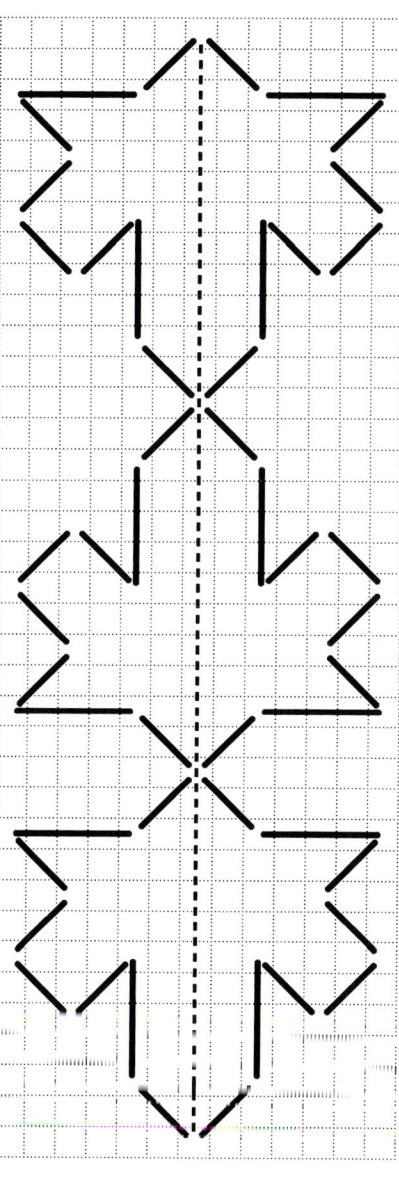

Step 1 Sequence. The flip-flop or inverted leaf outline is a simple one that divides in half easily. Use the overall and sequence charts above to outline both the left and right sides of each vertical row in a double running path. There are no side trips in the outline, and all of the diagonal stitches straddle two threads, but the straight stitches straddle 4 threads.

Step 2 Sequence. The step 2 sequence is actually the same step 3 blackwork pattern shown in Pattern 30 on page 107. Use the sequence chart on page 108 to execute this part of the pattern, but merge the pairs of diagonal stitches over two threads to single stitches over four threads. This pattern will overlap the step 1 pattern so it is a superimposed layer.

Below are two overall charts that show this pattern as a stripe. Five rows of the step 1 leaf outline are used, but no step 2 sequence is applied to the middle row. This creates an interesting stripe that could be used as a border.

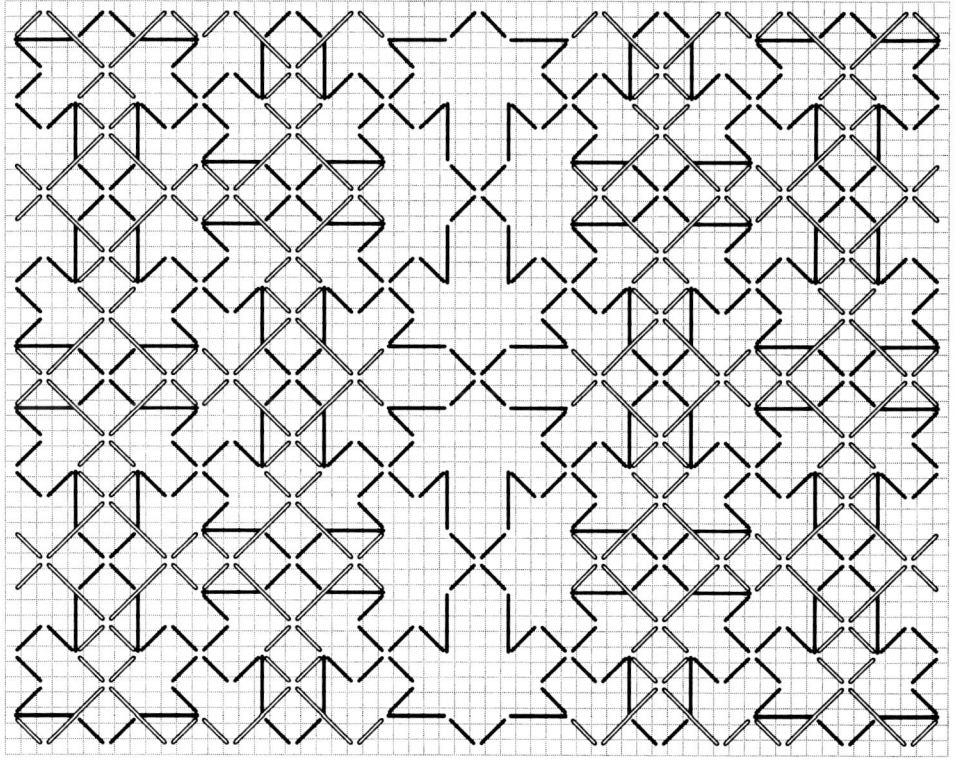

**PATTERN 49
BORDER
VARIATION**

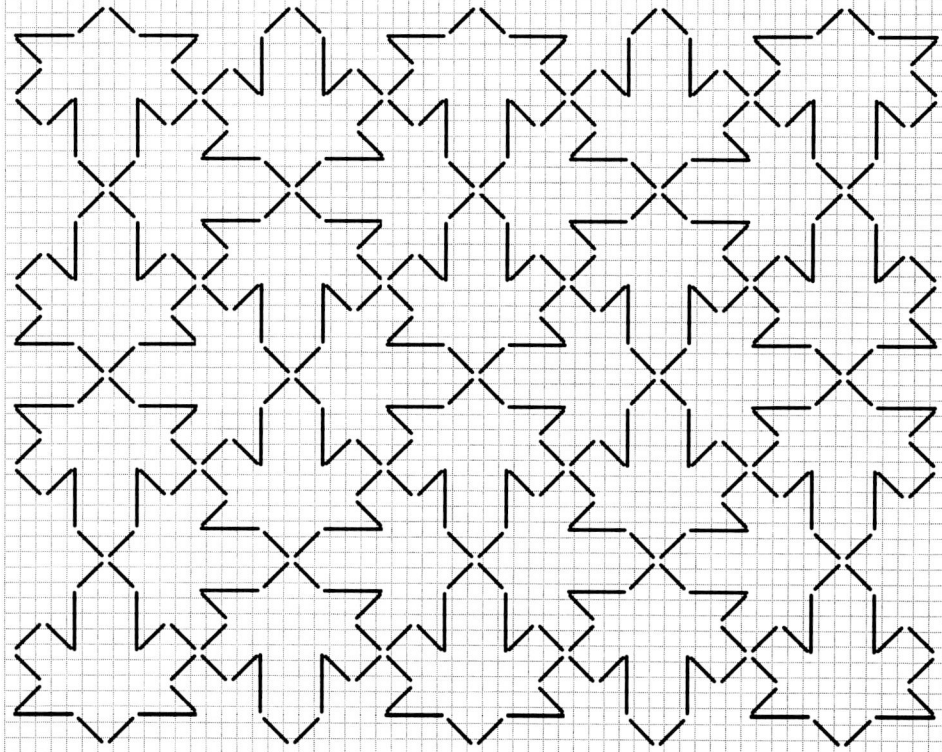

**PATTERN 49
BORDER
VARIATION
STEP 1**

The application of blackwork to define a shape is a concept that can apply to almost any pattern since each one is based on a particular pattern network with a specific motif. However, a blackwork pattern was actually created to suggest the leaves in the floral design shown on page 147. The shape itself is somewhat stylized, but so is the rest of the design in its effort to interpret something naturalistic with geometric shapes. Each repeat of the pattern does not resemble a leaf, but multiple repeats serve the purpose nicely. Only a small change in the last repeat at the base of the shape was needed to suggest a stem.

OVERALL CHART - PATTERN 50

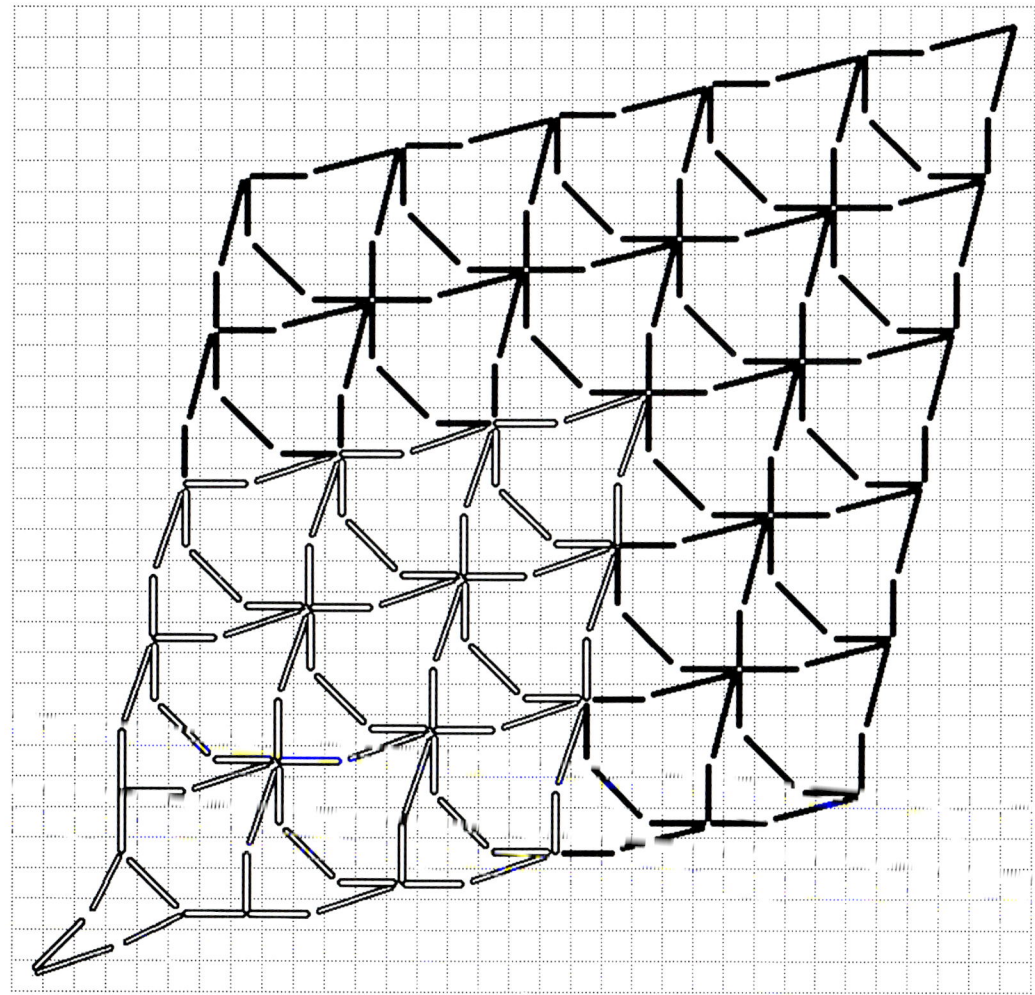

The view of the leaf shown above shows a shaded area at the base. This area was executed in a dark value thread in the original design whereas the remaining part of the pattern used a medium value. The sequence for executing these outlines involves two diagonal double running paths. The first path (step 1) outlines the top of each motif, and the second path (step 2) outlines the base of each motif. Because of the placement of the motifs, an attractive negative space that resembles an arrowhead or a boomerang results between the units. The sequence chart below isolates the two separate double running paths so that they are easy to follow. Therefore no numbered sequences are needed. Since the two rows connect it is easy to move from one to another.

As the rows widen, however, it will be necessary to travel with a "front stitch, back stitch" sequence along the upper edge to add part of the upper row and to get to the entry point for the second part of each new row (see the lettered sequence provided below on the right. Stitches n-o show the "front stitch-back stitch" trip that carries the thread to the entry point of step 2 of the second row).

Again double running is used not to make a pattern reversible, but to make it tidy. This interruption of the normal sequence adds to the overall efficiency in outlining the pattern yet it makes no difference in the appearance of the pattern on the front side. Therefore the advantages of altering the pattern sequence outweighs any minor discrepancies in consistency.

<table>
<tr><td align="center">**PATTERN 50**
SEQUENCE CHART</td><td align="center">**PATTERN 50**
LETTERED SEQUENCE
(First two repeats)</td></tr>
</table>

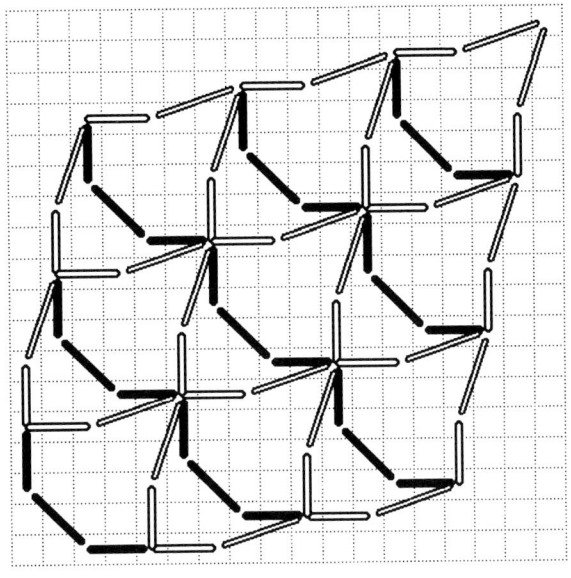

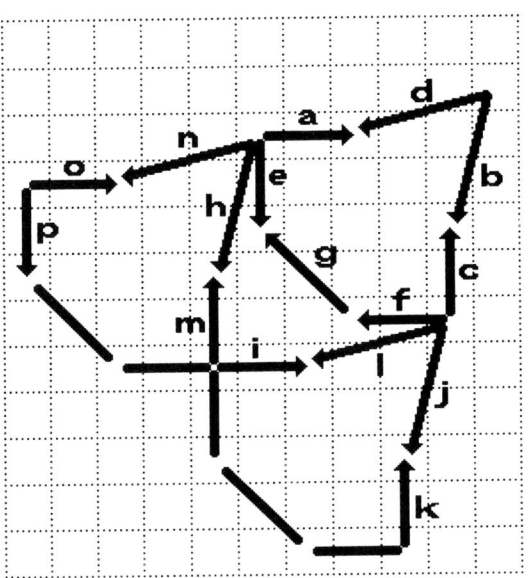

SINGLE
REPEAT

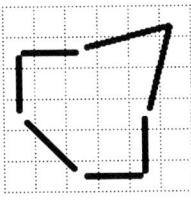

NOTE. The chart to the left shows one repeat of the leaf pattern. In the sequence chart above, the open stitches show the step 1 part of each row of motifs. The solid stitches show the step 2 part of each row of motifs.

Blackwork Used over a Gauze Foundation

In the *Comely Catfish* design (Color Plate XV) the large stomach area has a yellow transparent and iridescent fabric that has been applied to the canvas before the blackwork overlay is stitched through both the layer of fabric and the canvas holes (which are visible through the sheer fabric). This tightly woven fabric is available today in a variety of shades, and as long as a sharp needle is used to stitch the blackwork, the fabric does not run.

In order to secure the fabric, an outline of basting was stitched around the shape before the blackwork was added. After the blackwork was completed, the raw edges of the fabric were neatly trimmed close to the basting with a pair of sharp tapered scissors (I find cuticle scissors particularly useful and comfortable for this task when the shape is curved). This basting is hidden behind the rows of Japanese gold that were used to outline the entire fish after the individual body areas were embellished with a variety of couching treatments. The blackwork in the stomach area is also a form of "couching" since it is used to hold the fabric firmly in place as well as to embellish it. This technique is a nice way to add a color contrast to a canvas – and to add a metallic highlight in this case since the fabric chosen has a metallic glimmer.

The small heart sample shown on the right side below is an example of the use of this fabric technique. The pattern for doing this simple sample follows on the next page.

Floral Fantasy   *Heart With Gauze Foundation*

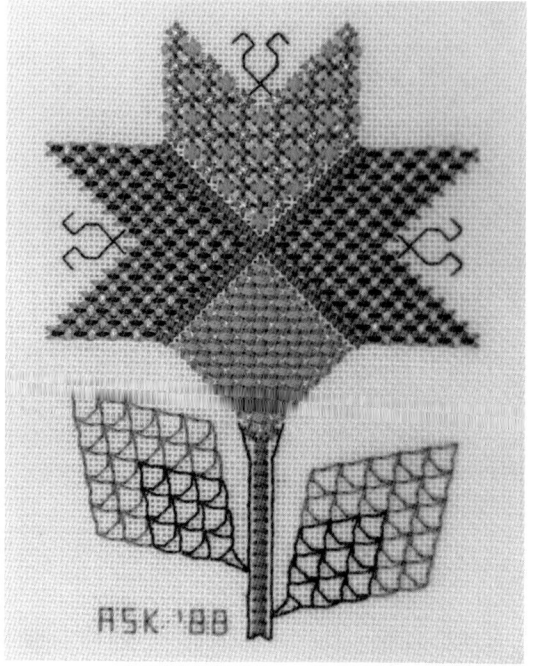 

The original heart sample was executed on a white 23-mesh Congress cloth ground. The outline (shown in open stitches along the edge) was done in a back stitch, using a #8 perle cotton in a light value. The double running rows (shown in the solid stitches inside the heart outline) were executed with a medium value floss, using two strands. The running stitch rows (shown in the open stitches inside the heart) were executed in a dark value floss, using two strands. Choose a pastel shade of the sheer fabric, and secure it to the canvas, using the back stitch outline rather than a basting outline. If the grain of the fabric is obvious, line it up with the canvas grain before the outline is started – a few pins in the corners will hold it securely until it is attached. Be sure no ripples form as the outline is stitched.

Step 1 Double Running Rows. Stitch these paths from left to right and back again for each row. Notice that the parallel rows are all two threads apart. Enter the fabric with the needle perpendicular to the canvas and fabric to keep the stitches clean through both layers.

Step 2 Running Stitch Rows. These diagonal rows are stitched in one direction only. In the center when the rows change direction, there will be a traveling thread that will carry across the open canvas. This is unavoidable, but it will create the same slight shadow on every row so it will not be unattractive or inconsistent. This traveling thread is indicated on the overall chart with a dotted line.

NOTE. Every row does not have a step 2 sequence. There are only five rows of this additional pattern.

This particular pattern illustrates one final point about blackwork patterns. If a pattern is a simple stripe outline, it can be rotated to form a mirror image pattern. The chevron pattern inside the heart is a "rotated" version of Pattern 23 on page 97 (without the tramé, of course). Since the heart is a symmetrical shape with a center axis, it looks particularly nice to have a chevron shaped pattern inside that fits it so gracefully. In Sampler 1 two variations of this pattern are used to fill Areas 4 and 6. They are rotated to fit the mirror image repeats of both shapes, and this makes the presentation that much more pleasing.

The heart in Color Plate X also uses the original version of a rotated Pattern 23 (with a tramé) in its background. However, the differences in tonal contrasts along with the addition of the tramé make this background appear almost unrelated to the same pattern used in the heart with the gauze foundation. The pattern in the heart with the bow has a definite vertical thrust whereas the pattern in the heart with the gauze foundation is a strong diagonal stripe. Notice how much denser the traméd pattern is as well.

This completes the section of miscellaneous pattern types. I hope it has provided some additional ideas for uses for blackwork in your future embroideries. Blackwork can be used effectively by itself or combined nicely with other canvas and counted thread techniques to form interesting designs and patterns. The possibilities are endless, and I hope my suggestions intrigue you. The next chapter on pattern design should also serve as a catalyst in igniting further enthusiasm for creating original pattern treatments and designs.

CHAPTER 7 - PATTERN DESIGN

Designing for blackwork is easier than for any other needlework technique because it is pure pattern with no consideration for color or texture in its traditional connotations. As you have discovered in this book, it can be combined with other canvas treatments for an unconventional effect, but a basic blackwork pattern is a simple linear outline that relies totally on contrast for its success.

Combining blackwork with other treatments complicates the issue of design a bit. However, I usually start with the blackwork pattern and then add other treatments to it once the dimensions of the blackwork outlines are established.

The exception to this approach is the group of patterns that have the open canvas lattice networks in them (chapter 5). In this case I usually create the open canvas pattern and then decide what extra embellishments would be appropriate. Sometimes a continuous blackwork pattern can be added to the remaining open areas. Other times an isolated blackwork filling is used in combination with other canvas treatments.

When couching is combined with the blackwork patterns, the blackwork is almost always planned first. Then the pattern itself will dictate a number of choices for the laidwork – either a one-way or two-way diagonal couching pattern, a vertical couching pattern, a horizontal couching pattern, or a combination of all three.

Pattern itself is everywhere, and it exists in two forms - both as irregular or random units or as structured measurable units. All forms of pattern can be an inspiration to an artist or embroiderer, but it must be controlled on canvas since it is a grid. Because blackwork is pure pattern it is possible to adapt almost any pattern to a blackwork outline. Often adjustments in proportion must be made to interpret a printed pattern on a grid, but since the essence of pattern is repetition, one starts with designing a single repeat of a pattern. Often a single unit or shape can be combined a number of ways to produce an interesting pattern.

When adapting from either natural sources of pattern or from printed sources, it is important to learn to isolate the underlying network upon which the pattern is based. Often color, texture and intricate details will disguise or obscure the basic "skeleton upon which the muscles and bones are placed."

Like books on color theory, pattern books tend to be complex and full of terminology that is not readily understood by a novice. Many books focus on the history of pattern rather than the structure of it. This is fascinating since different motifs were popularized by different cultures, and such information is very useful when one is planning a design that must reflect historical or ethnic accuracy.

However, to plan original patterns for counted embroidery, one must understand the construction of pattern and how to adapt it to an evenly woven fabric. In reality this fabric is not woven exactly so the grid is seldom true. Therefore a square pattern will seldom measure evenly after it is stitched – the weft sides are usually wider than the warp sides. The slight distortions in such stitched patterns are not obvious, but it is critical to know this when a design is being planned to fit a fixed finishing choice such as a place mat.

When designing a canvas for texture stitches and blackwork, a simple line drawing is usually the best starting point. Composite patterns need bold areas in order to be effective. An elegant handpainted canvas with sophisticated shading is restrictive since such intricate details can usually only be interpreted in small scale stitches like tent or encroaching gobelin that maneuver well in small areas. If texture stitch treatments are desired, it is better to design with large "blocks" of shapes or what is sometimes called "coloring book" simplicity. This does not mean that the design has to look like a child's drawing. It means that the subjects are reduced to less detailed stylized forms that accommodate pattern nicely. The embroidery itself will make these simple lines appear much more sophisticated when the design is completed.

One must also learn to choose shapes that adapt well to a canvas interpretation. Although paisleys with their graceful curved lines are an exciting and beautiful category of pattern, they can be a challenge on a counted fabric. Quilt patterns on the other hand are an ideal choice because the inherent geometric shapes of most traditional patterns adapt well to interpretation on a structured canvas grid.

Once the basic style and shapes of a canvas design have been determined it becomes easier to design specific patterns for the areas involved. One classic rule regarding pattern is that the scale of the pattern must be appropriate to the size of the shape. A good guideline here is that a minimum of 3-4 repeats must be visible in at least one direction for a pattern to be comfortable within a shape. The reason for this is that the essence of pattern is repetition, and if there are not enough repeats visible to clarify the rhythm or flow of the pattern, the eye cannot compensate and appreciate its beauty.

With such restrictions, how does one go about creating appropriate patterns? Two methods can be used to design an original blackwork pattern. The first way is to borrow a published pattern from a non-embroidered source and translate it into a blackwork outline, using individual stitches to reproduce the pattern lines onto a grid. The second way is to doodle a single pattern motif on a piece of graph paper and repeat it to form a pattern. A small motif will create a small scale pattern, and a large motif will create a bold pattern. Sometimes these doodles are influenced by physical surroundings, but more often I just begin to play with various geometric shapes until something pleasing emerges.

Regardless of what method is used, it is essential to have a good understanding of basic pattern networks and how pattern is constructed. A variety of reference books on pattern are included in the pattern bibliography. However, the book that I most recommend to beginners to learn the basics of pattern structure is Richard Proctor's *The Principles of Pattern*, which has recently been reprinted as *Principles of Pattern Design*. Mr. Proctor explains clearly and directly the eight basic networks on which repeat patterns can be constructed. These networks are the square, the diamond, the brick, the half-drop, the triangle, the hexagon, the ogee and the scale. All pattern is derived from one of these basic shapes. If these terms are not clear, an illustrated discussion of them is included at the end of the segment on pattern design.

Once the eight basic networks are familiar, the study of pattern becomes much more enjoyable. One will recognize key elements within complex patterns that will enable one to break them down into simple component parts and repeats. Once the structure is seen clearly, it is easy to adapt it to a useful needlework pattern and to eliminate any excessive lines.

Pattern is ubiquitous – so much so that we often take it for granted. Floral patterns tend to dominate in home decorating since they are natural and feminine. However, geometric patterning is also common and blends well with other types of patterning. When was the last time you appreciated the pattern on the kitchen floor? Bathroom tiles do not have to be simple squares. Did you ever notice the pattern on your mattress when you change the sheets? Walking through hotels is always an interesting experience since the carpets tend to have busy geometric patterns – not only are they more interesting but they do not tend to show soil or wear as much as solid colors do. Even bridge abutments tend to have interesting patterns in the concrete supports. Make it a habit to always carry a small pad of graph paper in your purse or brief case so that it is readily available to chart that irresistible "find." A quick sketch can often lead to a more refined and sophisticated pattern, but it is important to jot down the important elements while they are in front of you. Even though a moving target takes some finesse at times, I have several patterns that have been adapted from a man's tie or a lady's blouse that was noticed in an airport. Most subjects who notice you doodling are flattered by your interest and your acknowledgment of their good taste. Sometimes it is easier to photograph an architectural detail than it is to sketch it.

By now I think you have the idea. Books and printed material are helpful sources for developing blackwork patterns, but we constantly encounter pattern in our everyday lives so notice your surroundings. This seems to be an inborn trait for most stitchers as is our love of both color and threads. The trick is taking this stimuli and using it in an original way.

The best advice I can give you is to just try to do this. The more you endeavor, the more success you will have. I always develop patterns on graph paper with a pencil so that I can make changes easily. I generally work with a single repeat and refine it to a point where it is attractive. Then I extend the drawing to see how it looks as a multiple repeat. When you join segments of a symmetrical motif, you often get an interesting negative space between the repeated units that enhances the pattern that much more. Such spaces are usually large enough to accommodate some extra embellishment, if desired. This sort of trial and error approach generates lots of interesting possibilities, and an appealing linear outline will form the blackwork outline or the foundation for a composite treatment.

A computer can also be a useful tool for developing interesting outlines for blackwork patterns. Once a single repeat is drawn in a graphics program, it can be exploded into all kinds of interesting networks by using tools that allow you to create and connect multiple repeats in a fast efficient manner. It is also versatile in allowing you to rotate motifs and create many variations of a pattern outline in a relatively short time if the user is proficient.

Once the outline is established, the situation gets more complicated. Planning an appropriate double running sequence takes even more skill, but hopefully the contents of this book have provided a good foundation for you to start. Begin by studying the flow of the pattern to see how the units connect. Would horizontal, vertical or diagonal paths be more efficient? Would a series of side trips be needed, or can they be avoided with an alternative route? There is no question that someone who has a good puzzle-solving mind can see spatial relationships better and determine logical tracking sequences more readily. However, once you understand how pattern is constructed, you will begin to see the pattern flow more quickly. The more practice you give yourself, the more success you will have.

Once the blackwork foundation is established, there are endless choices in how to embellish the pattern further with additional accents. The variables multiply with considerations of color, texture and thread choice. However, no matter how much experience you have, you can seldom predict the final visual effect until a pattern is totally stitched. Small changes in color, value, thread weight, etc. can make a big difference in the final presentation and visual effect. The safest approach is to doodle first on a waste canvas rather than hope that your first instinct is going to be right in a finished design.

Some specific words of advice are listed as follows:

1. Always make sure that your pattern is the way you want it both close up and at viewing distance. Some helpful approaches to achieving this balance were discussed under section 4 on page 11.

2. Color interaction seldom shows up at close viewing so when working with close values in a composite stitch place it across the room before the final judgment is made.

3. Choose or develop patterns that reinforce the shapes within a design.

4. Choose patterns that compensate easily for difficult shapes. Patterns with upright and diagonal stitches compensate better than those with oblong stitches. Couching patterns maneuver well within any shape as long as the couching stitches are simple.

5. Center the patterns within a shape to create comfortable viewing. This can be measured within geometric shapes but it can also be judged by eye in irregular shapes.

6. Be careful with stripe patterns as they are dramatic and create motion. They can be used effectively to draw the eye to certain focal points and to add contrast, but four-way or allover patterns tend to make quieter backgrounds and do not upstage other elements.

7. Use variegated threads when you want random or irregular effects like shading. They tend to interrupt the flow of a regular pattern and negate the uniform repeats.

8. Maintain a balance within a design of different types of patterns or treatments. In pure blackwork create a variety of densities and balance them to keep the design from being monotonous.

On the next page there are two black and white photographs of Sampler 1 to illustrate the variety in the density of the patterns chosen. Notice too the nice balance of values that are achieved within the design. It is sometimes difficult to judge these value contrasts when a design is done in several colors, but a black and white photograph shows only value so it is a good evaluation tool. There is also a monochrome viewing filter that can be purchased at some photography stores that can be used to eliminate color when one wants to judge value contrasts.

The fuzzy out-of-focus view of the design also simulates what happens when you squint at a design to see if the contrasts are effective. This eliminates the detail of the patterns and shows only the value contrasts.

9. Too much busy pattern can be overkill - some "quiet" areas are needed to offset the most dramatic patterns within a mixed media design. A traditional blackwork pattern is striking in its clarity and contrast, but I have grown to like the variety that I can achieve by combining it with other treatments in a mixed media design. These additional options create more choices, but they also need balance and control.

10. If two colors are used, maintain a balance in the color distribution.

11. Wherever possible, use a pattern motif that is appropriate to the subject matter of a design. For example, in *Vowlentine*, (Color Plate XIII) I developed three blackwork patterns with heart motifs that were used in the "barn door" panels. These reinforced the theme of a "valentine" which the title also suggests in a humorous way.

In the *Raccsnack* design shown on the next page (another adaptation of a whimsical Charles Harper print), a blackwork pattern with a star motif was selected for the background area behind the raccoon and above the limb. It seemed to suggest the idea of a "starry night," which is also supported by the darning pattern used below the limb, which has a similar star-shaped repeat.

Raccsnack

Beyond these specific guidelines, I urge you **to study the principles of color and design as well as the principles of pattern. Few people have an eye or an instinct for this without some training.** Books are readily available today as are opportunities for classes on both subjects. General information can be helpful, but the most direct path to creative insight is likely to be the one which focuses on the unique idiosyncracies of textiles and embroidery. Seek other ways to expand your knowledge through local needlework shops and guilds. If the desire is there, the network to pursue such interests does exist.

Most of my growth was based on a healthy combination of ongoing education blended with a desire to be creative and go beyond what traditional embroidery styles offered. Once you have learned the basics, do not be afraid to challenge existing methods. Treat them as helpful guidelines and aim for something personal and unique. In the final analysis, it is the results that count, and "the end justifies the means."

IDENTIFICATION OF EIGHT BASIC PATTERN NETWORKS

The eight basic pattern networks include the following geometric shapes that form the understructure of all repeat patterns: the square, the diamond, the brick, the half-drop, the triangle, the hexagon, the ogee, and the scale. The illustrations that follow show these networks as blackwork outlines since this book is a study of blackwork patterns.

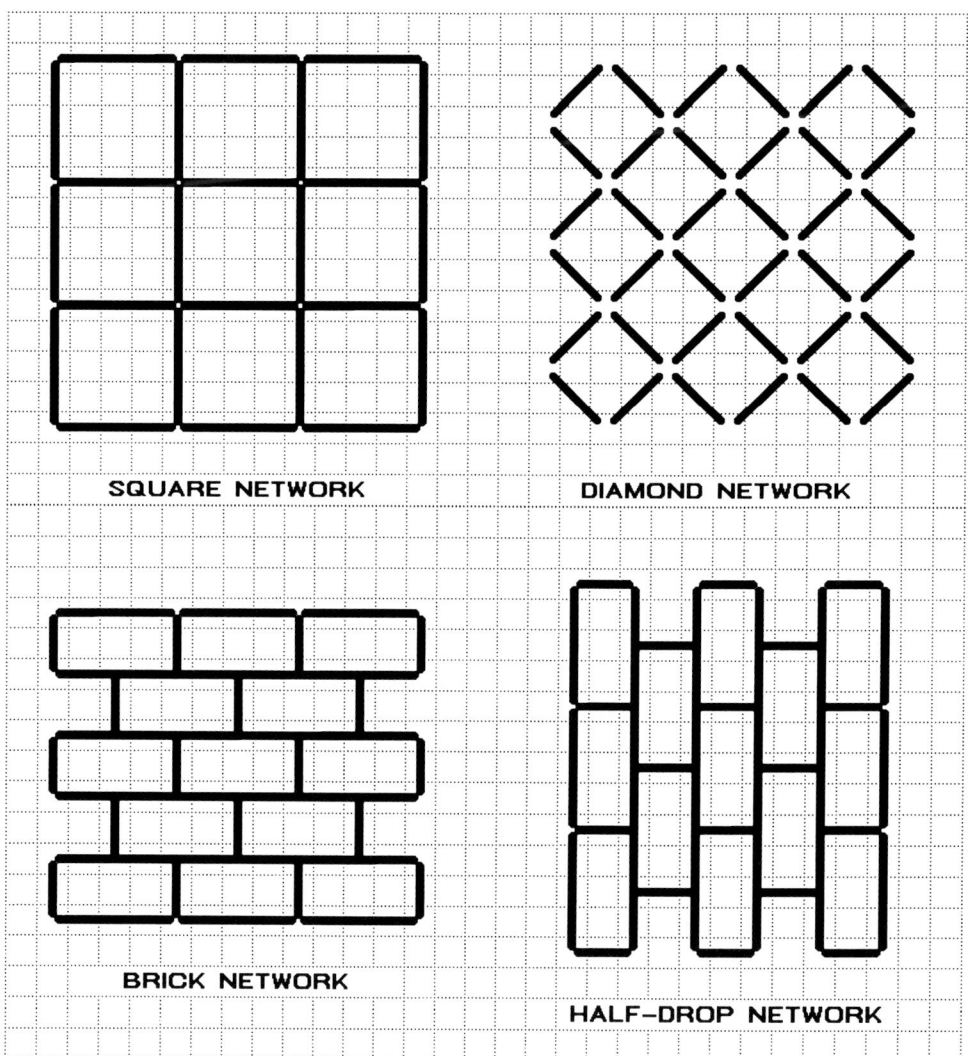

SQUARE NETWORK

DIAMOND NETWORK

BRICK NETWORK

HALF-DROP NETWORK

The chart above shows the first four basic pattern networks, and these are common in many canvas embroidery patterns. There are many box shaped stitches that form a square network when they are stitched as a solid filling. These include Scotch Stitch, Mosaic, William and Mary and Smyrna Cross. There are also many diamond shaped stitches that form diamond networks when stitched as solid fillings. These include Diamond Eyelet, Hungarian, Upright Cross and Double Straight Cross.

156

The brick and the half-drop networks are "cousins" in that if either network is rotated 90° it will form the other. Both networks are derived from simple variations of square or rectangular units that are arranged so that the alternating rows are staggered in either a horizontal arrangement for brick networks or in vertical arrangements for half-drop patterns. Although half-stepping is the usual proportion for these arrangements, many other combinations are common. In canvas embroidery, the cashmere stitch, or any rectangular or square unit, can be used to form either of these networks.

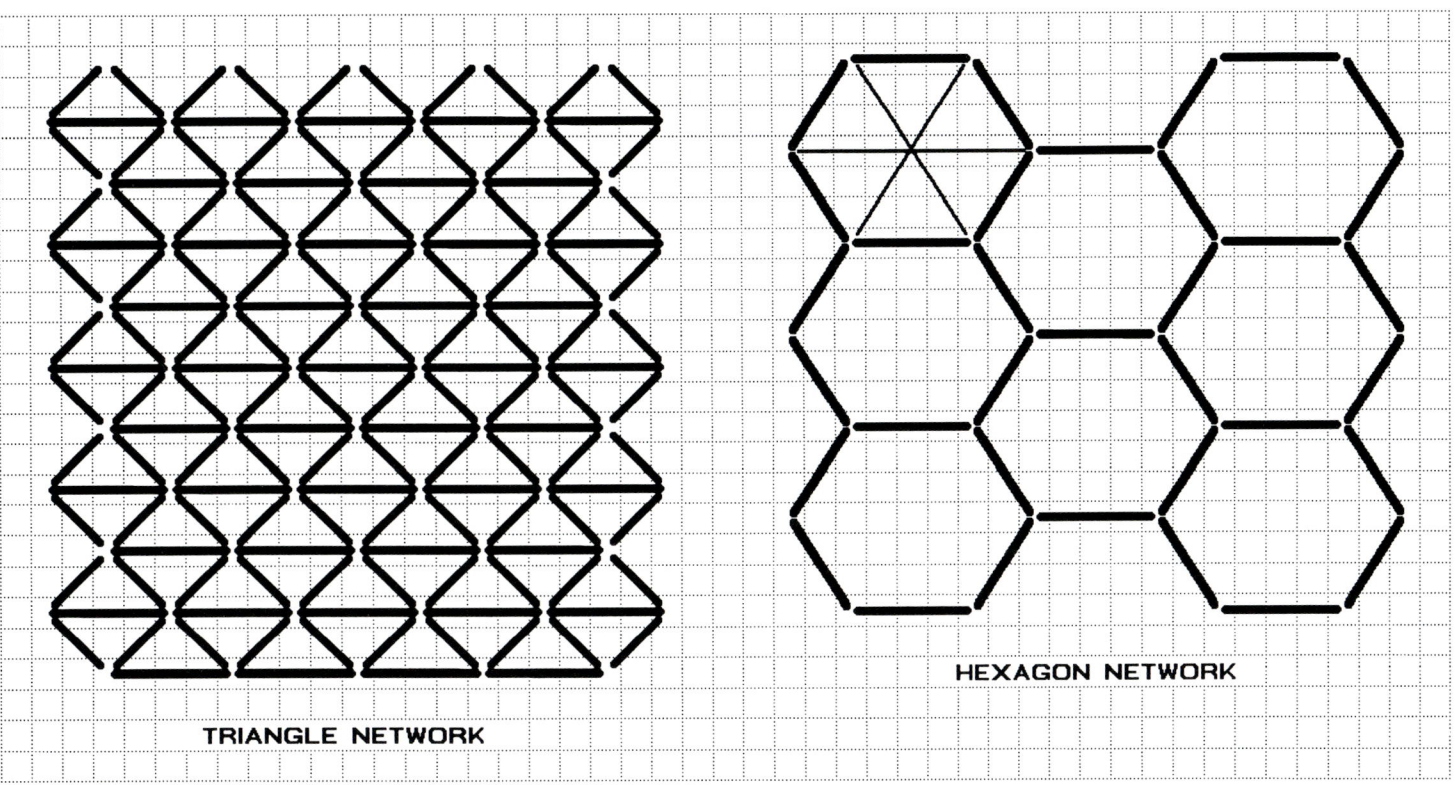

TRIANGLE NETWORK

HEXAGON NETWORK

The triangle is merely a half of a diamond shape, and the Milanese stitch is the "classic" canvas stitch that forms a natural triangle network. Combinations of parallel satin stitches can also be used to form a triangle shape.

The hexagon is a six-sided shape that can be formed by six triangles – hence the network chart above shows one unit that is divided into six equal size triangles. Any hexagonal pattern can be copied on canvas by using satin block triangles to form the hexagons and by changing colors at strategic points to follow the pattern repeats. As a matter of fact, there is a book called *Trianglepoint* that explores this premise (see the canvas bibliography).

The last two pattern networks are not common to actual canvas stitches, but they are very common in a category of canvas embroidery called Florentine Embroidery. Both the ogee and the scale pattern networks have curves in them that do not maneuver well on a grid.

157

However, straight stitches used in step formations can create lovely soft curves, so many Florentine or bargello patterns use these shapes.

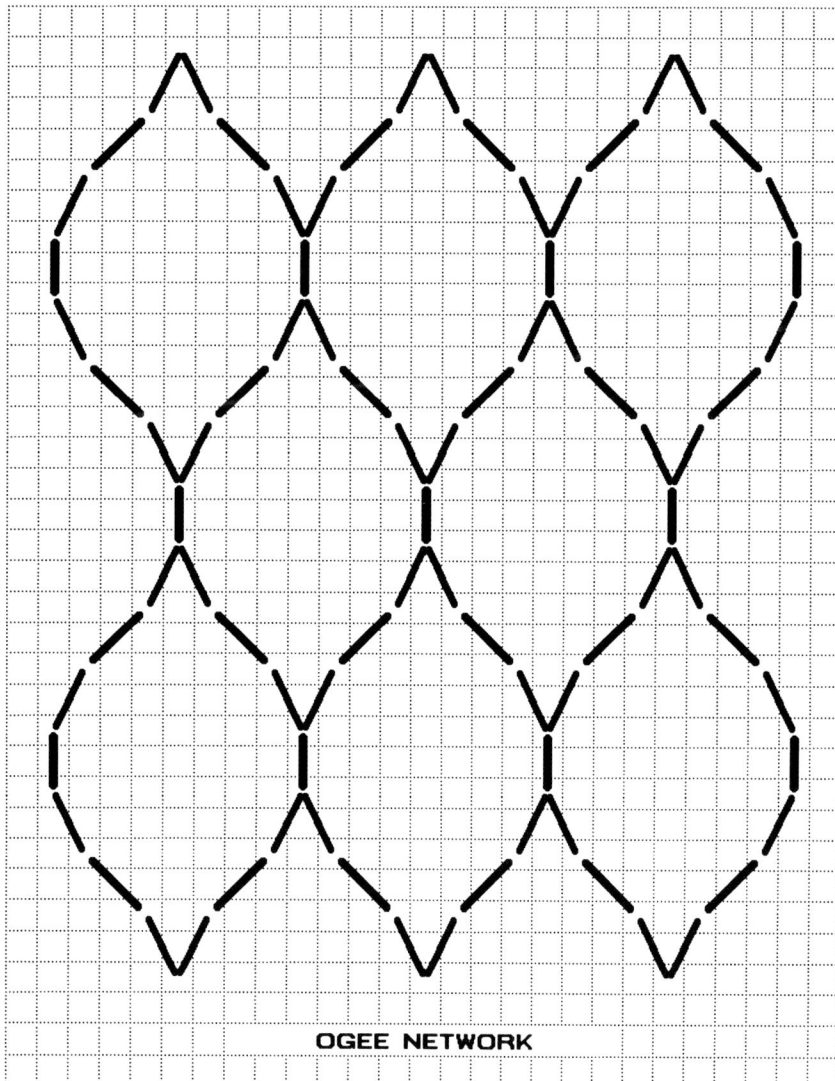

OGEE NETWORK

INSET

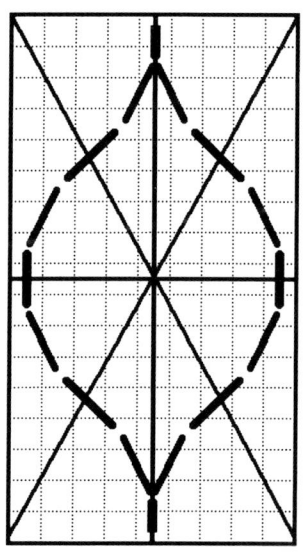

The inset chart above shows how the ogee network is based on the S curve. A diamond shape is divided into 4 equal shapes, and each shape has the same wavy line that has been rotated to form the ogee.

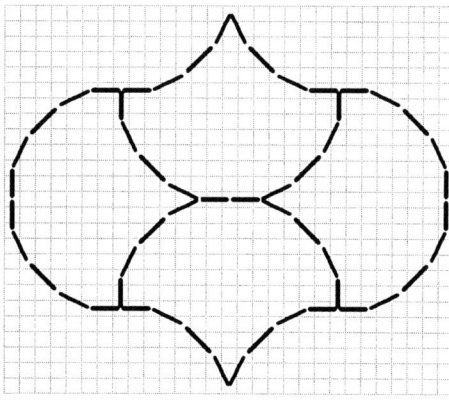

This elongated ogee is commonly associated with Christmas tree ornaments. However, the chart to the left shows a wide ogee that is formed by a four-way arrangement of scale units.

A tent outline could also be used on canvas to outline this shape, but notice how attractive the contours are in blackwork outlines that use a slanted gobelin stitch to suggest the curves.

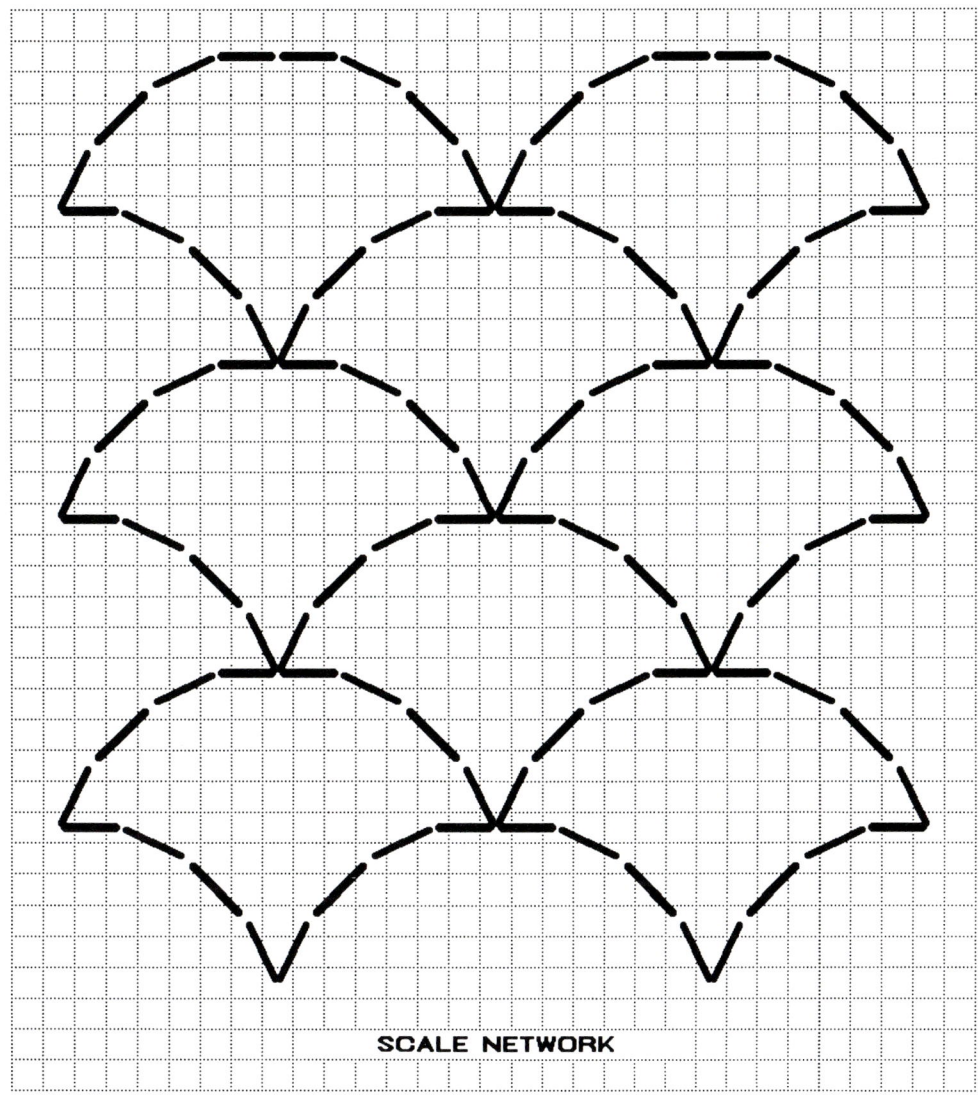

SCALE NETWORK

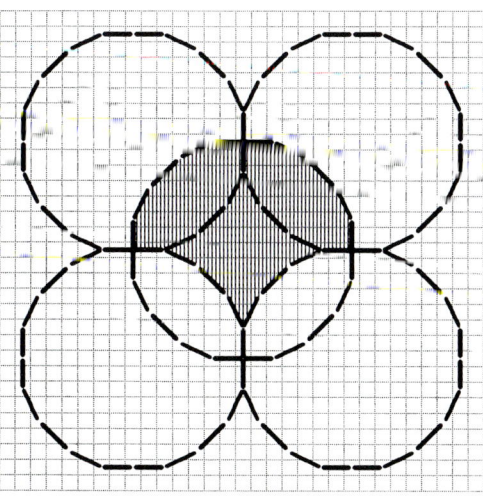

The chart above displays a scale pattern executed in a blackwork outline. The chart to the left illustrates the fact that a scale network is derived from a pattern of overlapping circles. The circle itself is not a basic pattern network because any arrangement of circles that are tangent to each other produces a pattern with negative or leftover spaces between the units (notice the small diamond that is part of the shaded scale). Therefore a circle cannot create a true "interlocking" network when it is repeated. A basic network must connect endlessly in any direction, but other types of networks can be constructed of noninterlocking shapes. For further study, please see the bibliography for pattern at the end of the book.

159

CHAPTER 8 - PROJECTS

The projects that follow are provided for those readers who prefer to stitch an overall design rather than individual stitch samples of each pattern. Fifteen of the patterns in the book are used in the two designs, and these include examples from a variety of types.

Both projects use simple bargello outlines to create interesting shapes. Patterns were selected for the shapes that are appropriate in scale and in density. Some, like the ogee pattern in Sampler 1, were deliberately chosen because they reinforce the shapes. This sort of graceful fit makes a pattern look comfortable, and when I don't have a readily available pattern for such shapes I usually create one.

All designs need diversity to be totally successful so I have used several values of two colors in the two samplers. Sampler 1 uses a complementary red-green arrangement, and Sampler 2 uses an analogous blue-purple arrangement. Since the outlines of both samplers are done in blended Watercolours, the individual blackwork patterns use only monochromatic colors that show up clearly beside the mixed outlines. All repeat shapes have identical fillings, however, to create balanced groups within the symmetrical contours of the designs.

None of the pattern areas are big enough to accommodate elaborate exposed canvas pattern networks, but some of the bold blackwork patterns have isolated canvas stitches in some of the negative spaces. Many of the patterns have tramé foundations, and these accents are usually in metallic thread.

Since all of the patterns are discussed in depth in the various pattern chapters, it was not necessary to repeat the instructions again here. In each case an overall pattern shape is provided that shows the placement of the pattern in my original model. When needed, additional remarks will accompany this chart.

A large colored picture is also provided for each sampler. Sampler 1 is shown on the back cover, and Sampler 2 is shown in Color Plate I . Use these photographs in combination with the stitch directions on the designated pages to plan your own samplers. There is no need to copy my combinations – just use the contrasts created as a guideline for creating a more personal statement. The more one experiments with color and value, the more one will learn about color interaction; some patterns will look surprisingly different when stitched with values that change the emphasis.

For those who want to explore further, I would recommend that you make small notebook samples of each pattern in the book to use as a reference. Many of the composite patterns can be done in a variety of combinations that will change the dominance and overall impression of the pattern so a record of these variations will prove helpful when you select the pattern for a finished design.

Have fun and be daring. I know I have only scratched the surface of what can be done with blackwork, and I hope my discoveries will inspire you to take it a step further.

SAMPLER 1 - BARGELLO WAVE GEOMETRIC

This sampler uses a bargello outline to create interesting shapes for blackwork patterns. The outline is a wave step pattern that undulates as the row direction changes. Two of the shapes formed are attractive ogees and hearts, and some dramatic stripes further enhance the design.

Most of the patterns in this design have straight stitches, but the ogee pattern (Area 2) has many slanted stitches so it is advisable to practice this one on a doodle cloth before trying to fit it into the shape provided. Other patterns are examples of superimposed patterns or patterns with tramé foundations. Two stripe patterns (Areas 4 and 6) are variations of the same network, and both patterns are used in a flip-flop placement to contour better to the mirror image shapes that they fill. The superimposed pattern in the border area also has beaded accents that are added as a third step after the blackwork layer is completed. Sometimes beads are incorporated into a pattern as it is stitched. This time, however, the beads looked better if they nested in the open centers of the small diamond outlines so they are added in a separate step.

The Springtime Watercolours is a combination of bright pink and mint green blended colors with some ivory accents. The patterns inside the outlines use similar pinks and greens, and the complementary color scheme minimizes the risk of any color interaction caused when close values of two colors are side by side. The analogous color scheme used in the second sampler was less predictable, and values had to be adjusted as the design was worked to keep the patterns from fading.

No sequence charts are provided in the instructions that follow. Only a pattern number and a page reference are needed for each area along with a thread key code. However, either a partial or whole area chart is available to indicate the pattern placement in each area. The appropriate compensation is also included, and if gaps appear on the charts, they are not mistakes. An omission merely means that the outline thread is heavy enough to overlap what appears to be an exposed thread so no compensation is needed.

Use the main road map and the detailed outline and individual area charts to execute the sampler along with the code key that follows. A materials list for my original sampler is provided for your convenience, and the instructions include the colors that were used in the original model.

CAUTION: Do not add any beads to the design until after all other areas are completed, as they tend to snag threads and get in the way if they are placed earlier. All of the areas in this design are repeated at least twice so it is tempting to forge ahead and try some of the later patterns before all of the repeat areas of earlier patterns are completed. The border area is numbered as the last area for a good reason, so heed!

161

SAMPLER 1 - MATERIALS LIST

12" Square stretcher frame (narrow strips)
12" Square piece of pink 23-mesh Congress cloth
Tapestry needles - size 22, 24, and 26   Crewel needle - size 8 (for beading)
Watercolours - 1 skein Springtime
#8 Balger metallic braid - 1 reel #024 Fuchsia
                                          1 reel #092 Star Pink
DMC floss - 1 skein #604 light pink
                    1 skein #603 medium pink
                    1 skein #498 red (or substitute a red silk instead)
                    1 skein #503 light green
                    1 skein #502 medium green
                    1 skein #501 dark green
Mill House seed beads - 2 packages #00561 Ice Green (260 beads are needed, but many
                    will not fit over the fine crewel needle)

Finished design size - 8" square

NOTE: If you decide to use a different color scheme, it is important to achieve a balance
in the values of each color family. Individual patterns can be effective in a variety of
combinations, but when several have to work together in a total design, diversity of value
is an important consideration. Direct substitutions will usually work, but when you have
to match another Watercolours, some changes are inevitable. As long as some diversity
in tone is maintained, however, a combination will usually be interesting and successful.

INSTRUCTIONS

OUTLINE. Use the outline charts on pages 165 and 166 to create the pattern areas for the
blackwork. Find the midpoint of the canvas, and mark it with an enlarged hole by wiggling
the needle slightly in the hole. Begin with the stitch that has the lines intersecting through
it on the chart, and build the rows out from this center stitch. The second chart on page
166 shows the upper left quadrant for those readers who would prefer a larger grid to work
from.

If the Watercolours is a new thread to you, you will find that it is not as durable as regular
perle cotton. Therefore do not try to reuse a piece that you have ripped out. Because it
is a twisted thread, however, you can stitch with the thread going in either direction without
it wearing excessively. Therefore when you begin a new thread, use the end that gives you
the nicest transition and do not let one color dominate a particular row or area. Once the
patterns are added, the outline will be less prominent, but the color areas of the outline
look nicer if they are scattered freely to begin with. Each strand of this cotton thread is
3-ply. Use only one ply for the outline. The thread is perfect for diagonal stitches on 18-
mesh canvas and ideal for straight stitches on 23-mesh Congress cloth.

All of the blackwork patterns should be executed in 2 strands of floss. However, in the red ogee pattern, you may want to consider using a single ply of silk instead if your tension control dulls the "star" points formed by the angled stitches.

When you execute the outline, you will notice that the backing changes when the row direction shifts from downhill to uphill. Since you will be using the backing of the outline to secure threads in and to travel through, it is important to have adequate density. Therefore use the "bargello tuck" stitch that is described on page 164 to pivot when the row direction turns uphill. If all of the rows are stitched in the same downhill flow, a strong backing will be achieved throughout the design.

When threads are ended in the middle of a continuous bargello row, they should be buried in a forward direction so park them until the row ahead is completed enough to weave through. A new thread should come from behind to maintain a consistent tension on the thread. Therefore it can be woven in as you begin. However, do not cut a starting tail until the thread is firmly in place, as it tends to loosen as you stitch the first few stitches. Pull it gently before trimming it to keep the joins from being obvious. Frankly, I prefer to start my new threads with an "away tail" or an "away knot." This is a thread that is parked in a hole away from the area being stitched so that it is not wrapped into the row being stitched. The starting tail is then rethreaded after the new row is completed, and it can be buried in the correct direction and cut at the same time. **The one technique that should not be used in bargello rows is the "waste knot" whereby the starting thread is parked ahead and wrapped into the new stitches as they are laid.** There is too much risk of piercing this thread in zigzag or undulating rows, and this also buries the thread in the wrong direction so that joins may be conspicuous because stitches are leaning in a manner that shows the interruption in the normal rhythm. Consistency is an important goal in achieving excellence in canvas embroidery so I cannot stress it enough.

CAUTION: When starting tails are used, park them either in the selvage area outside of the design area, or in a shared hole already used in a segment of the already stitched outline. If these tails, or any of the metallic tails, are parked in an open area, the perforations from the needle entry may show later. These enlarged holes can be closed by scoring in both directions lightly, but it is easier to avoid the unsightly problem by parking safely each time. Since the blackwork will be done with a long folded strand to create the necessary 2 strands, there will be no starting tails to worry about in these outlines. Some of the bargello outlines will end along the outside edges of the design. In this case bury the tails back into the previously stitched row rather than out in the selvage area. This thread is too thick to secure in the bald canvas, and the reversal of the tension on the thread does not show when another thread does not join for a continuous row.

When the Watercolours tails are buried, merely weave them through the stitched rows on the back side. It is not necessary to take a locking back stitch with this heavier thread. When the blackwork tails are secured into the outline, however, a locking backstitch is recommended since the finer slippery threads do not cling as readily. Other tails may also travel through the same area and possibly loosen tails that were secured earlier. Since there are clusters of three and four straight stitches in the bargello, it is usually better to take the locking back stitch in the middle of one of the clusters since any extra stress here will be less apt to show than it would on a single stitch or a side stitch. This trick is one that I learned for hardanger kloster blocks, and the principle works for this situation as well.

This completes the instructions for Sampler 1. Proceed to the next page, and begin the stitching. For best results, mount the canvas on a stretcher frame before you start, using either tacks or staples. The firm support of the frame will help with tension control, and it will also allow you to stitch with two hands. Tacks allow you to remove the canvas easily, as needed, to tighten the canvas, so they are my preferred fastener. Tape or bind the edges of the canvas beforehand so that the raw edges will not snag the threads as you stitch. If you need further assistance in these basic canvas techniques, please consult a book on general methods and procedures. My personal favorite as a canvas reference is *The Needlepoint Book* by Jo Ippolito Christensen, first published in 1976 by Prentice-Hall, Inc. This classic is still readily available at a reasonable price, and it is a comprehensive handbook that is easily understood by all levels of experience.

Sampler 1 Outline. Use the two large charts that follow on pages 165 and 166 to execute the outline. The first chart shows the complete outline, and the second one shows a detail of the upper left quadrant. Start the outline in the middle of the canvas to make sure that it will fit. The dotted lines in the chart on page 165 converge at the center hole of the design.

Use a #22 tapestry needle with the Watercolours outline thread. The curved lines of the outline will step up and down as the outlines are stitches. If no adjustments are made downhill rows of stitches will have an adequate backing, but uphill rows will have a sparse backing. It is ideal to have a full backing since it will accommodate starting and ending tails comfortably with no distortion of the stitches on the front when tails are secured in the backing. Therefore when the direction of a row changes a "bargello tuck" should be taken in the last stitch of each row.

A bargello tuck is a pivot stitch over a single thread that is done on one of the inside threads wrapped by the final stitch since it is not conspicuous there. This stitch is what I call a "rollover" stitch (a term coined by a former teacher, Betty Bohannon). If seated firmly, it will sink and not interfere with the next stitch when it is laid on top. This stitch is laid in the reverse direction from the previous row of stitches, and the last stitch will then be laid on top of the tuck stitch. It is also laid in the new direction to start the uphill row. In the chart to the right, stitches 4 and 8 are both tuck stitches. Notice how both the stitch before and after the tuck stitch are still snugly wrapped so good tension is maintained on all of the stitches that are visible. Another benefit of snugly wrapped stitches is that the blackwork patterns will share these holes cleanly with no risk of piercing the outline thread.

BARGELLO TUCK

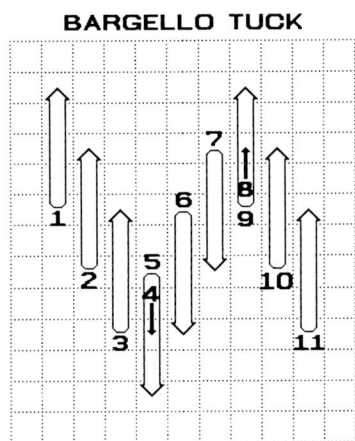

Note: Once the rollover stitch is made, you may want to rotate the frame to face the upward row as a downhill row. Some stitchers can stitch backwards readily but others need to rotate the frame to maintain consistency.

Incidentally, this clever trick was published in *Needlepoint News* several years ago by Marion Scoular. It was recommended specifically for bargello chair seats and pillows since it made the functional needlework wear better to have a strong backing throughout the design.

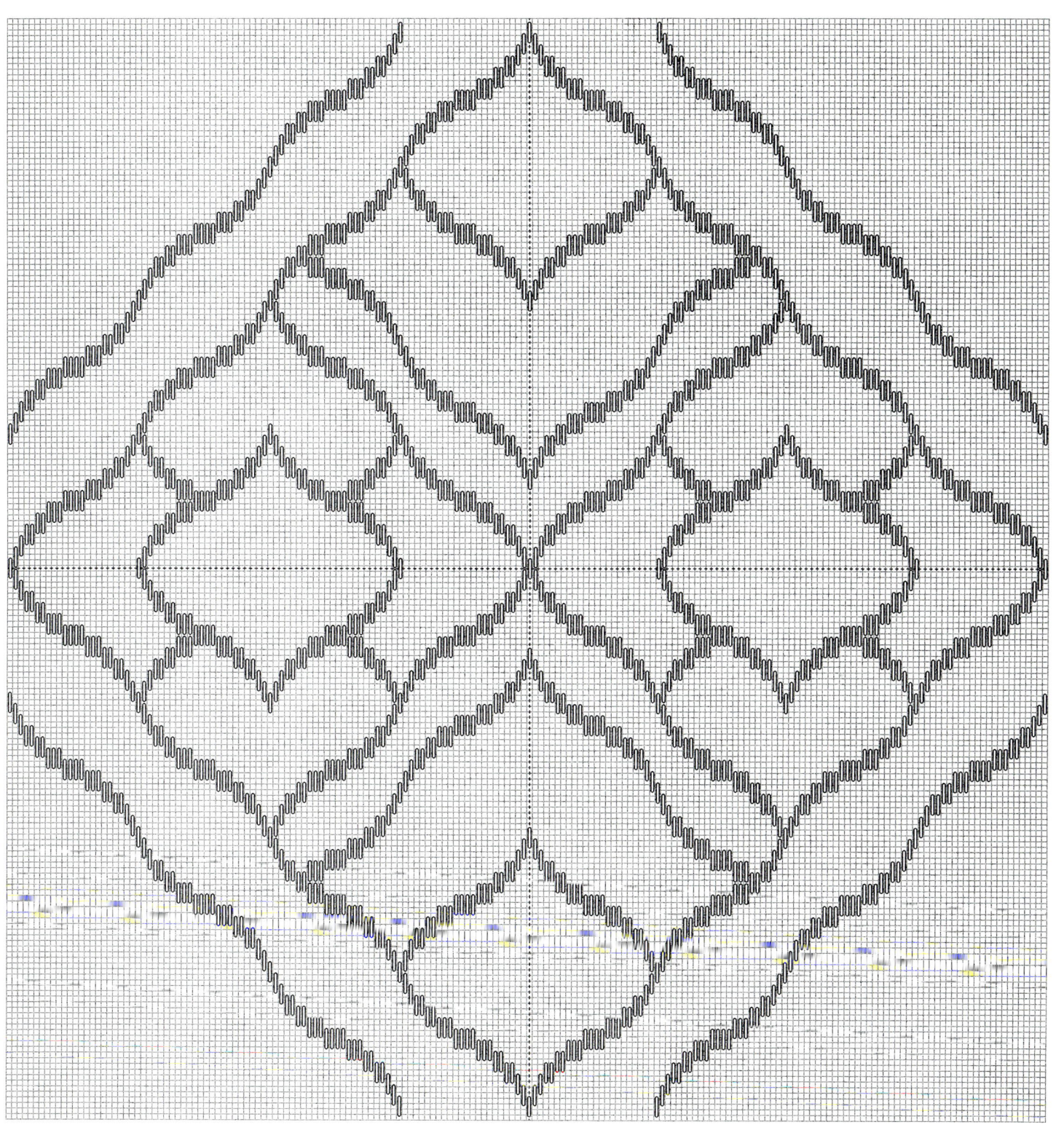

SAMPLER 1 - GENERAL PATTERN AND THREAD KEY
(Use with the Main Road Map on the next page)

OUTLINE - Done in Watercolours, Springtime

AREA 1 - Pattern 14, pages 80-81.
    Foundation layer of blackwork done in DMC Floss, #502 Medium Green
    Top layer of blackwork done in DMC Floss, #503 Light Green
    Running stitch row done in DMC Floss, #501 Dark Green
AREA 2 - Pattern 12, pages 74-77.
    Blackwork done in DMC Floss #498 Red (or a comparable silk)
AREA 3 - Pattern 24, pages 98-99.
    Tramé rows done in #8 Balger Metallic Braid, #092 Star Pink couching stitches
    done in DMC Floss #501 Dark Green
    Blackwork done in DMC Floss, #502 Medium Green
AREA 4 - Pattern 23, Variation 2, pages 96-98.
    Tramé rows done in #8 Balger Metallic Braid, #024 Fuchsia
    Blackwork steps both done in DMC Floss #604 Light Pink
AREA 5 - Pattern 22, pages 95-96.
    Tramé rows done in #8 Balger Metallic Braid, #092 Star Pink
    Blackwork done in DMC Floss, #502 Medium Green
    Back stitch rows done in #501 Dark Green
AREA 6 - Pattern 23 without Step 3, pages 96-97.
    Tramé rows done in #8 Balger Metallic Braid #024 Fuchsia
    Blackwork done in DMC Floss #603 Medium Pink
AREA 7 - Pattern 2 Superimposed on Pattern 1, pages 42-47.
    Foundation layer of blackwork done in DMC Floss #501 Dark Green
    Top layer of blackwork done in DMC #502 Medium Green

Beads - Mill House #00561 Ice Green (Add with the #502 Medium Green Floss)

Blackwork Patterns. Unless otherwise stated, use a #24 or #26 tapestry needle to execute the blackwork. The smaller size needle is less apt to pierce the outline or any other previously laid stitches in the shared holes, but the #24 needle is more comfortable for many people and is acceptable. Unless otherwise noted, the correct thread weight for all the blackwork is 2 strands of floss when the patterns are done on either 18-mesh or 23-mesh Congress cloth. If the angled stitches do not have adequate points on Congress cloth, consider using 1-strand silk floss instead, but 1-strand cotton floss is too skimpy. Use the folded floss thread since this is ideal for the 2-strand thread (review this technique in section C on page 12, if needed). Since the pattern placement is already defined on every chart for you, it is easier to start along a side edge rather than in the center of each pattern.

SAMPLER 1 - MAIN ROAD MAP

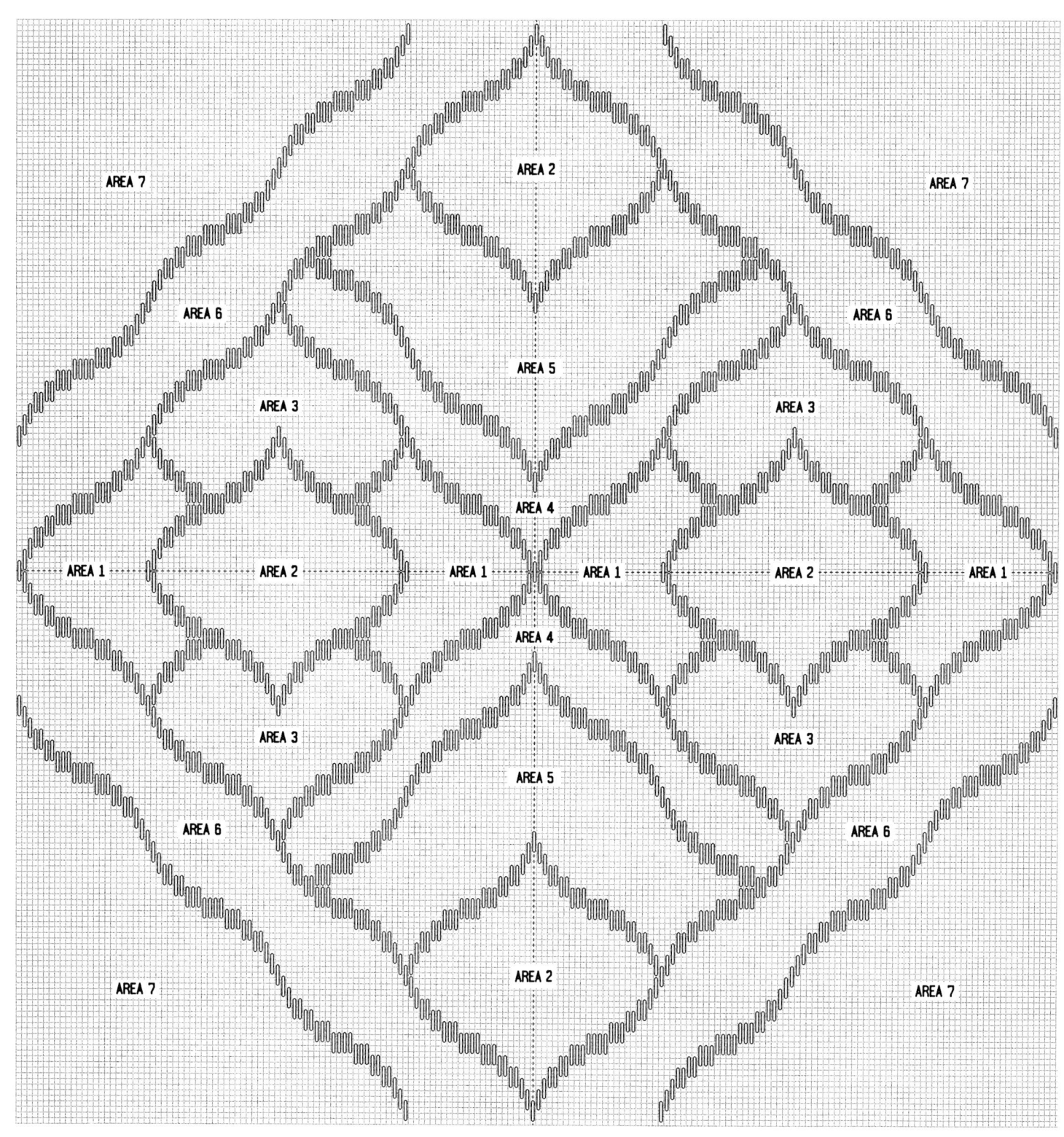

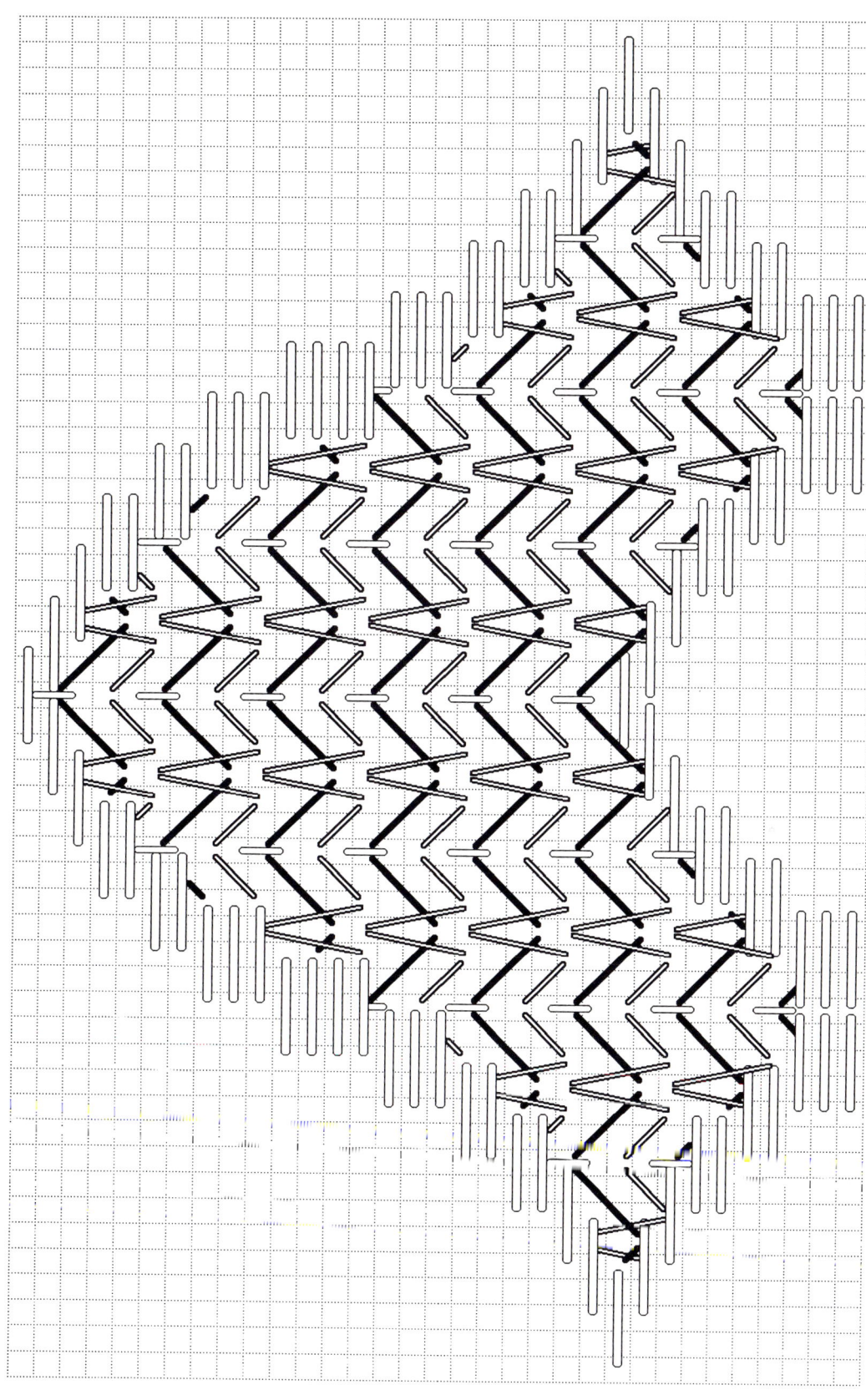

AREA 1 PATTERN 14 (Page 80)

169

AREA 1. PATTERN 14 (Page 80). Area 1 is repeated four times in the design. It is the shape that surrounds the left and right ogees along both sides. The two middle sections meet along the center stitch of the design in a mirror image position. The overall chart on the previous page shows the section to the right of the center axis. However, the pattern instructions show the pattern sequence in horizontal zigzag rows so rotate the chart and the canvas 90° to make them correspond to the view in the sequence charts. It is also easier to work the pattern with the canvas in the same rotated position so line it up accordingly.

Because this pattern builds in layers, and because the slanted stitches of step 2 obscure the view of the foundation layer, two separate charts are provided that show steps 1 and 2. However, this time the charts display only the right half of the area. Once the pattern rows are worked to the center axis, it should be easy to continue the rhythm and fill the left side. If you need to, however, refer back to the overall pattern until you have memorized the sequence.

This pattern has some tricky compensation along the edges. When you see a "blunt" stitch on the chart, it means that the stitch sinks behind the outline stitches so slant the needle to enter cleanly into the designated hole. If easier, use a second needle or a tekobari to hold back the outline stitch as you plant the needle. Some rows are quite far apart too so weave through the outline to get to the new starting holes each time. As you leave each row, do not forget the underside stitch needed to complete the pattern on the reverse side. When the outline is in place, you must "fake" this stitch by piercing the back of the outline at the correct angle to hold the thread. Then you can travel to the next row without pulling the thread off course. Any short cuts at the end of the rows may show so beware!

The final step is shown clearly on the overall pattern chart. A running stitch sequence will give this accent a bolder look. It also makes it easier to enter and exit since no pivots are needed. This pattern is particularly pretty when the 2 plies are laid carefully in side by side plies. The dark shade was chosen for step 3 because it gives the pattern a strong vertical thrust. The couching rows in areas 3 and 5 create a similar visual stripe so I wanted to repeat the effect in this pattern to create the same line and scale. Since this stripe is perpendicular to the others, it also presents an interesting contrast.

Stripes tend to create motion and attract attention. Therefore they can be a dramatic force when used properly. If used in a background, a stripe pattern can sometimes carry the eye away from the focal point or out of a design in a negative way so something quieter is usually a better choice. However, in the *Rainy Winter Landscape* (Color Plate VI), a metallic stripe background is effectively used to suggest the wind and the rain. Again in *Comely Catfish* (Color Plate XV), a wave stripe in blackwork is used for the background to suggest water. In Sampler 1 the stripes are contained and tend to reinforce the geometric shapes in a positive way.

In *Coyote Chorus* (Color Plate II), this same pattern was used in the middle mountain range. The back stitches were not done in a dark value here because it was important to maintain medium values to suggest distance. The "star points" created an adequate vertical thrust to reinforce the two peaks, and the horizontal zigzag rows followed the range contours nicely too.

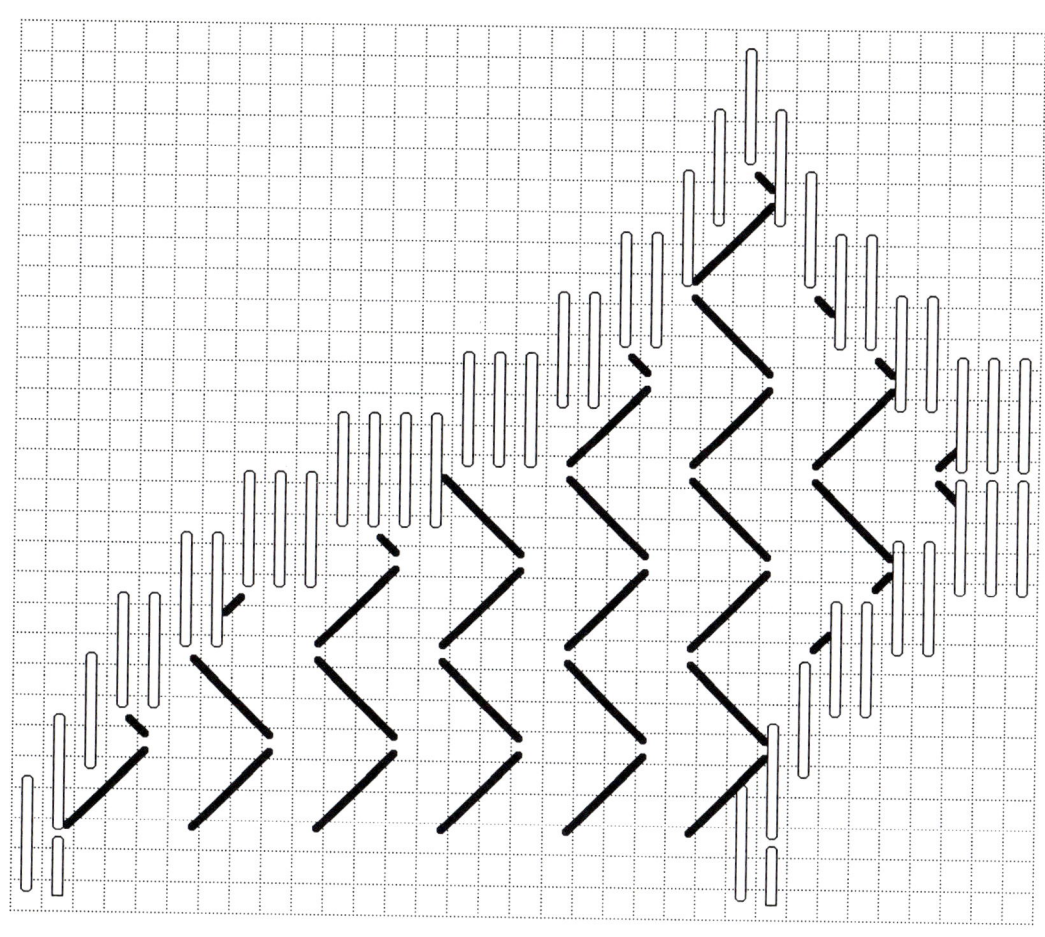

**AREA 1 - STEP 1
PLACEMENT**

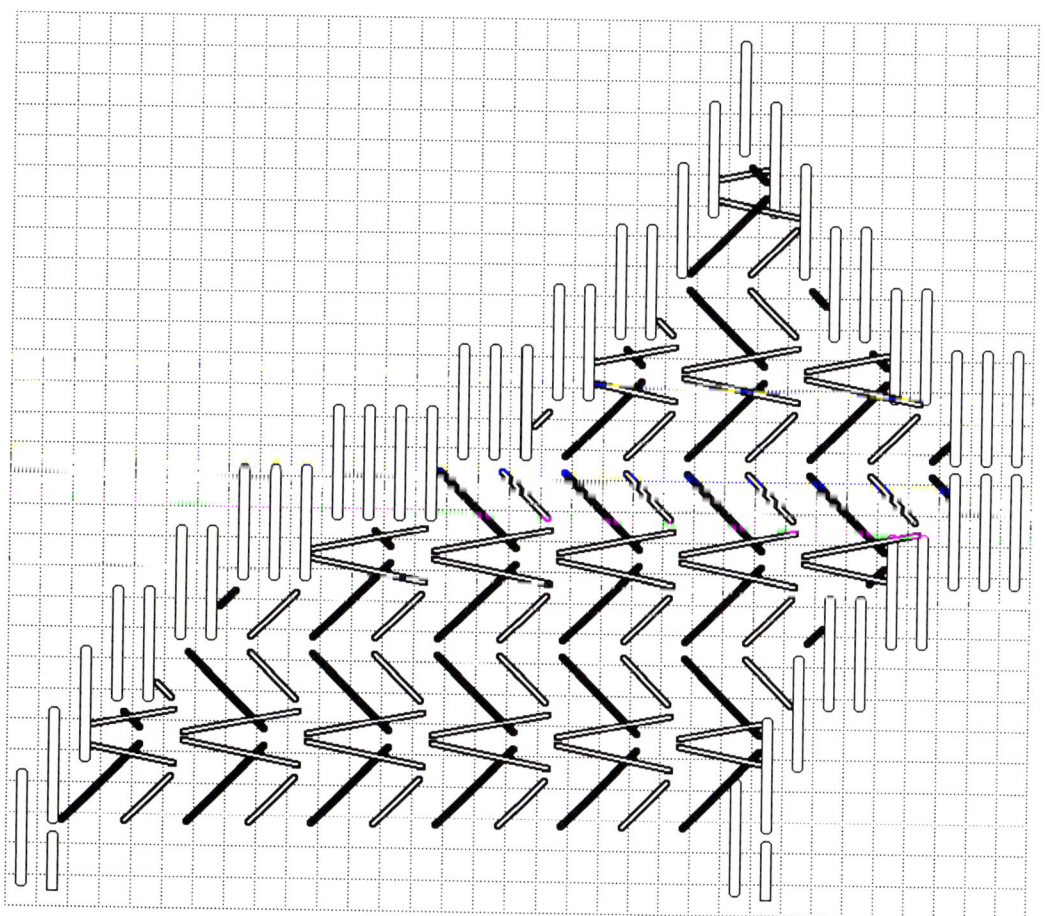

**AREA 1 - STEP 2
PLACEMENT**

AREA 2 - PATTERN 12
(Page 74)

AREA 2. PATTERN 12 (Page 74). This ogee pattern is repeated in the design four times. It is a prominent area both because of the large scale of the pattern and because the blackwork is executed in red. The area is too big to show an enlarged overall view, but there is an enlarged view of the right half of the shape on the next page.

Use the horizontal sequence to execute the pattern for this shape. Work the wide middle row first to get the pattern established. This is a tricky pattern too so review all of the directions (and warnings!) again before you start. It is easy to make a placement error in the beginning so proceed carefully. Double check the compensation at the beginning and end of each row, and make sure that the top and bottom edges match each other throughout the area.

It is often said that it is difficult to get a nice curve on canvas. Notice how soft the curves are in this blackwork pattern. It is easy to copy patterns with circles, scales and ogees in blackwork, but it does require using the slanted stitches, and these are more tedious to lay. However, if you focus on the sinking holes rather than on the angle of the stitch as you progress, the likelihood of an error is decreased somewhat. Notice the relationship of these holes to previously laid filled areas, and such "clues" will help you stitch accurately. Almost every slanted stitch meets one of the diagonal stitches at one end so this fact should be helpful in finding your way.

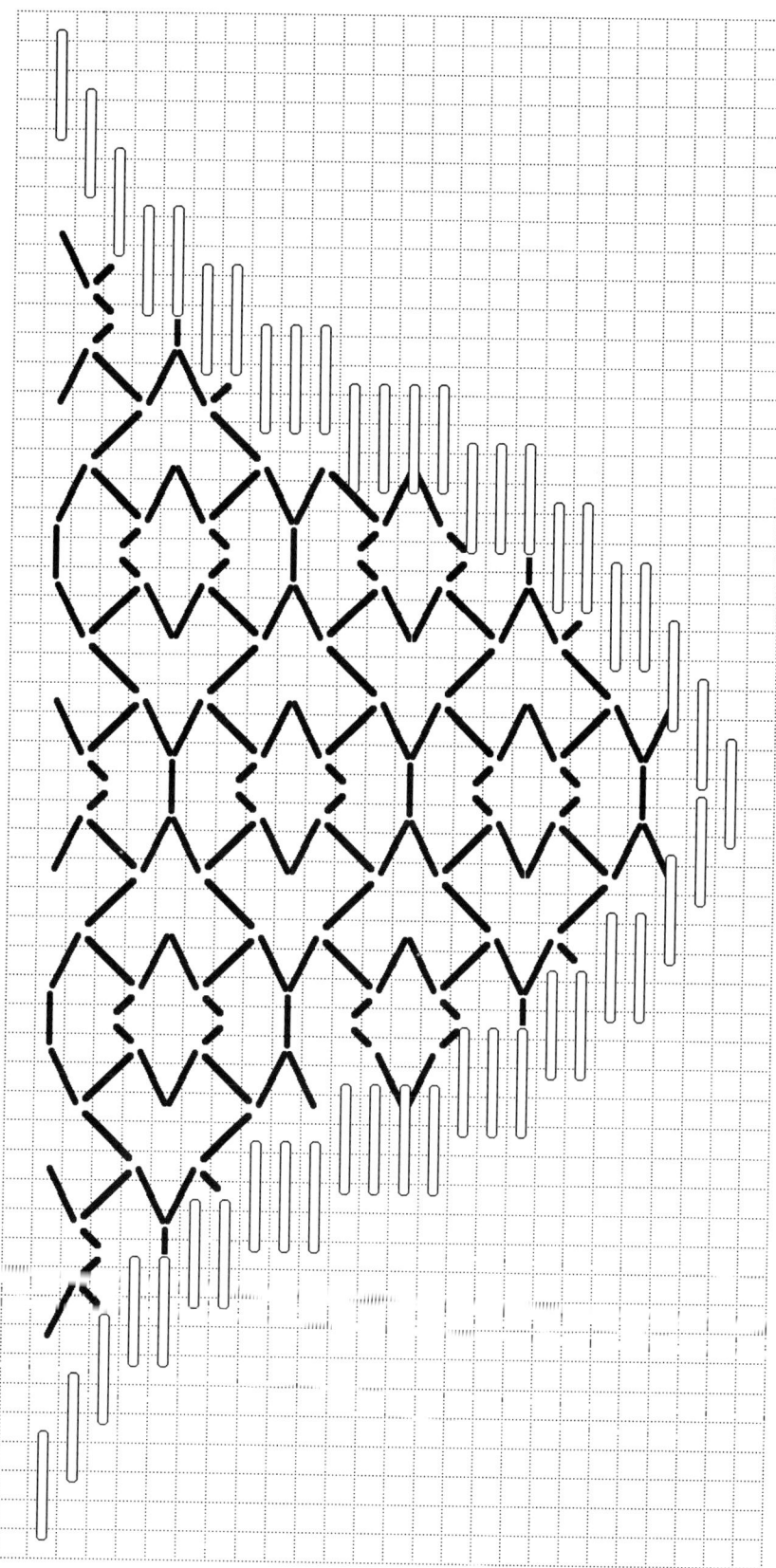

**AREA 2
ENLARGED VIEW
RIGHT HALF**

173

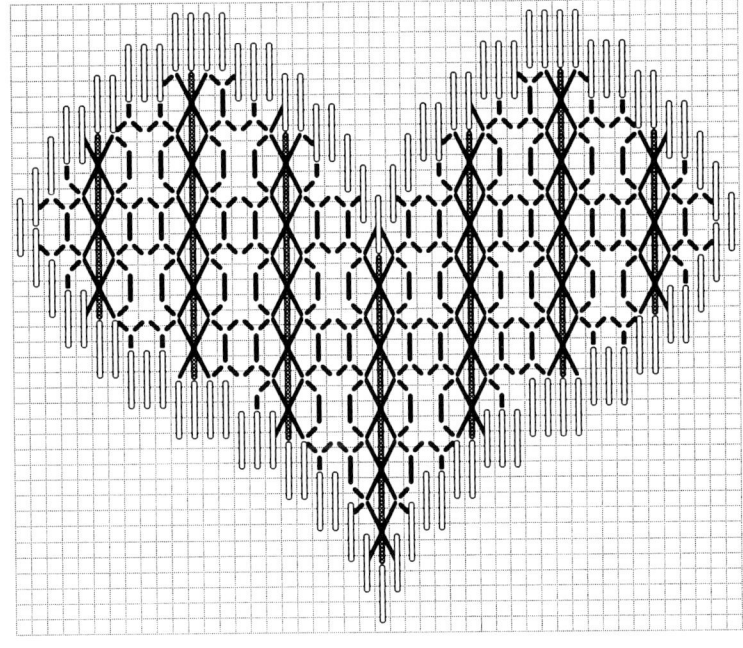

AREA 3. PATTERN 24 (Page 98). This pattern is repeated four times in the design. The heart shapes are located on the top and bottom sides of the left and right ogee shapes, and the view above matches the position of the hearts on the lower side.

A medium and a dark value of green are combined in this blackwork pattern. This combination of shades is repeated again in the beaded border, making a nice contrast to the lighter greens used in areas 1 and 5.

Again the whole shape is too big to be reproduced in an enlarged view, but there is a magnified view of the left side on the next page. The pattern fits the heart shape nicely so that there is no awkward compensation anywhere.

This is the first tramé pattern in the design. In the model a soft star pink metallic is used for the tramé foundations in the fine #8 weight. This creates a subtle inconspicuous effect, but either the #16 size, or two strands of the #8 metallic braid laid in pairs, could be used if a bolder effect is desired.

Rotate the canvas 180° to execute the hearts on the upper side of the design. The hearts are closer to you in this position and the view is upright.

The blackwork pattern here has all straight vertical or diagonal stitches so it is easy to stitch. The sequence turns a corner after every stitch too so the stitches should all lay cleanly with no clutter in any shared holes.

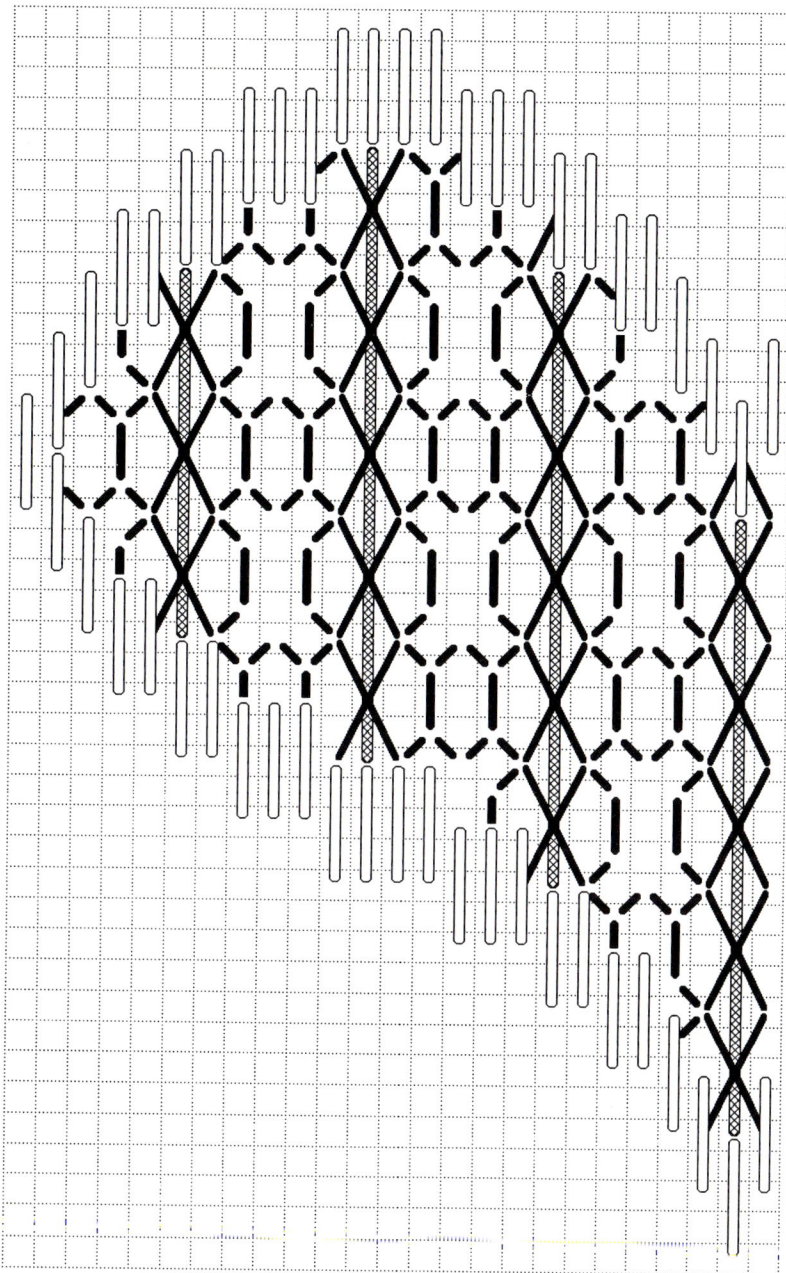

HINT: This pattern has several compensation stitches that straddle a single thread. Remember the trick about wrapping these twice to maintain the same density to the appearance of the partial stitch. The first stitch will wrap snugly and sink down. It will then help to support the second stitch, which will spread out nicely on this comfortable foundation. Usually overstitching is a "no!no!" in embroidery, as stitches will often appear overly padded or distorted when laid on top of another stitch. However, this application is an exception and works beautifully to eliminate the risk of losing a stitch that straddles just a single thread. Since the first layer recedes, it is not visible, so nobody can tell that anything has been fixed.

NOTE: The stitches that need to be wrapped twice will usually wrap cleaner if the stitch is taken as a back stitch rather than a running stitch. Since these stitches are along the outline edges a change in rhythm will be easy to accomplish, so I would recommend entering these rows with a back stitch and then start the running stitch rhythm on the second stitch. This will mean that the final stitch of these rows is a running stitch on top of the canvas but since it comes from an angled turn it can be wrapped twice with no interference. Hence change the sequence **ONLY** at the beginnings of these rows where the benefit is worthwhile.

AREA 4. PATTERN 23, VARIATION 2 (Page 98). Area 4 is a long narrow shape that forms an interesting chevron swirl in the middle of the design. This four way "ribbon" is balanced by the wide ribbon that forms a diamond outline along the outside edges, and the same pattern is used in both areas since the shapes are similar. Both use the rose metallic for the tramé foundation, with a pink top layer of blackwork, but the color treatments and the patterns vary slightly in the two areas. In both cases the pattern is placed in a mirror image position to contour better to the directional changes in the shapes.

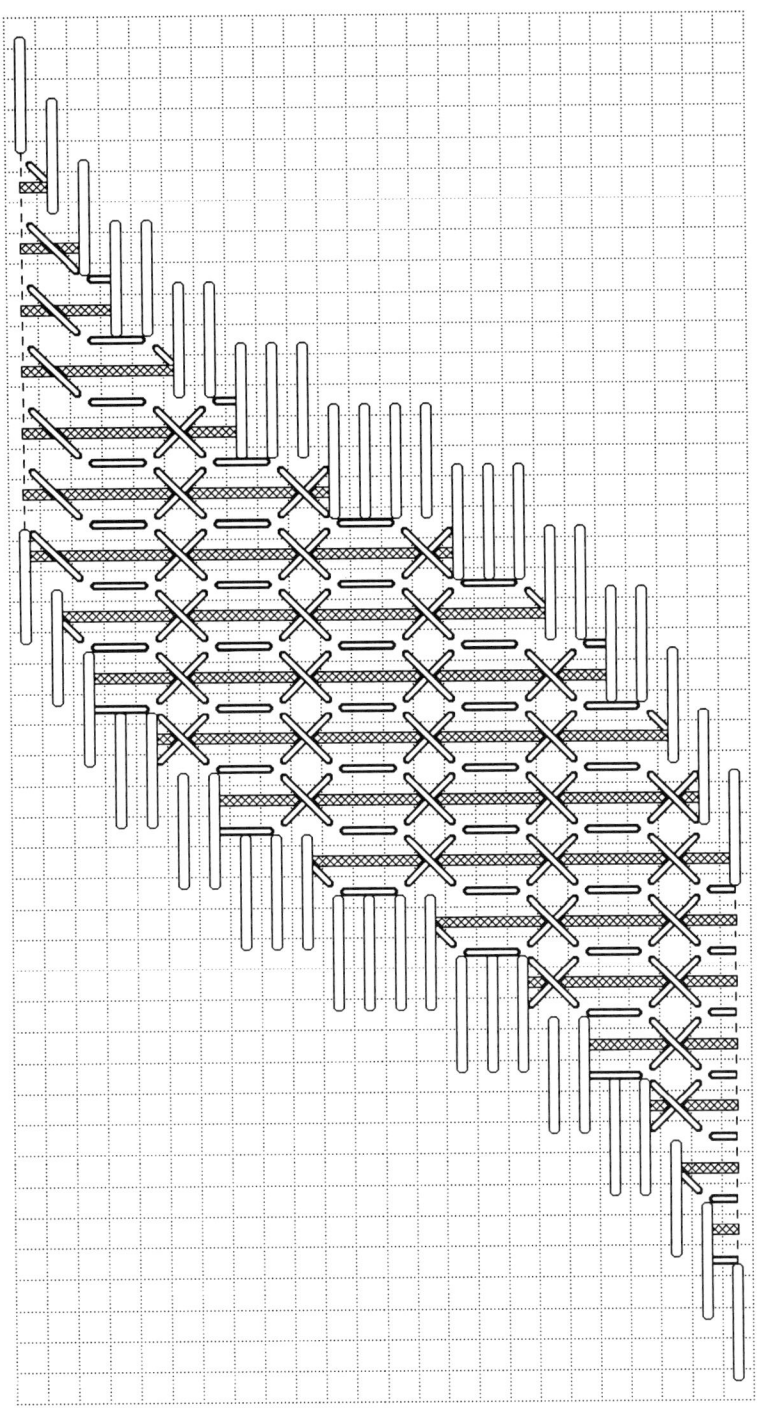

**AREA 4
PATTERN 23
VARIATION 2
(Page 98)
RIGHT HALF VIEW**

NOTE: The stitches of step 3 in the right half of this pattern all slant from lower right to upper left. The "uncrossed" slanted stitches along the center diagonal look nicer if they run parallel to the upward thrust of the pattern. However this represents a change in the usual pattern rhythm. Therefore start the pattern rows along the center seam with a downhill stitch and continue the usual uphill zigzag path after the first stitch. The top crosses will then be added as step 3.

Reminder: This pattern has an easier return trip if the diagonal stitches are on top of the canvas on the running stitch row. Review the discussion of this on page 97, if needed.

176

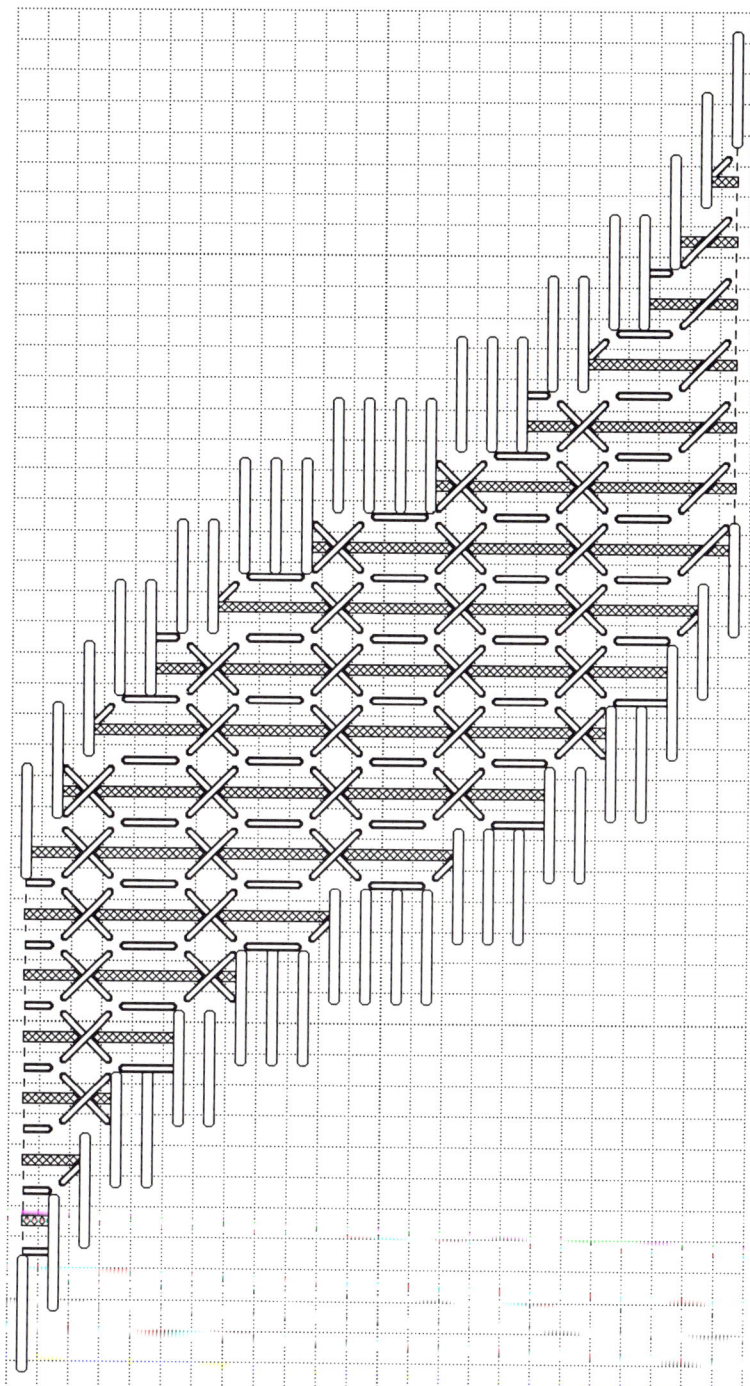

AREA 4 - PATTERN 23
VARIATION 2
(Page 98)
LEFT HALF VIEW

NOTE: The stitches of step 3 in the left half of this pattern all slant from lower left to upper right so that they match the single slanted stitches in the middle that meet those of the right half to form an attractive peak that reinforces the shape. In order to stitch the step 2 reversible rows in the usual path from left to right, rotate the chart and the canvas 180° so that the pattern is viewed upside down. This time do step 3 as the second step and not the third. Then add the double running path as step 3. Begin with the center single stitch along the middle seam in the same manner that you did in the right half. Then pivot and work the zigzag rows in an uphill path in the usual way. This was the simplest solution to the placement dilemma since it accommodated the directional changes needed without altering the rhythm of the reversible sequence. Other solutions are possible so perhaps you will think of an alternative.

Design shapes can often require a modification in pattern placement to enhance the way the pattern fits the contours. Symmetrical shapes and mirror image shapes require special consideration, and this sort of "flow reversal" of a pattern to fit shapes with a center axis often improves the presentation of the pattern. The addition of the step 3 crosses in this pattern also creates a strong vertical stripe that negates or dilutes the zigzag thrust of the reversible rows. Again this not only reinforces the upward thrust of the shape, but it also

177

echoes the stripes in some of the earlier patterns, which have similar wave peaks. In Area 6, only the zigzag rows are used because the flow of these zigzag steps parallels the undulating direction of the ribbon shape. Simple color and value changes can alter the visual effect or dominance within a pattern so many variations are possible within the same pattern. Additional steps also create attractive variations so many tools can be used to achieve the desired end in a pattern. The black and white charts usually only show the network of a pattern when done in dark threads so there are always surprises waiting when the patterns are actually stitched. To my way of thinking, there is no such thing as an ugly pattern, but it may take several tries until you get the impression desired. The more you experiment, the better your instincts will develop in predicting how a pattern will look, however, so don't get discouraged.

AREA 5 OVERALL CHART

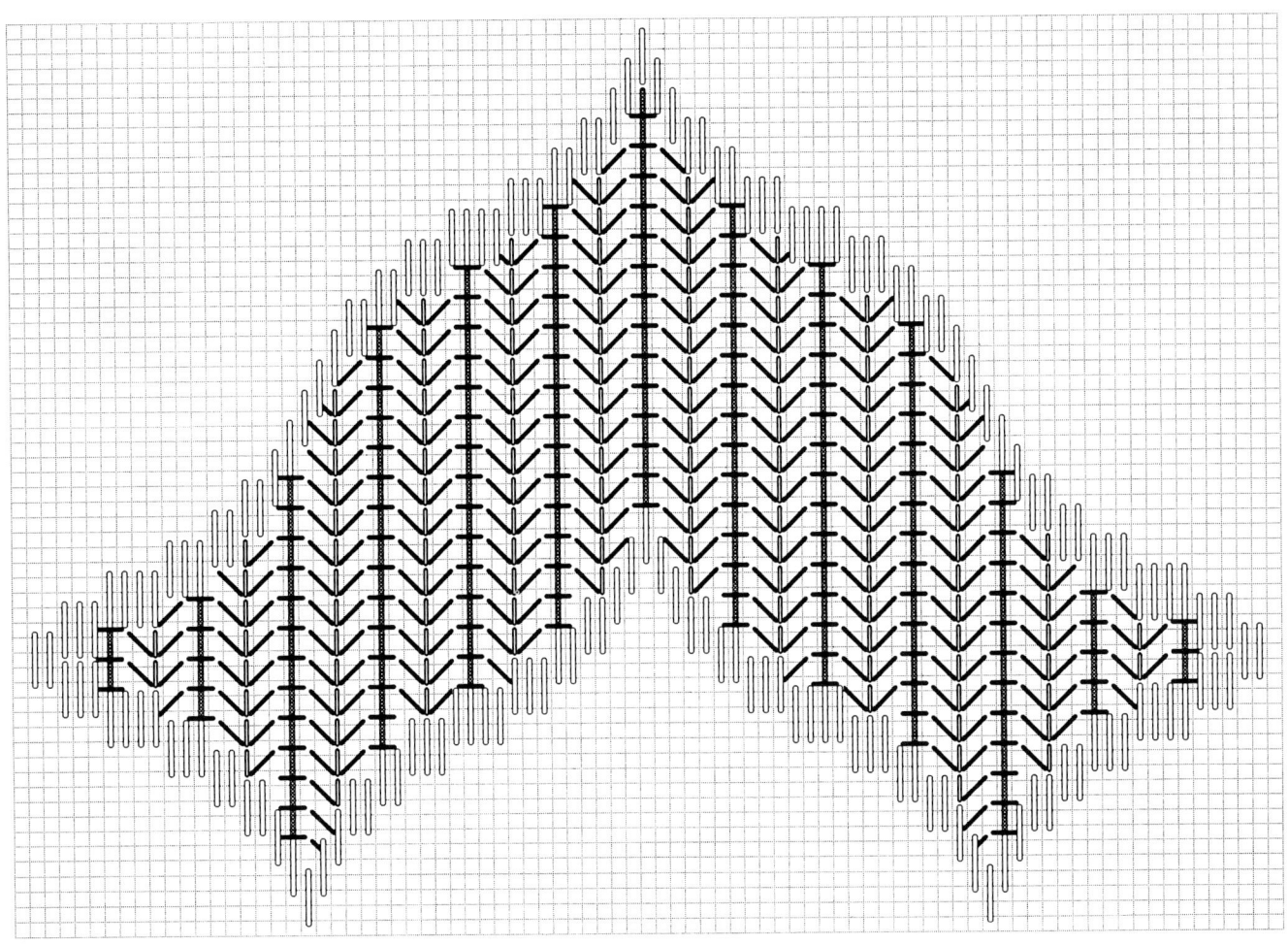

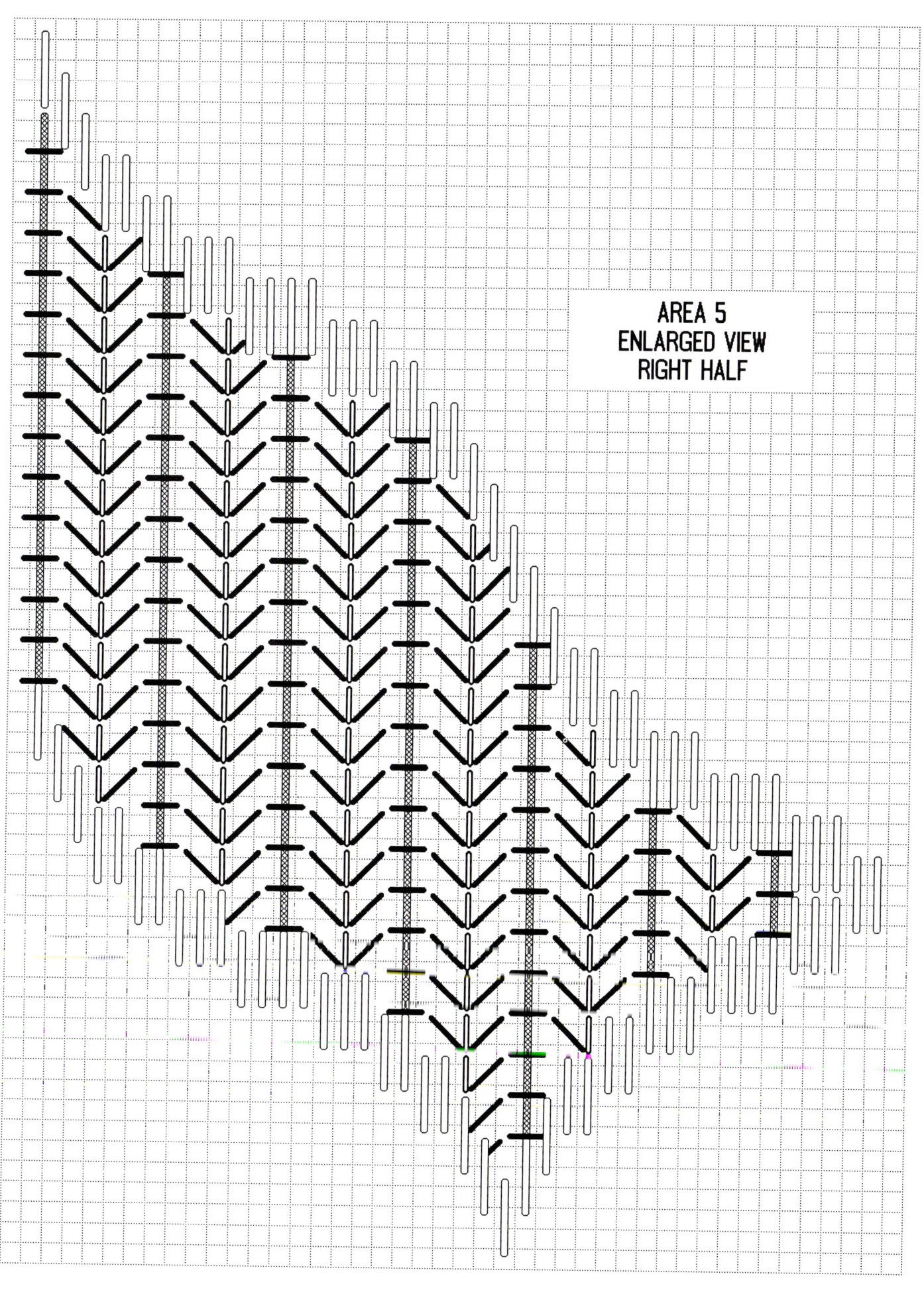

AREA 5
ENLARGED VIEW
RIGHT HALF

AREA 5. PATTERN 22 (Page 95). Area 5 is the largest shape in the design so it requires a full page to reproduce an enlarged view of just the right half. Even though the shape is a mirror image one, I did not choose to split a pattern this time. A traméd blackwork pattern was chosen, and one of the tramé rows is centered in the middle channel that divides both halves of the shape. These laid threads dominate here to give another strong vertical thrust to the pattern. In the previous couched patterns the overlays were heavier so the direction of the long laid threads was interrupted. Usually the couching creates a "bricking" effect that subdues the metallic and creates an attractive glimmer or glow underneath the pattern. A heavier weight metallic or a brighter color can make it more dominant, if desired. This pattern is repeated twice, and the view on the chart shows the lower area. Rotate the canvas 180° to match this view with the upper area.

AREA 6. PATTERN 23 WITHOUT STEP 3 (Page 97). This area was discussed briefly when Area 4 was covered. The same pattern is used in both shapes, but step 3 is omitted here. This area is repeated four times, and the areas form a large diamond "ribbon" around the interior geometric shapes. The areas touch at the midpoint of every side, but the patterns never join since the ribbons end with a "blunt cut" along the edge. The patterns are placed in a mirror image position within the top and bottom pairs of the area shape.

The pattern area is too large to present a complete segment. However, each area undulates in four repeats so one of these repeats is shown on the next page to display how the pattern fits one repeat. Since all of the stitches in the pattern are straight, the compensation is easy, but it will vary within the repeated shapes somewhat since the count of the outline is "odd" and the pattern placement is "even." Just work the blackwork paths from left to right in the manner diagrammed, and make sure that the diagonal stitches are always on the top side of the canvas on the running stitch rows to create a comfortable journey back over the path. If the starting edge calls for a straight stitch, merely begin on an underneath stitch to assure that the ideal rhythm is maintained.

NOTE: Some compensation stitches do not connect with the blackwork rows. Add these isolated stitches as you weave through the outline with a simple side trip maneuver. Most of these tuck under an outline stitch too so it is better to begin with an underneath half stitch. This will place the needle on top for the return trip so you can angle it to make a clean entry behind the outline stitch – less risk of piercing an outline thread so a sensible thing to do. Some of the half stitches are horizontal so be sure to wrap these twice, if needed – if you keep the tension loose as you tighten the first stitch, this may be adequate, especially since the outline obscures many of these compensation stitches somewhat anyway.

The chart on the next page shows the right side of each pair of pattern areas when the design is in the upright position shown on the overall chart on page 168. The chart on page 183 shows one repeat of the left side. The pattern builds in uphill rows from right to left in the two left sides so I found it easier to reverse the usual sequence and stitch these rows from right to left. It is easier to match the patterns since the starting points of new rows are closer to the already stitched rows on the adjacent mirror image side. If you complete a right side first, you will be so familiar with the pattern that this flip-flop path should be easy.

HINT. When you start the first right side, begin in one of the repeats that is inside rather than trying to start along a blunt edge where you may not anticipate the compensation as readily. Once the pattern is establish it is easy to add new rows on either side of the filled areas.

**AREA 6
PLACEMENT CHART
ONE REPEAT
RIGHT SIDE**

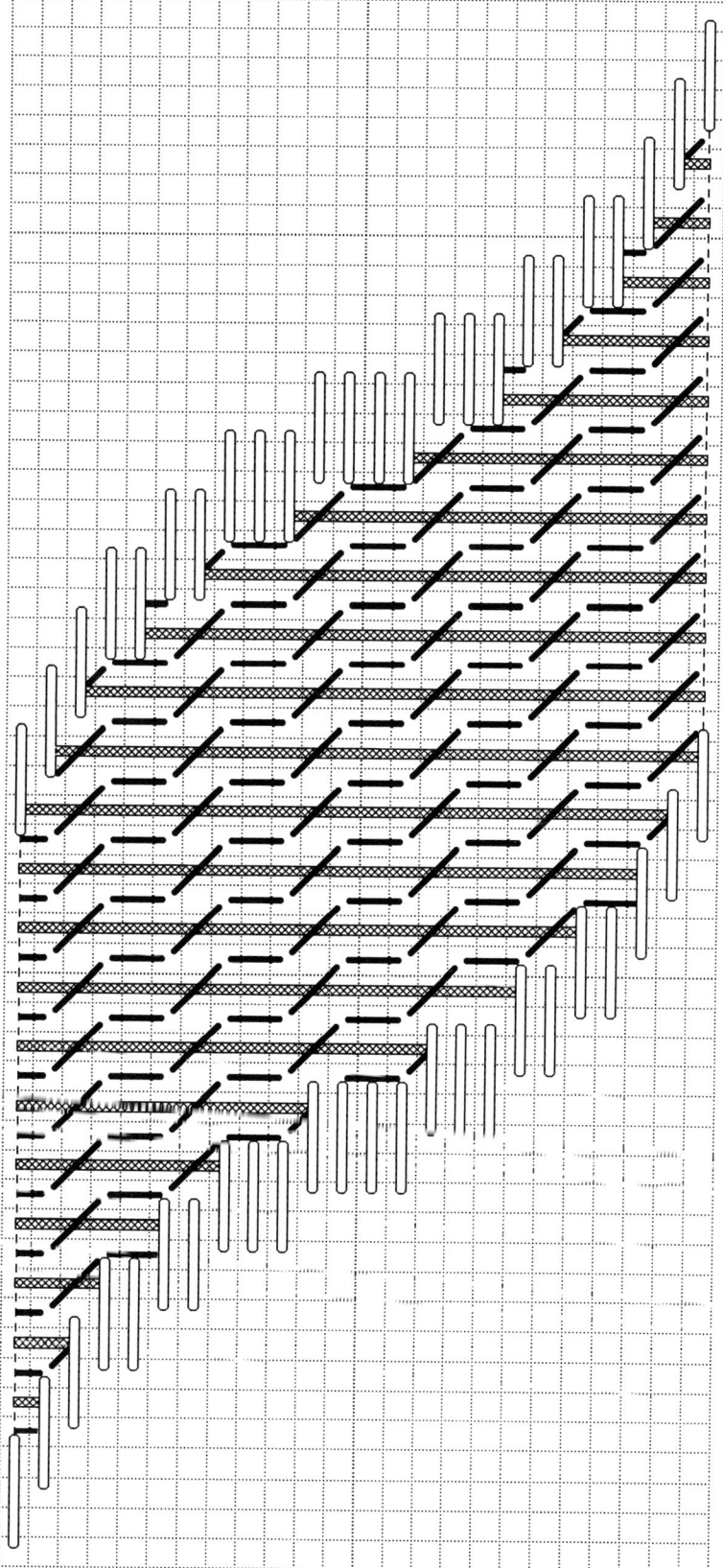

181

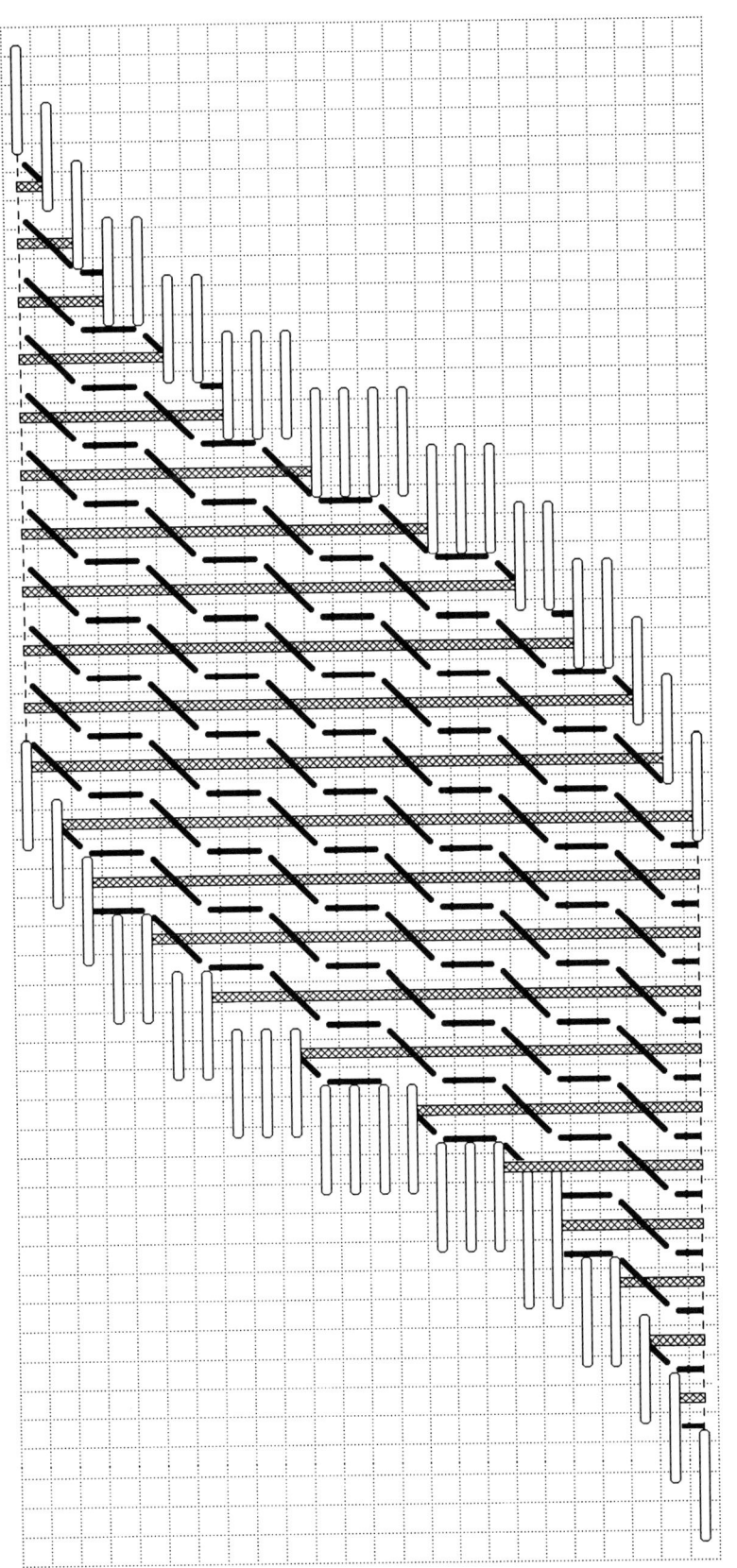

**AREA 6
PLACEMENT CHART
ONE REPEAT
LEFT SIDE**

AREA 7. PATTERN 2 SUPERIMPOSED ONTO PATTERN 1 (Page 45). The last area is a border area that surrounds the diamond design. An allover pattern was chosen for this shape because it is a large area with no particular definition like the other areas. The greens were repeated here to balance the color areas, and since a lovely metallic green bead is available that matches the DMC #500 family of greens, I decided to bead the pattern in this design.

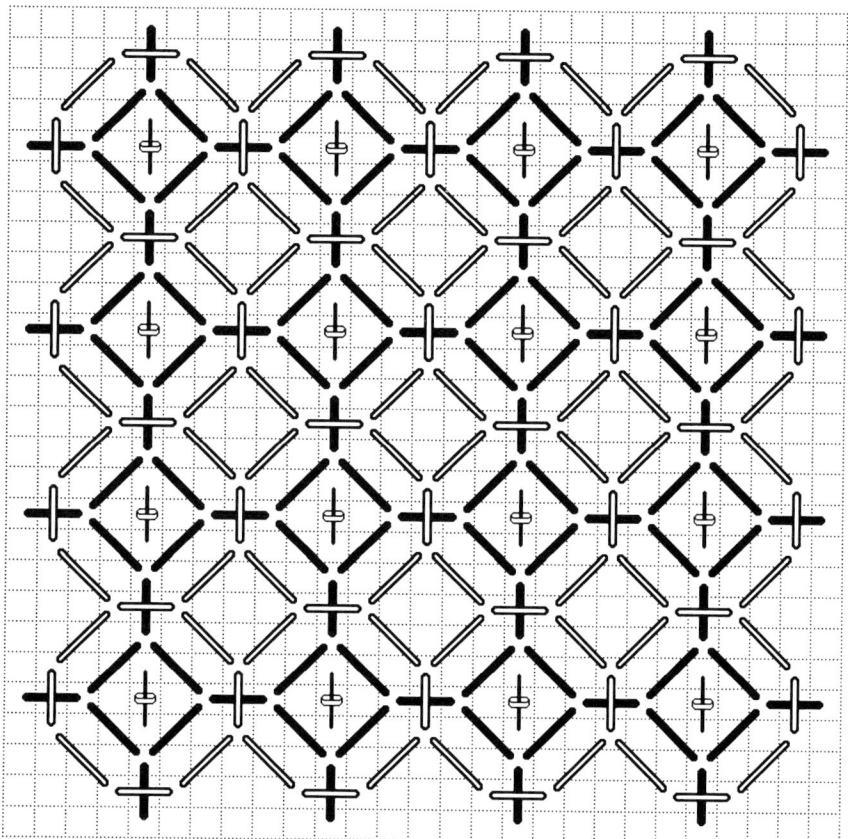

AREA 7 BLACKWORK PATTERN. Score from the side edges where the outlines end towards each corner to find the corner hole of each side (the spot where the two channel lines intersect). Mark these holes by wiggling the needle in them to enlarge them slightly. Measure the starting point of the pattern from the corner hole and begin a vertical path four threads in from the outside hole.

Only an overall pattern chart is provided for this area, as the shape is too large to feature the entire pattern placement. If the pattern is placed so that the square shown here fits exactly into the outside corner of each area, all four areas will match. Even though the pattern itself is a four way one, the bead rows are placed in upright vertical rows in all 4 corners so that the beads lay in the same direction throughout. The beads nest in the middle of each dark diamond, and they are anchored with a separate path from the blackwork. These back stitch rows will hold the beads securely, and all the traveling threads will fall behind the blackwork of the previous two steps. Be sure to tighten each bead snugly. My beads were too small to wrap twice, and this is a tedious step that is not necessary when a heavy enough thread is used to secure them. The density of the thread will usually keep them from drooping as long as the tension is firm when the holding stitches are laid. Use a #8 crewel needle for the beading step. The needle has a small enough eye to pass through the beads, but it is much easier to thread than a beading needle (less dangerous too). This final pattern completes the design, and I hope you enjoyed stitching the sampler. It exposed you to a nice cross section of pattern types, and the next sampler will introduce you to more complex patterns with angled stitches.

SAMPLER 2

BARGELLO DIAMOND GEOMETRIC

This sampler, like the previous one, uses a bargello outline to create interesting shapes for blackwork patterns. This time the outline is a simple step pattern of single stitches over four threads with no clusters of stitches. Natural diamond shapes form as opposing rows of slanted lines intersect at regulated intervals. Other interesting bolder shapes and dramatic zigzag lines form when some rows are left out.

Most of the blackwork patterns used in this sampler have angled stitches so they are more difficult to execute than the straight stitches that were dominant in the first sampler. The angled stitches tend to reinforce the shapes better, and the splitting of an angled stitch is seldom needed since the outline usually accommodates whole stitches comfortably.

The Blue Lavender Watercolours used for this outline is an analogous blend of blue and lavender shades. It matches the blue Congress cloth nicely, but slightly brighter blues and purple threads are needed to make the patterns show up well against the soft pastel canvas and outline thread.

The lavender metallic is quite neutral with both color families and does not show up well on the blue canvas. However, it does provide a subtle glimmer in the patterns that is secondary to the more prominent outlines. In another situation these patterns would be more forceful with a stronger contrast in the metallic, but I wanted to have the bold blackwork dominate here.

Use the main road map, the detailed outline charts, and the individual area charts to execute the sampler along with the code key that follows. A materials list for my original sampler is also provided below for your convenience.

SAMPLER 2 - MATERIALS LIST

13" Square stretcher frame (narrow strips)
13" Square piece of light blue 23-mesh Congress cloth
Tapestry needles - size 22, 24, and 26
Watercolours - 2 skeins Blue Lavender
#8 Balger metallic braid - 2 reels of #9294 Periwinkle
DMC #8 perle cotton - 1 ball #798 medium blue (floss may be substituted)
                                              1 ball #797 dark blue
DMC floss - 1 skein #799 light blue
Anchor floss - 2 skeins #109 medium dark purple

Finished design size - 9" square

SAMPLER 2 - INSTRUCTIONS

OUTLINE. Use the outline chart on the next page to create the pattern areas for the blackwork. Only the left half of the design is shown on the chart in order to present it as boldly as possible for you to follow. It was not possible to enlarge the entire outline since this design is bigger than the previous one.

In order to add the right half of the design to the canvas, merely rotate this chart 180° and repeat the same outline. **However, do not repeat the stitches that straddle the center channel of the design when you add the second half.** The dotted line falls in the middle of these stitches so they fall on the center axis of the symmetrical shape.

If you prefer to have a complete overall design, make two copies of the chart of the left side. Cut the shapes out carefully. Rotate one of them 180° to produce a right side image and tape them together, being sure to overlap the vertical dotted lines. On page 187 I also included a second chart that shows a quarter of the outline enlarged. This outline is busier than the one for sampler 1 so the bigger grid may be helpful. If an overall chart of this scale is desired, merely make two enlarged copies of the left side chart on page 186, using legal size paper. The scale of the upper left quadrant chart is 1 1/2 times that of the left side chart so adjust the copy machine accordingly. If an even bigger map is desired, use 11" X 17" paper to enlarge the legal size sheets further. Rotate one of these charts 180° and piece the two graphs together to create one large overall chart.

BEWARE! When you do this kind of piecing, avoid using a copy machine that automatically shrinks the image slightly. However, as long as the pieces are all reproduced from the same original, they will fit nicely together regardless of what brand of machine is used.

If you did not do Sampler 1 first, please read pages 160-164 before you start this sampler. The general instructions about the Watercolours, the thread weights, and the bargello tuck for the outline apply to this sampler as well, but they will not be repeated here. Since the outline in Sampler 2 creates many more pattern areas and geometric units, the outline will zig and zag much more as it is stitched. Therefore it is even more important to use the "bargello tuck" when the row directions turn uphill (see page 164, if needed).

Again start the outline by marking the center hole of the canvas. This corresponds to the dense point where the dotted lines converge in both outline charts. Since this design has a trickier outline, it may be helpful to baste these dotted lines on to the canvas first. This way if a mistake is made in the outline, you will discover it <u>sooner</u> rather than <u>later</u>!

SAMPLER 2 - OUTLINE CHART

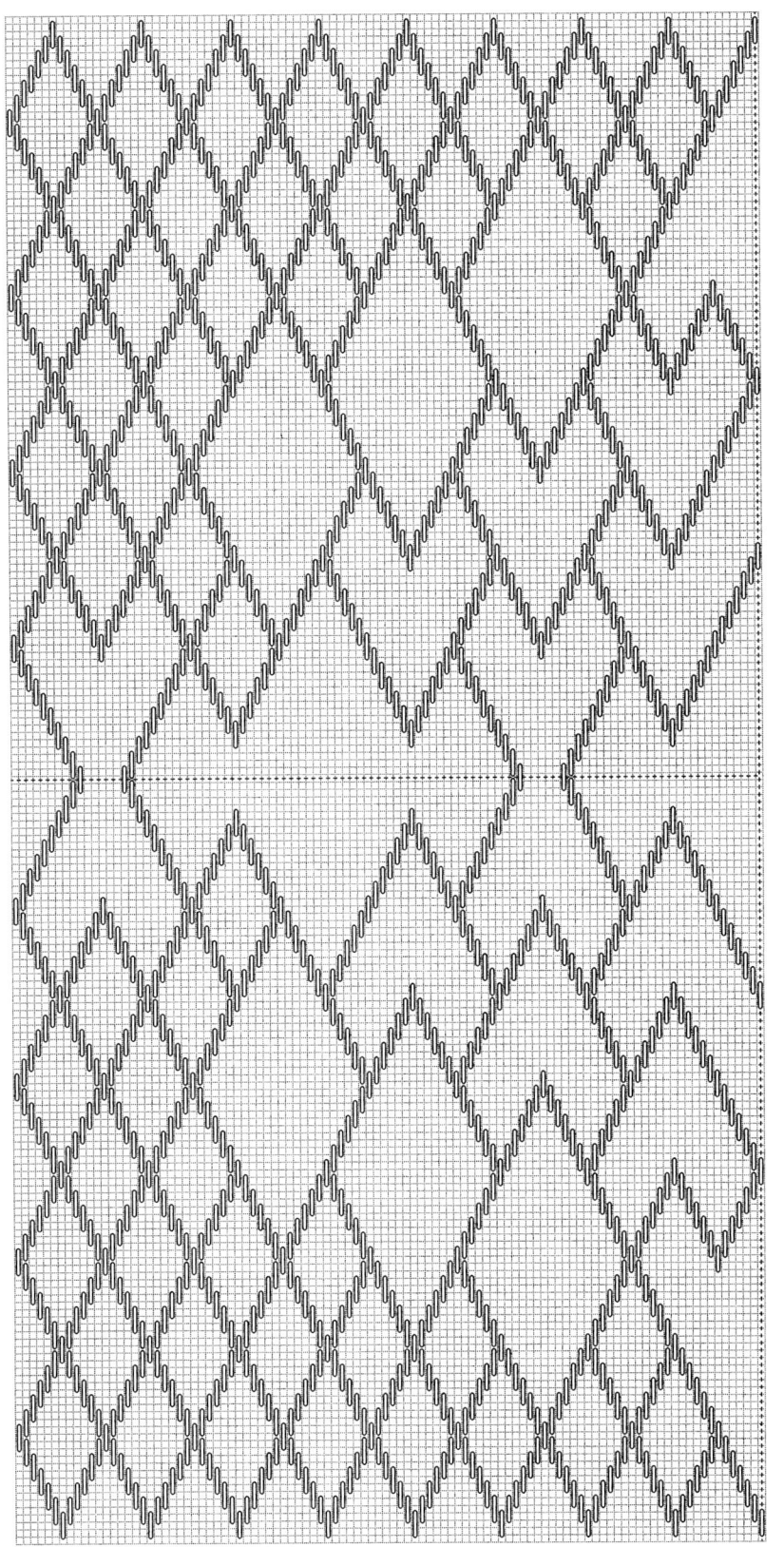

LEFT HALF OF THE DESIGN
Use Watercolours
1 ply

*Midpoint of the Canvas

Complete the entire outline before going on to the blackwork fillings.

SAMPLER 2 - OUTLINE CHART - ENLARGED VIEW
UPPER LEFT QUADRANT

Rotate this chart 180° to create a view of the lower right quadrant. However, if a view of the upper right and lower left corners is needed, a transparency must be made of this chart to create the mirror image views. An easier solution to creating an enlarged map is found on page 185.

SAMPLER 2 - MAIN ROAD MAP

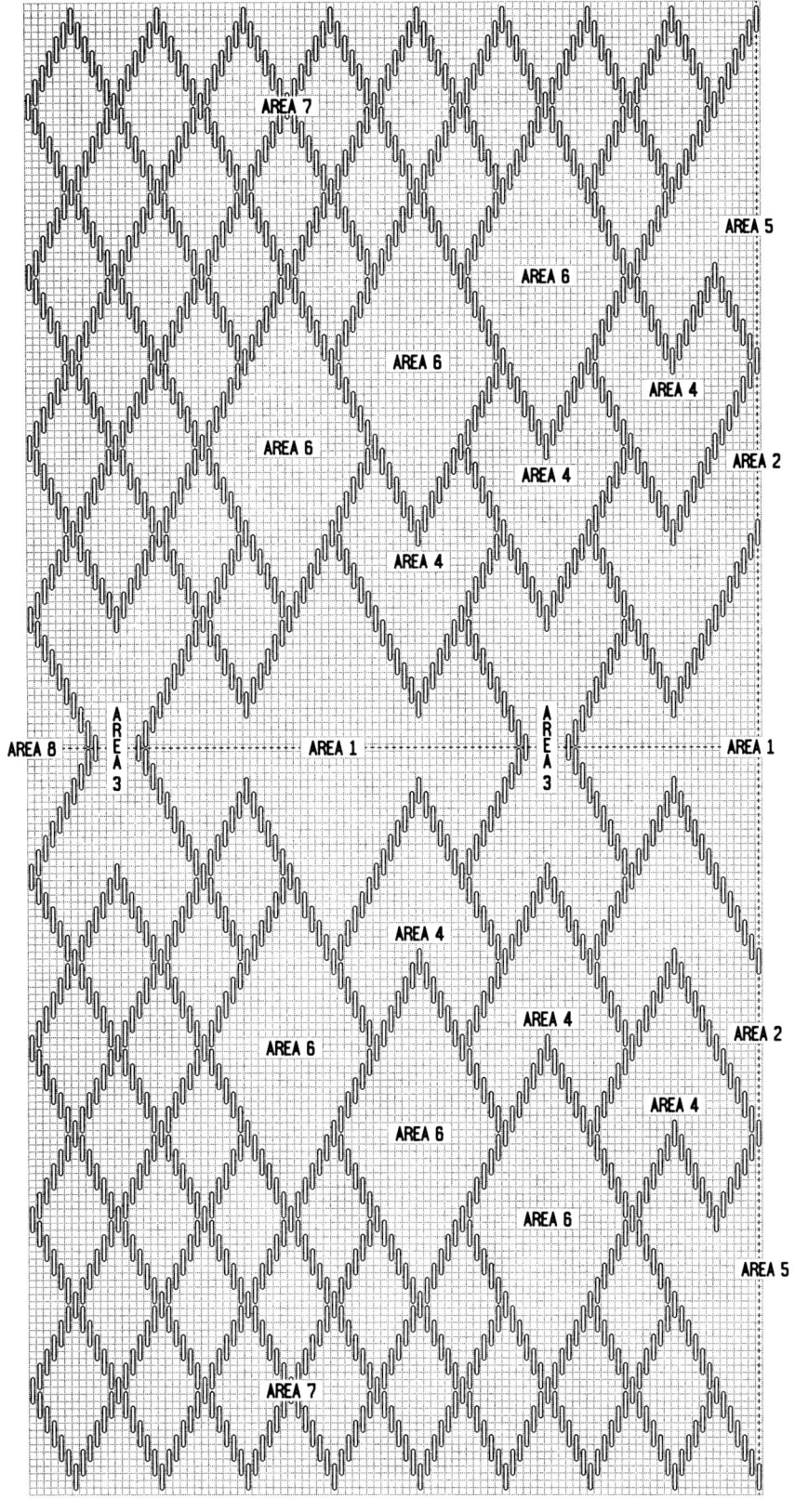

The General Pattern and Thread Key list for Sampler 2 follows on the next page.

As with Sampler 1, only an overall chart is provided for each area pattern. Use this along with the sequence chart included in the detailed pattern instructions.

SAMPLER 2 - GENERAL PATTERN AND THREAD KEY

OUTLINE - Done in Watercolours, Blue Lavender
AREA 1 - Pattern 39 (pages 120-121)
    Blackwork done in DMC #8 Perle Cotton, #797 Dark Blue
    Tied Oblong Crosses done in #8 Balger Metallic Braid, #9294 Periwinkle, 1 strand
AREA 2 - Pattern 31 (page 109)
    Tramé done in #8 Balger Metallic Braid, #9294 Periwinkle, 2 strands
    Oblong Cross Couching Sequence done in #8 DMC Perle Cotton, #798 Medium
      Blue
    Blackwork done in DMC Floss, #799 Light Blue, 2 strands
AREA 3 - Pattern 32 (page 110)
    Tramé done in #8 Balger Metallic Braid, #9294 Periwinkle, 2 strands
    Blackwork Couching Sequence done in DMC #8 Perle Cotton, #798 Medium Blue
    Third Layer of Tiedown Stitches done in DMC Floss, #799 Light Blue, 2 strands
AREA 4 - Pattern 37 (pages 118-119)
    Blackwork done in Anchor Floss, #109 Medium Dark Purple, 2 strands
    Tied Oblong Crosses done in #8 Balger Metallic Braid, #9294 Periwinkle, 1 strand
AREA 5 - Pattern 38 (pages 119-120)
    Blackwork done in DMC #8 Perle Cotton, #797 Dark Blue
    Tied Oblong Crosses done in #8 Balger Metallic Braid, #9294 Periwinkle, 1 strand
AREA 6 - Pattern 31 (page 109)
    Tramé done in #8 Balger Metallic Braid, #9294 Periwinkle, 2 strands
    Blackwork and Oblong Cross Couching Sequence done in DMC Floss, #799 Light
      Blue, 2 strands
AREA 7 - Pattern 41 (page 123)
    Blackwork done in DMC Floss, #109 Medium Dark Purple, 2 strands
AREA 8 - Modified Pattern 41, Sequence Chart on page 198
    Blackwork done in DMC Floss, #109 Medium Dark Purple, 2 strands

NOTE: In the area charts that follow, the patterns are presented in two different sizes. Small areas are shown "double" the size of the original graphic, but large areas are presented in the original size since an enlargement could not fit on a single page.

In addition, some of the compensation stitches appear to be tucked under the outline stitches along the pattern edges. Accomplish this by slanting the needle as you sink it, being careful not to pierce the outline. Some slanted stitches appear to sink on either side of an outline stitch when the outline stitch is directly above or below these "star points." It is important to guide these stitches in this way to keep the pattern from appearing distorted.

Unless otherwise stated, use a #24 or #26 tapestry needle to execute the blackwork. The smaller size needle is less apt to pierce the outline or any other previously laid stitches in the shared holes, but the #24 needle is more comfortable for many people and is acceptable. Unless otherwise noted, the correct thread weight for all the blackwork is two strands of floss when the patterns are done on either 18-mesh or 23-mesh Congress cloth. If the angled stitches do not have adequate points on Congress cloth, consider using 1-strand silk floss instead, but 1-strand cotton floss is too skimpy. Use the folded floss thread since this is ideal for the 2-strand thread (review this technique in section C on page 12, if needed). Since the pattern placement is already defined on every chart for you, it is easier to start along a side edge rather than in the center of each pattern.

**AREA 1
PATTERN 39
(Page 120)**

This pattern is repeated three times in the design. Work the long middle row first in each area. Then the remaining rows will be easier to add.

This pattern was actually developed specifically for this shape so it is no accident that whole units fall in the peaks and valleys of the zigzag lines. The side corners are not quite as graceful, but the eye is drawn to the dramatic peaks in the pattern first so a good fit there makes other compensation areas less conspicuous. When compensation areas within symmetrical shapes match exactly, they appear more comfortable and detract less from the whole repeats of the pattern.

**AREA 4
PATTERN 37
(Page 118)**

This pattern is repeated twelve times. Again rotate **either** the chart or the canvas 180° to make the view of the chart correspond to the area that is being worked.

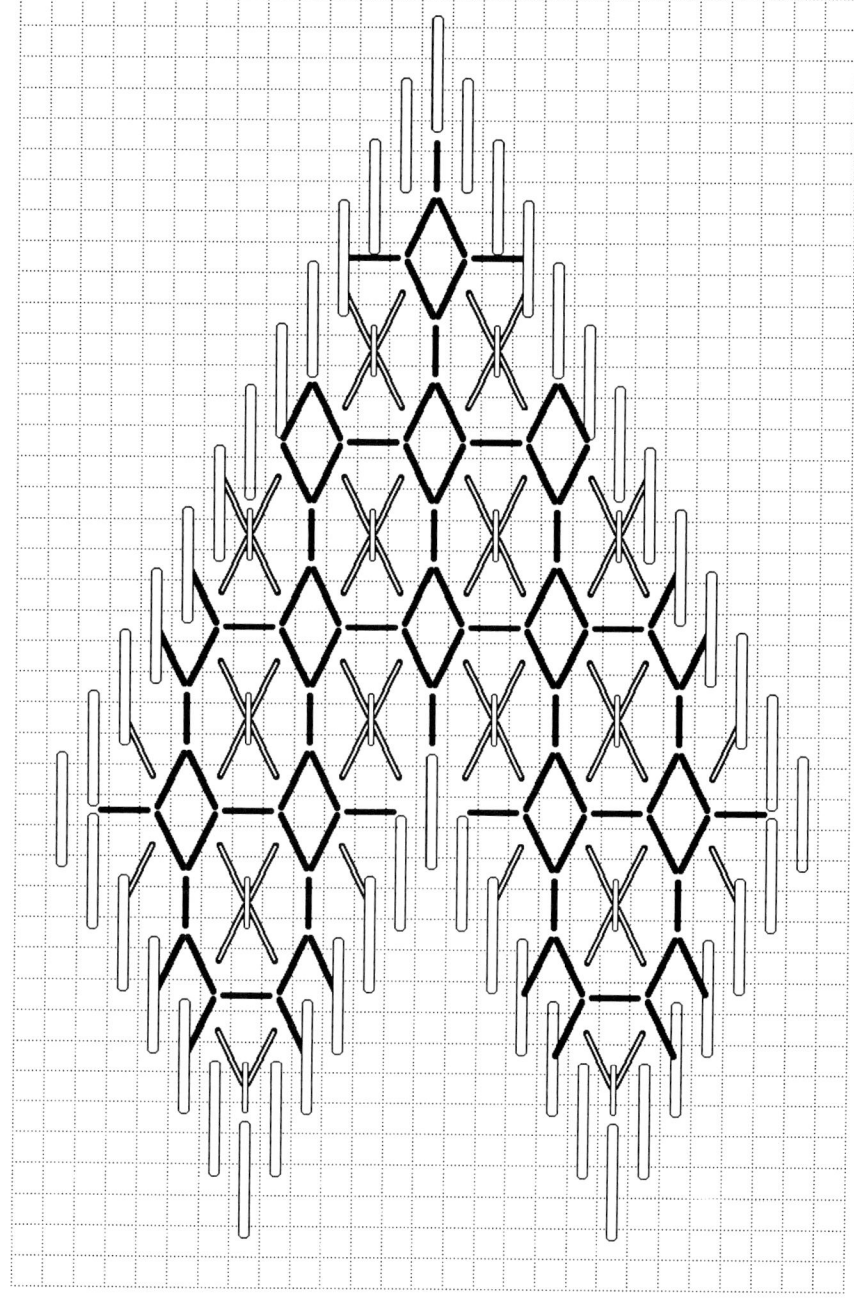

NOTE: The tied oblong crosses in this pattern are not connected so no sequence could be devised that eliminates the visibility of the traveling threads in the open area. Therefore the pale periwinkle metallic was chosen to minimize the conspicuousness of the paths in this unavoidable situation. The same problem exists in Areas 1 and 5 so the same thread was used again to solve the dilemma.

193

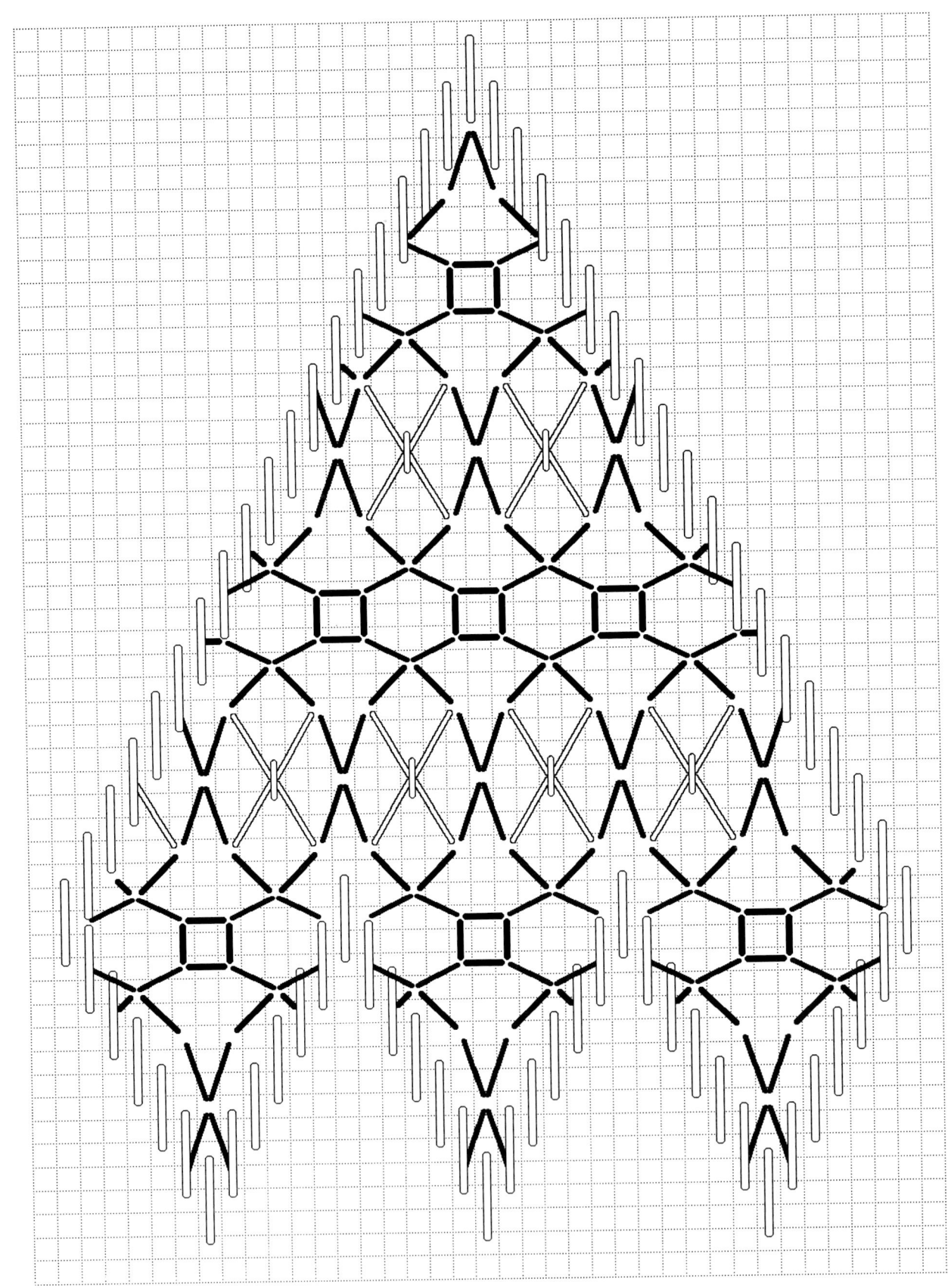

AREA 5 - PATTERN 38 (Page 119)

194

The pattern in Area 5 on the previous page is a bold pattern, and it is repeated twice in the design. The chart matches the position of the upper Area 5 section so rotate **either** the canvas or the chart 180° to stitch the lower section. The color treatments here are the same as those in Area 1, but the pattern is slightly bolder for the smaller shape. However, the pattern fits perfectly with no need for foreshortened stitches along the edges.

AREA 6
PATTERN 31
(Page 109)

The pattern used in the diamonds is the same as that used in Area 2. However, this time both the blackwork and the oblong cross couching sequences are in the same thread.

This area is repeated 12 times in the design, and the pattern is used again in Area 2, but the value treatment is different. Arrange the tramé rows in the same position shown in the chart on page 109. Secure the tramé rows with the oblong crosses. Then add the diamond blackwork pattern in

195

the same thread to complete the pattern. Area 2 uses a darker treatment that is similar to that used in the center Area 3 patterns. The lighter treatment used in Area 6 is similar to that used in the side sections of Area 3.

NOTE. By keeping these particular sections in the same color and value treatments, an attractive "ring" of blue medium values forms in the center of the design. An outer "ring" of lighter values of blue is also created that stands out nicely against the bold dark blue ares and the lavender areas.

AREA 7 - PATTERN 41 (Page 123)

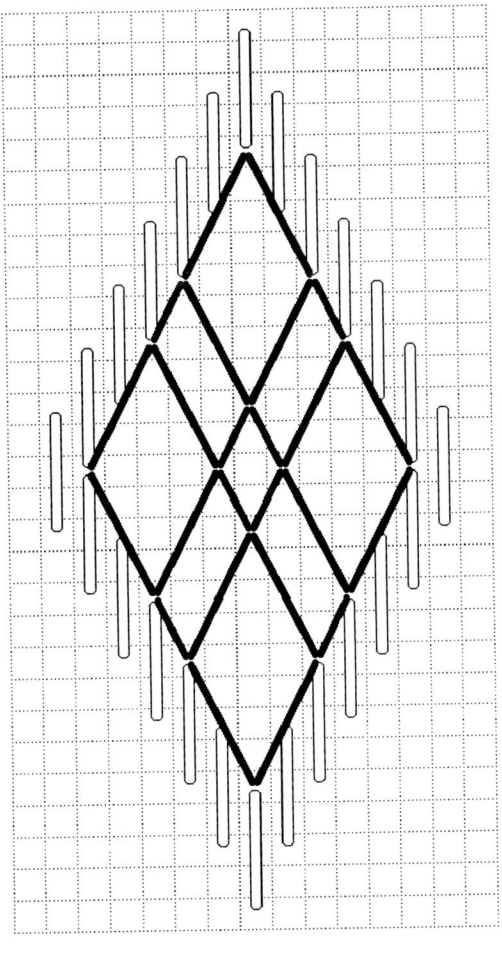

Area 7 is a small shape that is repeated many times. Unlike the previous patterns, the canvas pattern of open diamonds forms an allover pattern that serves as an outline for the bolder interior fillings. This time the blackwork pattern is isolated within each diamond outline so the repeats do not touch to form a continuous network. Use the sequence shown for pattern 41 to work the separate repeats in diagonal or slanted rows. Along the outside edges there are partial units of diamonds so the blackwork fillings inside are also partial segments. A similar combination sequence can be used to add these "abbreviated" patterns. None of these is reversible, however, as it is easier to execute isolated blackwork motifs with a combination or running stitches and back stitches.

The outside edges of the design have two different compensations. Along the side edges the half diamonds hold exactly half of the blackwork filling, and no foreshortened stitches are needed (see the Side Edge View chart on the next page). Along the top and bottom edges, however, the diamonds extend a bit beyond the midpoint of the blackwork pattern so some compensation is needed. However, the compensation is graceful since it is exactly one half of a long stitch, or a simple gobelin stitch which maintains the same angle as the longer stitch (see the Bottom Edge View chart on the next page). In determining the edge of the design, I felt these views made the most attractive presentation.

When repeated segments cannot be connected in continuous rows, a reversible sequence is not the ideal method of execution. Instead a combination of back stitches and running stitches is used to fill each individual diamond pattern. Each sequence starts in the upper left part of each diamond and ends in the lower right part near the starting point for the next diamond. In plotting the sequence it was important to turn a corner after each stitch to avoid having paths of several straight stitches in a row. The zigzag paths kept shared holes clean, and no stitches look distorted.

The final stitch also angles cleanly toward the first stitch in the next diamond so the pattern fills efficiently in diagonal (or slanted) rows. The traveling from diamond to diamond is minimal so no traveling threads have to be buried in the Watercolours outlines.

NOTE: A graceful fit for both the blackwork and the diamond outline along the edges was a prime consideration in "squaring off" the design. Along the top and bottom edges of the design I also took what I consider some additional "artistic license" with the final contour. Technically there should be a half stitch along each side of the outside diamond peaks if they are to fully simulate the other diamonds. However, I felt this "total" compensation was somewhat clumsy so I chose the lighter look that is presented. This delicacy seemed appropriate since it makes the interrupted patterns along the background edge less obtrusive. Therefore this benefit overrode my usual priority of accurate and complete compensation.

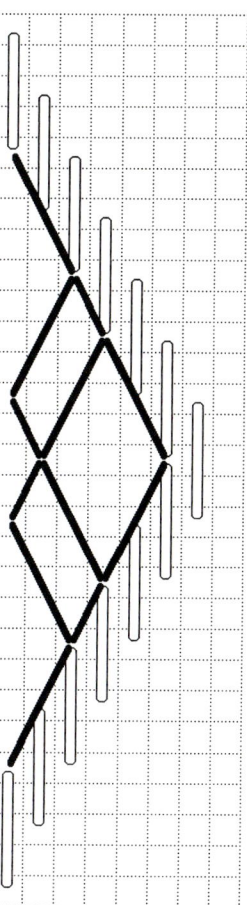

AREA 7 - PARTIAL DIAMONDS
SIDE EDGE VIEW - LEFT SIDE

Rotate **either** the canvas or the chart 180° to view the placement for the right side.

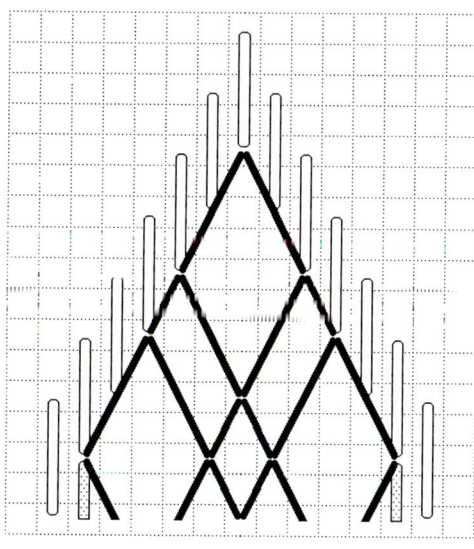

AREA 7 - PARTIAL DIAMOND
BOTTOM EDGE VIEW

The lower side of this chart shows four compensated blackwork stitches. The two middle stitches are not altered (hence the rounded ends), but the others are half the usual size of a "merged" stitch (hence the straight ends). Rotate **either** the canvas or the chart 180° to view the placement for the top edge.

NOTE: The half stitches of the outline that are filled with dots in this chart show the compensation stitches that were omitted in the final design.

197

AREA 8 - MODIFIED PATTERN 41

This area is a leftover space along the outside edge of both side sections of Area 3. Since the shape is a half diamond, and an enlarged version of the half diamonds of Area 7, the same blackwork pattern is used to echo the other background areas. Use the modified version of the combination sequence for Pattern 41 that I developed for this shape (see the sequence chart below). Again this view is of the left side so rotate the canvas 180° to make the sequence chart fit the pattern on the right side.

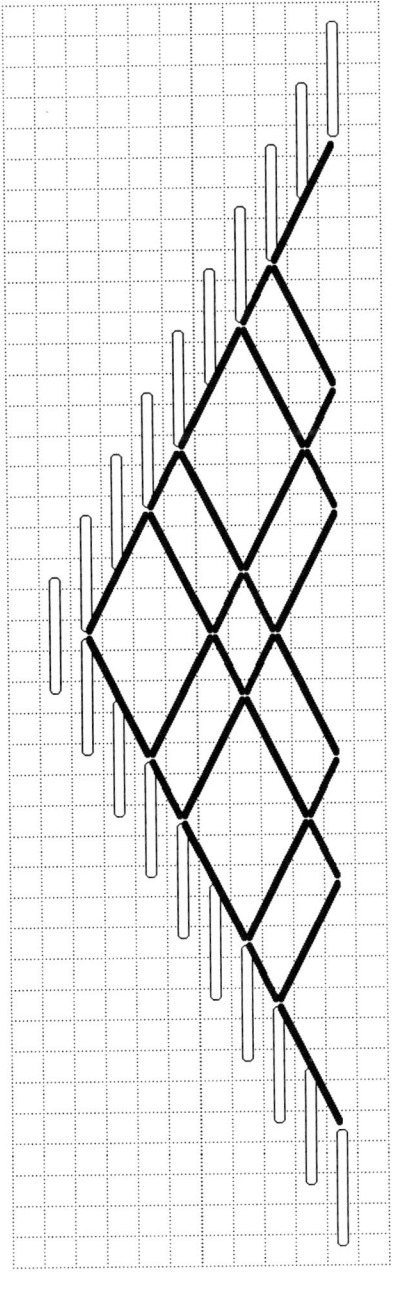

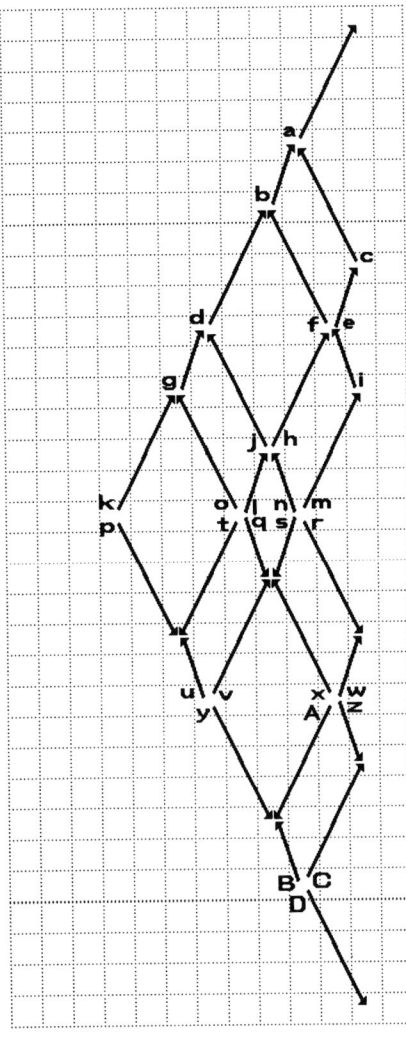

SEQUENCE CHART
AREA 8

The chart to the left has adapted the combination sequence of Pattern 41 to the large half diamond shape that is Area 8 in Sampler 2. The sequence is lettered rather than numbered to minimize clutter. After the lower case alphabet is exhausted, the final four stitches are identified with upper case letters A-D. The inside stitches of the blackwork pattern are executed in consistent double running rows. However, the stitches along the left edge are often manipulated to provide clean traveling to new rows without weaving through the outline and to set up a clean entry for the first stitch of the next row. This kind of adjusted sequence is sensible because it allows rows to connect efficiently while keeping the pattern uniform and unchanged in appearance on the front side. The pattern rhythm is still consistent except along the edges where pivot stitches are acceptable. This kind of modified sequence is usually recommended in small areas when patterns have few repeats. **Remember that the main goal of reversible blackwork is not to create an identical pattern on the back side but to eliminate the visibility of traveling threads in the open areas and to provide an orderly as well as a tidy way to connect pattern repeats. If another method can accomplish all of these priorities in a more efficient way, there is no reason to stick to a totally reversible sequence. If another method or a modified sequence can actually improve the appearance of a pattern, it should be substituted for the pure reversible technique. The ultimate goal in needlework should be the best possible appearance to the front of the embroidery so a stitcher must evaluate every situation and do what is necessary to achieve the most favorable results. The end usually justifies the means in this pursuit of excellence so I prefer a logical or intuitive approach to stitching that is not bound by rigid rules.**

Once the basic principles are learned, stitching becomes less of a game of right vs. wrong. If one fully understands the reasons for the general rules, one can better assess when and how to bend or break the rules to honor a higher priority or to handle a specific situation such as adapting a pattern to a particular shape.

I hope you enjoyed the two projects as practice pieces. The geometric designs also demonstrated how patterns can be created and arranged to fit symmetrical shapes gracefully. In freely drawn shapes, always select patterns that maneuver well so they look comfortable and do not require awkward compensation. Patterns with slanted stitches like those used in Sampler 2 are usually the most difficult to compensate so use these with discretion.

Each of the patterns presented in this book has exposed you to my way of analyzing its characteristics and formulating a logical sequence. I hope my rationale has provided a good foundation for you to start to create some original patterns and to formulate sequences for them. I hope my ideas for innovative pattern treatments will lead you to new experiments in blackwork.

A good book should serve not only as a reference but as a catalyst for inspiring readers to strike out on their own. I hope I have encouraged you to "take it a step further" in the same way that Ilse Altherr encouraged me. Blackwork is fun, and the possibilities are endless.

GLOSSARY OF GENERAL NEEDLEWORK TERMS

Back Stitch Pull on Both Ends of a Stitch - a term developed by me to explain my concept of charting stitch sequences so that both ends of every stitch are snugly wrapped and all stitches in a pattern appear to be uniform. If the tension is not even or taut on every stitch, patterns will look uneven or distorted so I adjust sequences to be sure that the needle comes from behind as the upward motion is taken. Then the stitch is wrapped by sinking the needle away from this entry point, and the path afterward is ahead to the next stitch. Adjustments are usually needed only at the beginning or end of the stitched rows, and they are controlled by the pattern shape as well as by the structure of the stitch itself. When the normal rhythm of the stitch is interrupted to make this adjustment, I call the changeover stitch a "pivot stitch." Most books show only one sequence for each row of stitches, or perhaps two sequences – one for the row in one direction and another for the row in the opposite direction. Although these sequences would appear to be consistent, slight discrepancies occur under certain circumstances. I prefer to eliminate such discrepancies by altering the sequence, as needed. Differences are less obvious when areas are filled with solid stitches that cover fully. However, when areas have open treatments, and threads are used that do not necessarily fill the canvas holes, individual stitches are far more affected by the direction in which they are laid. It is more necessary to manipulate stitches in order to maintain a consistent appearance of both the straightness of the lines and the uniformity of the stitch lengths – hence the development of the concept of always creating a "back stitch pull" on both ends of every stitch to control the size and regularity of the stitches. Any changes in the normal rhythm are only apparent on the back side, and the benefit of the improved appearance on the front overrides all other considerations as a result.

Composite Pattern - a pattern that combines two or more stitches or two or more treatments – e.g. an open canvas pattern that has a blackwork filling in the negative space.

Compressed Pattern - term used when a pattern is reduced so that there is less negative space between the stitched units. In open canvas treatments, the negative space is as integral a part of the pattern as the positive space (which is the actual stitched or filled area). Changes in the placement of the stitched units can create interesting variations within the same pattern.

Counterchange - a figure-ground reversal in a pattern with roughly equal quantities of the two contrasting colors, textures or shapes. Outlines form the boundaries for the alternating elements. A checkerboard is a simple example of such a counterchange pattern since it has alternating squares in two different colors.

Diaper Pattern - any pattern that, when repeated enough times, forms visual diagonals in both directions. If a pattern contains such diagonal repeats, it will also have a vertical and horizontal repeat so it is actually a four-way allover pattern. All eight basic pattern networks can form diaper patterns so these patterns are common in all counted thread and canvas treatments. It is not coincidental that the term is also applied to a baby's breech cloth. The early cloth diapers were made from a white figured fabric that had a reverse diagonal diamond woven pattern in it. This fabric is commonly referred to as a "birdseye" weave.

Expanded Pattern - term used when a pattern has been enlarged to create more negative space between the stitched units.

Glitch - potential hazard or irregularity in a blackwork sequence if the double running stitch is handled in a casual manner. With a conscious effort to plant the needle in a strategic manner on the return trip of a sequence, patterns will appear uniform and even throughout.

Inherent Vice - unavoidable glitch or trap built into certain stitching situations.

> Ex. 1. When a stitch with directional changes (such as an eyelet) is laid, it is impossible to attain 100% coverage around every unit without overpacking or distorting the actual stitch. A back stitch outline around each unit is an attractive and acceptable compensation when 100% coverage is desired.

> Ex. 2. In a bargello pattern that has blocks or clusters of straight stitches in a row rather than steps of stitches, it is impossible to attain full coverage between successive rows. A stitch squeezes slightly as it sinks into a canvas hole so coverage at the ends is somewhat more sparse. In a step pattern the wide center part of the neighboring stitches overlaps the thinner ends of the adjacent stitches so 100% canvas coverage is possible. Again I recommend a back stitch compensation between the blocks of satin stitches if 100% canvas coverage is needed, but all judges may not agree so it may be better to avoid such patterns in a judged situation.

> Ex. 3. When an area that has solid diagonal stitches butts up to an area that has solid straight stitches, it is difficult to attain 100% canvas coverage. Compensation measures here can be tricky so it is again better to avoid this in a judged situation.

Merged Stitch - a term developed for the conversion of two stitches in a straight line in blackwork to one long stitch over four threads or intersections instead of the traditional pair of stitches over two threads or intersections. Straight lines of double running stitches tend to look crooked so such conversions improve the appearance of a pattern. Similarly a longer line of three stitches over two threads or intersections will look nicer if it is converted to two stitches over three threads instead.

Pattern Network - the underlying skeleton or outline upon which a pattern is based. There are eight basic pattern networks. These include the square, the diamond, the half-drop, the brick, the triangle, the scale, the ogee and the hexagon. A circle is not a pattern network since side by side circles leave a negative space between them. However, networks like the scale and the ogee are formed from overlapping circles, which leave no negative space. A thorough discussion of the eight basic pattern networks is presented on pages 156-159.

Pivot Stitch - in traditional canvas embroidery this is a stitch taken that allows the needle to change the direction of a thread path gracefully without altering the normal tension on the previous stitch. Such "alterations" or interruptions in the normal sequence are often needed to maintain consistency at the beginning or end of certain rows, and the change is usually dictated by the shape of the area and by the location of the entry point of the next row. In open canvas techniques the term is also used for the method of entering or leaving a stitched row gracefully. By taking a back stitch over a single thread or intersection in a specific direction to allow the thread to exit consistently from one row and to enter from the correct direction on the next row.

Stab Stitch - this is a term applied to the method of stitching on canvas when the canvas is mounted firmly on a stretcher frame. It is no longer possible to "sew" or "scoop" stitches in a simultaneous in and out method to complete a stitch in the same manner that a stitch is taken when a fabric is not mounted in this way. A separate up and down "stab" motion is needed to complete each stitch, and both hands are generally used to guide the needle, particularly when the frame is secured to a table with a clamp or frame weight.

Half-drop - a pattern term used for a half-step placement of the alternating rows of a pattern network when the placement involves a vertical alternation. The term brick is used when the pattern has a horizontal alternation. A more complete explanation is discussed in the pattern network discussion that begins on page 156.

Tramé - a long laid stitch that is unstable so it must be couched or tied down by "holding" stitches. Usually these are placed at regulated intervals to form a uniform pattern. One-way tramé patterns have laid threads that are parallel, and they lie in one direction only. Two-way patterns have laid threads in two directions and form what are called square or diamond lattice networks. Four-way patterns have a combination of a square lattice and a diamond lattice used together to form four layers. In these latter two types of patterns, the laid threads are tied down at overlapping intersections.

Unit - a term developed by me to label stitches that are made up of more than one stitch (e.g. a Hungarian unit is composed of two brick stitches that surround one long stitch in the middle that straddles four threads).

INDEX OF PATTERNS

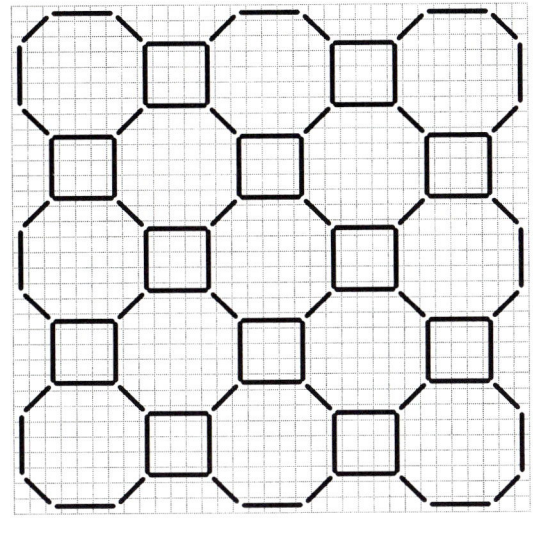

PATTERN 1

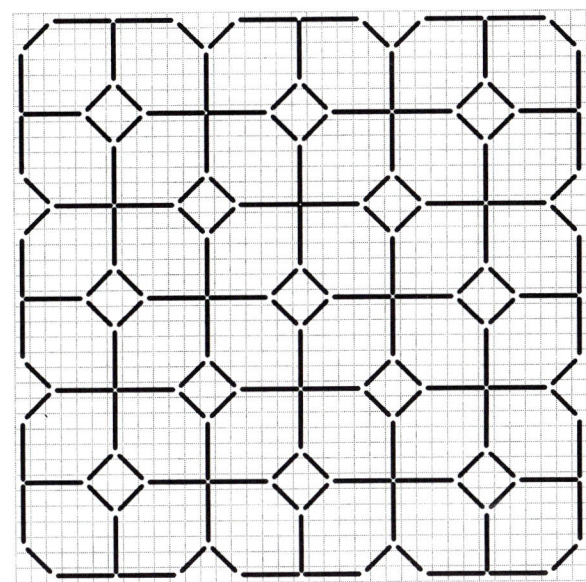

PATTERN 2

PATTERN 3

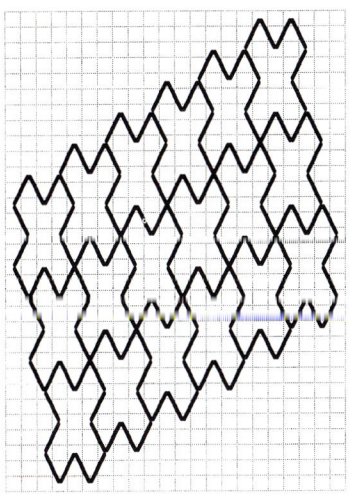

PATTERN 4

PATTERN 5

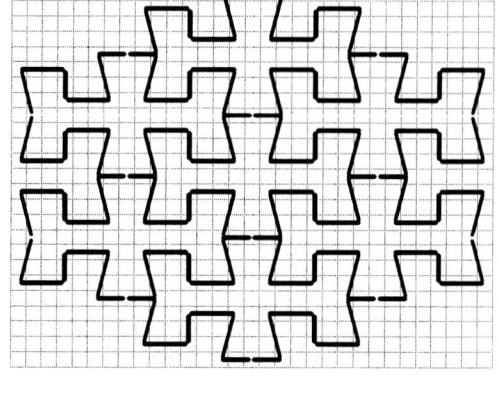

PATTERN 6

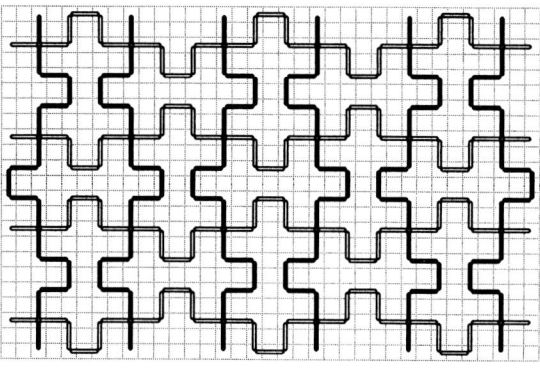

PATTERN 7

PATTERN 8

PATTERN 9

PATTERN 10

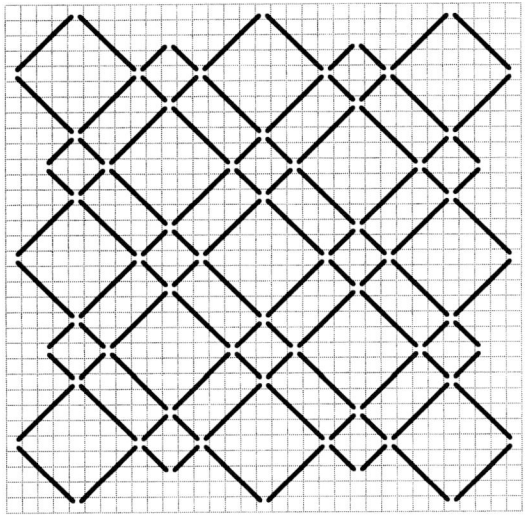

PATTERN 11

PATTERN 12

PATTERN 13

PATTERN 14

PATTERN 15

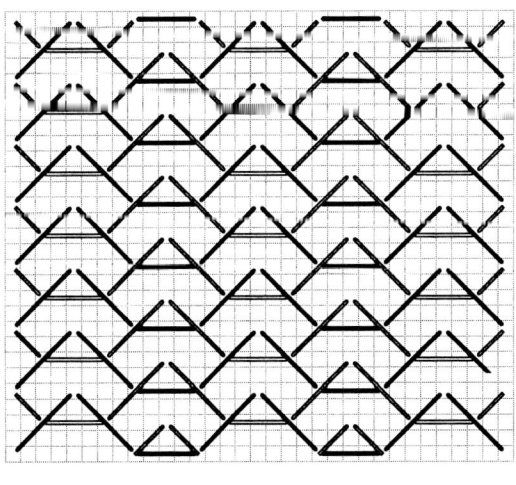

PATTERN 16

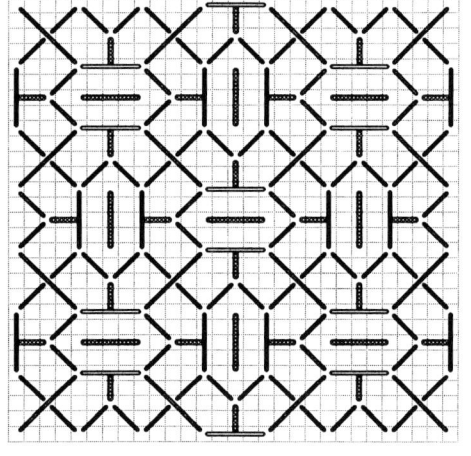

PATTERN 17

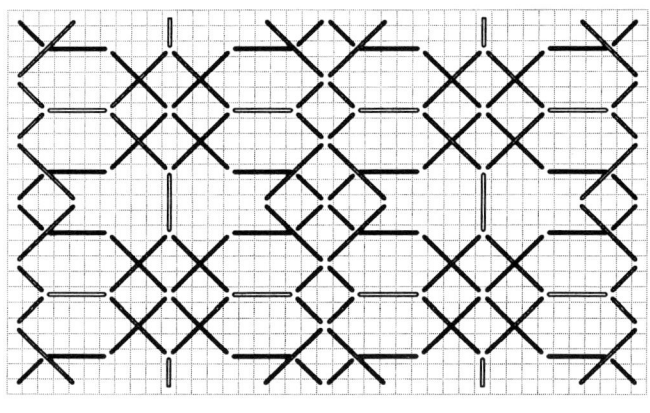

PATTERN 18

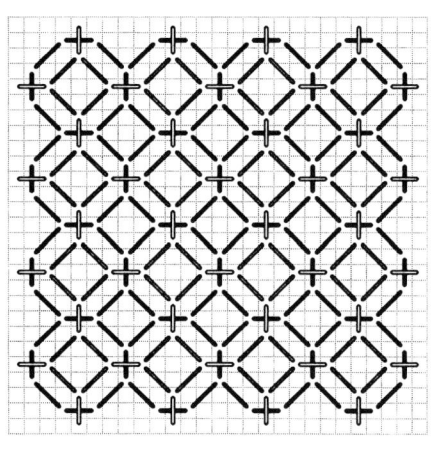

PATTERN 19

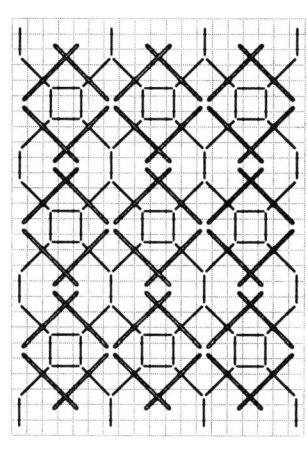

PATTERN 20a

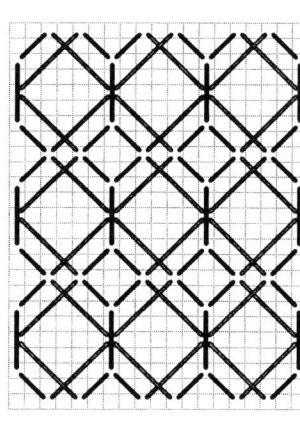

PATTERN 20b

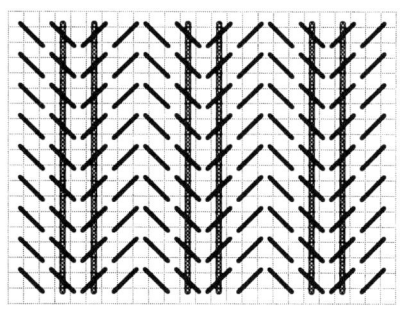

PATTERN 21

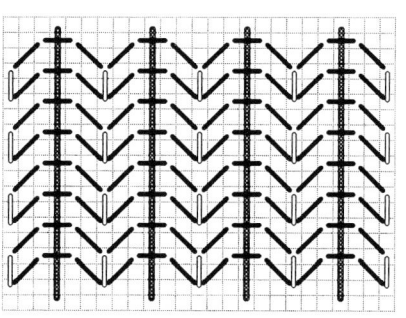

PATTERN 22

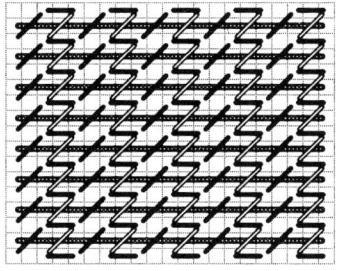

PATTERN 23

PATTERN 24

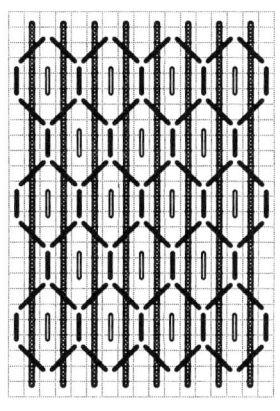

PATTERN 25

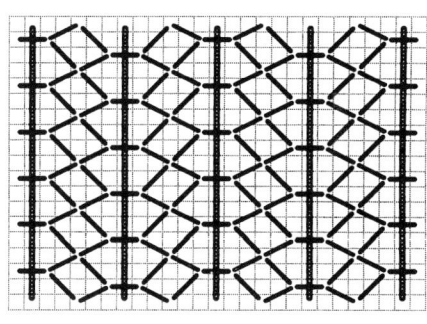

PATTERN 26

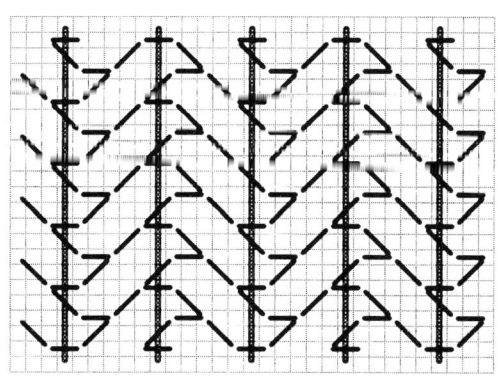

PATTERN 27

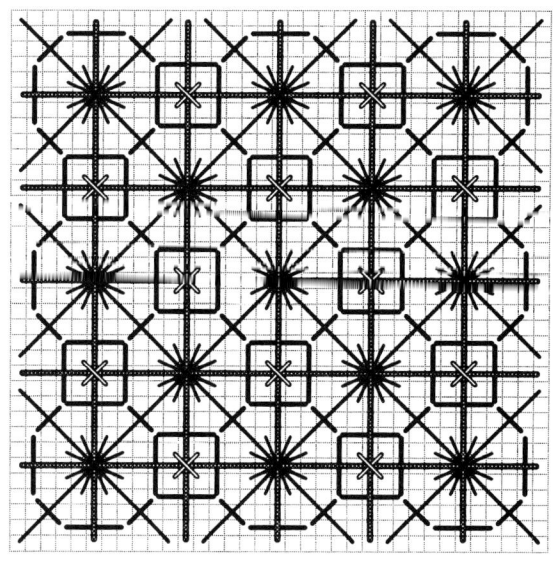

PATTERN 28

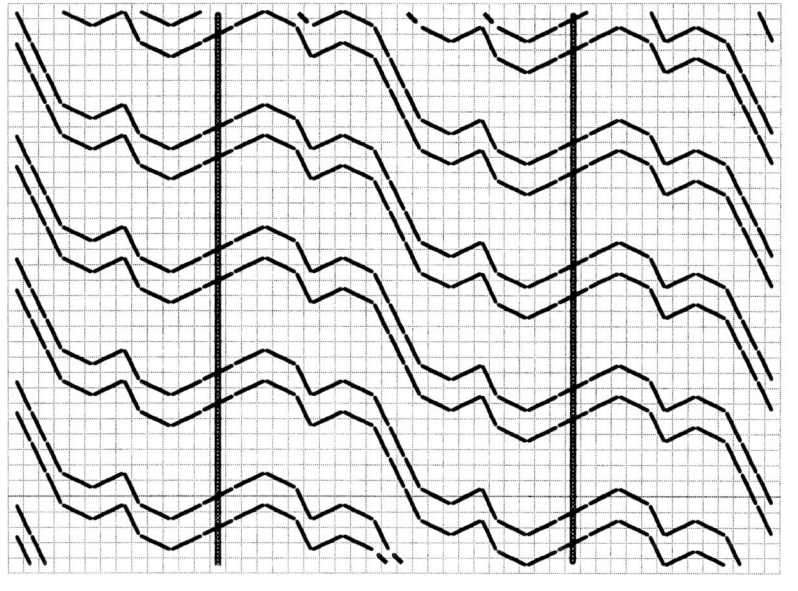

PATTERN 29

PATTERN 30

PATTERN 31

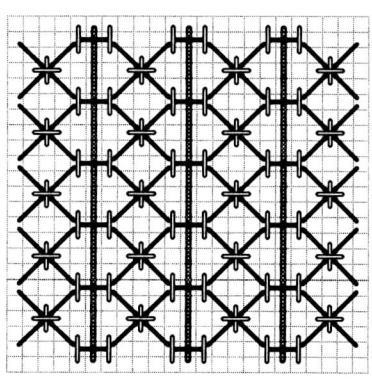

PATTERN 32

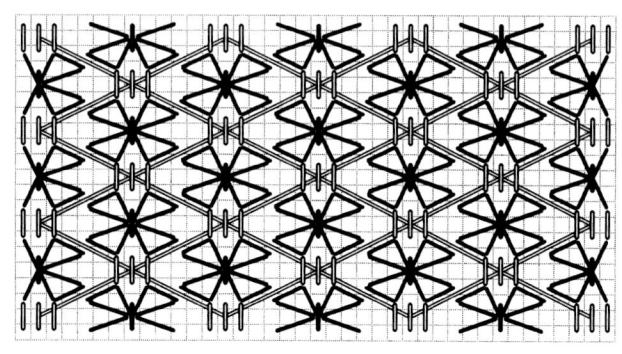

PATTERN 33

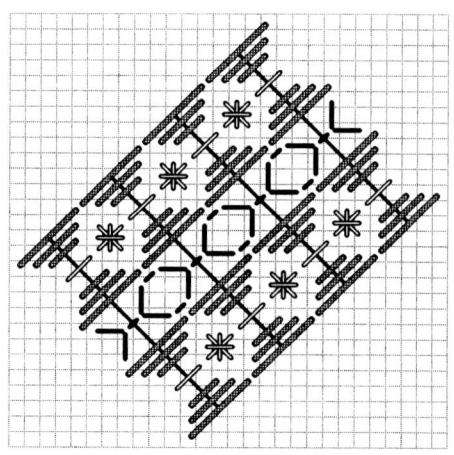

PATTERN 34

PATTERN 35

PATTERN 36

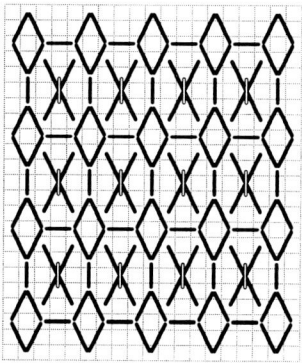

PATTERN 37

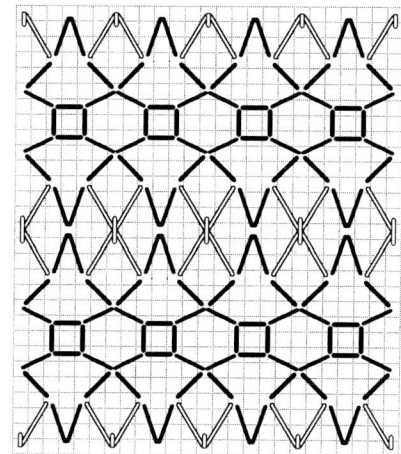

PATTERN 38

PATTERN 39

PATTERN 40

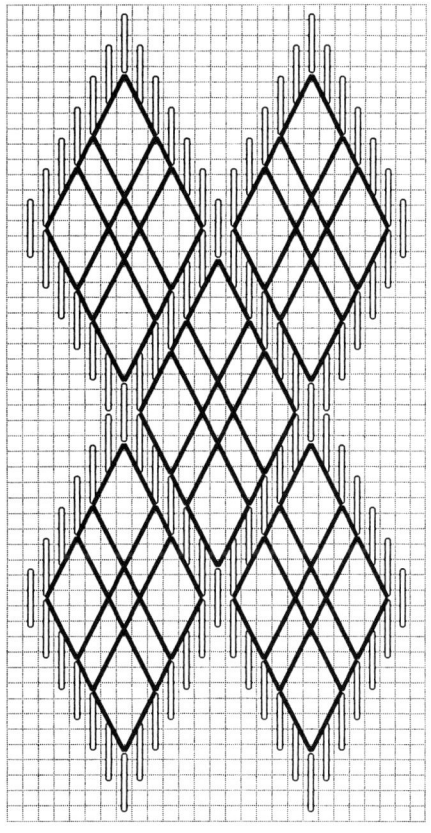

PATTERN 41

PATTERN 42

PATTERN 44

PATTERN 43

PATTERN 45

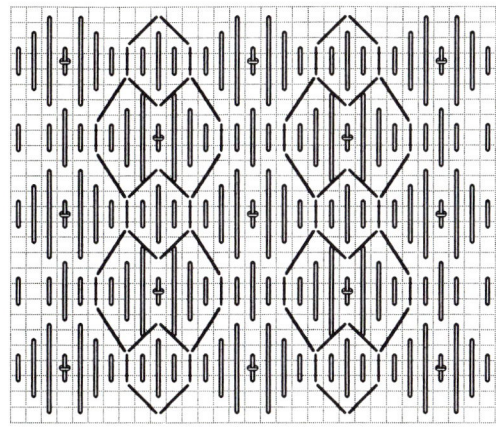

PATTERN 46

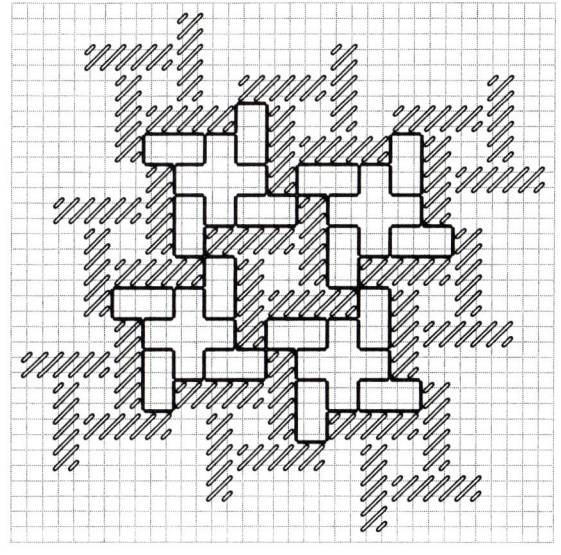

PATTERN 47

PATTERN 48

PATTERN 49

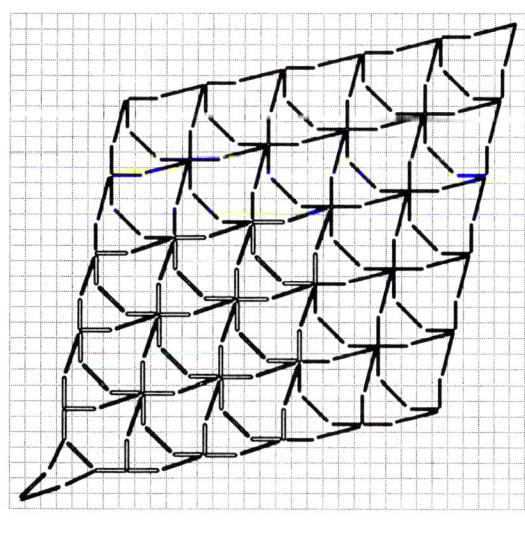

PATTERN 50

BLACKWORK

Selected Bibliography

Altherr, Ilse. *Reversible Blackwork.* Self-published, 1980.

Altherr, Ilse. *Blackwork and Holbein Embroidery.* Self-published, 1981.

Cornelius, Rosemary (with Peg Hardy and Sue Doffek). *Exploring Blackwork.* The Sinbad Series, no. 1. Ellington, CT, 1974.

Drysdale, Rosemary. *The Art of Blackwork Embroidery.* New York: Charles Scribner's Sons, 1975.

Geddes, Elisabeth and Moyra McNeill. *Blackwork Embroidery.* London: Mills and Boon, 1965; reprint, Dover Publications, New York, 1976.

Gostelow, Mary. *Blackwork.* New York: Van Nostrand Reinhold, 1976.

Pascoe, Margaret. *Blackwork Embroidery.* London: B. T. Batsford, Ltd., 1986.

Pesel, Louisa F. *Historical Designs for Embroidery.* Reprinted by the Counted Thread Society of America with the permission of B.T. Batsford, Ltd., London, 1979.

Scoular, Marion. *Blackwork.* Leisure Arts, Leaflet 82, 1976.

Scoular, Marion. *Folio of Blackwork Patterns.* Self-published.

Stears, Elizabeth. *Double Running.* Series 1 - Counted Thread Techniques. Denver: Counted Thread Society of America, 1986.

Thomas, Mary. *Mary Thomas's Embroidery Book.* London: Hodder and Stoughton, 1936.

Wilson, Erica. *Erica Wilson's Embroidery Book.* New York: Charles Scribner's Sons, 1975.

Zimmerman, Jane D. *Blackwork Embroidery Patterns.* Self-published, 1975.

PATTERN

Selected Bibliography

Christie, Archibald H. *Pattern Design.* New York: Dover Publications, 1969.

Day, Lewis F. *Pattern Design.* New York: Taplinger, 1979.

Edwards, Edward B. *Pattern and Design with Dynamic Symmetry.* New York: Dover Publications, 1967.

Justema, William. *The Pleasures of Pattern.* New York: Reinhold Book Corporation, 1968.

Proctor, Richard M. *The Principles of Pattern.* New York: Van Nostrand Reinhold, 1969.

Schoenfeld, Susan. *Pattern Design for Needlepoint and Patchwork.* New York: Van Nostrand Reinhold, 1972.

Stevens, Peter S. *Handbook of Regular Patterns.* Cambridge: MIT Press, 1981.

Ware, Dora and Maureen Stafford. *An Illustrated Dictionary of Ornament.* New York: St. Martin's Press, 1974.

SOURCES FOR ADAPTATION OF BLACKWORK PATTERNS

Selected Bibliography

Durant, Stuart. *Ornament.* Woodstock, NY: The Overlook Press, 1986.

Dye, Daniel S. *Chinese Lattice Designs.* New York. Dover Publications, 1974.

Humbert, Claude. *Ornamental Design.* New York: The Viking Press, 1970.

Jones, Owen. *Grammar of Ornament.* New York: Van Nostrand Reinhold, 1972.

Meller, Susan and Joost Elffers, *Textile Designs,* New York: Harry N. Abrams, Inc., 1991.

CANVAS EMBROIDERY

Selected Bibliography

Ambuter, Carolyn. *Carolyn Ambuter's Complete Book of Needlepoint.* New York: Thomas Y. Crowell Co., 1972.

Bucher, Jo. *Complete Guide to Creative Needlepoint.* Des Moines: Meredith Corp., 1979.

Christensen, Jo Ippolito. *The Needlepoint Book.* Englewood Cliffs, NJ: Prentice-Hall, Inc., 1976.

English, Mindy. *The Canvas Embroidery Notebook.* Self-published, 1976.

Fischer, Pauline and Anabel Lasker. *Bargello Magic.* New York: Holt, Rinehart and Winston, 1972.

Ireys, Katherine. *The Encyclopedia of Canvas Embroidery Stitch Patterns.* New York: Thomas Y. Crowell Co., 1977.

Lantz, Sherlee and Maggie Lane. *Pageant of Pattern for Needlepoint Canvas.* New York: Atheneum, 1973.

Lantz, Sherlee. *Trianglepoint.* New York: The Viking Press, 1976.

Snook, Barbara. *Florentine Embroidery.* New York: Charles Scribner's Sons, 1967.

Pendray, Shay. *Stitching Toward Perfection.* Self-published, 1989.

Zimmerman, Jane D. *The Canvas Work Encyclopedia.* Self-published, 1989.